Hm? What's this? Oho, a bed for staff
members to nap on? Let's see...
Zzzzzz...nyup nyup... From today on,
this is mine.

Still... I have a rival. She also has her sights
set on this spot. The little girl is smack in
the middle of her terrible twos. We'll see who
becomes master of this bed. Fight me!!!

—*Yūki Tabata's dog, 2022*

YŪKI TABATA

was born in Fukuoka Prefecture
and got his big break in the 2011
Shonen Jump Golden Future Cup
with his winning entry, *Hungry
Joker*. He started the magical fantasy
series *Black Clover* in 2015.

BLACK CLOVER
VOLUME 31
SHONEN JUMP Edition

Story and Art by YŪKI TABATA

Translation ✽ TAYLOR ENGEL,
HC LANGUAGE SOLUTIONS, INC.

Touch-Up Art & Lettering ✽ ANNALIESE "ACE" CHRISTMAN

Design ✽ KAM LI

Editor ✽ ALEXIS KIRSCH

First published in Japan in 2015 by SHUEISHA Inc., Tokyo.
English translation rights arranged by SHUEISHA Inc.

Printed in Canada

Published by VIZ Media, LLC
P.O. Box 77010
San Francisco, CA 94107

10 9 8 7 6 5 4 3 2 1
First printing, December 2022

VIZ MEDIA
viz.com

SHONEN JUMP

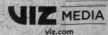

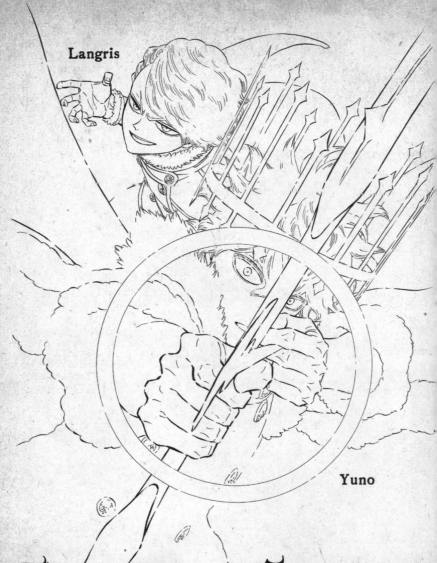

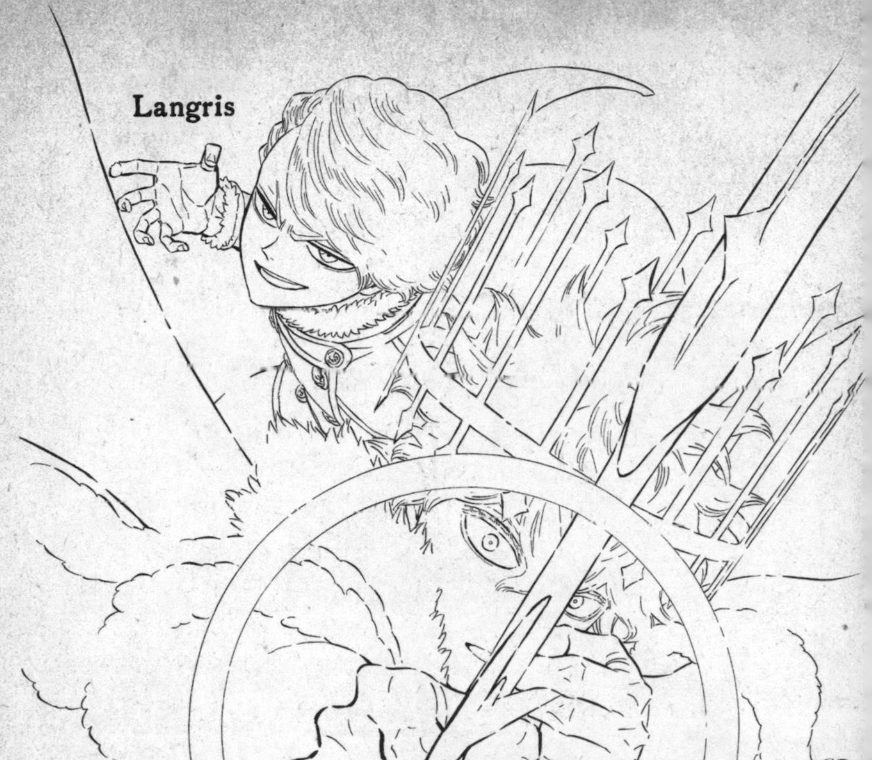
Langris
Yuno

Black Clover

31

YŪKI TABATA

UNYIELDING RIGHT AND WRONG

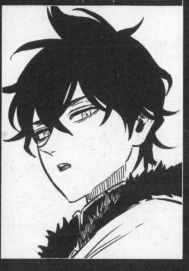

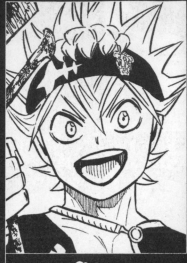

Asta

Member of: The Black Bulls
Magic: None (Anti-Magic)

He has no magic, but he's working to become the Wizard King through sheer guts and his well-trained body. He fights with anti-magic swords.

Yuno

Member of: The Golden Dawn
Magic: Wind

Asta's best friend, and a good rival who's also been working to become the Wizard King. He controls Sylph, the spirit of wind.

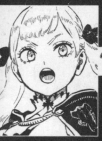

Yami Sukehiro

Member of: The Black Bulls
Magic: Dark

A captain who looks fierce, but is very popular with his brigade, which has a deep-rooted confidence in him. Heavy smoker.

Noelle Silva

Member of: The Black Bulls
Magic: Water

Of royal blood. Getting through life-or-death situations has made her talents blossom. She likes Asta.

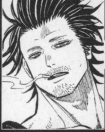

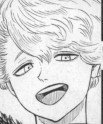

Nacht

Member of: The Black Bulls
Magic: Shadow

The vice captain of the Black Bulls. He's served by several devils and fights using variations of Devil Union.

Langris Vaude

Member of: The Golden Dawn
Magic: Spatial

Finral's younger half-brother. He wasn't fond of Finral, who folded under the pressure of becoming head of their family.

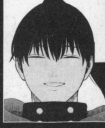

Gaja

Magic: Lightning

Lolopechka's close adviser. He has Zero Stage magic and is one of the Heart Kingdom's spirit guardians.

Lolopechka

Magic: Water

The queen of the Heart Kingdom. She's fundamentally klutzy and clueless. She's been cursed by the devil Megicula.

Dante Zogratis

Magic: Body and Gravity

The leader of the Dark Triad, the rulers of the Spade Kingdom. He believes that malice is supreme.

Liebe

Devil

The devil that's sealed in the five-leaf grimoire. He's bound to an equal contract with Asta.

Vanica Zogratis

Magic: Blood and Curse-Warding

A member of the Dark Triad. She's the host of Megicula, a devil both Lolopechka and Noelle have deep connections to.

Zenon Zogratis

Magic: Bone and Spatial

A member of the Dark Triad. His power is so vast that he destroyed the Golden Dawn by himself.

❖   ❖   ❖

STORY

In a world where magic is everything, Asta and Yuno are both found abandoned on the same day at a church in the remote village of Hage. Both dream of becoming the Wizard King, the highest of all mages, and they spend their days working toward that dream.

The year they turn 15, both receive grimoires, magic books that amplify their bearer's magic. They take the entrance exam for the Magic Knights, nine groups of mages under the direct control of the Wizard King. Yuno, whose magic is strong, joins the Golden Dawn, an elite group, while Asta, who has no magic at all, joins the Black Bulls, a group of misfits. With this, the two finally take their first step toward becoming the Wizard King…

As Charlotte's group is driven into a corner, Noelle and Gaja rush to their aid. They use their new strength to fight Vanica, but then Megicula manifests and even Gaja's suicidal attack isn't enough. However, Rill follows up ferociously with his Twilight Valhalla, and the House of Silva's blood feud comes to an end!!

CONTENTS

BLACK ❀ CLOVER

31

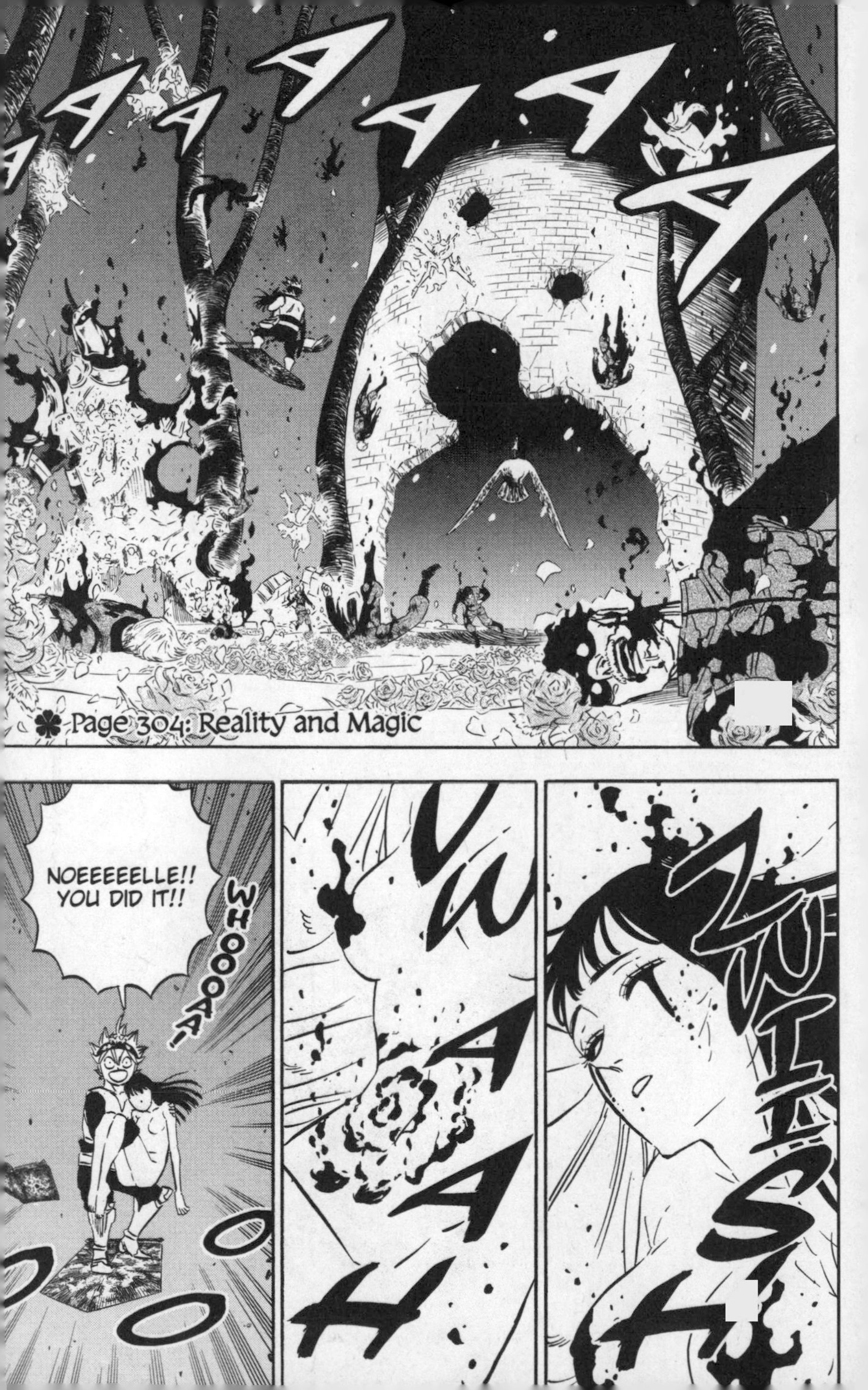
Page 304: Reality and Magic
NOEEEEELLE!! YOU DID IT!!
WHOOOAA-

UH...

OOPS
Oh! HAH!

HAVE NO F-F-FEAR!! I DIDN'T SEE A TH-TH-THING!!

GNRRGH

Agh agh agh agh!

I'M SORRY! I'M SORRY I'M NAKED! I'M SORRY!

Aah!

QUEEN LOLOPECHKA! YOU'RE AWAKE, YOUR MAJESTY?!

LOLO-PECH-KAAA!!

Undine used up all her power.

GL OMP

LOLOPECHKA! I'M SO GLAD YOU'RE ALIVE!!

NOELLE... UNDINE!

NOTHING! I DID NOTHING!

POW

WHAT ARE YOU DOING, DORK-STA?!!

8

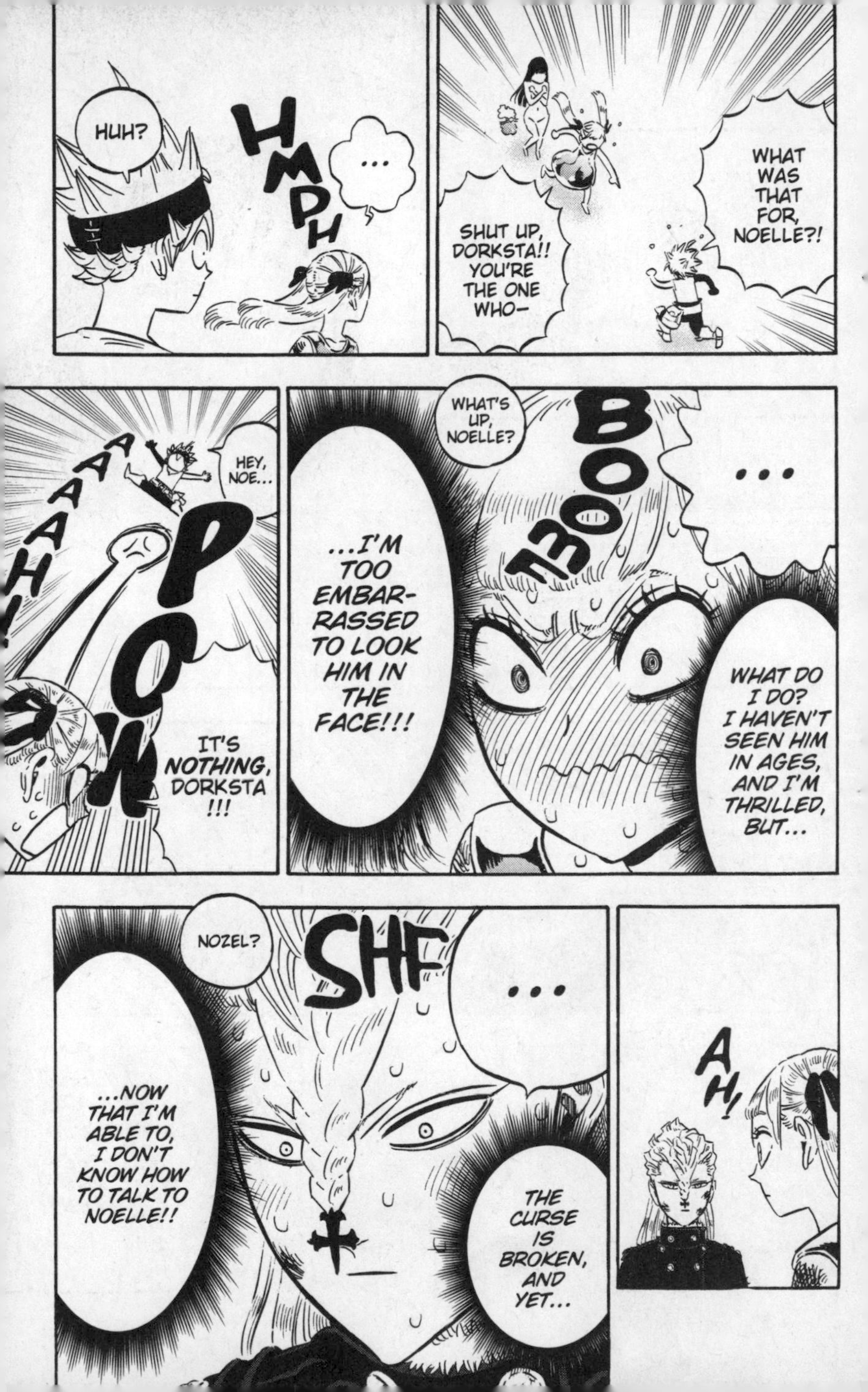
WHAT WAS THAT FOR, NOELLE?!
SHUT UP, DORKSTA!! YOU'RE THE ONE WHO—
HUH?
HMPH
...
WHAT'S UP, NOELLE?
BOOM
...
WHAT DO I DO? I HAVEN'T SEEN HIM IN AGES, AND I'M THRILLED, BUT...
...I'M TOO EMBARRASSED TO LOOK HIM IN THE FACE!!!
HEY, NOE...
AAAAH!
POW
IT'S NOTHING, DORKSTA!!!
AH!
NOZEL?
SHF
...
THE CURSE IS BROKEN, AND YET...
...NOW THAT I'M ABLE TO, I DON'T KNOW HOW TO TALK TO NOELLE!!

I STILL HAVEN'T MANAGED TO CREATE MY GREATEST WORK.

I GUESS MY ULTIMATE MASTERPIECE IS...

THE SPELL'S EFFECT IS GOING TO END SOON.

I'M SORRY, CHARLOTTE.

WE CAN'T AFFORD TO DIE YET.

AM I WRONG?

BESIDES...

NO NEED TO APOLO-GIZE, RILL.

YOU MADE IT POSSIBLE FOR ME TO FIGHT. I'M GRATEFUL TO YOU.

GAJA!

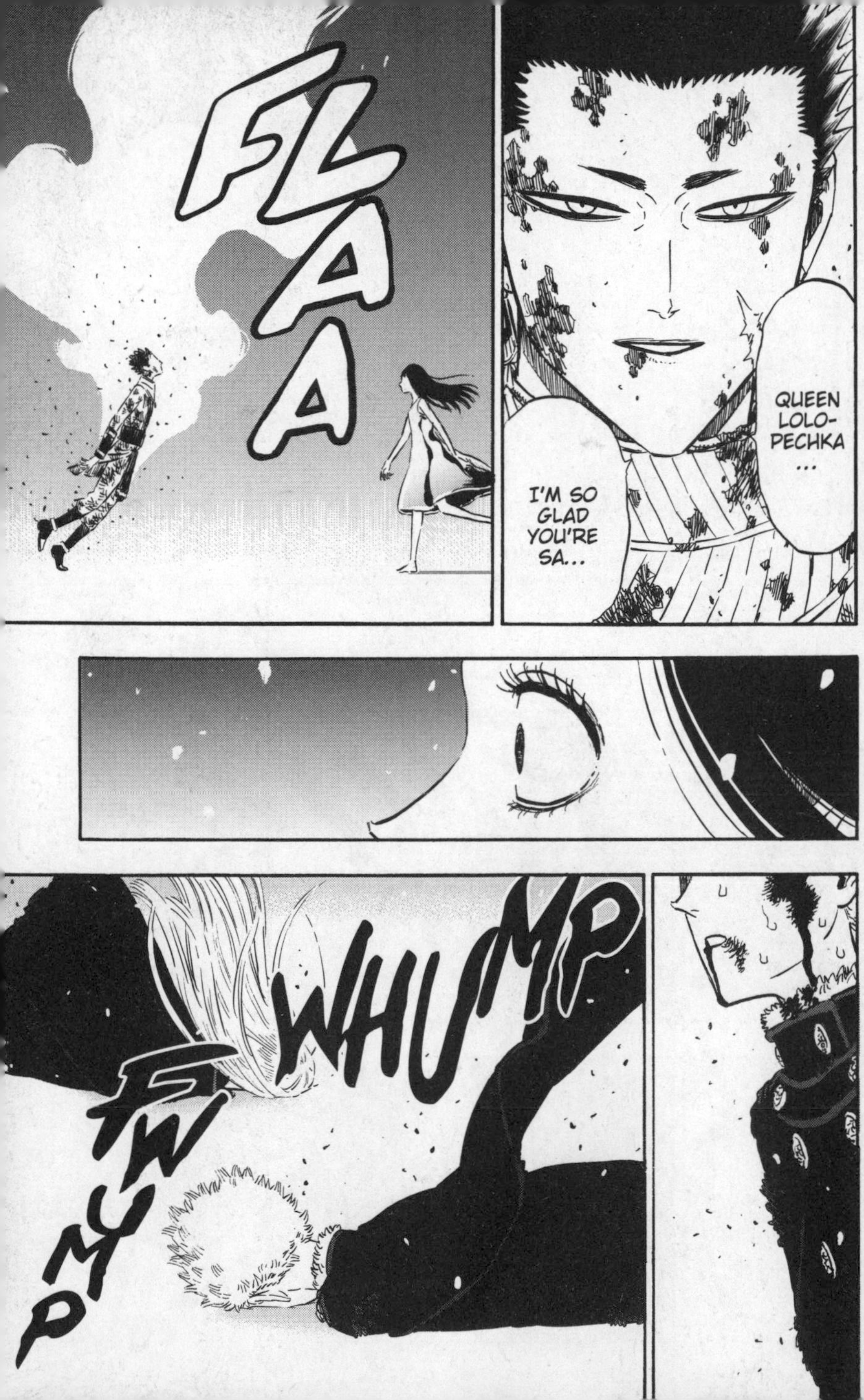
QUEEN LOLO-PECHKA...
I'M SO GLAD YOU'RE SA...
FLAA
WHUMP
FWUMP

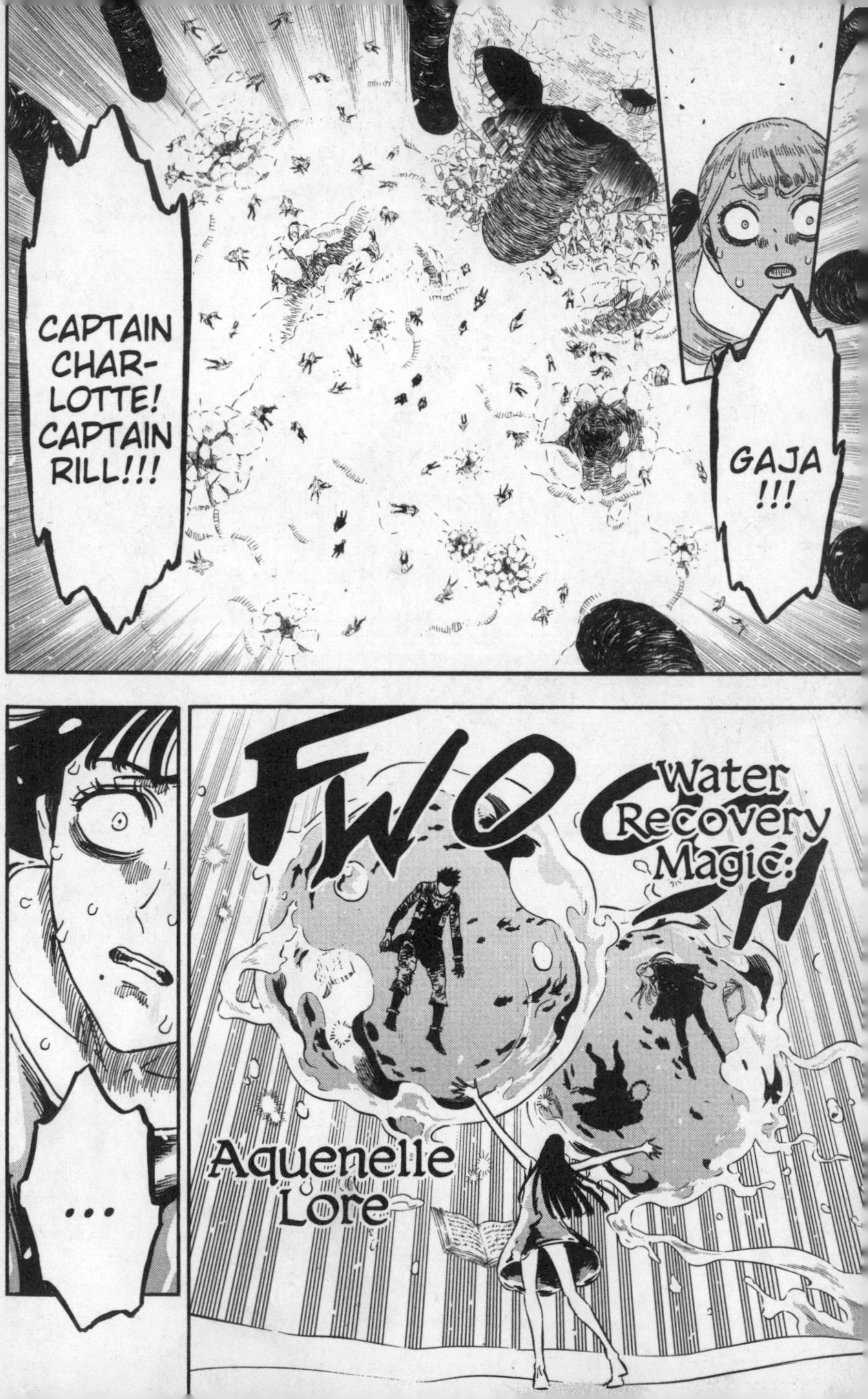
GAJA!!!
CAPTAIN CHARLOTTE! CAPTAIN RILL!!!
FWOOSH
Water Recovery Magic:
Aquenelle Lore
...

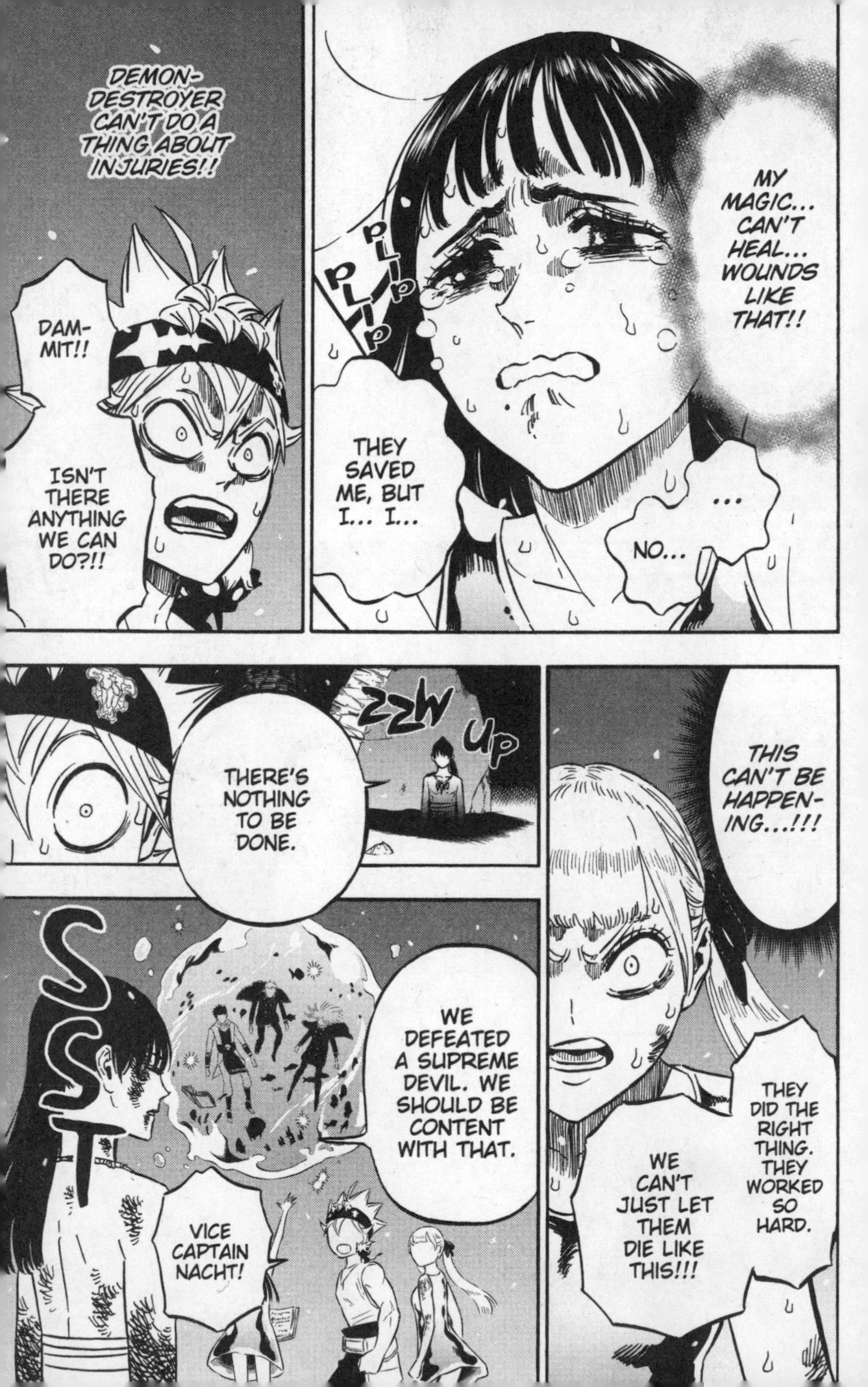
MY MAGIC... CAN'T HEAL... WOUNDS LIKE THAT!!
PLIP PLIP
...
NO...
THEY SAVED ME, BUT I... I...
DEMON-DESTROYER CAN'T DO A THING ABOUT INJURIES!!
DAMMIT!!
ISN'T THERE ANYTHING WE CAN DO?!!
THIS CAN'T BE HAPPENING...!!!
THEY DID THE RIGHT THING. THEY WORKED SO HARD.
WE CAN'T JUST LET THEM DIE LIKE THIS!!!
ZZW
UP
THERE'S NOTHING TO BE DONE.
SST
WE DEFEATED A SUPREME DEVIL. WE SHOULD BE CONTENT WITH THAT.
VICE CAPTAIN NACHT!

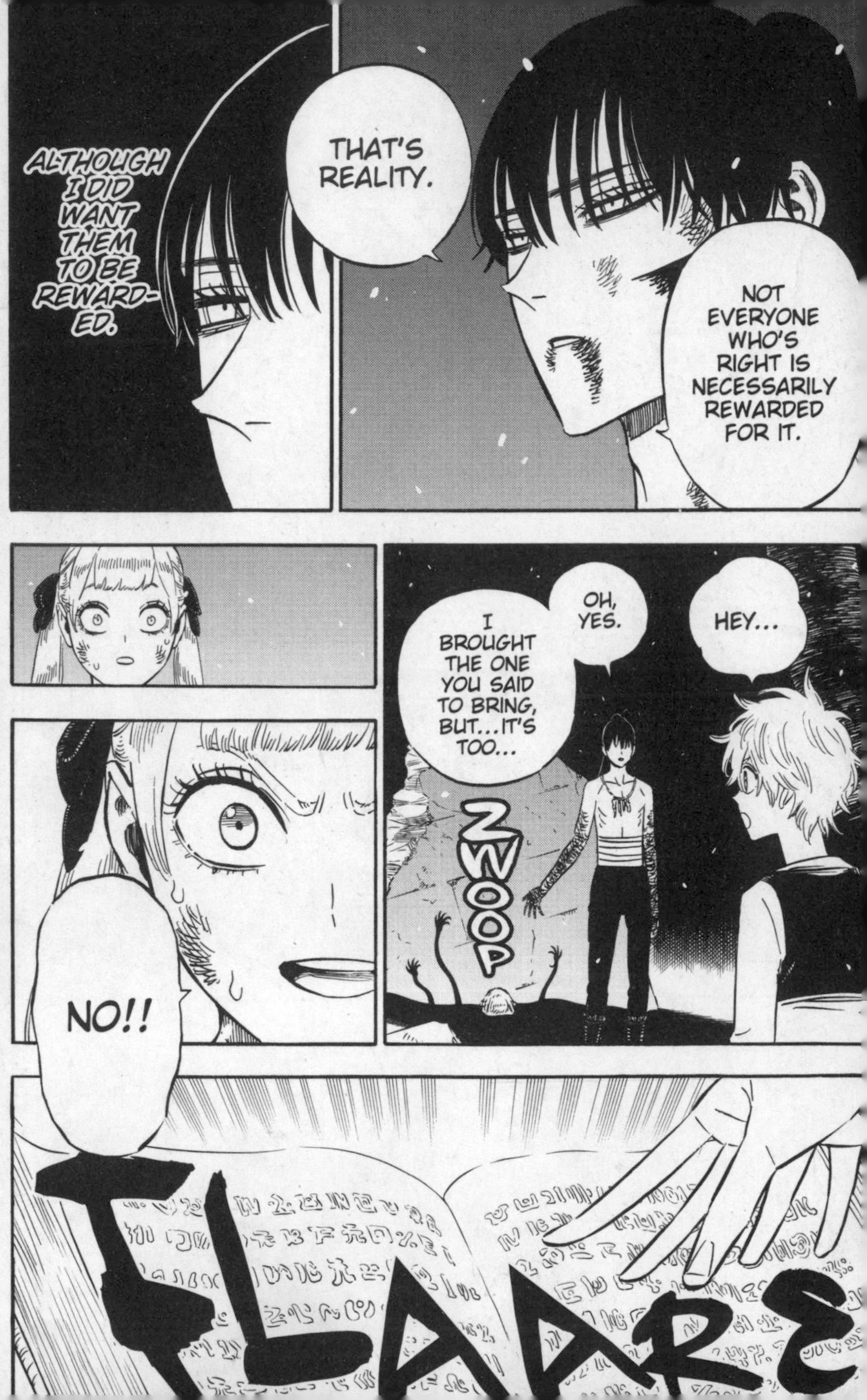
NOT EVERYONE WHO'S RIGHT IS NECESSARILY REWARDED FOR IT.
THAT'S REALITY.
ALTHOUGH I DID WANT THEM TO BE REWARD-ED.
HEY...
OH, YES.
I BROUGHT THE ONE YOU SAID TO BRING, BUT...IT'S TOO...
ZWOOP
NO!!
FLARE

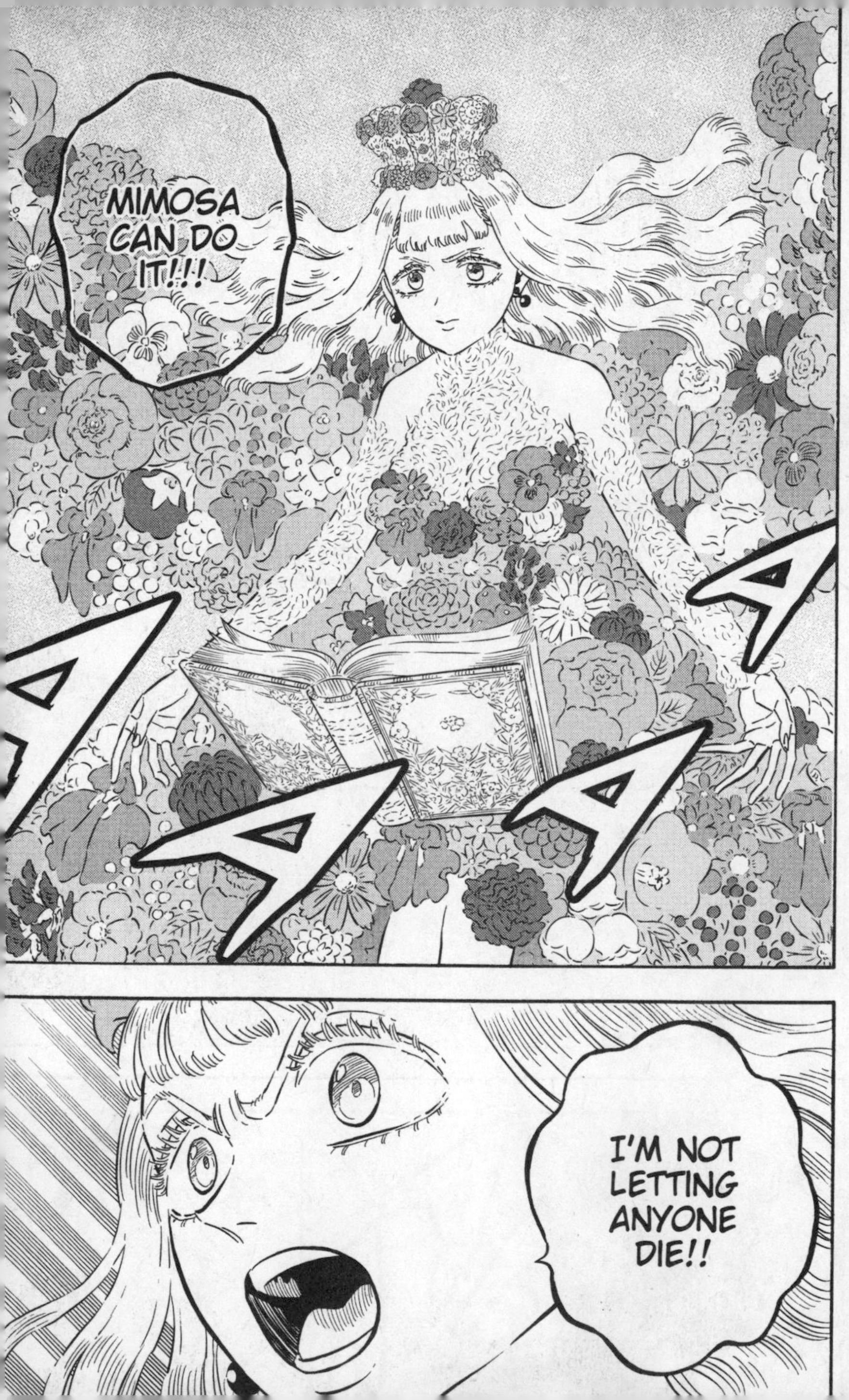
MIMOSA CAN DO IT!!!
AAAA
I'M NOT LETTING ANYONE DIE!!

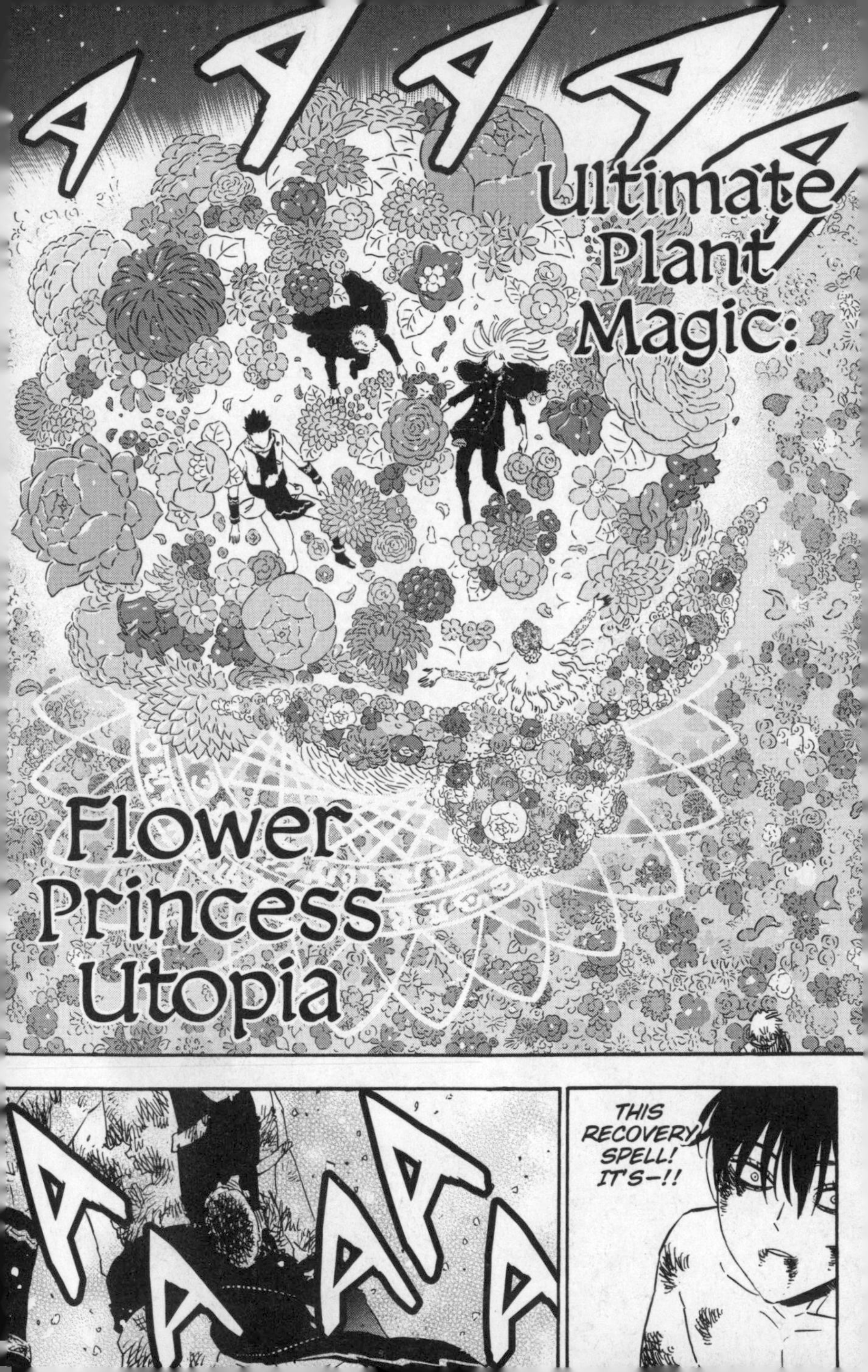
AAAAA
Ultimate Plant Magic:
Flower Princess Utopia
THIS RECOVERY SPELL! IT'S—!!
AAAAA

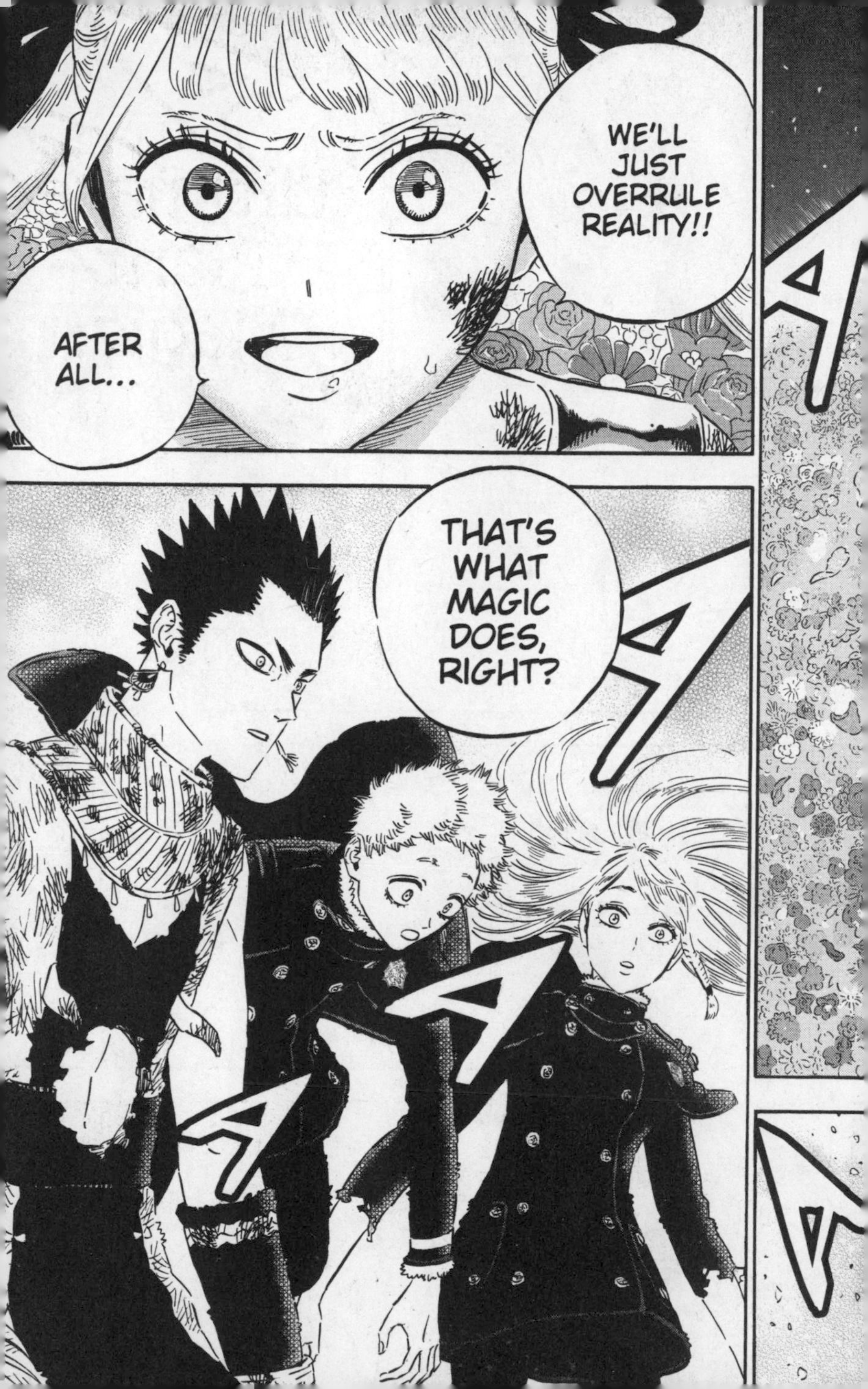
WE'LL JUST OVERRULE REALITY!!
AFTER ALL...
THAT'S WHAT MAGIC DOES, RIGHT?

IT WAS NO MORE THAN MY DUTY AS A SPIRIT GUARDIAN.

Please stop.

BOW BOW

ALL THAT FOR SOMEBODY LIKE ME— I'M SORRY! I'M SORRY!

DON'T YOU PEOPLE HAVE ANYTHING ELSE TO SAY?

RILLLLLL!! CAPTAIN CHARLOOOOOTE!!

Thank goodneeess!

GAJA!

Eh heh heh

MIMOSA, THAT WAS WAY TOO COOL!!!

I LOVE YOU.

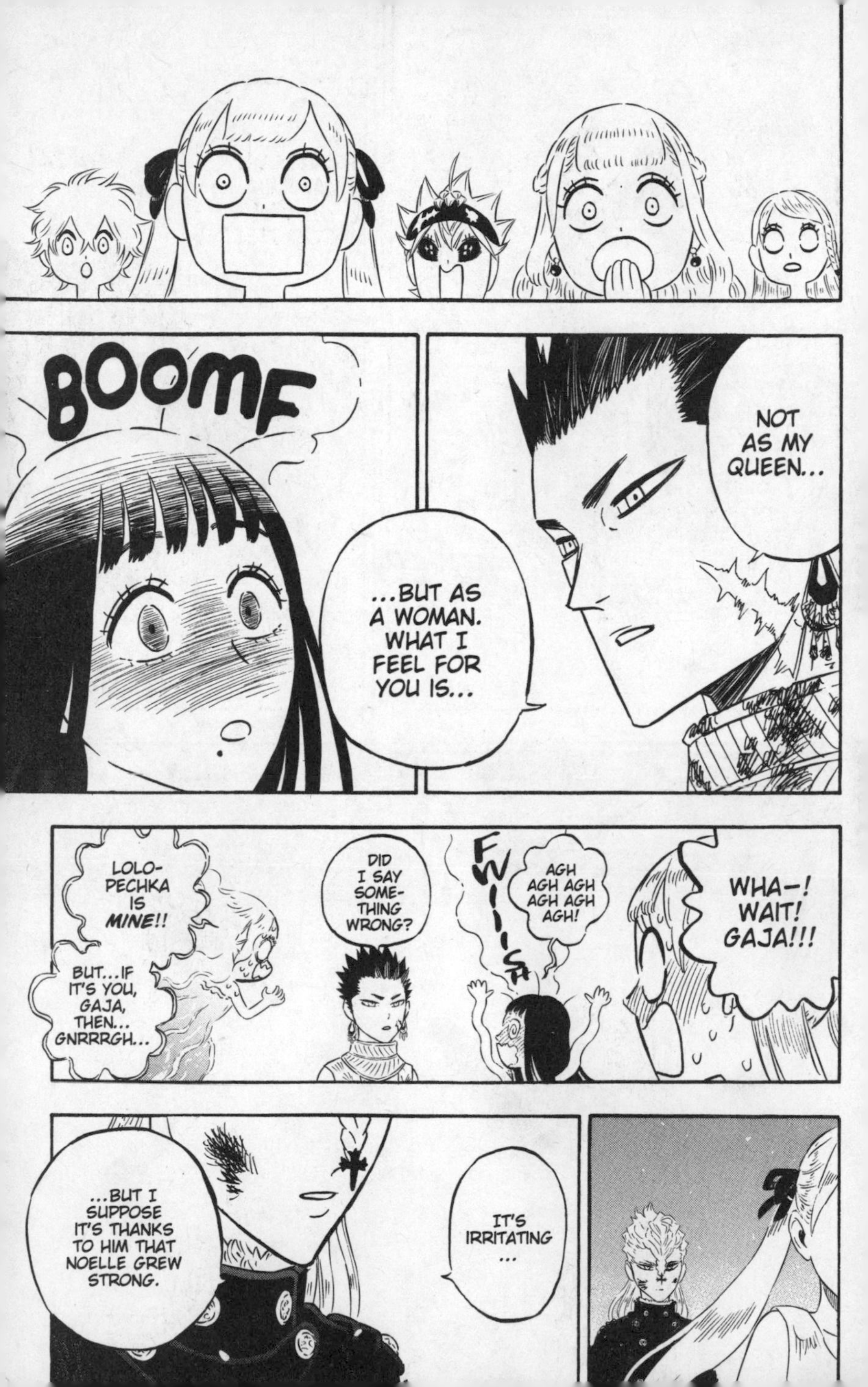
NOT AS MY QUEEN...
...BUT AS A WOMAN. WHAT I FEEL FOR YOU IS...
BOOMF
WHA-! WAIT! GAJA!!!
AGH AGH AGH AGH AGH AGH!
FWIISH
DID I SAY SOMETHING WRONG?
LOLOPECHKA IS MINE!!
BUT...IF IT'S YOU, GAJA, THEN... GNRRRGH...
IT'S IRRITATING ...
...BUT I SUPPOSE IT'S THANKS TO HIM THAT NOELLE GREW STRONG.

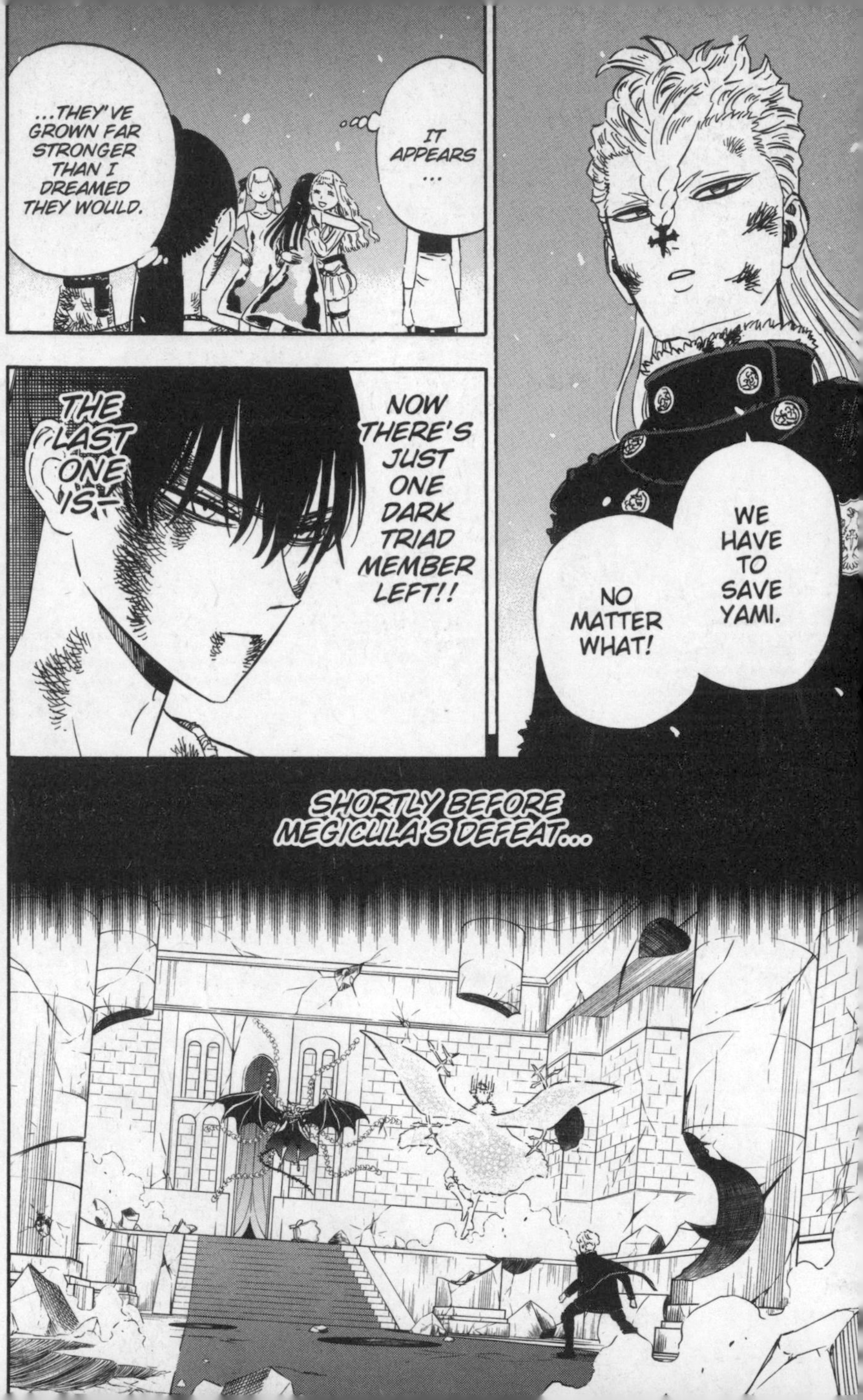
WE HAVE TO SAVE YAMI.
NO MATTER WHAT!
IT APPEARS...
...THEY'VE GROWN FAR STRONGER THAN I DREAMED THEY WOULD.
NOW THERE'S JUST ONE DARK TRIAD MEMBER LEFT!!
THE LAST ONE IS—
SHORTLY BEFORE MEGICULA'S DEFEAT...

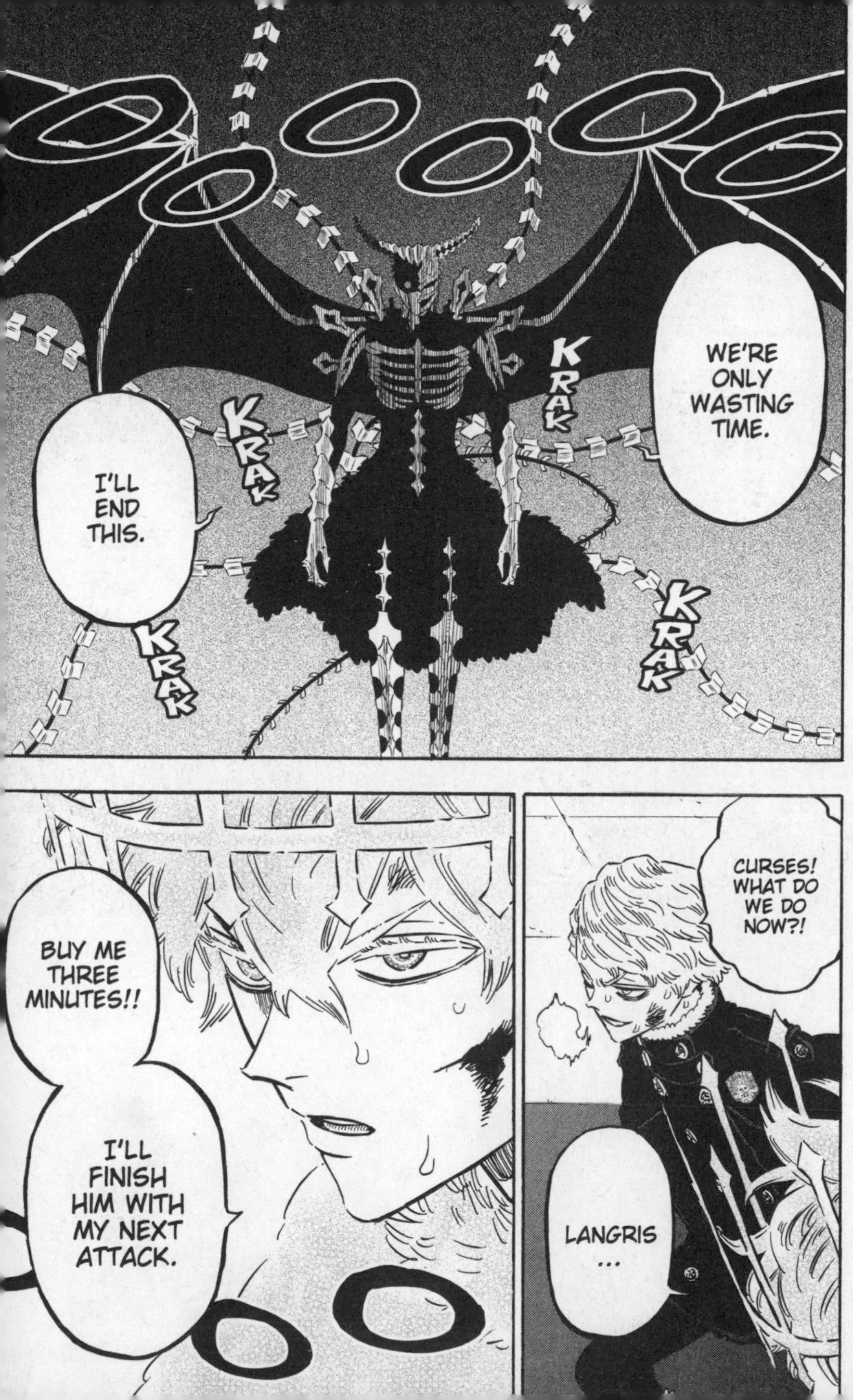
WE'RE ONLY WASTING TIME.
KRAK
KRAK
I'LL END THIS.
KRAK
KRAK
CURSES! WHAT DO WE DO NOW?!
LANGRIS ...
BUY ME THREE MINUTES!!
I'LL FINISH HIM WITH MY NEXT ATTACK.

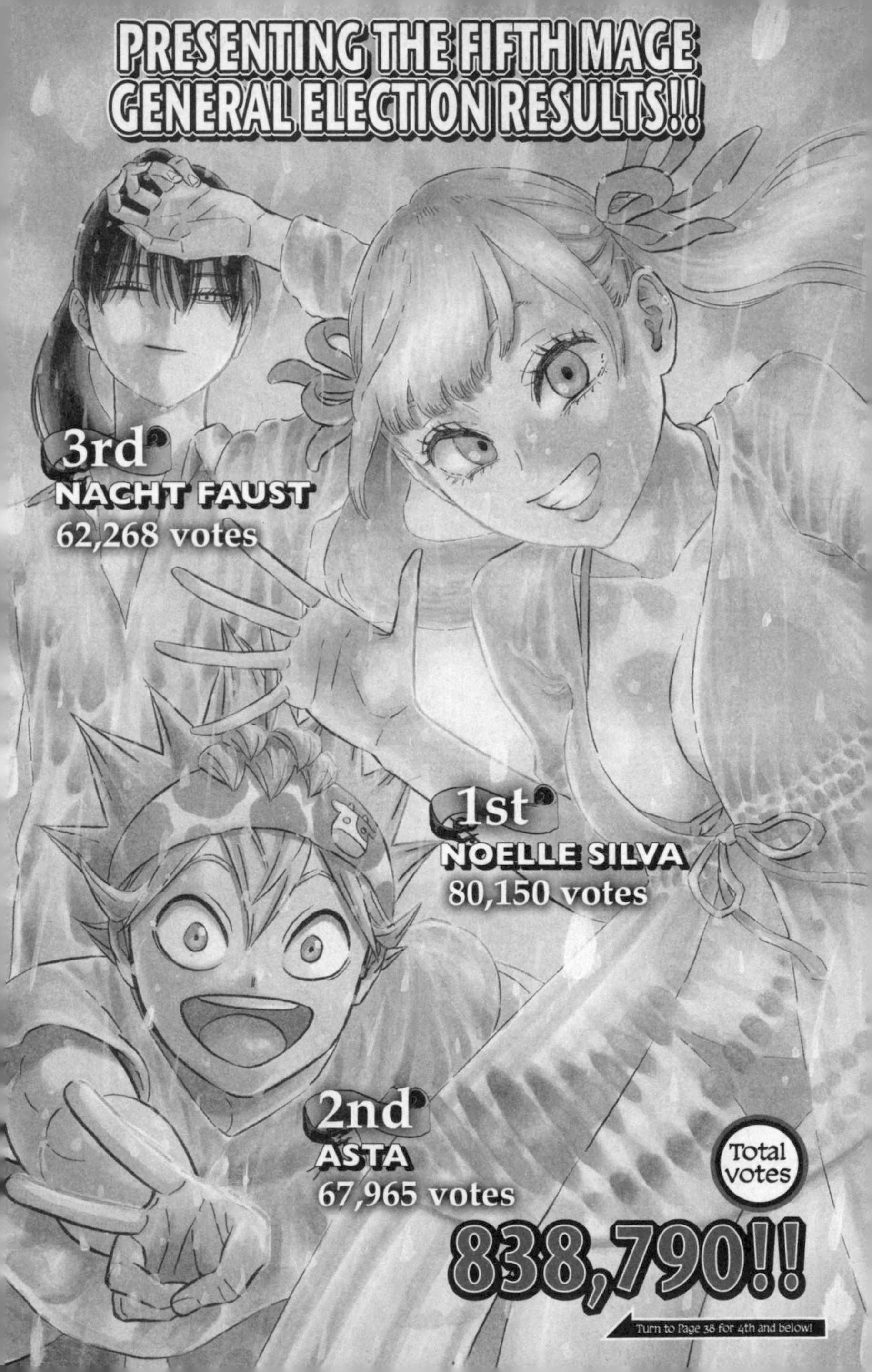

PRESENTING THE FIFTH MAGE GENERAL ELECTION RESULTS!!
3rd
NACHT FAUST
62,268 votes
1st
NOELLE SILVA
80,150 votes
2nd
ASTA
67,965 votes
Total votes
838,790!!
Turn to Page 38 for 4th and below!

Page 305: The Vice Captain of the Golden Dawn

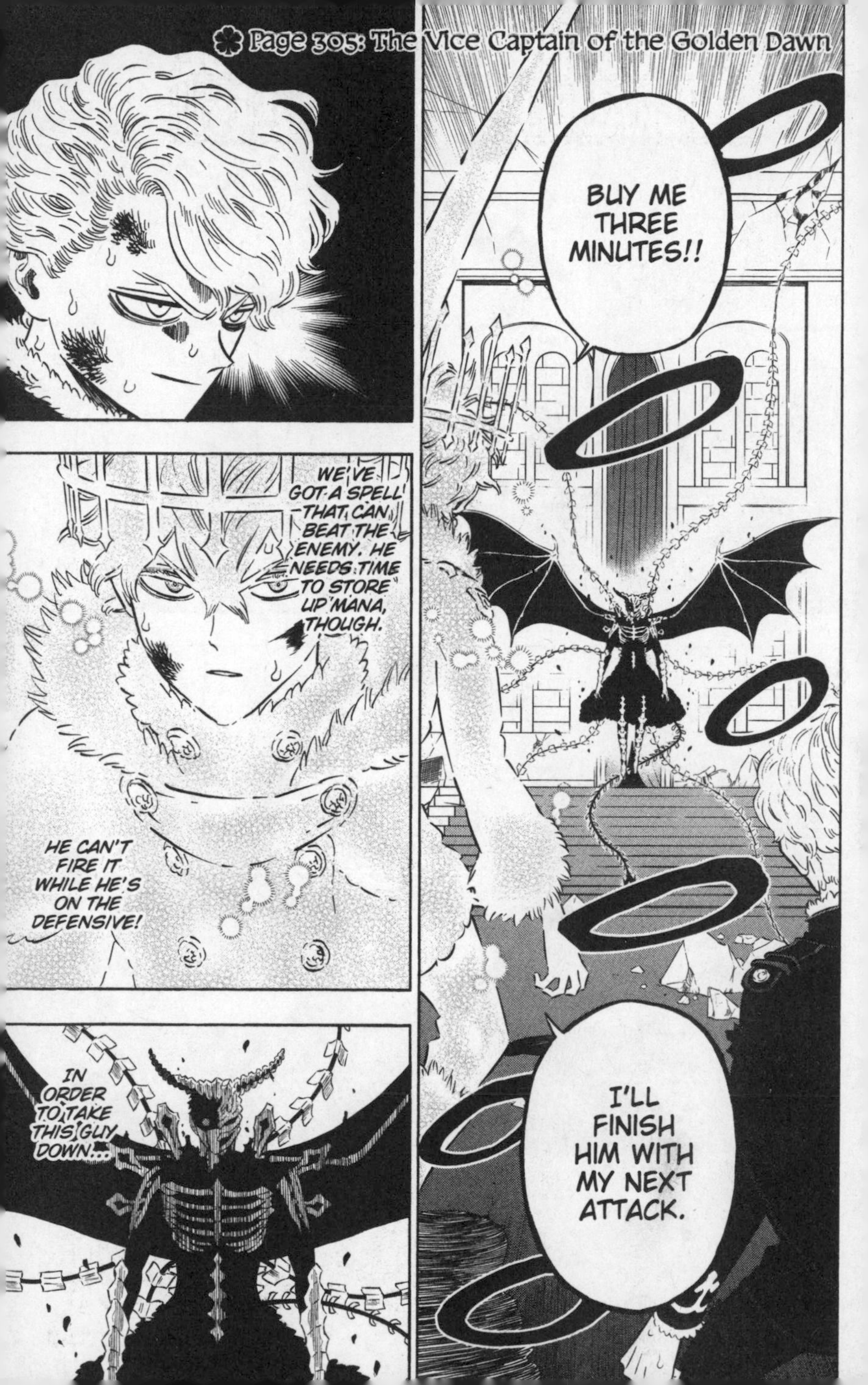

BUY ME THREE MINUTES!!
I'LL FINISH HIM WITH MY NEXT ATTACK.
WE'VE GOT A SPELL THAT CAN BEAT THE ENEMY. HE NEEDS TIME TO STORE UP MANA, THOUGH.
HE CAN'T FIRE IT WHILE HE'S ON THE DEFENSIVE!
IN ORDER TO TAKE THIS GUY DOWN...

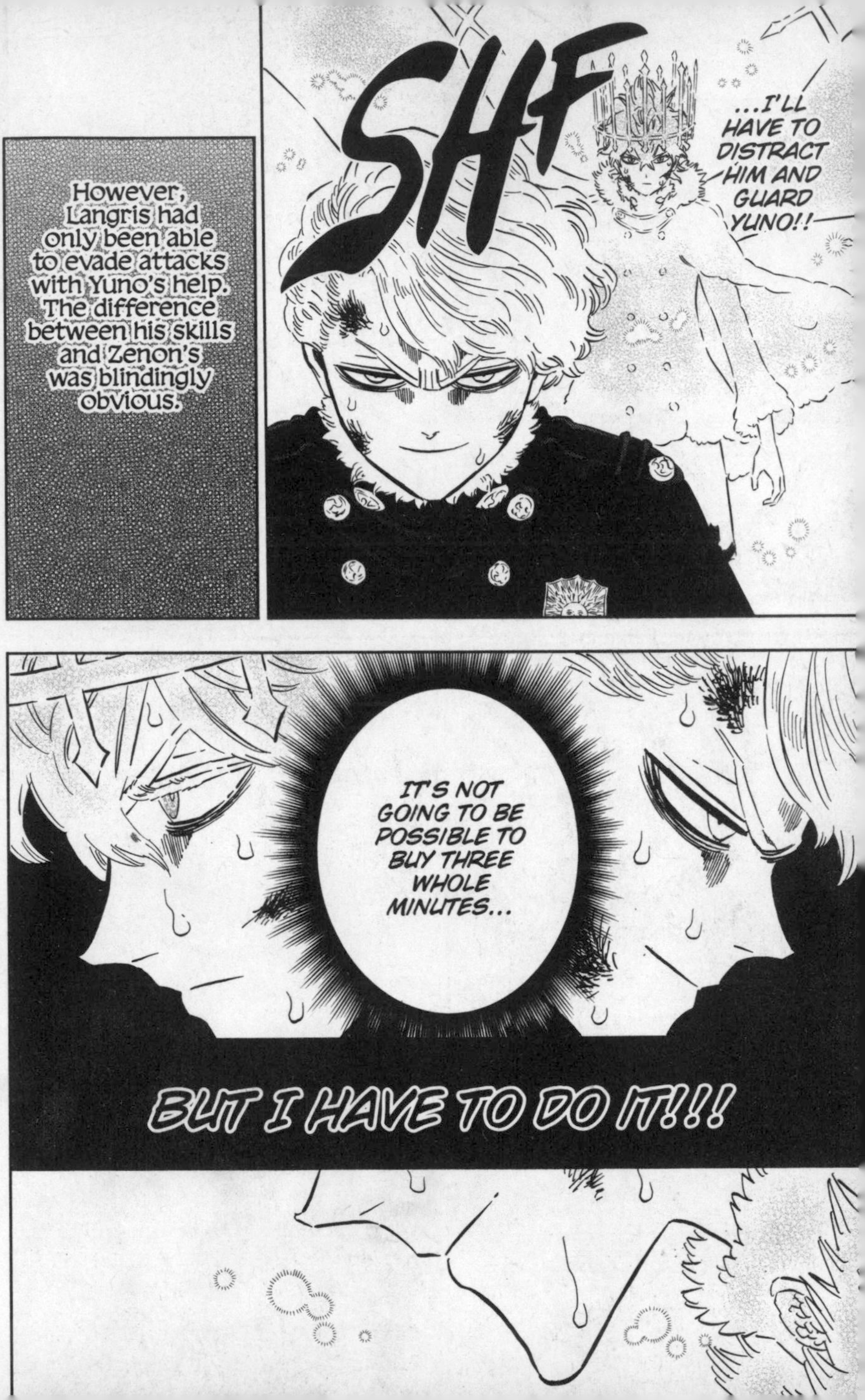
SHF
...I'LL HAVE TO DISTRACT HIM AND GUARD YUNO!!
However, Langris had only been able to evade attacks with Yuno's help. The difference between his skills and Zenon's was blindingly obvious.
IT'S NOT GOING TO BE POSSIBLE TO BUY THREE WHOLE MINUTES...
BUT I HAVE TO DO IT!!!

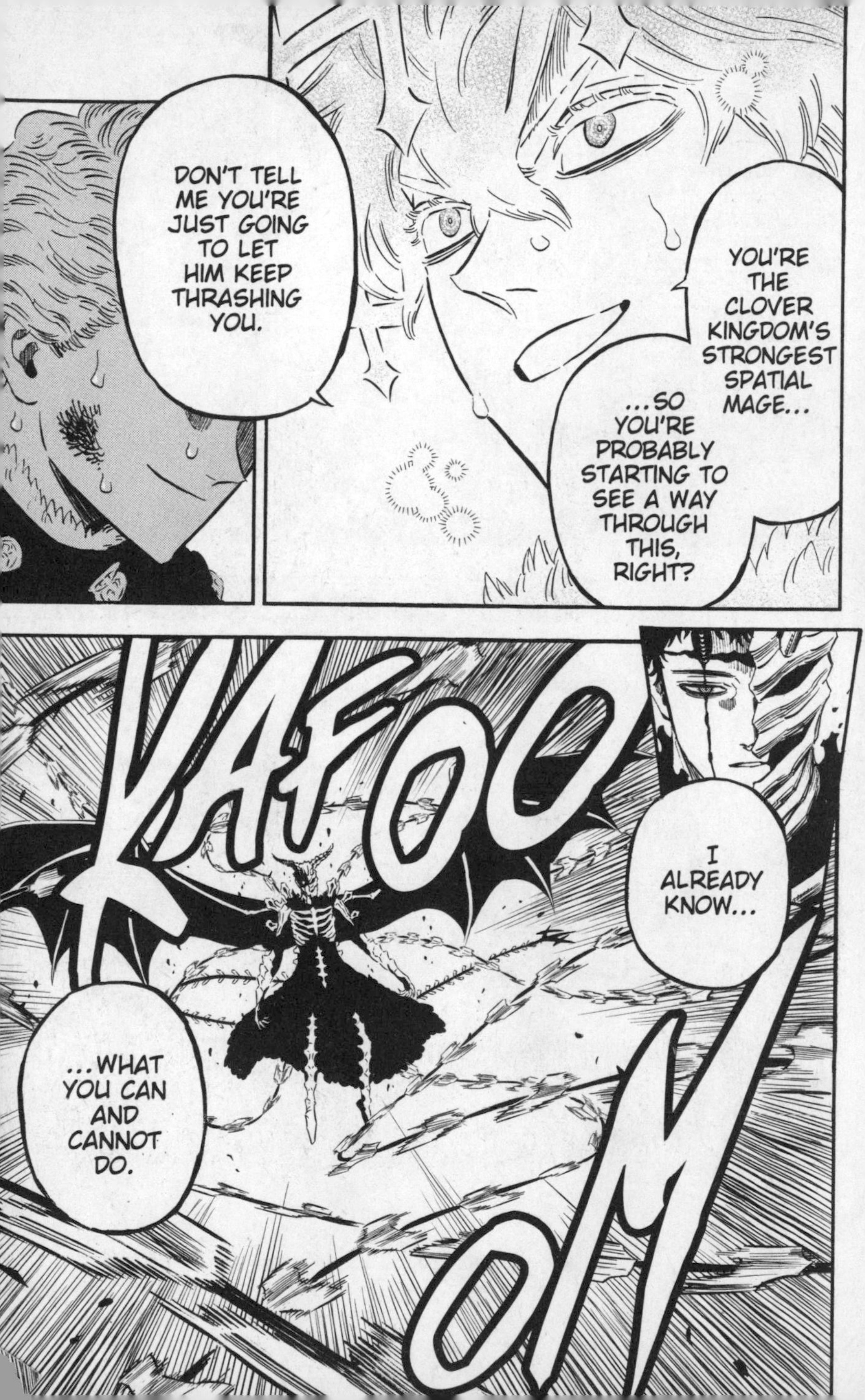
YOU'RE THE CLOVER KINGDOM'S STRONGEST SPATIAL MAGE...
...SO YOU'RE PROBABLY STARTING TO SEE A WAY THROUGH THIS, RIGHT?
DON'T TELL ME YOU'RE JUST GOING TO LET HIM KEEP THRASHING YOU.
VAFOOOM
I ALREADY KNOW...
...WHAT YOU CAN AND CANNOT DO.

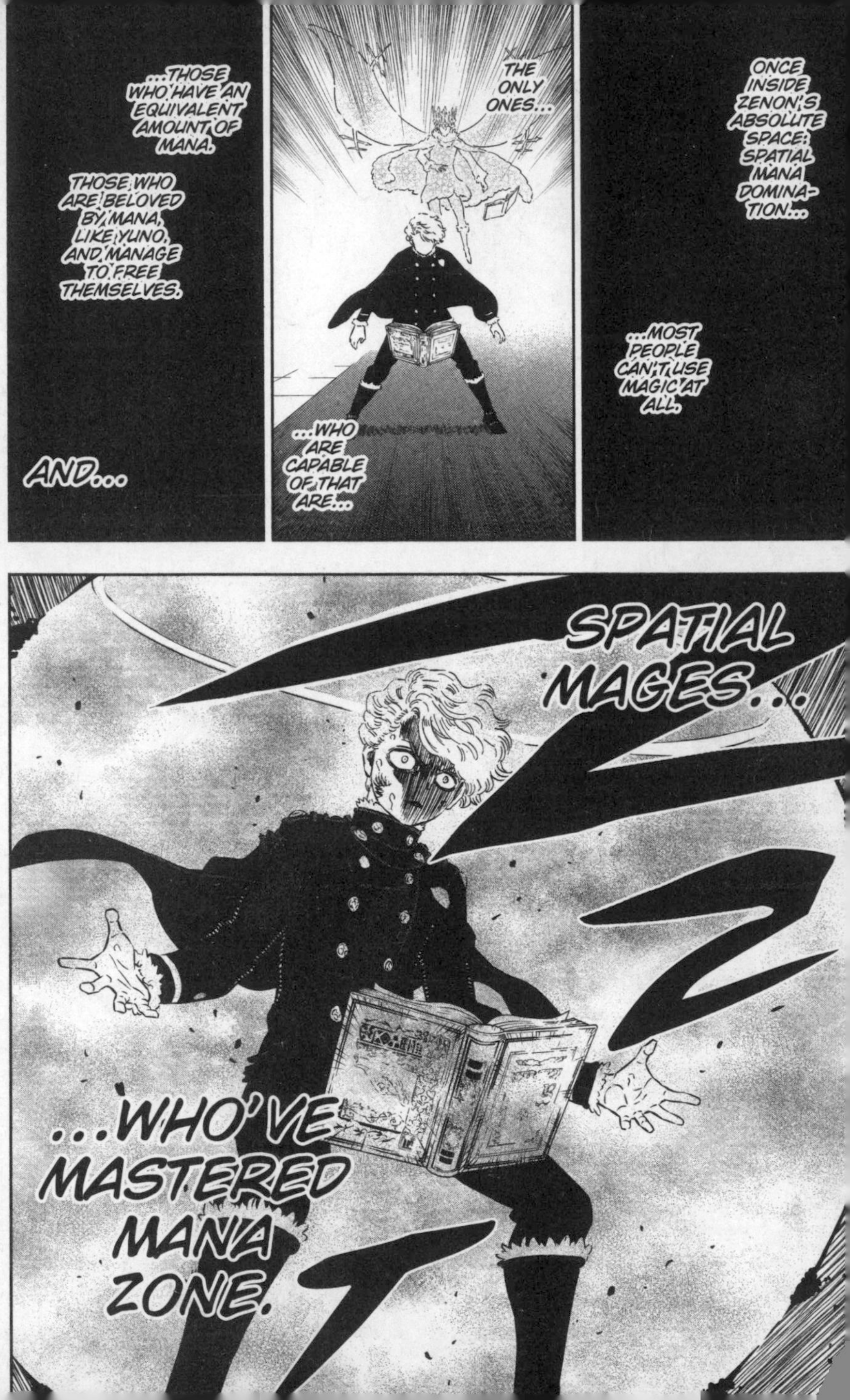
ONCE INSIDE ZENON'S ABSOLUTE SPACE: SPATIAL MANA DOMINATION...
...MOST PEOPLE CAN'T USE MAGIC AT ALL.
THE ONLY ONES...
...WHO ARE CAPABLE OF THAT ARE...
...THOSE WHO HAVE AN EQUIVALENT AMOUNT OF MANA.
THOSE WHO ARE BELOVED BY MANA, LIKE YUNO, AND MANAGE TO FREE THEMSELVES.
AND...
SPATIAL MAGES...
...WHO'VE MASTERED MANA ZONE.

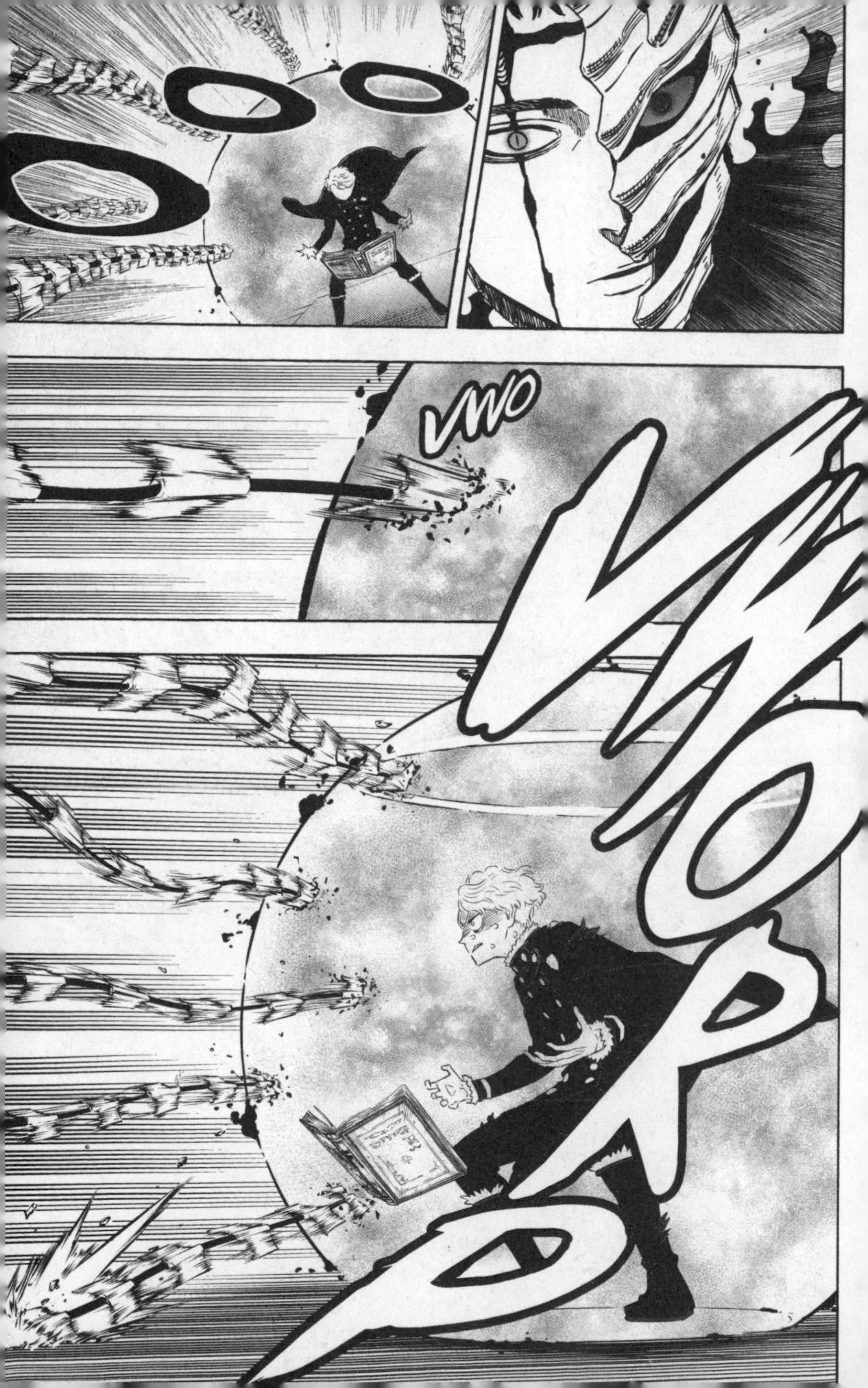
VWO
VWOOP

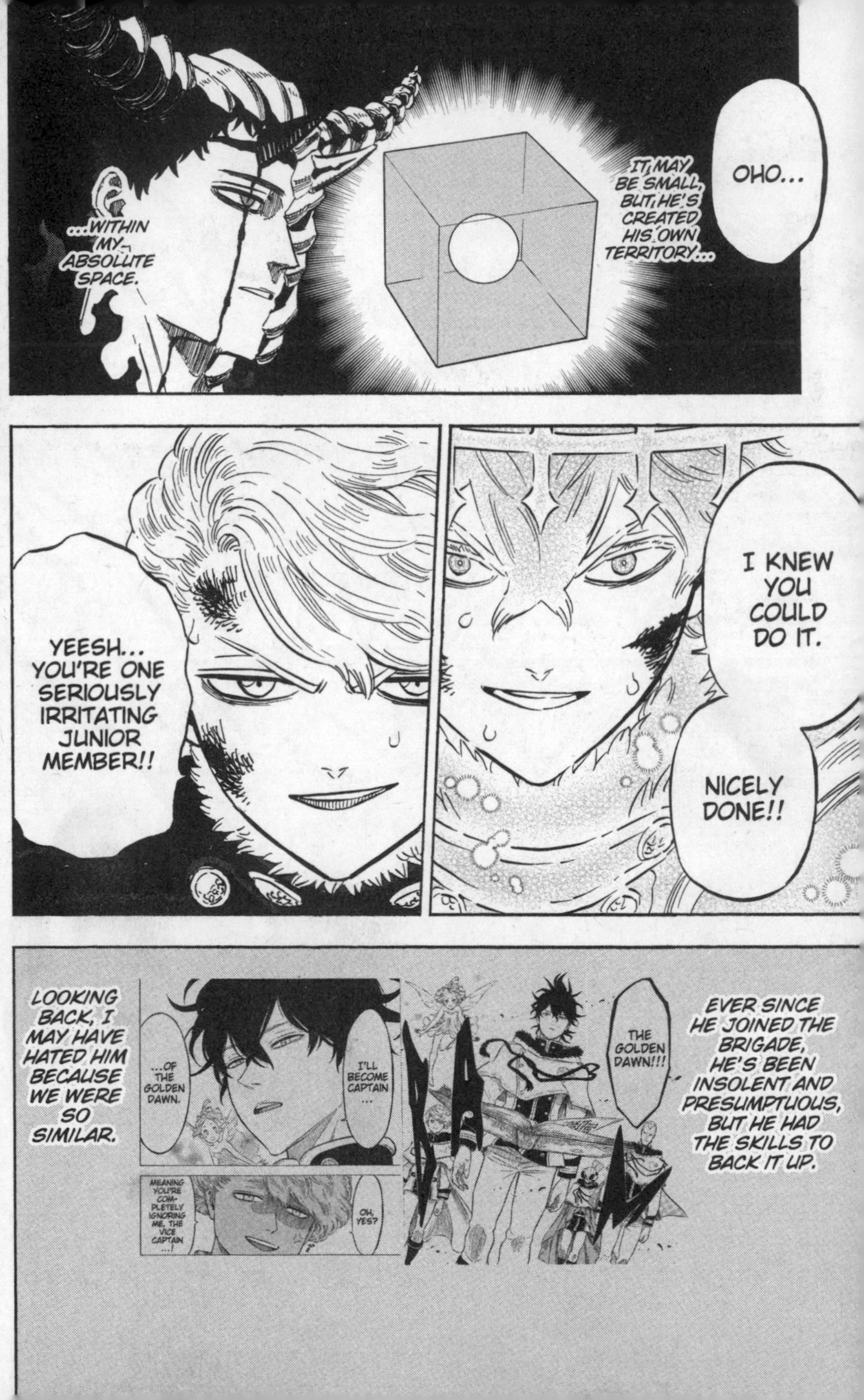
OHO...
IT MAY BE SMALL, BUT HE'S CREATED HIS OWN TERRITORY...
...WITHIN MY ABSOLUTE SPACE.
I KNEW YOU COULD DO IT.
NICELY DONE!!
YEESH... YOU'RE ONE SERIOUSLY IRRITATING JUNIOR MEMBER!!
EVER SINCE HE JOINED THE BRIGADE, HE'S BEEN INSOLENT AND PRESUMPTUOUS, BUT HE HAD THE SKILLS TO BACK IT UP.
THE GOLDEN DAWN!!!
I'LL BECOME CAPTAIN ...
...OF THE GOLDEN DAWN.
OH, YES?
MEANING YOU'RE COM-PLETELY IGNORING ME, THE VICE CAPTAIN...!
LOOKING BACK, I MAY HAVE HATED HIM BECAUSE WE WERE SO SIMILAR.

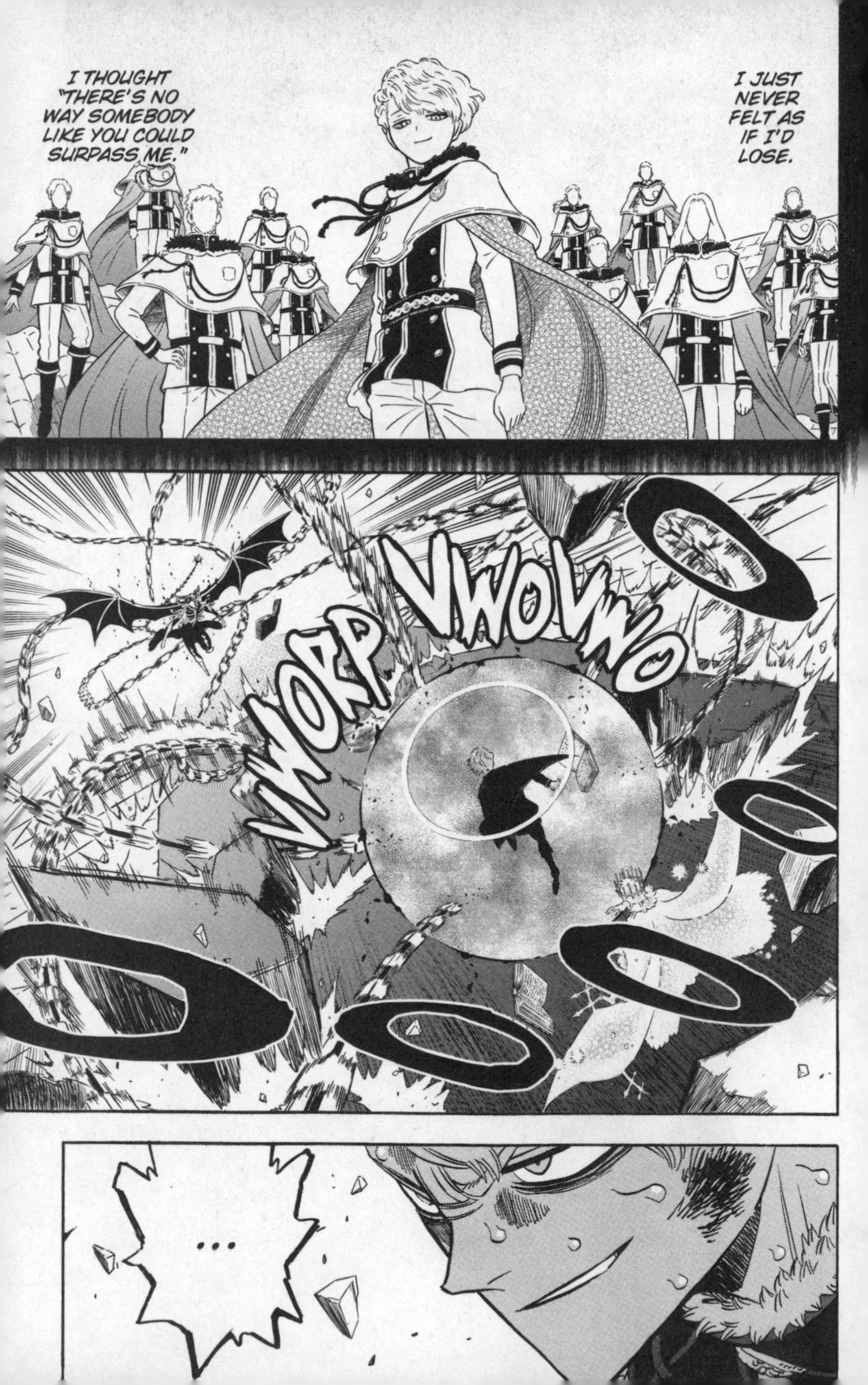
I JUST NEVER FELT AS IF I'D LOSE.
I THOUGHT "THERE'S NO WAY SOMEBODY LIKE YOU COULD SURPASS ME."
VWORP VWOVWO
OOOOOO
...

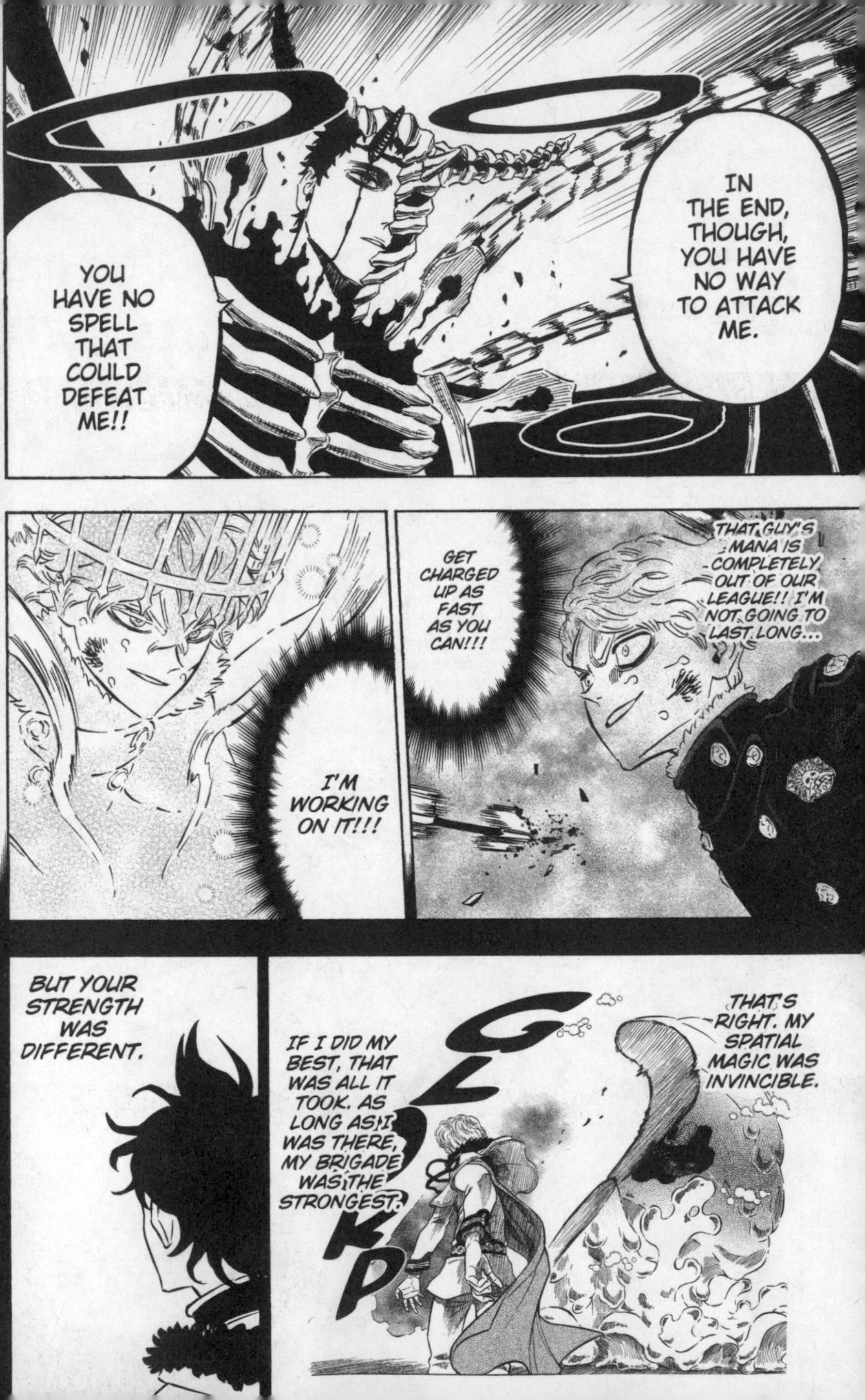
IN THE END, THOUGH, YOU HAVE NO WAY TO ATTACK ME.
YOU HAVE NO SPELL THAT COULD DEFEAT ME!!
THAT GUY'S MANA IS COMPLETELY OUT OF OUR LEAGUE!! I'M NOT GOING TO LAST LONG...
GET CHARGED UP AS FAST AS YOU CAN!!!
I'M WORKING ON IT!!!
THAT'S RIGHT. MY SPATIAL MAGIC WAS INVINCIBLE.
IF I DID MY BEST, THAT WAS ALL IT TOOK. AS LONG AS I WAS THERE, MY BRIGADE WAS THE STRONGEST.
GLKP
BUT YOUR STRENGTH WAS DIFFERENT.

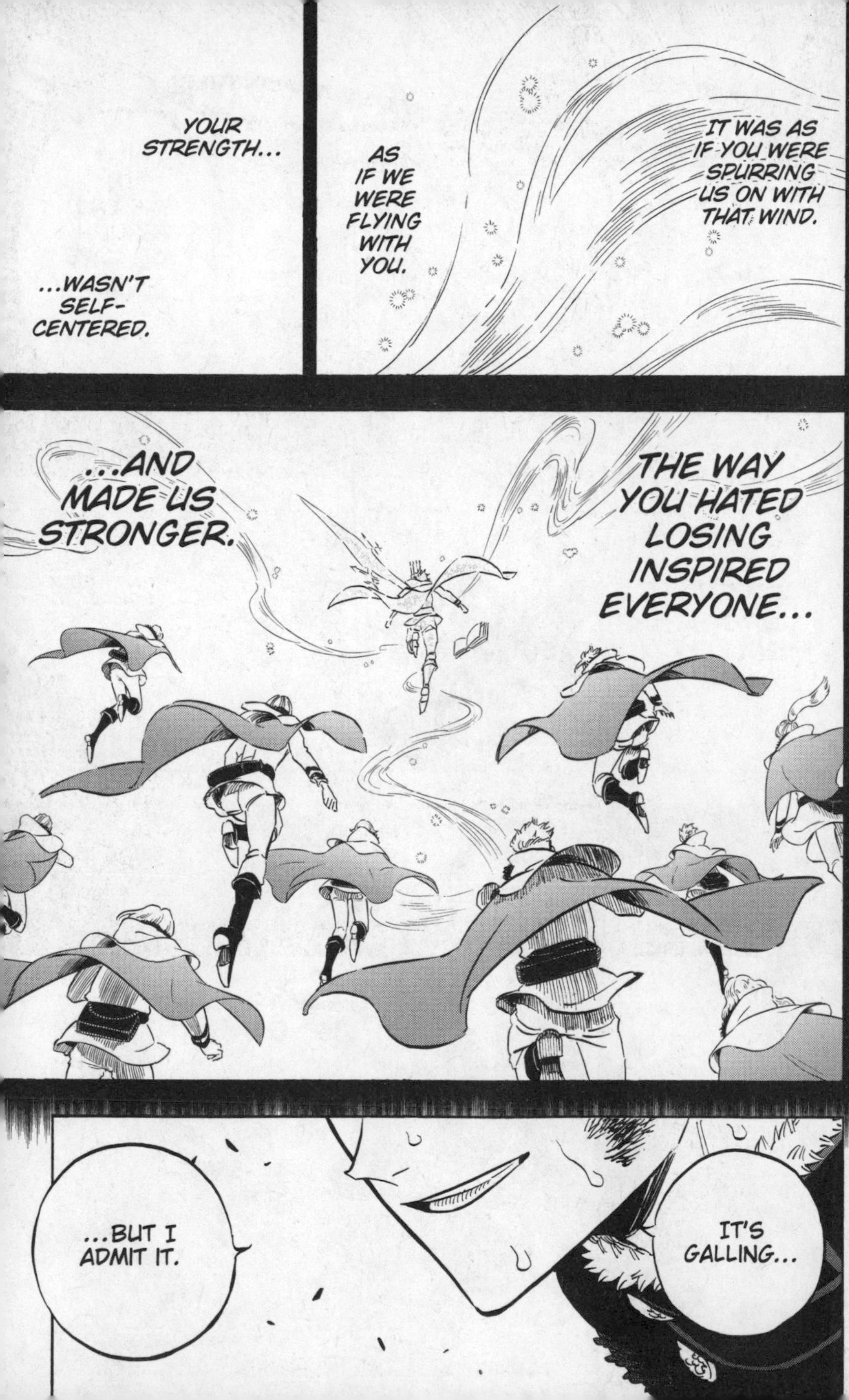
IT WAS AS IF YOU WERE SPURRING US ON WITH THAT WIND.
AS IF WE WERE FLYING WITH YOU.
YOUR STRENGTH...
...WASN'T SELF-CENTERED.
THE WAY YOU HATED LOSING INSPIRED EVERYONE...
...AND MADE US STRONGER.
IT'S GALLING...
...BUT I ADMIT IT.

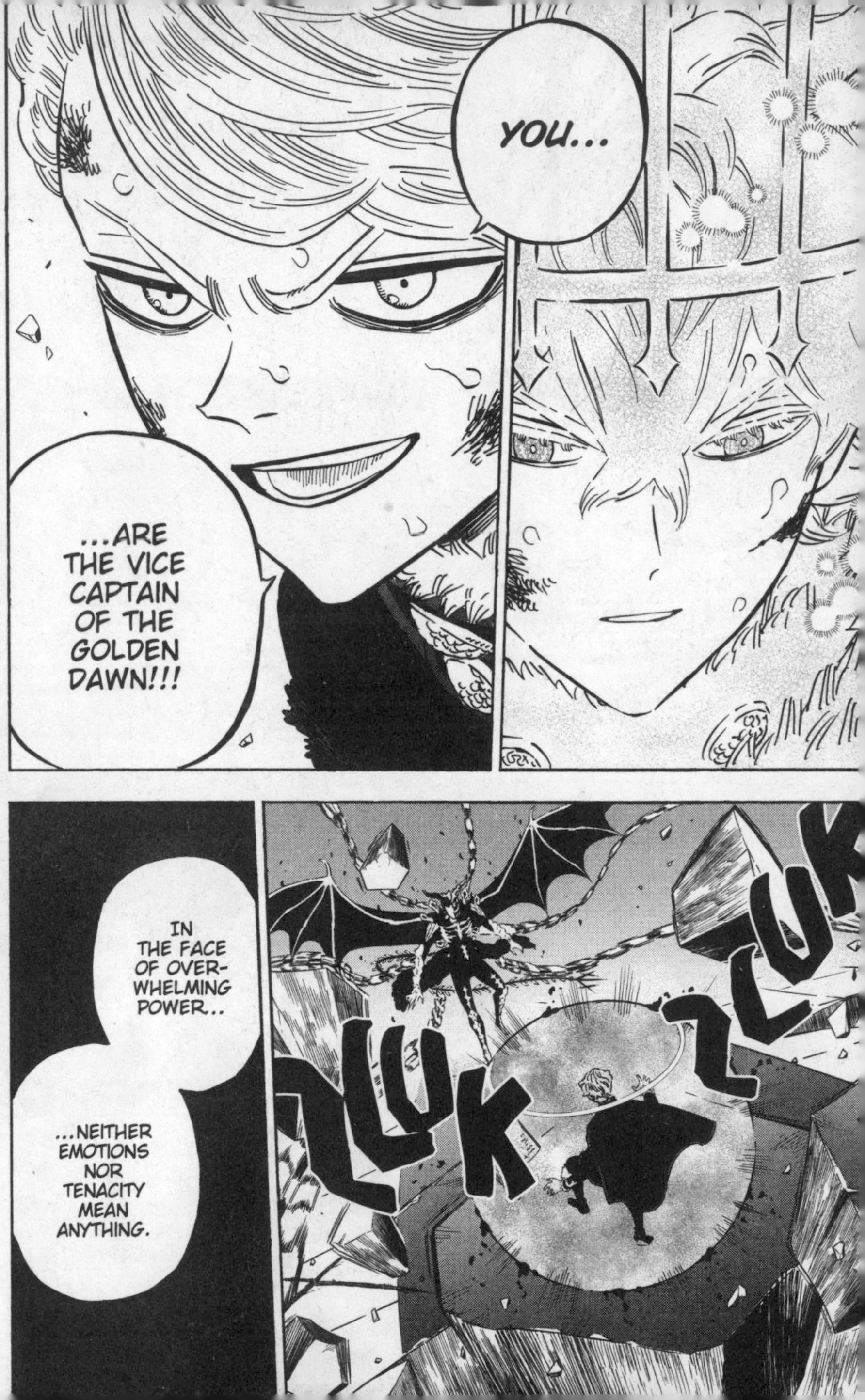
YOU...
...ARE THE VICE CAPTAIN OF THE GOLDEN DAWN!!!
ZUK
ZUK
ZUK
IN THE FACE OF OVER-WHELMING POWER...
...NEITHER EMOTIONS NOR TENACITY MEAN ANYTHING.

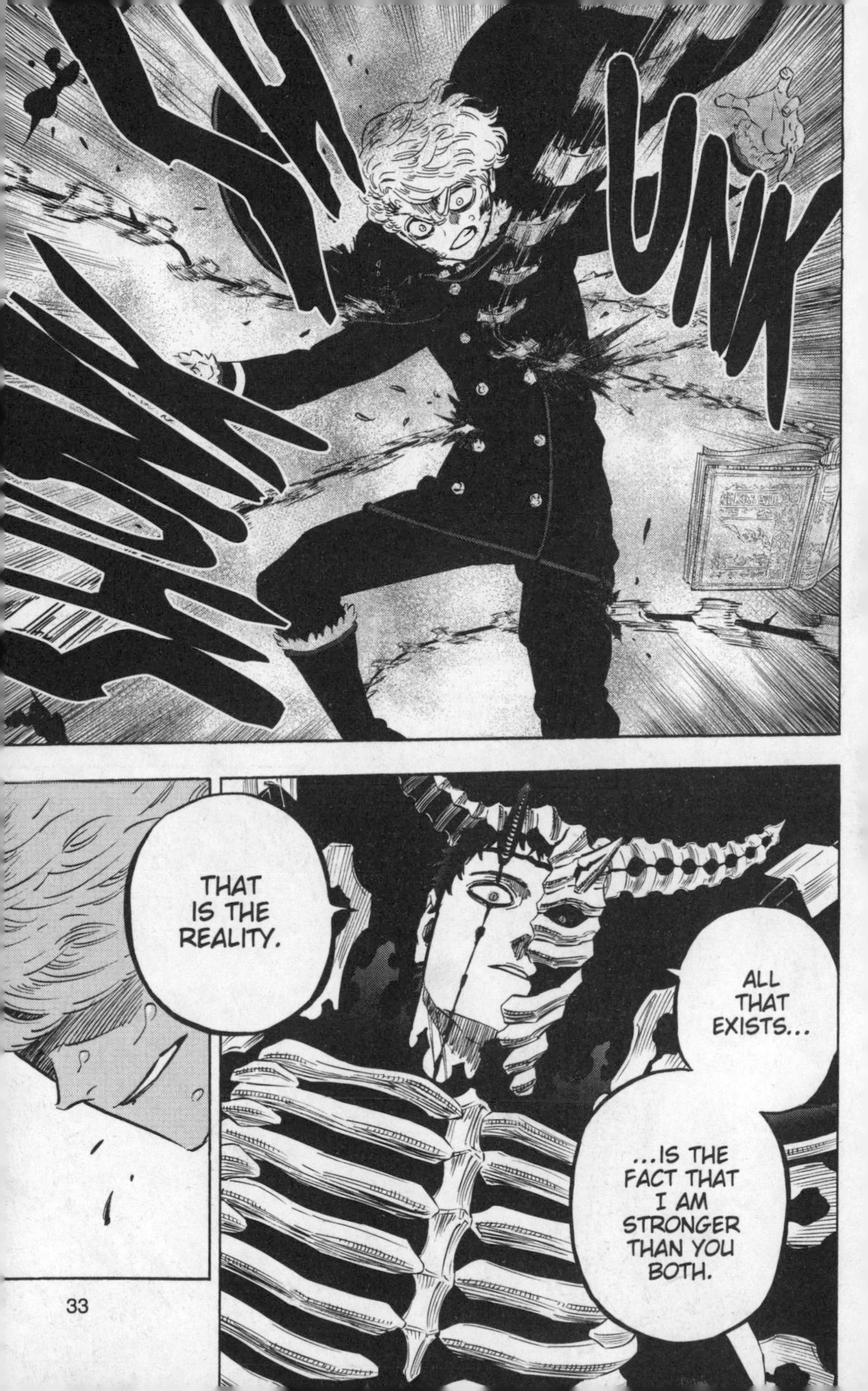
ALL THAT EXISTS...
...IS THE FACT THAT I AM STRONGER THAN YOU BOTH.
THAT IS THE REALITY.

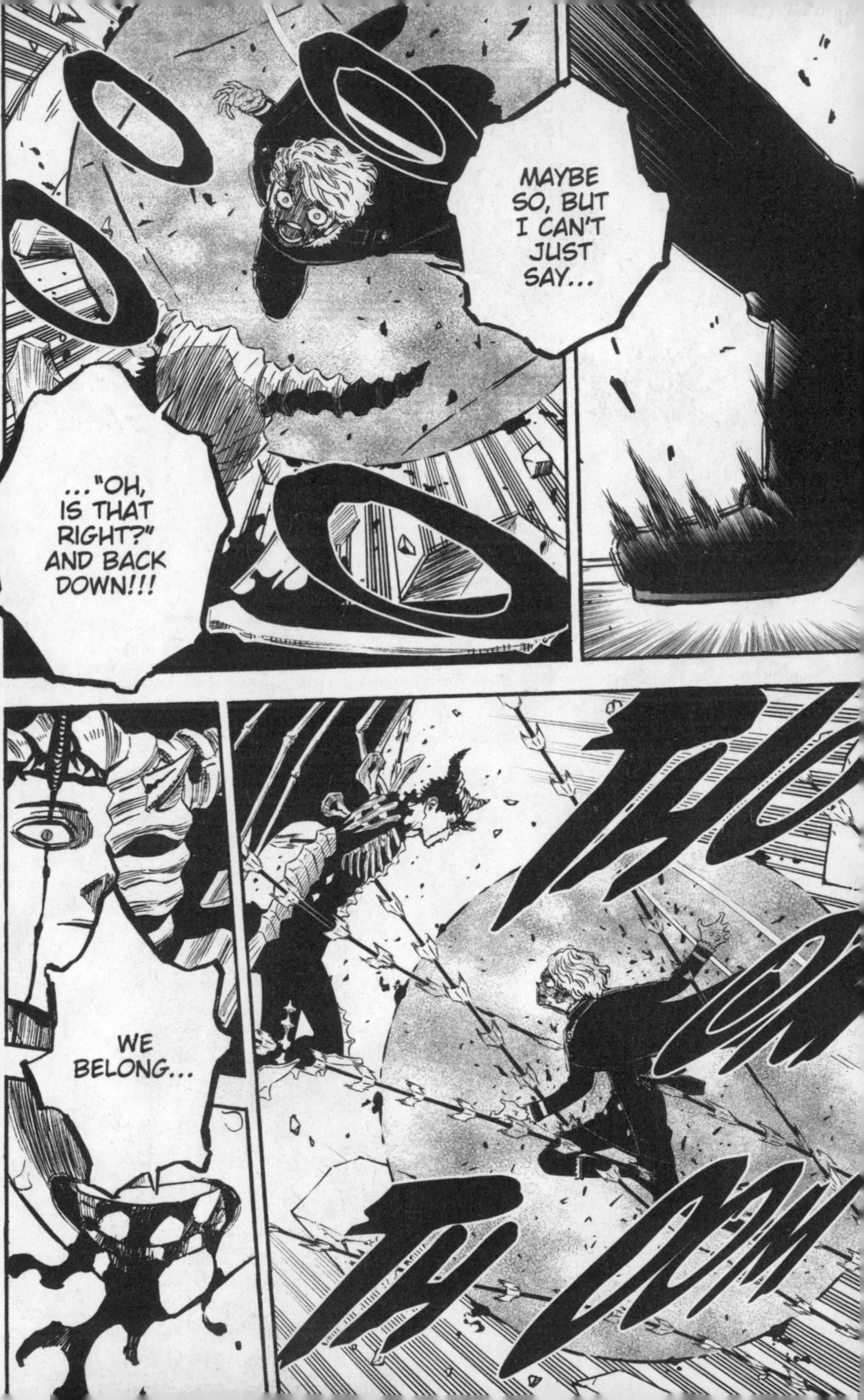
MAYBE SO, BUT I CAN'T JUST SAY...
..."OH, IS THAT RIGHT?" AND BACK DOWN!!!
WE BELONG...

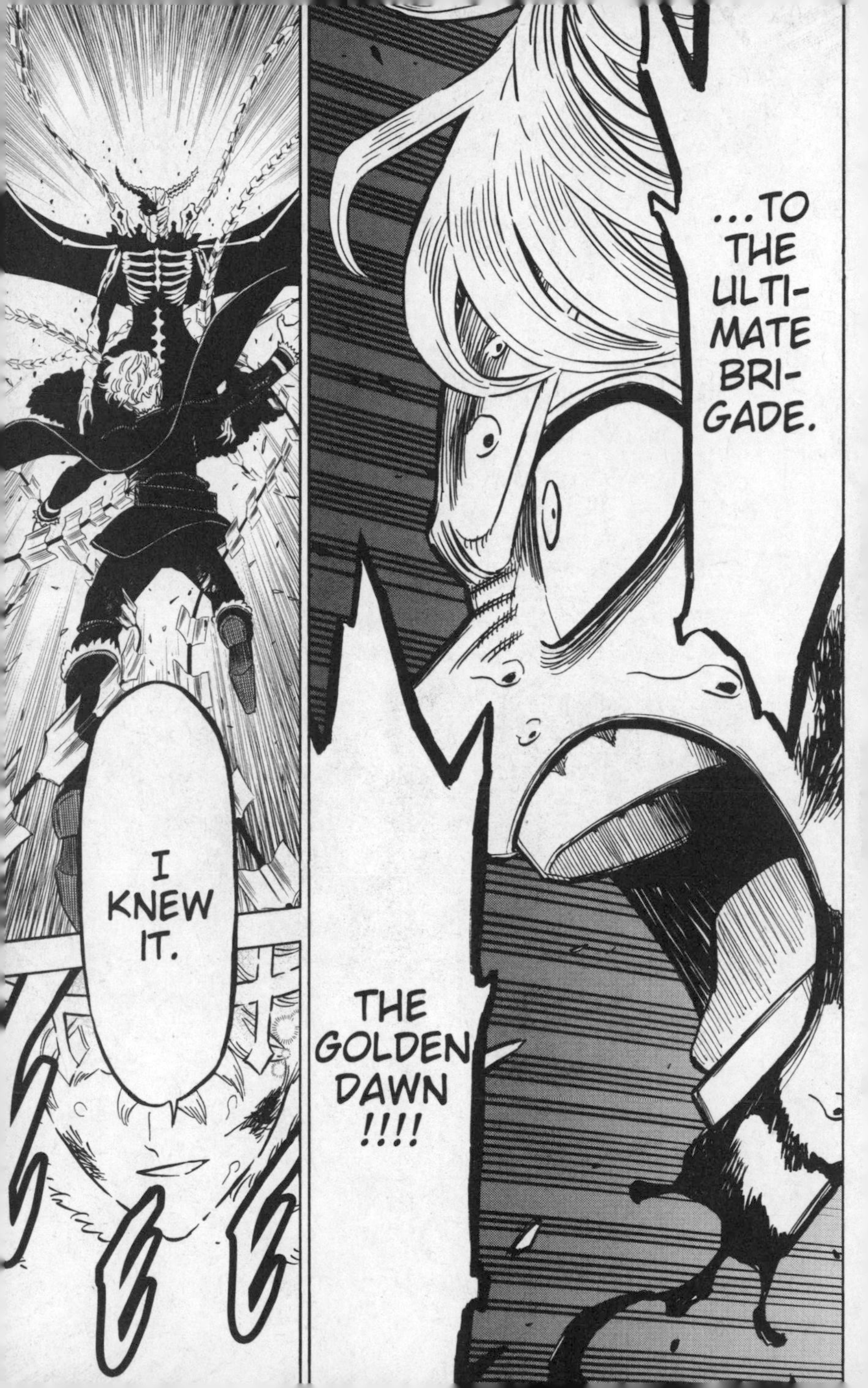
...TO THE ULTIMATE BRIGADE.
THE GOLDEN DAWN !!!!
I KNEW IT.

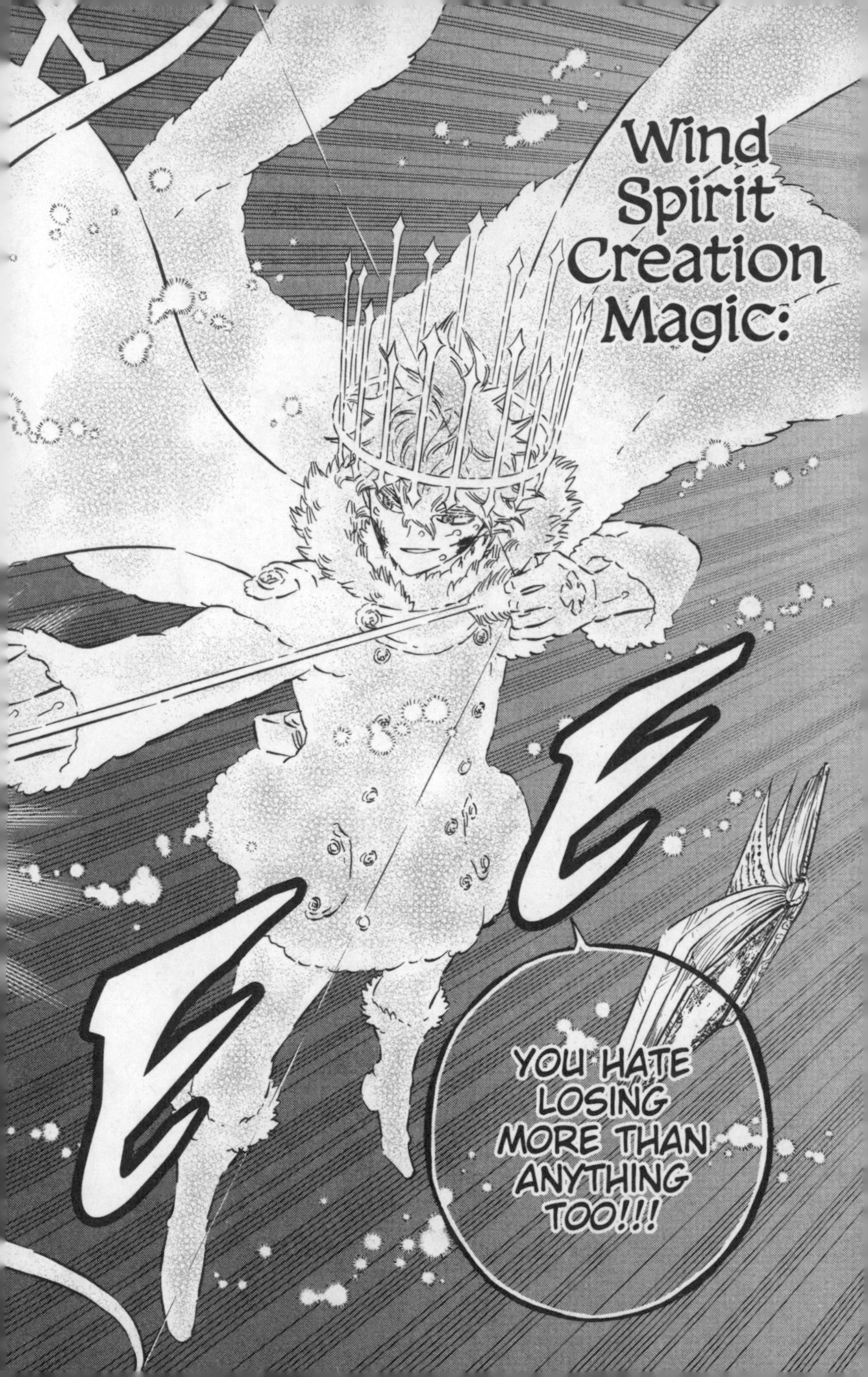
Wind Spirit Creation Magic:
YOU HATE LOSING MORE THAN ANYTHING TOO!!!

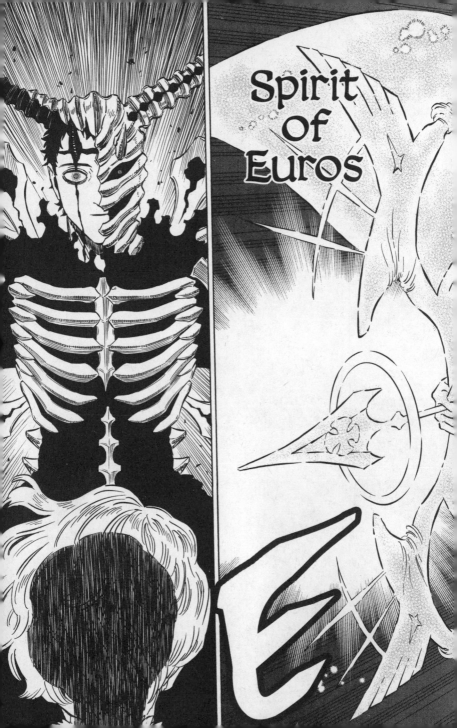

Spirit
of
Euros

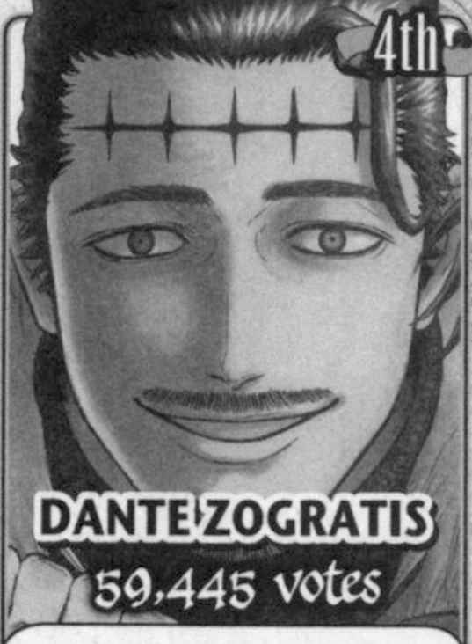
4th
DANTE ZOGRATIS
59,445 votes

THE OLDEST DARK TRIAD MEMBER IS BRAZENLY IN 4TH! THE VILLAIN WHO FOUGHT FIERCE BATTLES WITH ASTA AND THE REST PICKED UP VOTES FROM A LOT OF FANS!

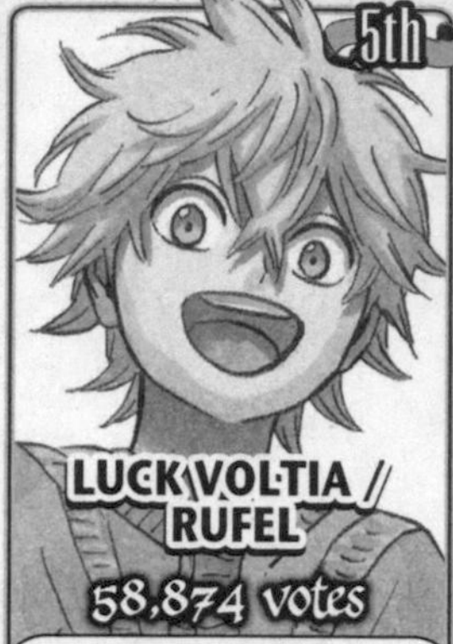
5th
LUCK VOLTIA / RUFEL
58,874 votes

LUCK'S A FREQUENT TOP TEN CHARACTER, AND HE'S ZOOMED UP THE RANKINGS THIS TIME! HE'S CURRENTLY KICKING BUTT WITH HIS NEW ULTIMATE MAGIC!

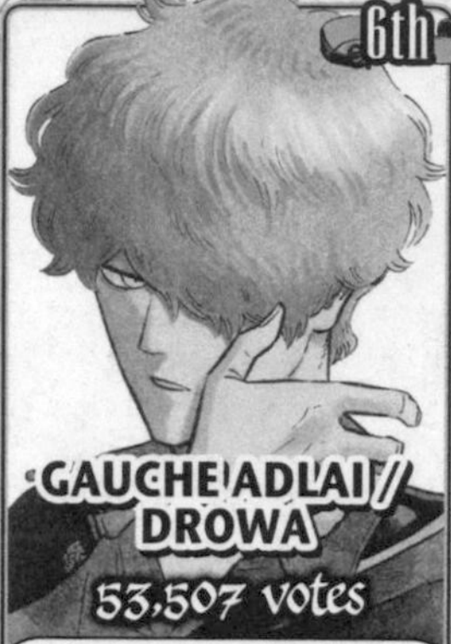
6th
GAUCHE ADLAI / DROWA
53,507 votes

IT WAS POSSIBLE TO VOTE EVERYDAY THIS TIME, AND HIS DEEP-SEATED POPULARITY GOT RESULTS! MANY PEOPLE WANT TO SEE WHAT HE DOES NEXT!

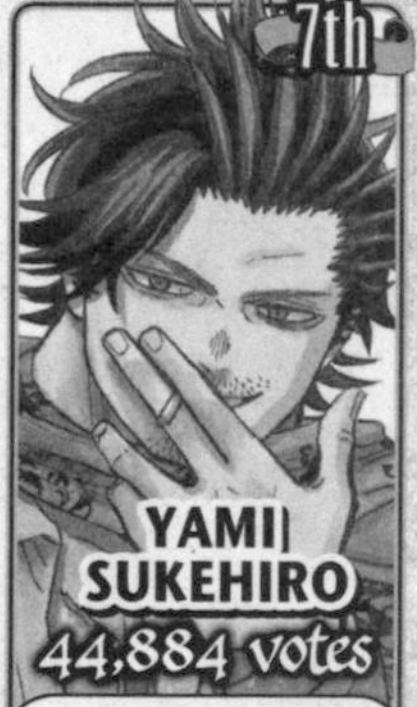
7th
YAMI SUKEHIRO
44,884 votes

EVEN WHILE THE ENEMY'S HOLDING HIM PRISONER, HE'S POPULAR!! WE CAN'T WAIT TO SEE HIM IN ACTION AGAIN!

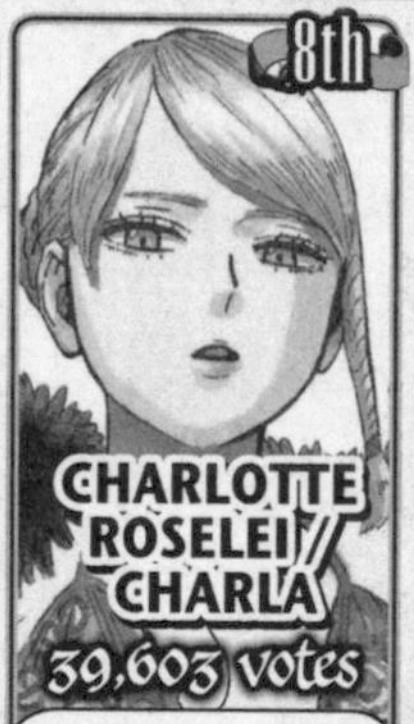
8th
CHARLOTTE ROSELEI / CHARLA
39,603 votes

SHE'S WAS A MAJOR PLAYER IN THE BATTLE WITH MEGICULA!! SHE AND YAMI ARE OPENLY TOGETHER IN THE TOP TEN AGAIN!!

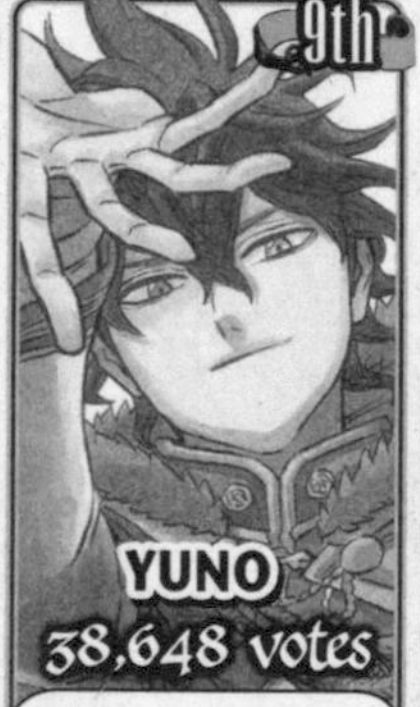
9th
YUNO
38,648 votes

AS ASTA'S RIVAL, WE'D LIKE HIM TO DO A LITTLE BETTER THAN THIS! CAN HE MAKE IT UP NEXT TIME?!

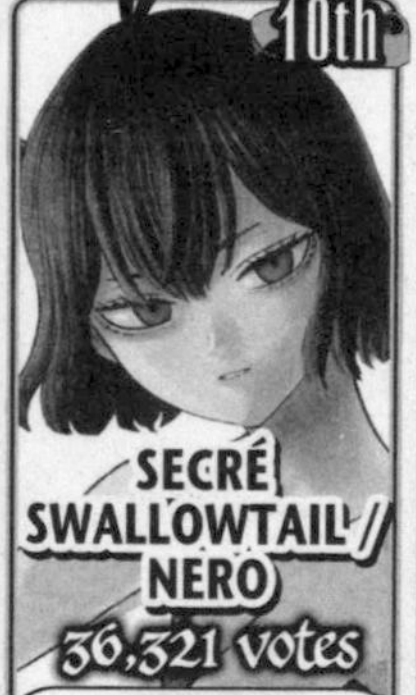
10th
SECRÉ SWALLOWTAIL / NERO
36,321 votes

THERE'S SOME SOLID POPULARITY HERE TOO! WE BET SHE'LL BE AN MVP IN FUTURE FIGHTS WITH THE DEVILS!!

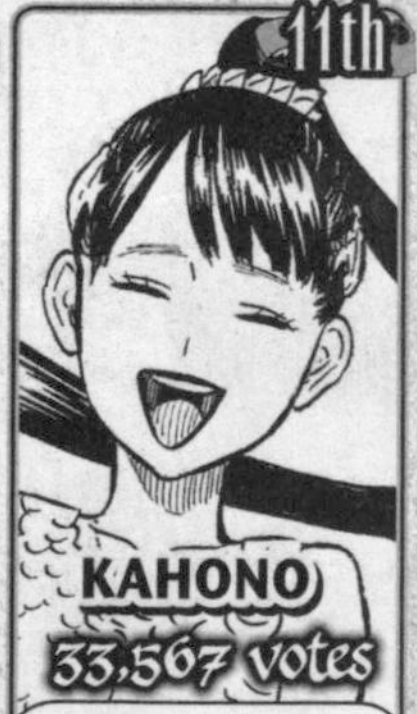
11th
KAHONO
33,567 votes

THE DYNAMIC MAGE FROM THE UNDERWATER TEMPLE ARC MAKES THE RANKINGS! HER FIRM POPULARITY WITH FANS WON HER 11TH PLACE!

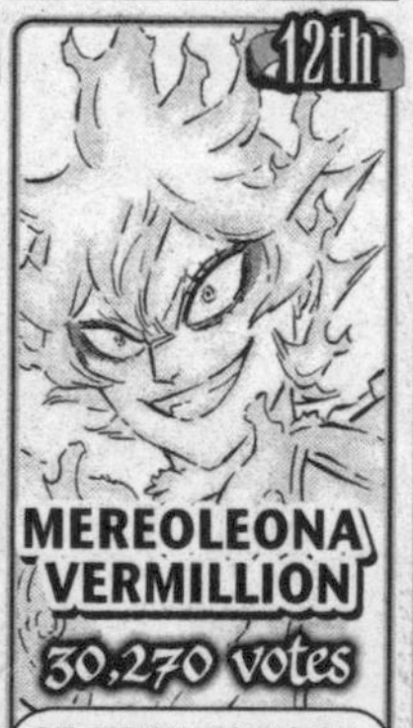
12th
MEREOLEONA VERMILLION
30,270 votes

THE GREAT MAGIC KNIGHT IS SHOWING 'EM HOW IT'S DONE IN THE SPADE KINGDOM! HOW STRONG WILL HER WHITE-HOT, DEMON-INCINERATING FLAMES GET?!

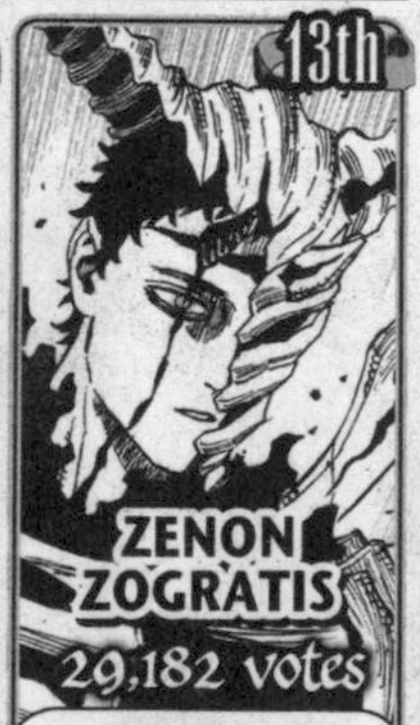
13th
ZENON ZOGRATIS
29,182 votes

THE YOUNGEST DARK TRIAD MEMBER ALSO JUMPED UP THE RANKINGS! HOW IS HIS FIERCE FIGHT AGAINST YUNO AND COMPANY GOING TO END?!

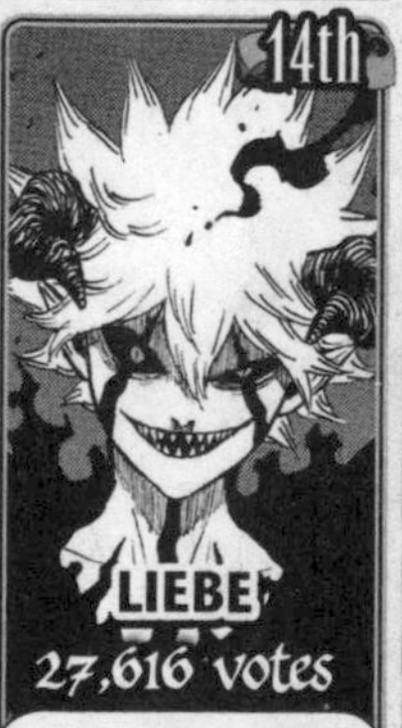
14th
LIEBE
27,616 votes

ASTA'S DEVIL AND HIS TRAGIC PAST ARE MAKING THEIR FIRST APPEARANCE IN THIS POPULARITY VOTE! TRAINING WITH NACHT MADE HIS POPULARITY SKYROCKET!

Continues on Page 54!!

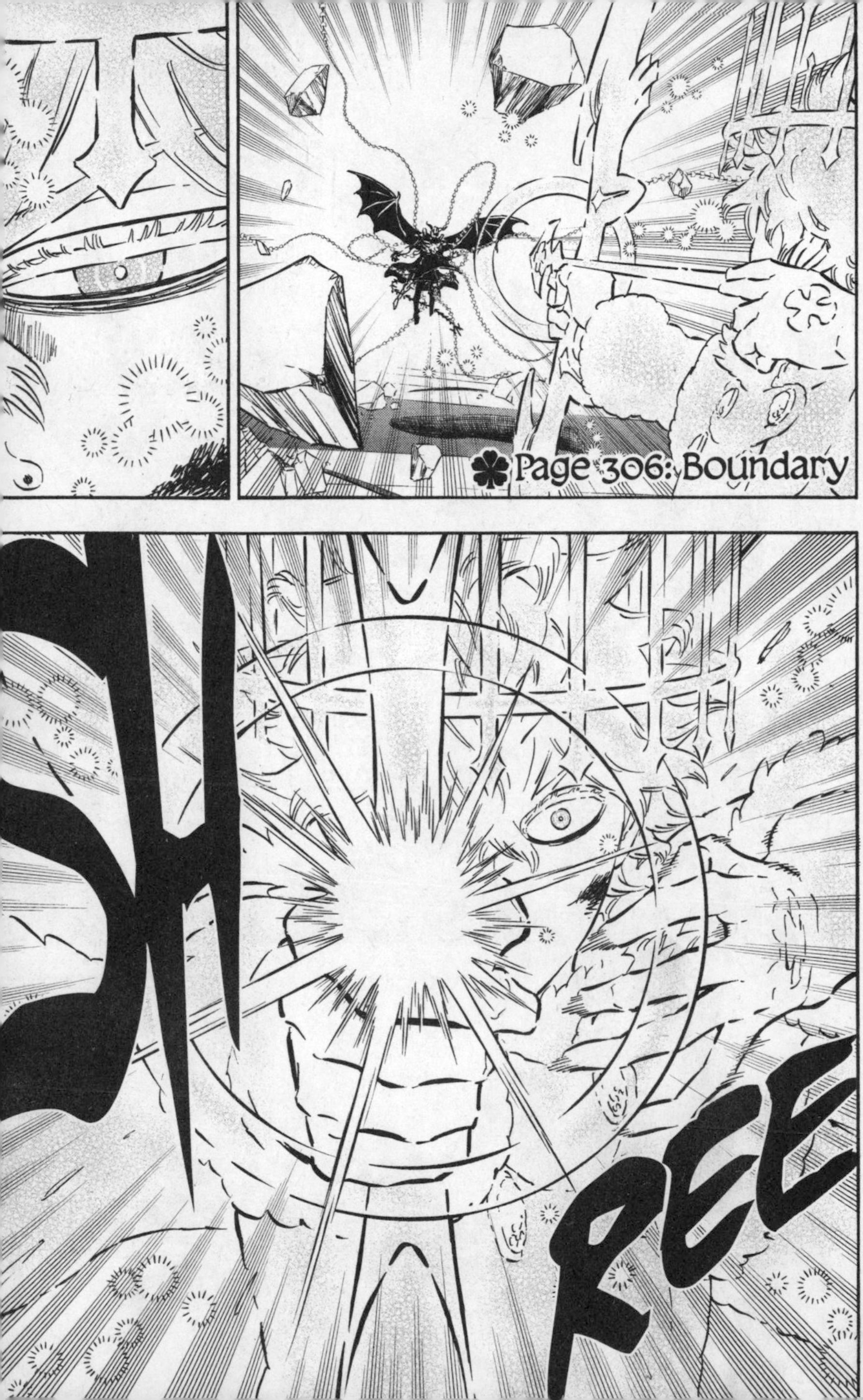
Page 306: Boundary
SHREE

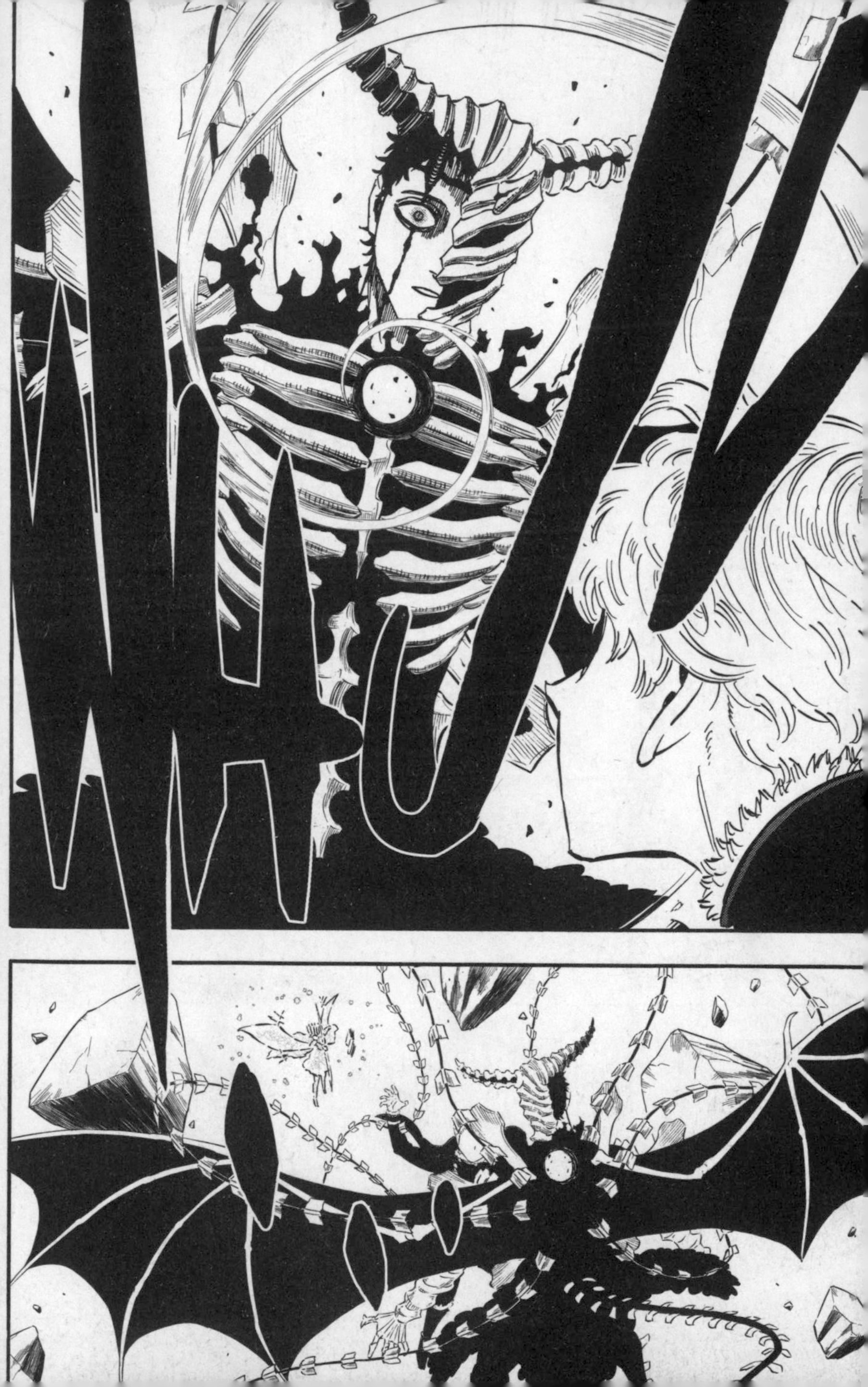

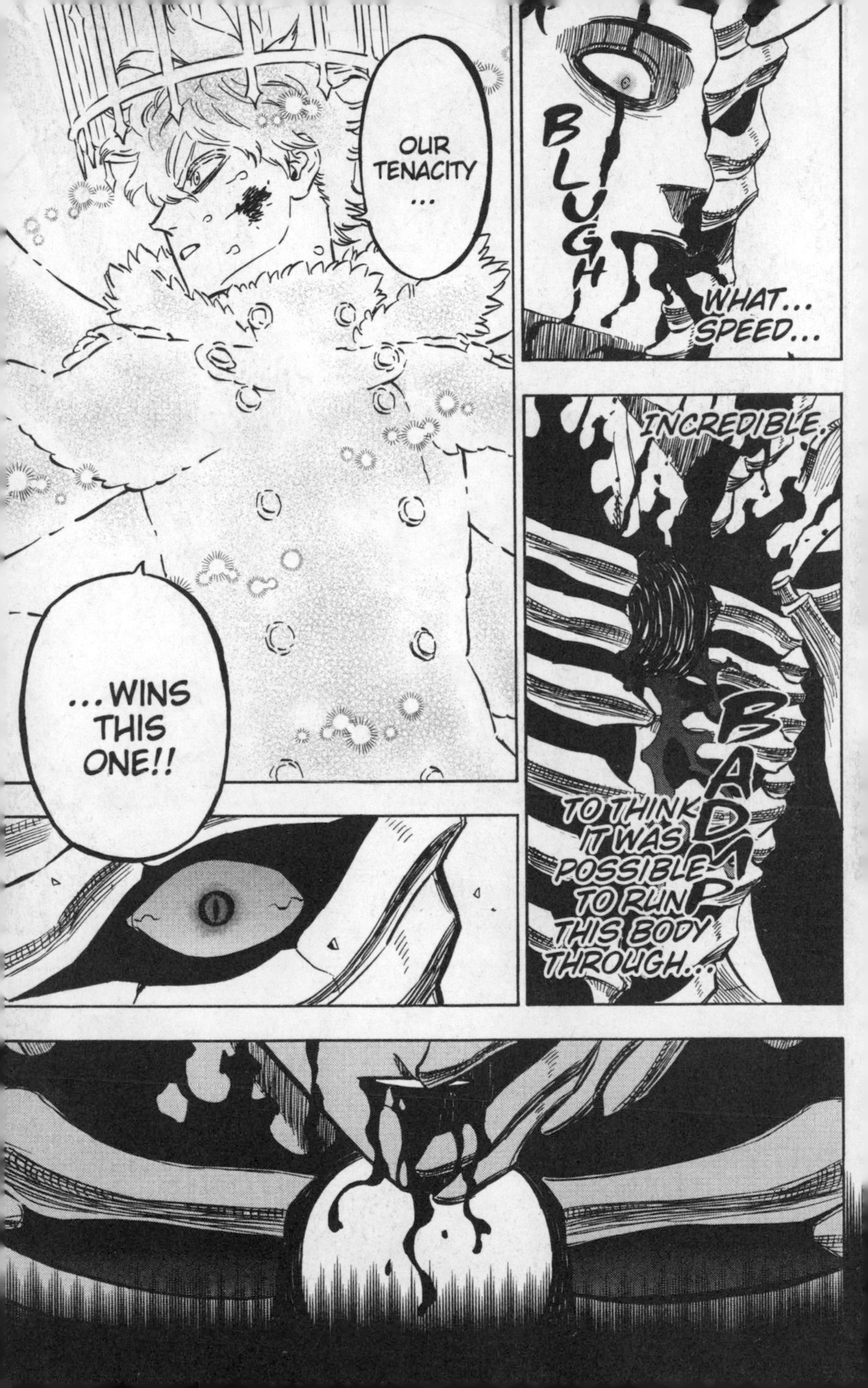
BLUGH
WHAT... SPEED...
OUR TENACITY ...
...WINS THIS ONE!!
INCREDIBLE.
BADMP
TO THINK IT WAS POSSIBLE TO RUN THIS BODY THROUGH...

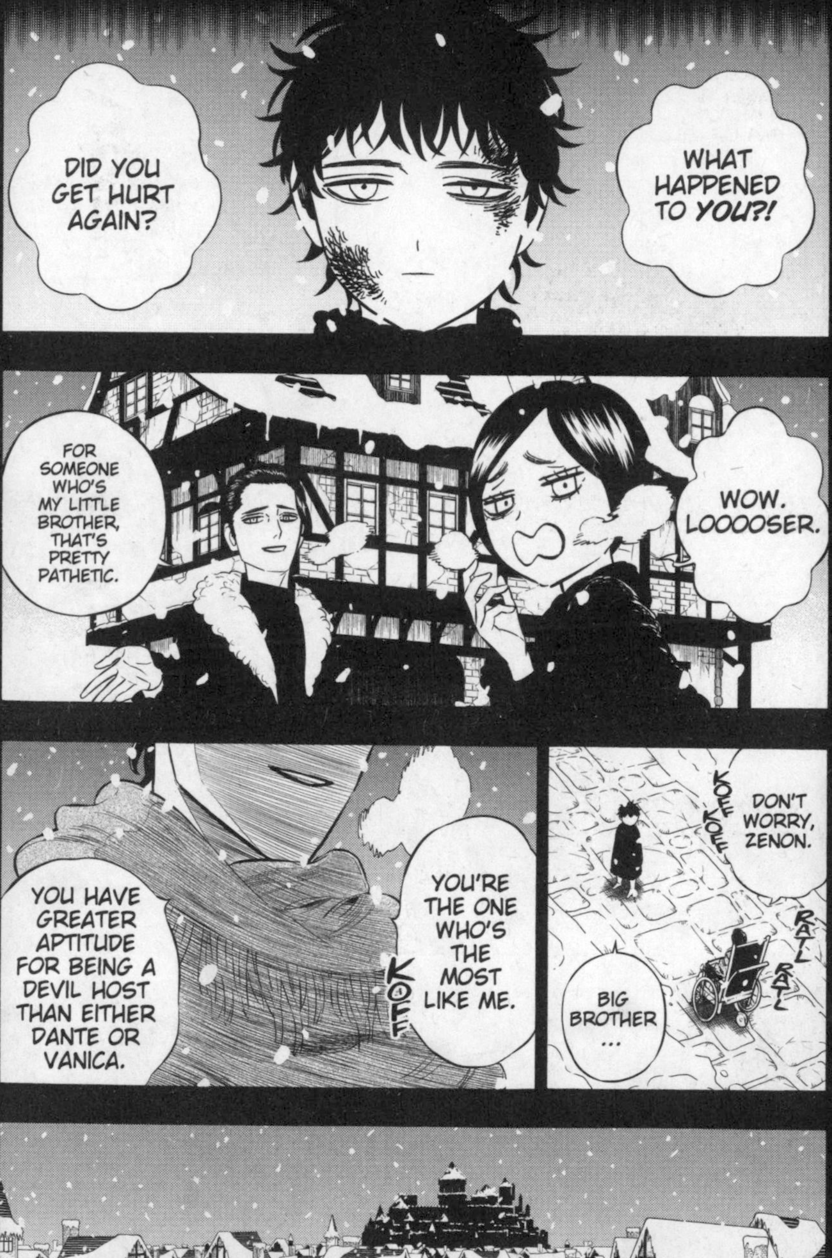
WHAT HAPPENED TO YOU?!
DID YOU GET HURT AGAIN?
WOW. LOOOOSER.
FOR SOMEONE WHO'S MY LITTLE BROTHER, THAT'S PRETTY PATHETIC.
KOFF KOFF
DON'T WORRY, ZENON.
RATL RATL
BIG BROTHER ...
YOU'RE THE ONE WHO'S THE MOST LIKE ME.
KOFF
YOU HAVE GREATER APTITUDE FOR BEING A DEVIL HOST THAN EITHER DANTE OR VANICA.

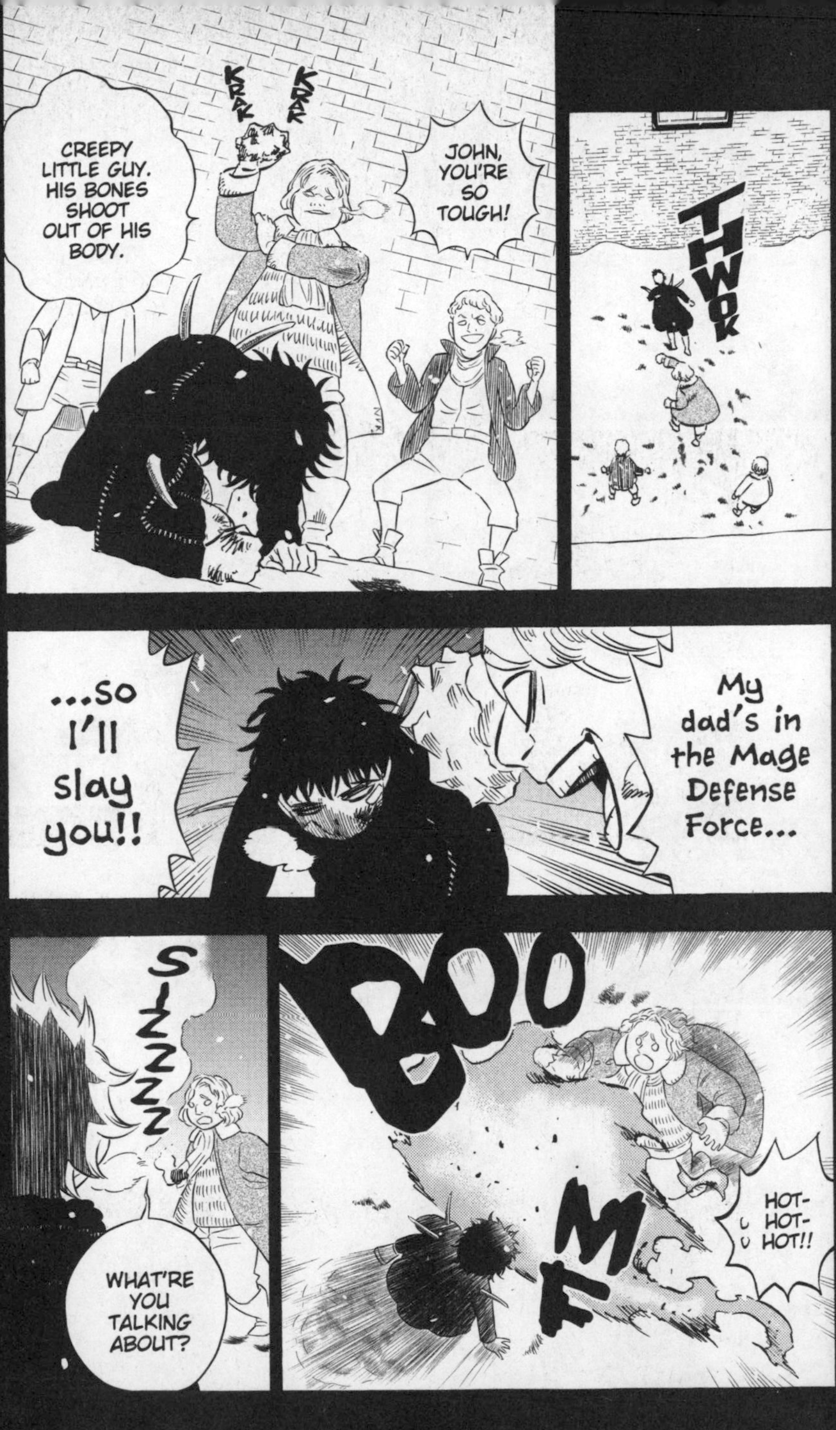
THWOK
JOHN, YOU'RE SO TOUGH!
KRAK KRAK
CREEPY LITTLE GUY. HIS BONES SHOOT OUT OF HIS BODY.
My dad's in the Mage Defense Force...
...so I'll slay you!!
BOOMF
HOT-HOT-HOT!!
SIZZZZ
WHAT'RE YOU TALKING ABOUT?

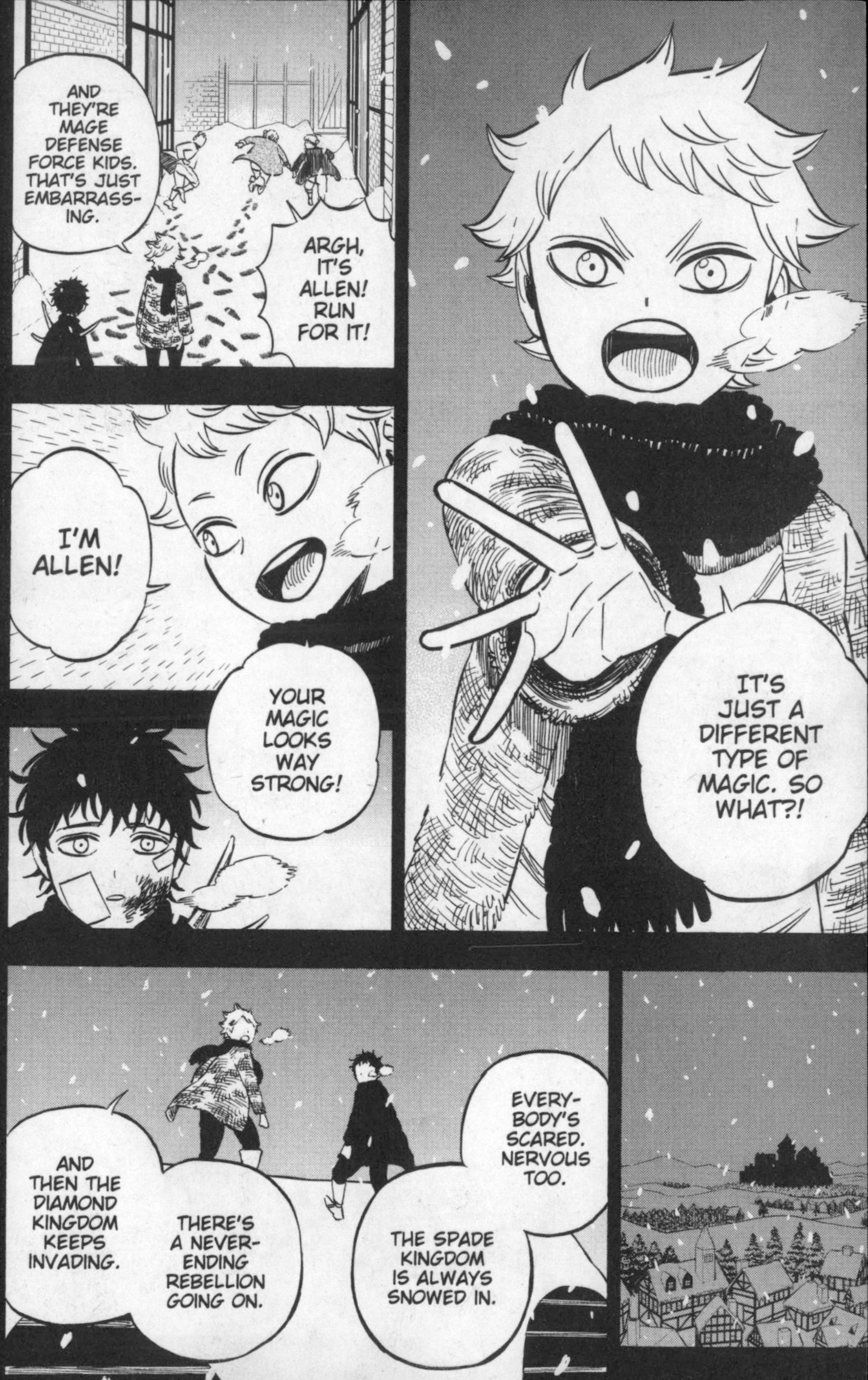
IT'S JUST A DIFFERENT TYPE OF MAGIC. SO WHAT?!
ARGH, IT'S ALLEN! RUN FOR IT!
AND THEY'RE MAGE DEFENSE FORCE KIDS. THAT'S JUST EMBARRASS-ING.
I'M ALLEN!
YOUR MAGIC LOOKS WAY STRONG!
THE SPADE KINGDOM IS ALWAYS SNOWED IN.
THERE'S A NEVER-ENDING REBELLION GOING ON.
AND THEN THE DIAMOND KINGDOM KEEPS INVADING.
EVERY-BODY'S SCARED. NERVOUS TOO.

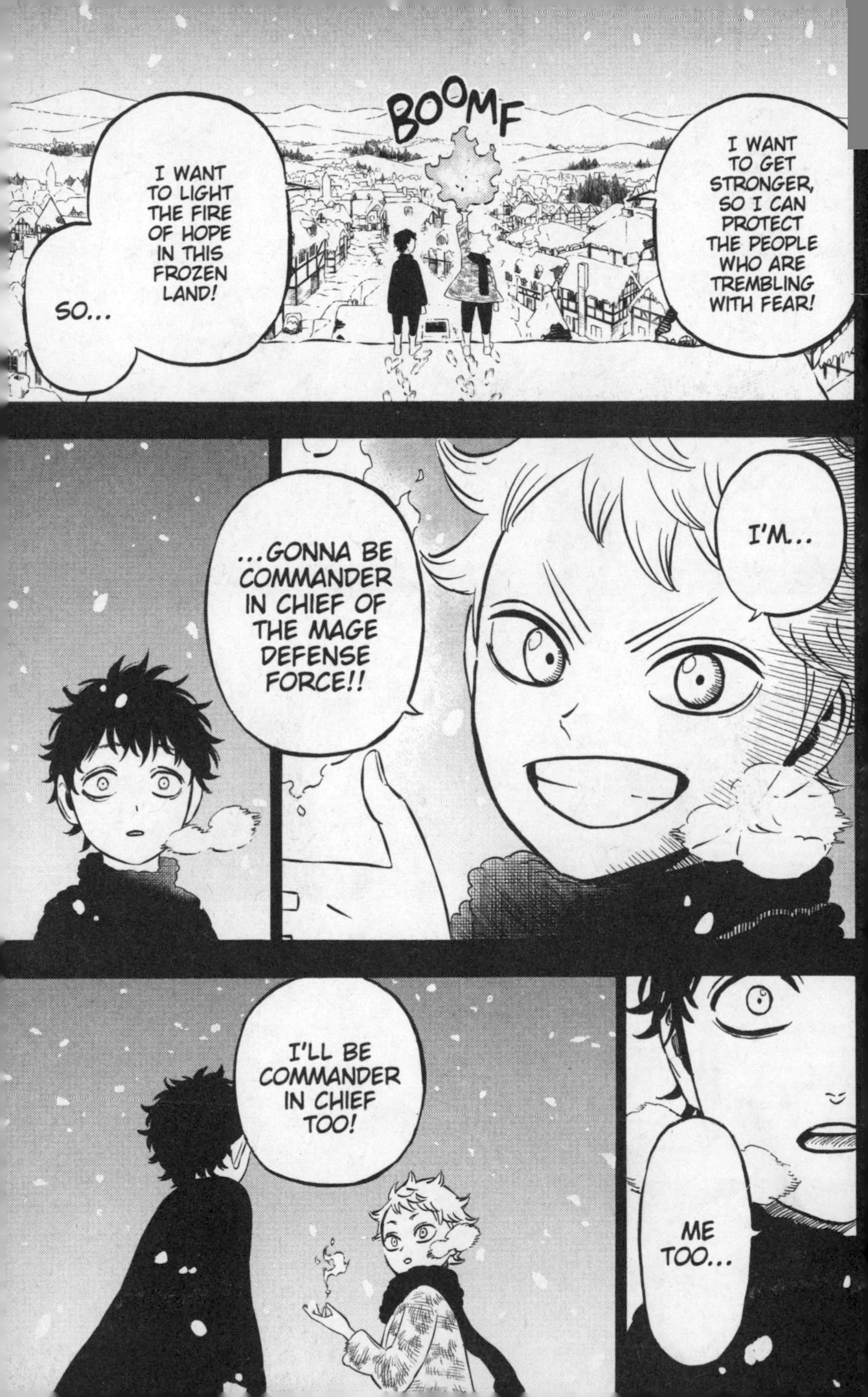
I WANT TO GET STRONGER, SO I CAN PROTECT THE PEOPLE WHO ARE TREMBLING WITH FEAR!
BOOMF
I WANT TO LIGHT THE FIRE OF HOPE IN THIS FROZEN LAND!
SO...
I'M...
...GONNA BE COMMANDER IN CHIEF OF THE MAGE DEFENSE FORCE!!
ME TOO...
I'LL BE COMMANDER IN CHIEF TOO!

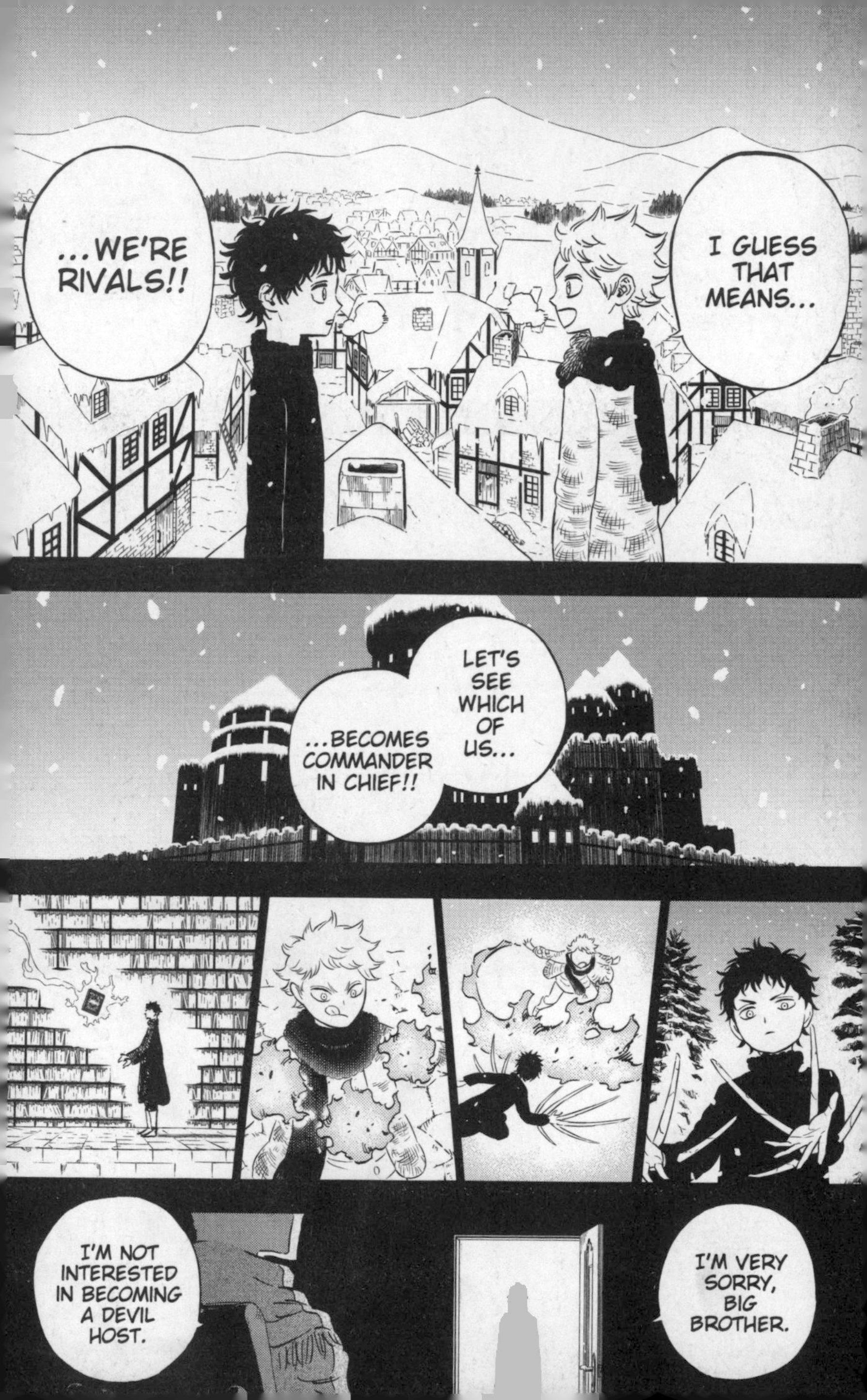
I GUESS THAT MEANS...
...WE'RE RIVALS!!
LET'S SEE WHICH OF US...
...BECOMES COMMANDER IN CHIEF!!
I'M VERY SORRY, BIG BROTHER.
I'M NOT INTERESTED IN BECOMING A DEVIL HOST.

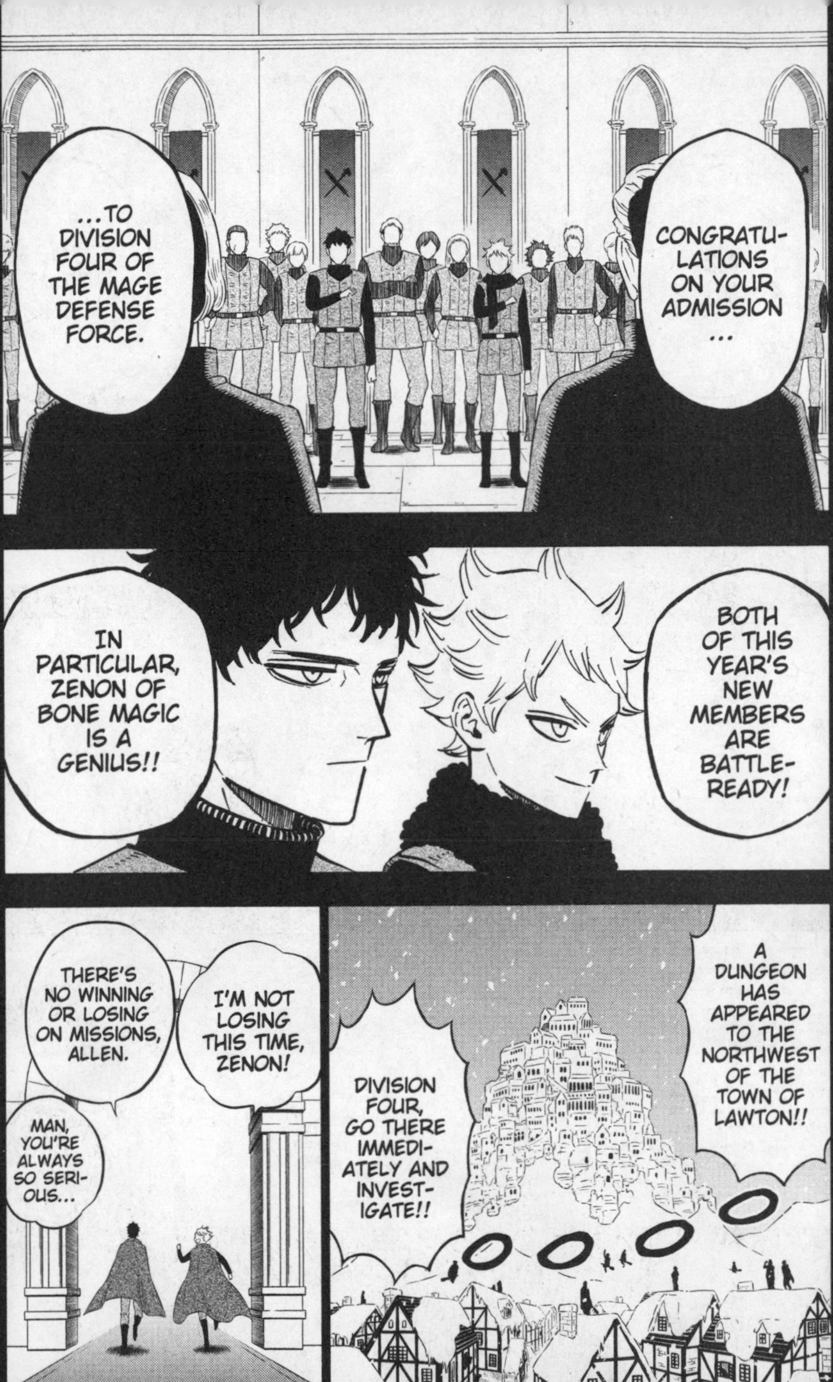
CONGRATULATIONS ON YOUR ADMISSION...
...TO DIVISION FOUR OF THE MAGE DEFENSE FORCE.
BOTH OF THIS YEAR'S NEW MEMBERS ARE BATTLE-READY!
IN PARTICULAR, ZENON OF BONE MAGIC IS A GENIUS!!
A DUNGEON HAS APPEARED TO THE NORTHWEST OF THE TOWN OF LAWTON!!
DIVISION FOUR, GO THERE IMMEDIATELY AND INVESTIGATE!!
I'M NOT LOSING THIS TIME, ZENON!
THERE'S NO WINNING OR LOSING ON MISSIONS, ALLEN.
MAN, YOU'RE ALWAYS SO SERIOUS...

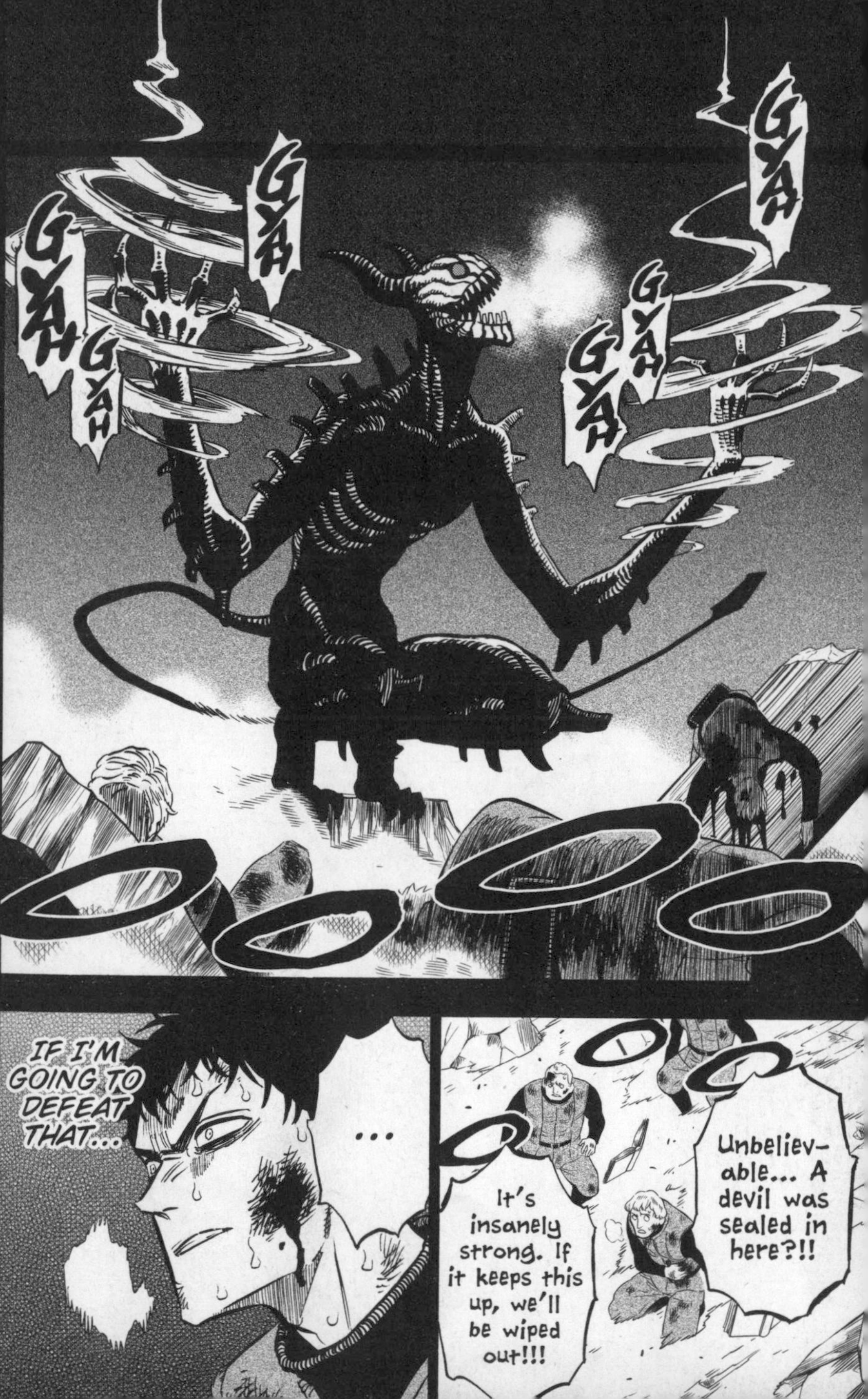
GYAH
GYAH
GYAH
GYAH
GYAH
GYAH
Unbeliev-able... A devil was sealed in here?!!
It's insanely strong. If it keeps this up, we'll be wiped out!!!
...
IF I'M GOING TO DEFEAT THAT...

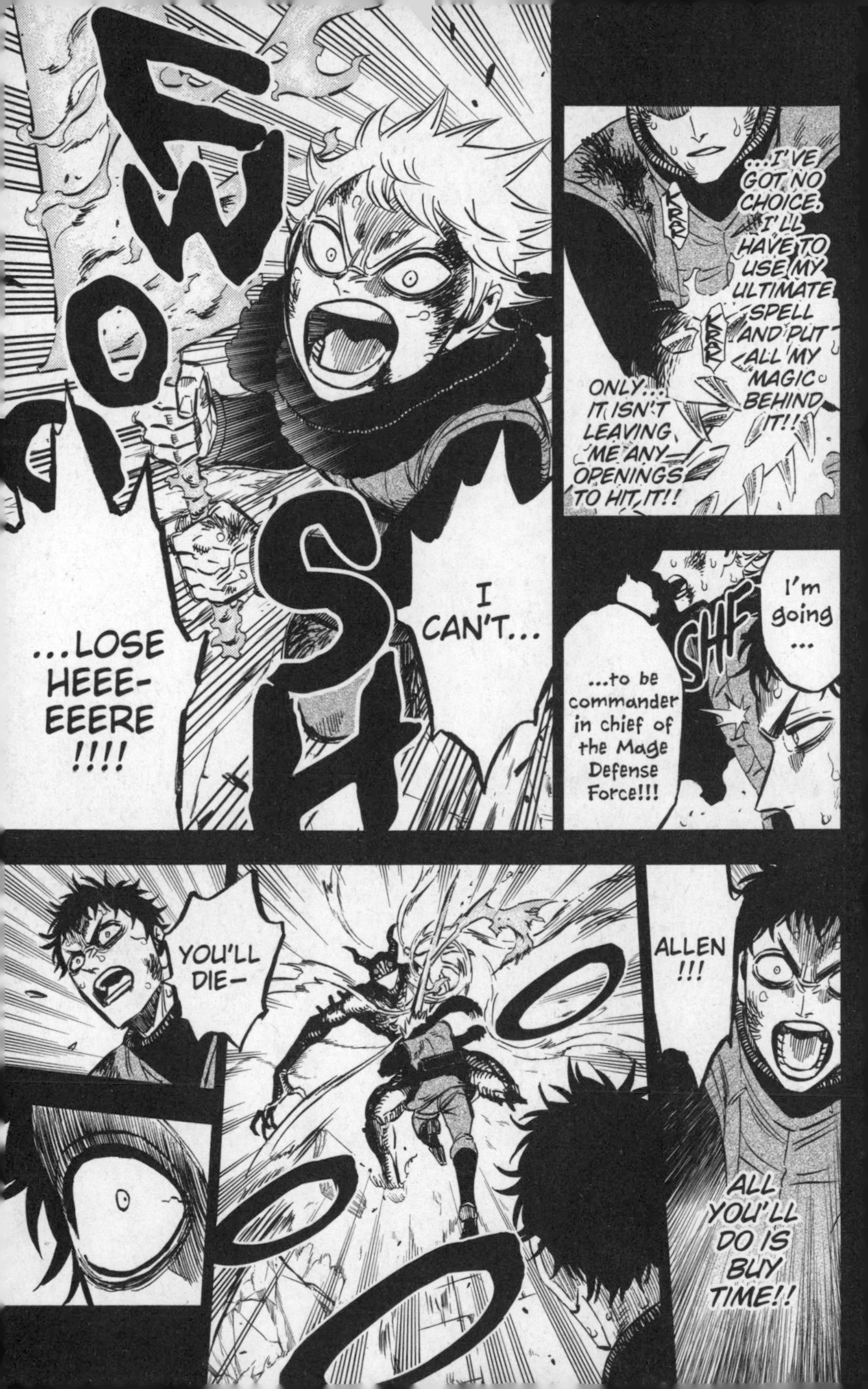
...I'VE GOT NO CHOICE. I'LL HAVE TO USE MY ULTIMATE SPELL AND PUT ALL MY MAGIC BEHIND IT!!
KRAK
KRAK
ONLY... IT ISN'T LEAVING ME ANY OPENINGS TO HIT IT!!
I'm going...
SHF
...to be commander in chief of the Mage Defense Force!!!
FWOOSH
I CAN'T...
...LOSE HEEEEEERE!!!!
ALLEN!!!
ALL YOU'LL DO IS BUY TIME!!
YOU'LL DIE-

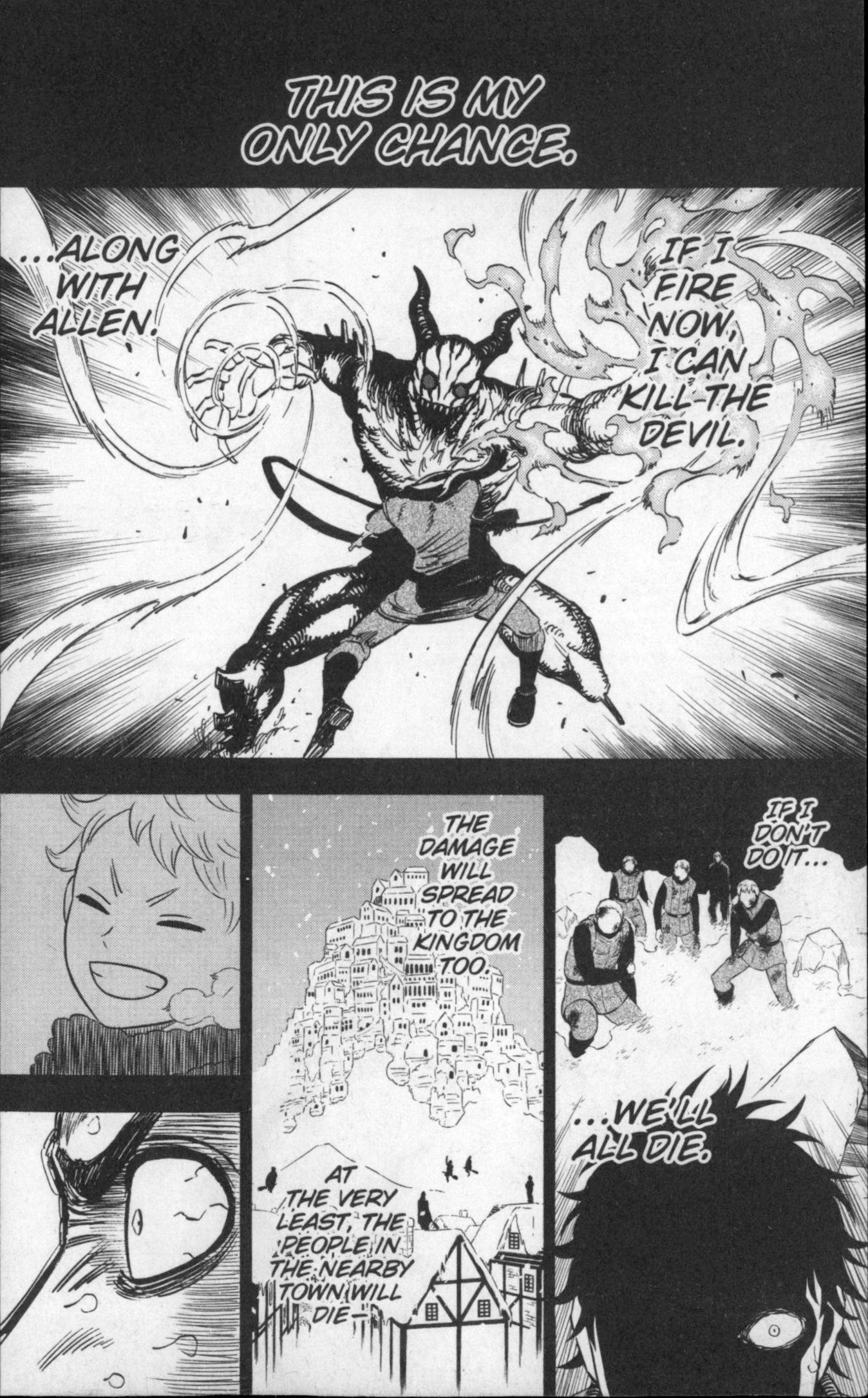
THIS IS MY ONLY CHANCE.
IF I FIRE NOW, I CAN KILL THE DEVIL.
...ALONG WITH ALLEN.
IF I DON'T DO IT...
...WE'LL ALL DIE.
THE DAMAGE WILL SPREAD TO THE KINGDOM TOO.
AT THE VERY LEAST, THE PEOPLE IN THE NEARBY TOWN WILL DIE—

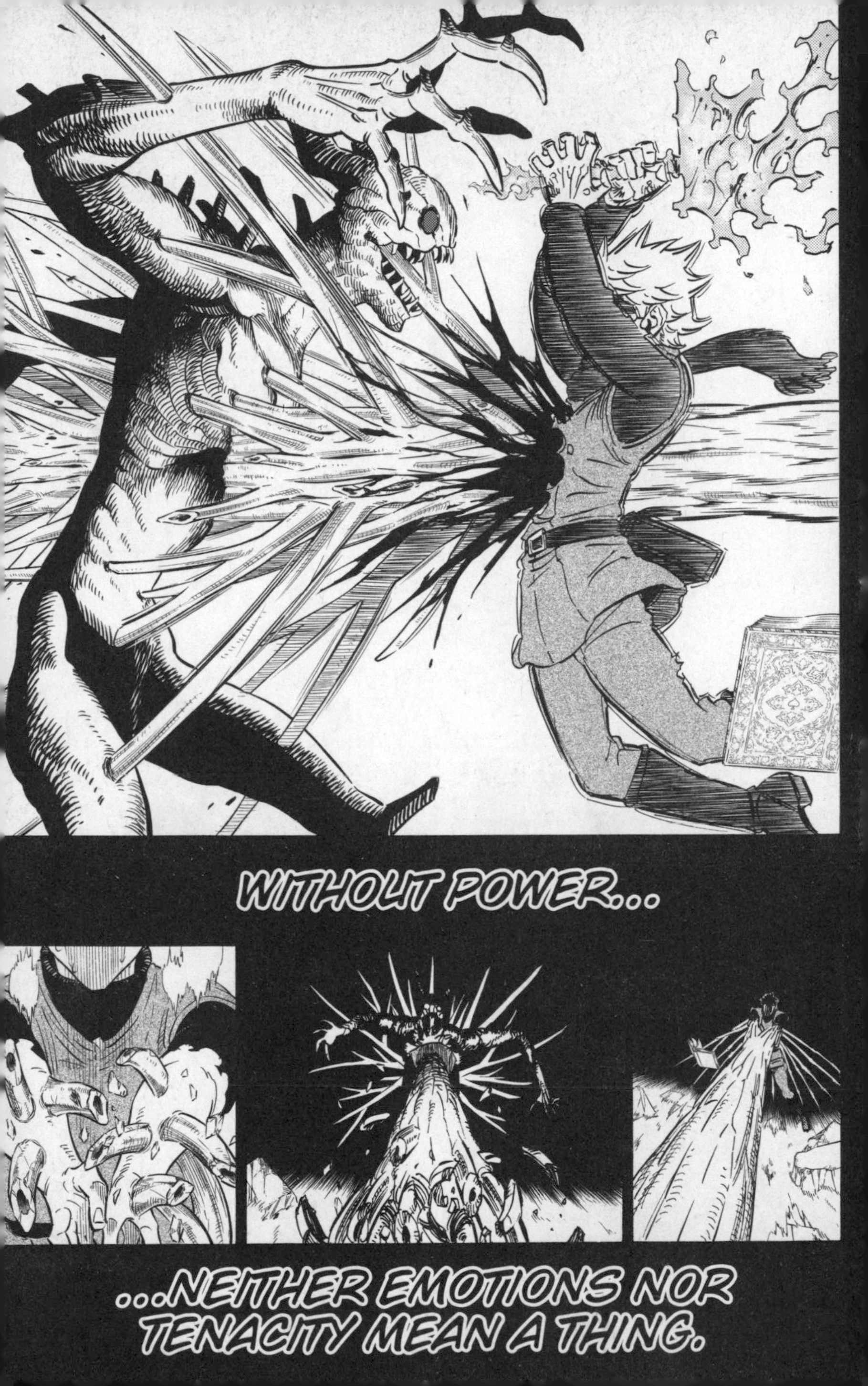
WITHOUT POWER...
...NEITHER EMOTIONS NOR TENACITY MEAN A THING.

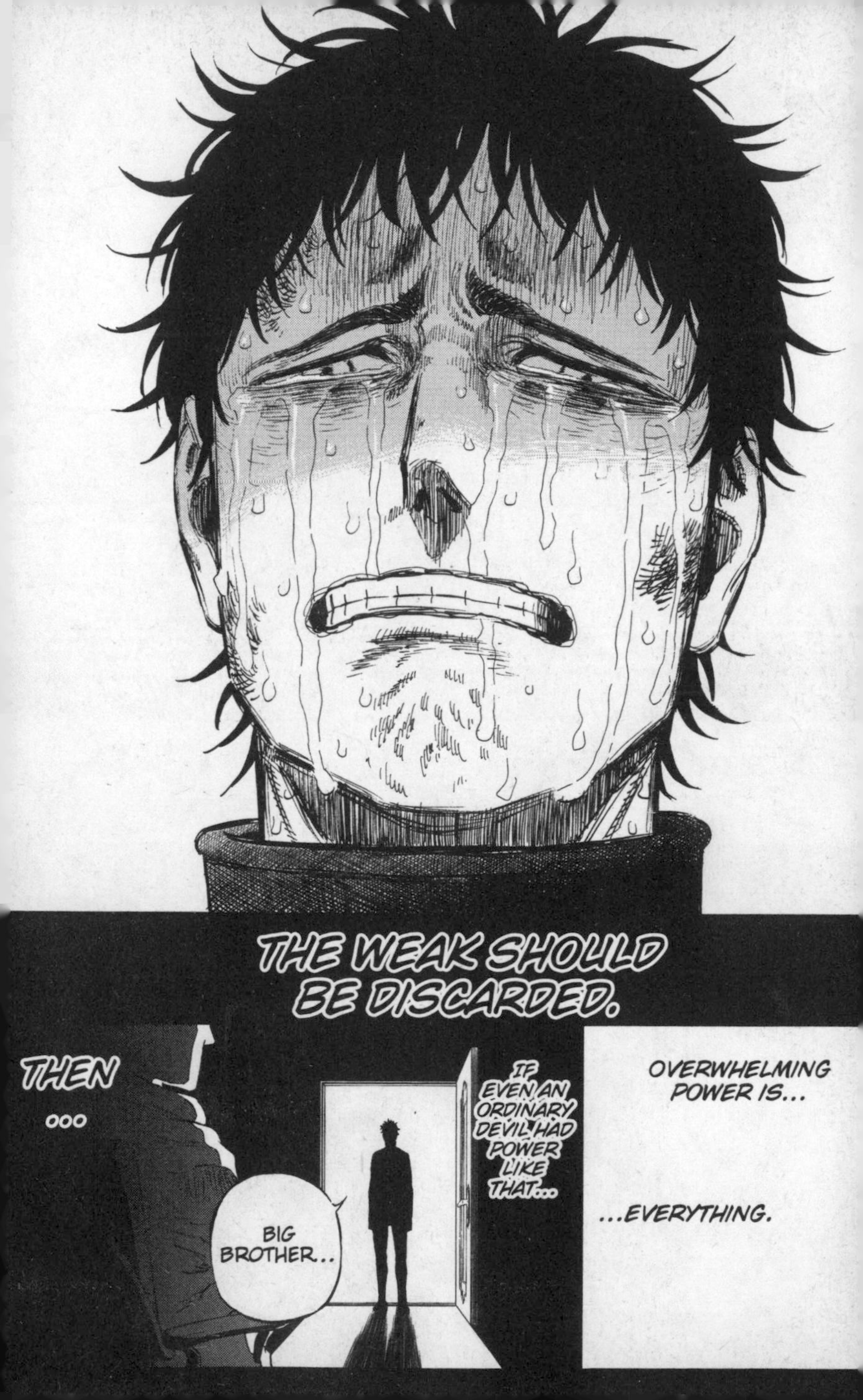
THE WEAK SHOULD BE DISCARDED.
OVERWHELMING POWER IS...
...EVERYTHING.
IF EVEN AN ORDINARY DEVIL HAD POWER LIKE THAT...
BIG BROTHER..
THEN ...

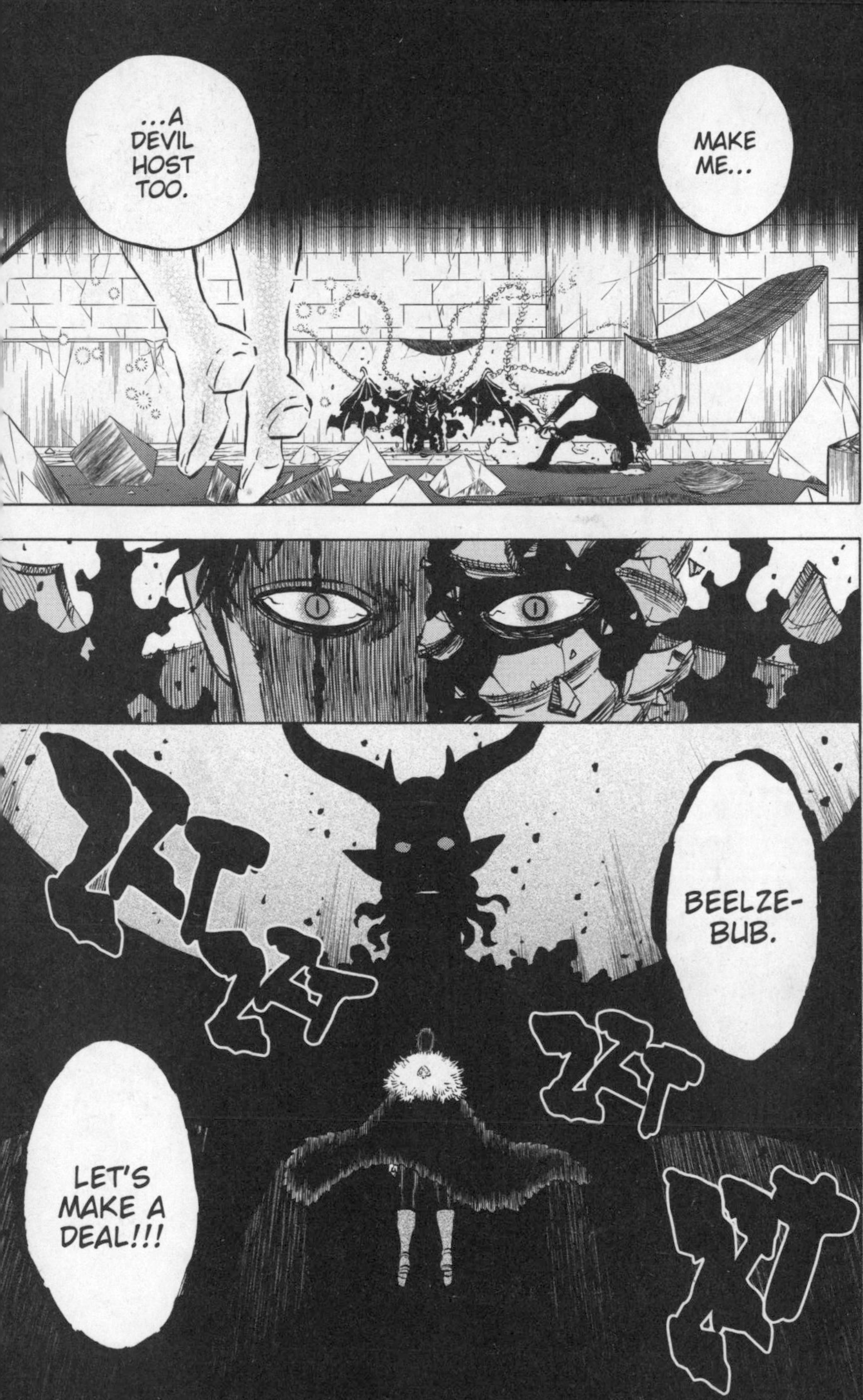
MAKE ME...
...A DEVIL HOST TOO.
BEELZEBUB.
LET'S MAKE A DEAL!!!

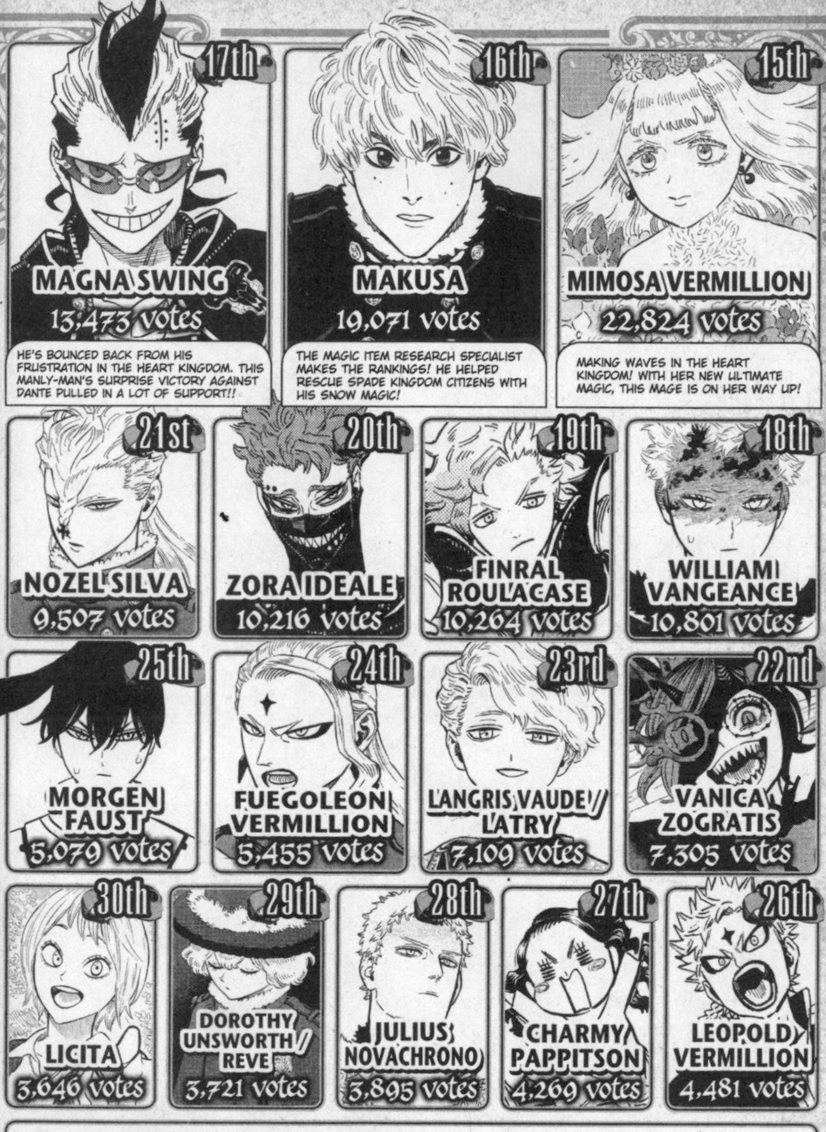
15th
MIMOSA VERMILLION
22,824 votes
MAKING WAVES IN THE HEART KINGDOM! WITH HER NEW ULTIMATE MAGIC, THIS MAGE IS ON HER WAY UP!
16th
MAKUSA
19,071 votes
THE MAGIC ITEM RESEARCH SPECIALIST MAKES THE RANKINGS! HE HELPED RESCUE SPADE KINGDOM CITIZENS WITH HIS SNOW MAGIC!
17th
MAGNA SWING
13,473 votes
HE'S BOUNCED BACK FROM HIS FRUSTRATION IN THE HEART KINGDOM. THIS MANLY-MAN'S SURPRISE VICTORY AGAINST DANTE PULLED IN A LOT OF SUPPORT!!
18th
WILLIAM VANGEANCE
10,801 votes
19th
FINRAL ROULACASE
10,264 votes
20th
ZORA IDEALE
10,216 votes
21st
NOZEL SILVA
9,507 votes
22nd
VANICA ZOGRATIS
7,305 votes
23rd
LANGRIS VAUDE / LATRY
7,109 votes
24th
FUEGOLEON VERMILLION
5,455 votes
25th
MORGEN FAUST
5,079 votes
26th
LEOPOLD VERMILLION
4,481 votes
27th
CHARMY PAPPITSON
4,269 votes
28th
JULIUS NOVACHRONO
3,895 votes
29th
DOROTHY UNSWORTH / REVE
3,721 votes
30th
LICITA
3,646 votes

31st	Vanessa Enoteca	3,614 votes	41st	Sekke Bronzazza	916 votes	51st	Mars	506 votes
32nd	Grey	2,724 votes	42nd	Nebra Silva	841 votes	52nd	Rouge	440 votes
33rd	Jack the Ripper	2,584 votes	43rd	Henry Legolant	838 votes	53rd	Gaja	425 votes
34th	Solid Silva	2,072 votes	44th	Patry	771 votes	54th	Lolopechka	373 votes
35th	Damnatio Kira	1,628 votes	45th	Rill Boismortier / Lira	735 votes	55th	Plumede	353 votes
36th	Klaus Lunettes	1,449 votes	46th	Sally	703 votes	56th	Sister Lily (Lily Aquaria)	346 votes
37th	Morris	1,252 votes	47th	Zagred	689 votes	57th	Rades Spirito	340 votes
38th	Gimodelo	1,079 votes	48th	Licht	645 votes	58th	Fana (human)	338 votes
39th	Gordon Agrippa	1,001 votes	49th	Sol Marron	605 votes	59th	Fana (elf)	311 votes
40th	Lumiere Silvamillion Clover	948 votes	50th	Raia	529 votes	60th	Robero Ringert	301 votes

*These results first ran in Issue 41 of *Weekly Shonen Jump* 2021.

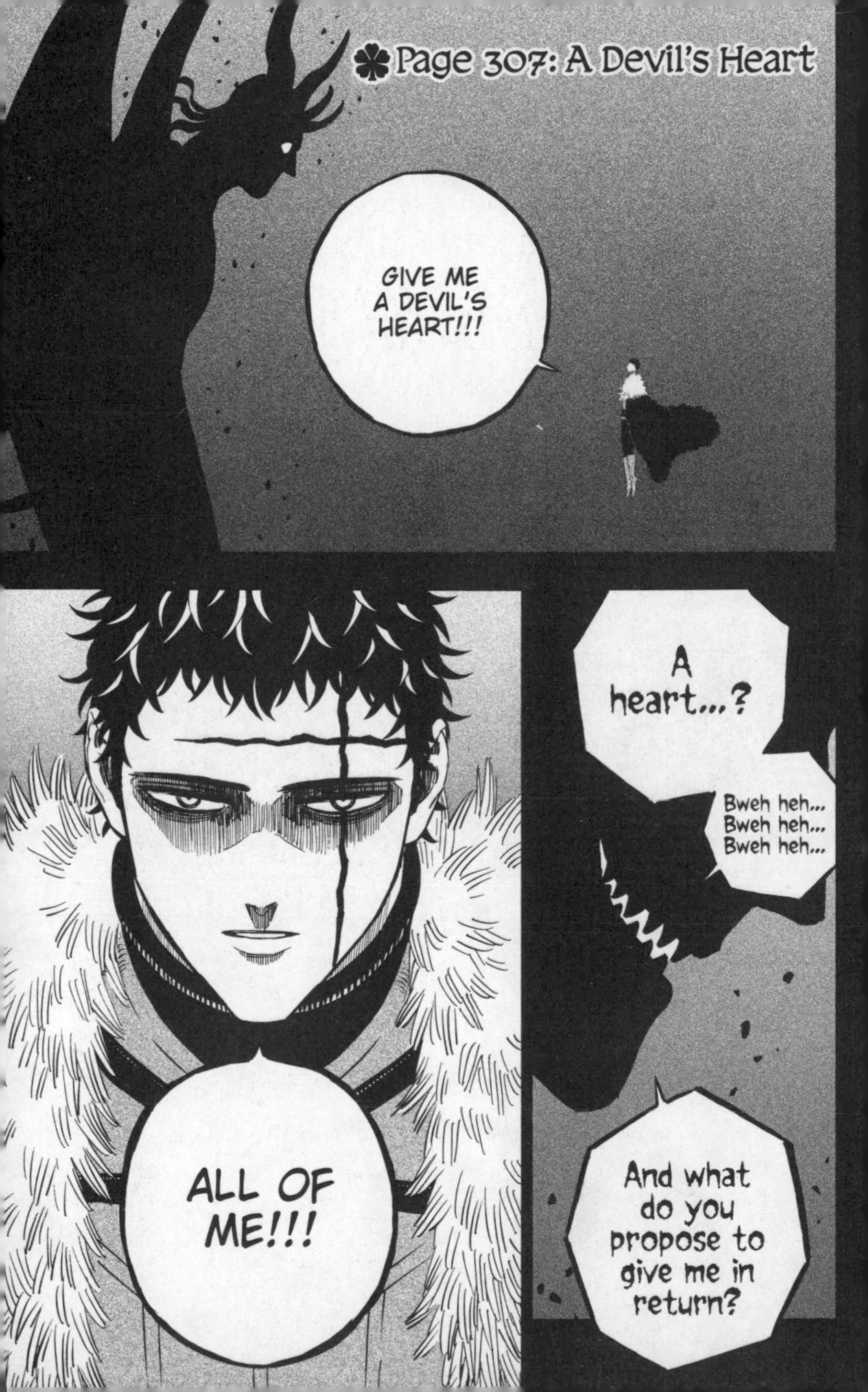
Page 307: A Devil's Heart
GIVE ME A DEVIL'S HEART!!!
A heart...?
Bweh heh... Bweh heh... Bweh heh...
And what do you propose to give me in return?
ALL OF ME!!!

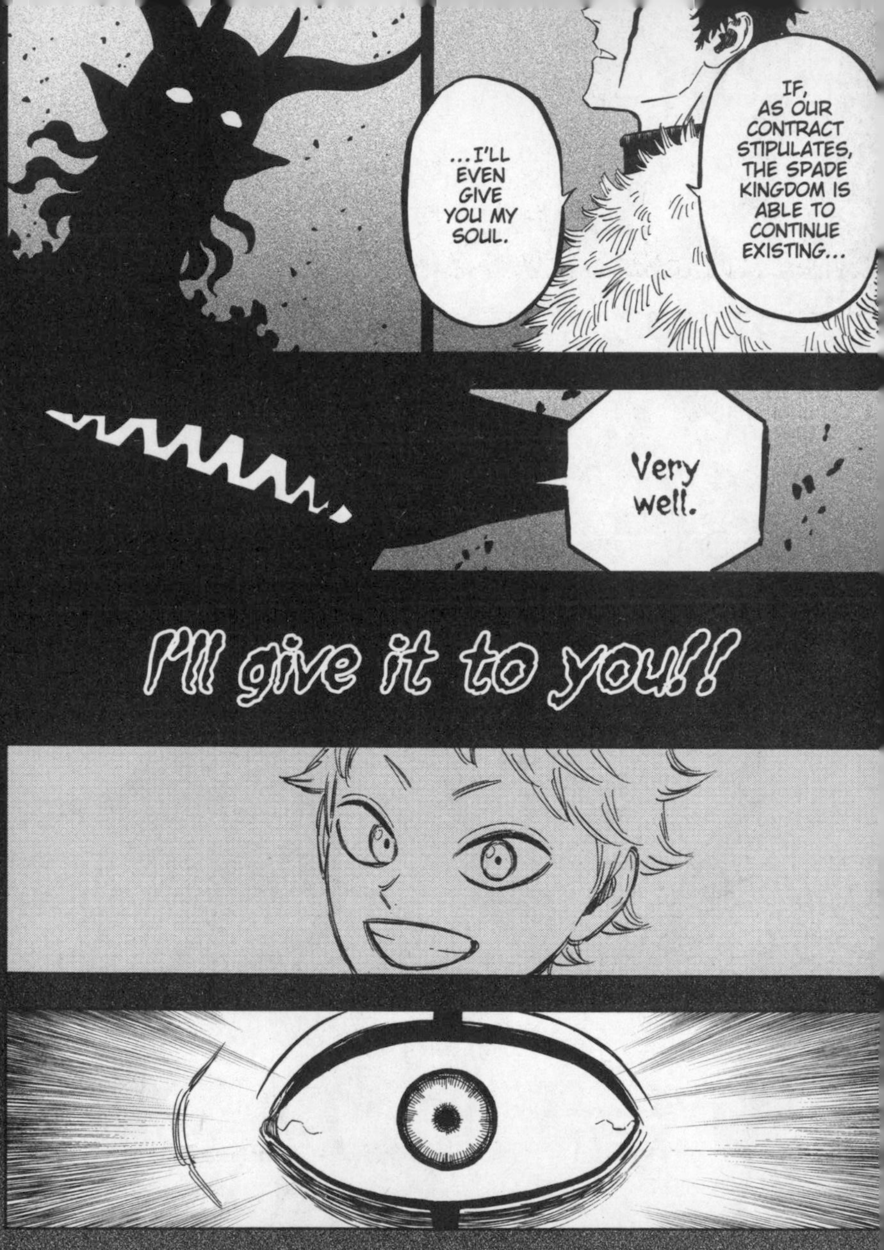
IF, AS OUR CONTRACT STIPULATES, THE SPADE KINGDOM IS ABLE TO CONTINUE EXISTING...
...I'LL EVEN GIVE YOU MY SOUL.
Very well.
I'll give it to you!!

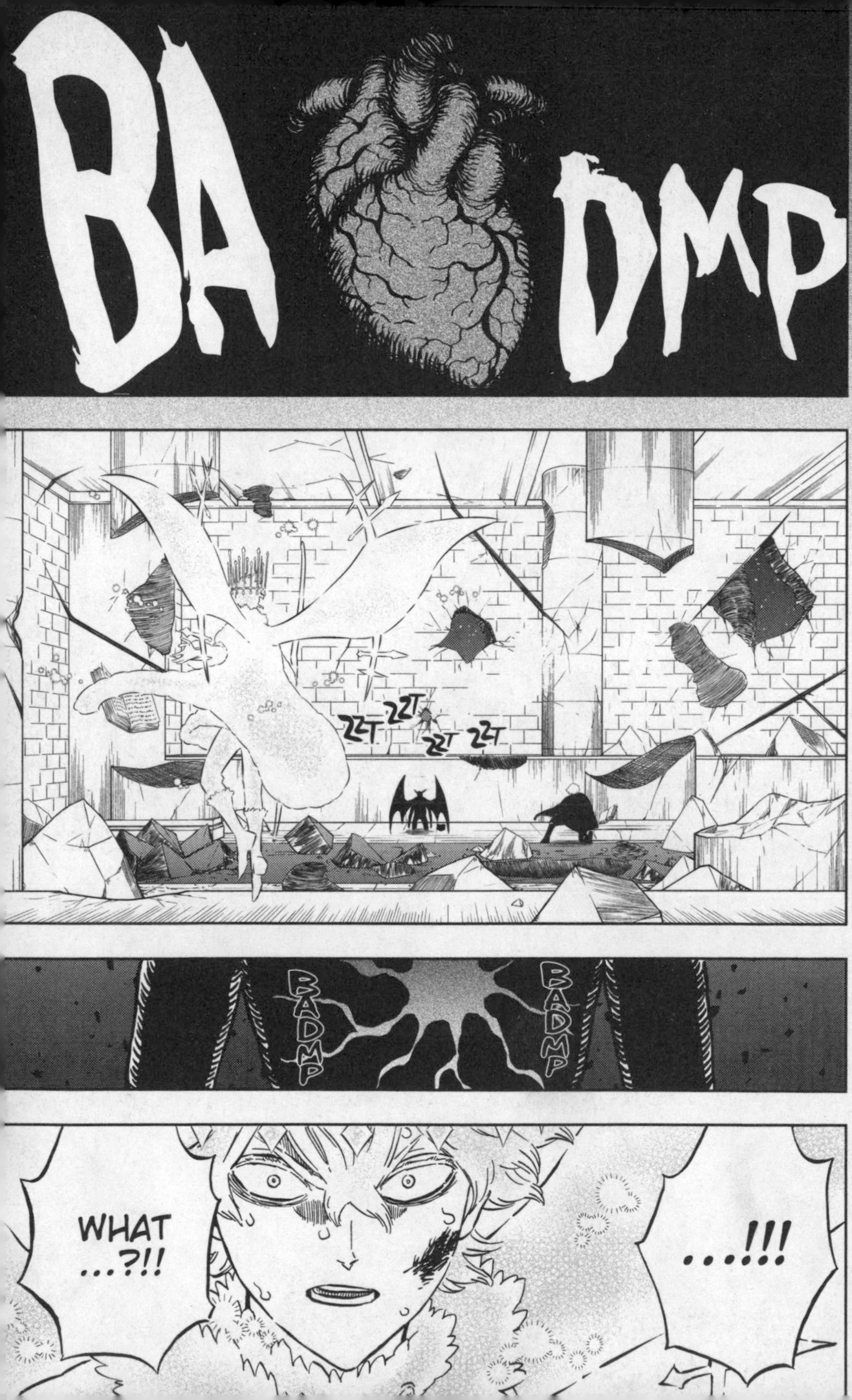
BA
DMP
ZZT
ZZT
ZZT
ZZT
BADMP
BADMP
...!!!
WHAT ...?!!

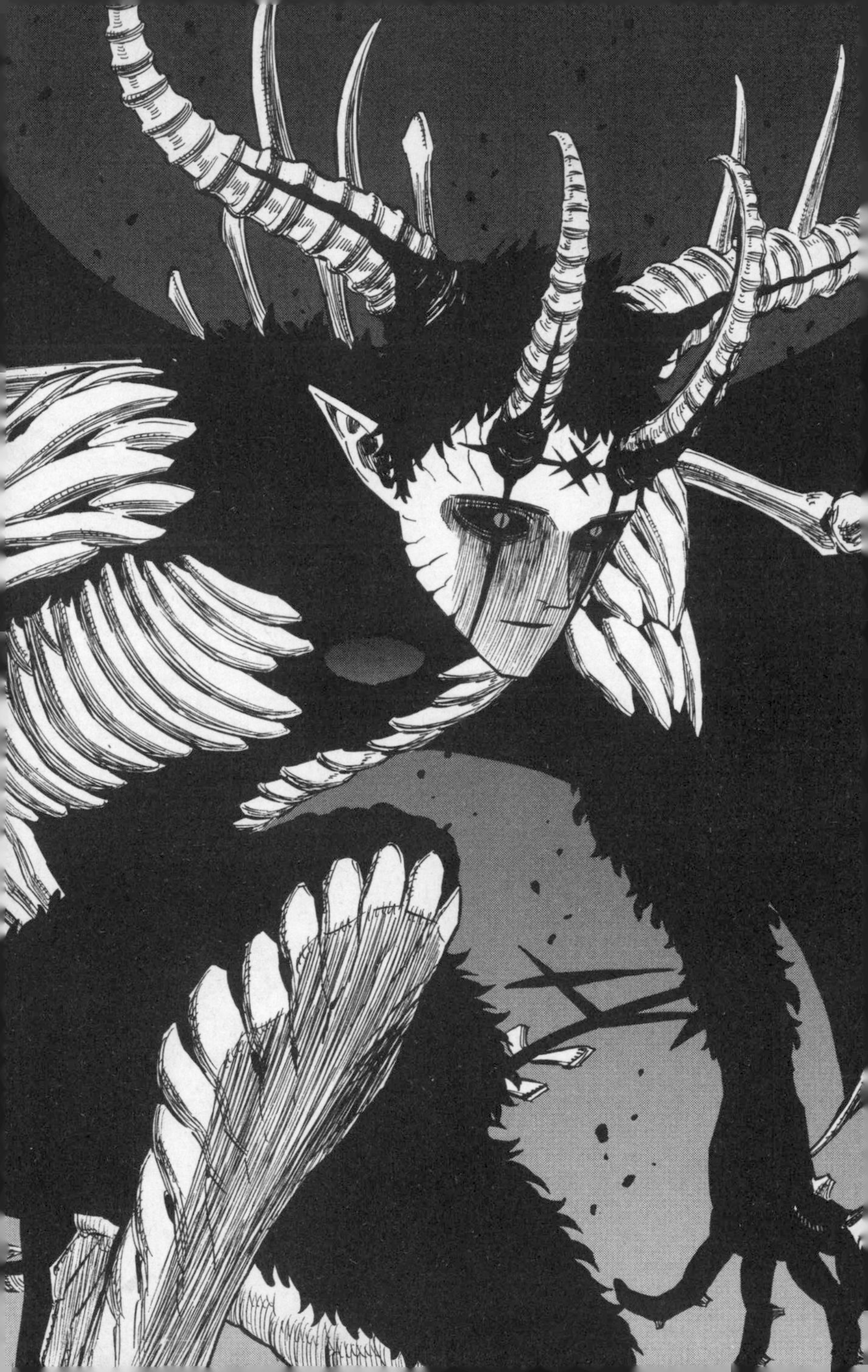

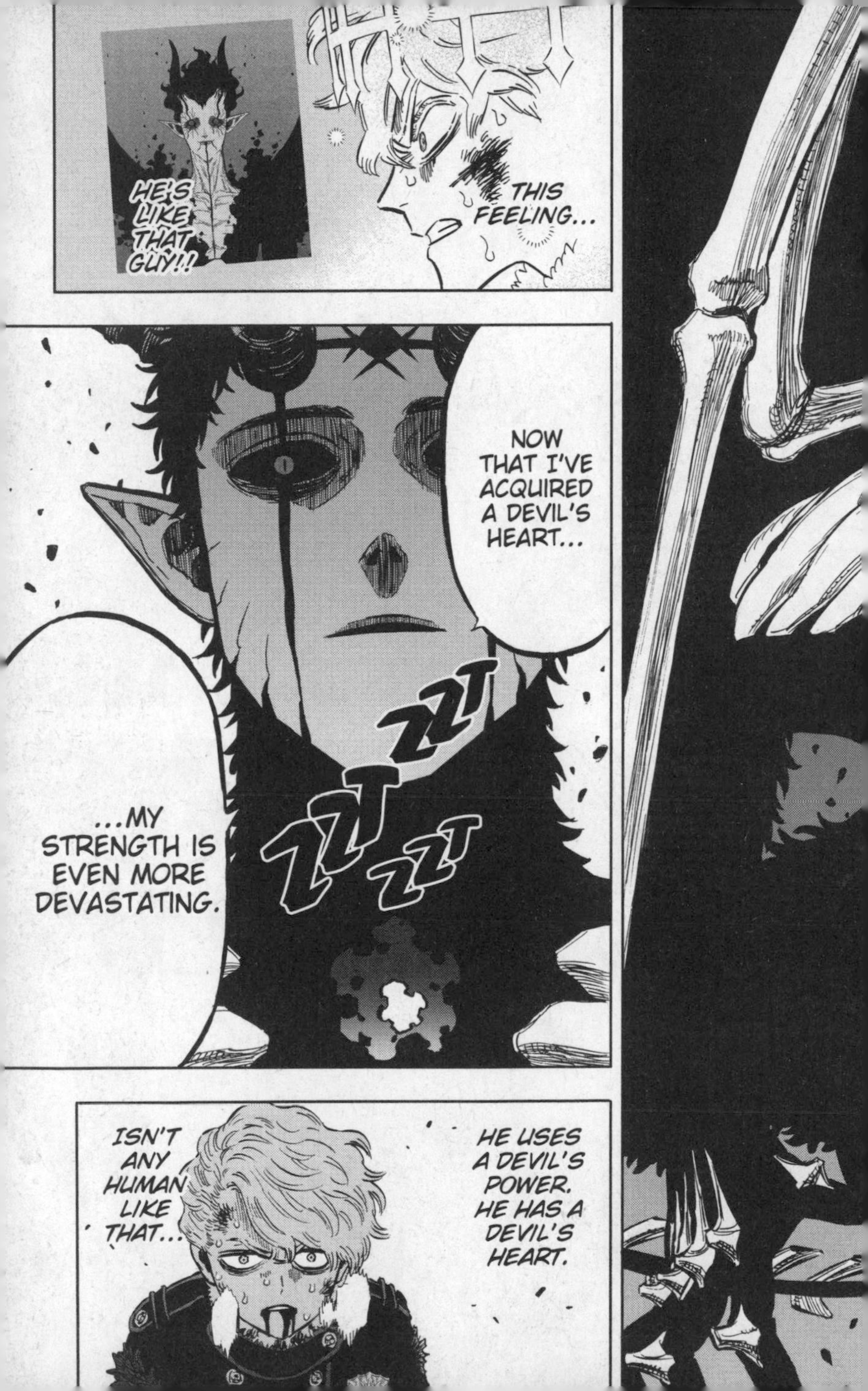
THIS FEELING...
HE'S LIKE THAT GUY!!
NOW THAT I'VE ACQUIRED A DEVIL'S HEART...
...MY STRENGTH IS EVEN MORE DEVASTATING.
ZZT
ZZT
ZZT
HE USES A DEVIL'S POWER. HE HAS A DEVIL'S HEART.
ISN'T ANY HUMAN LIKE THAT...

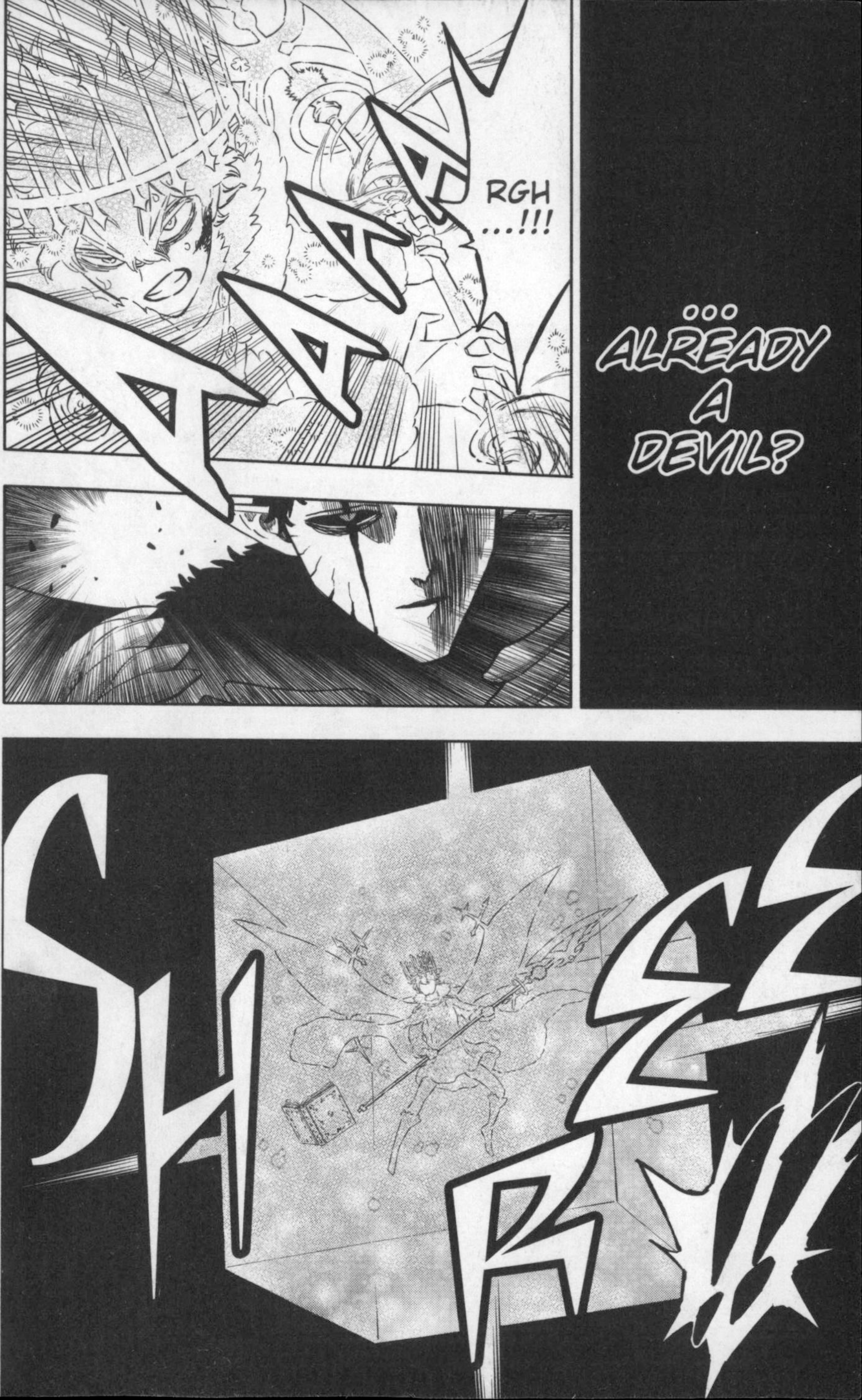
... ALREADY A DEVIL?
AAAAAAA
RGH ...!!!
SHRZZ!!

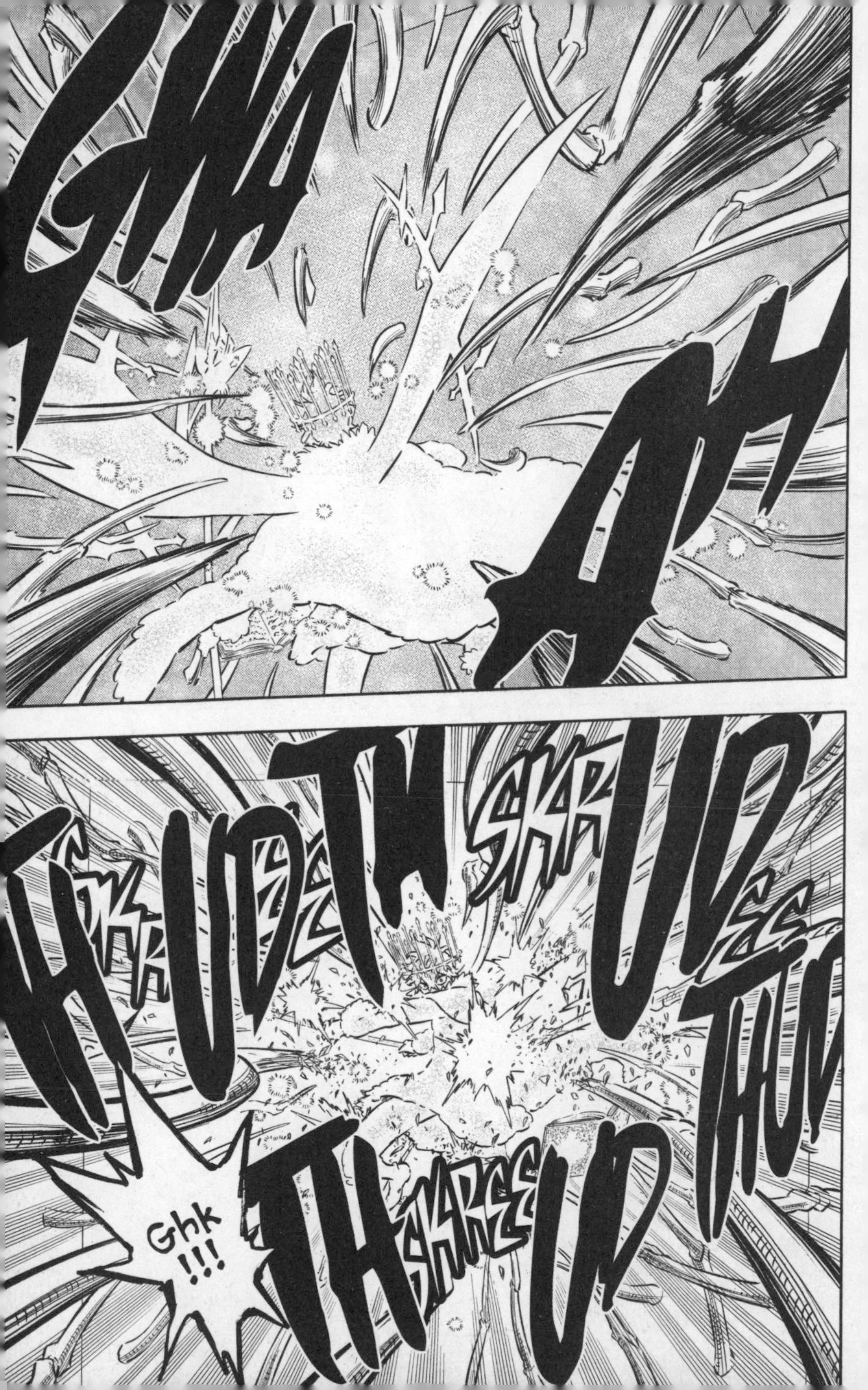
Ghk
!!!

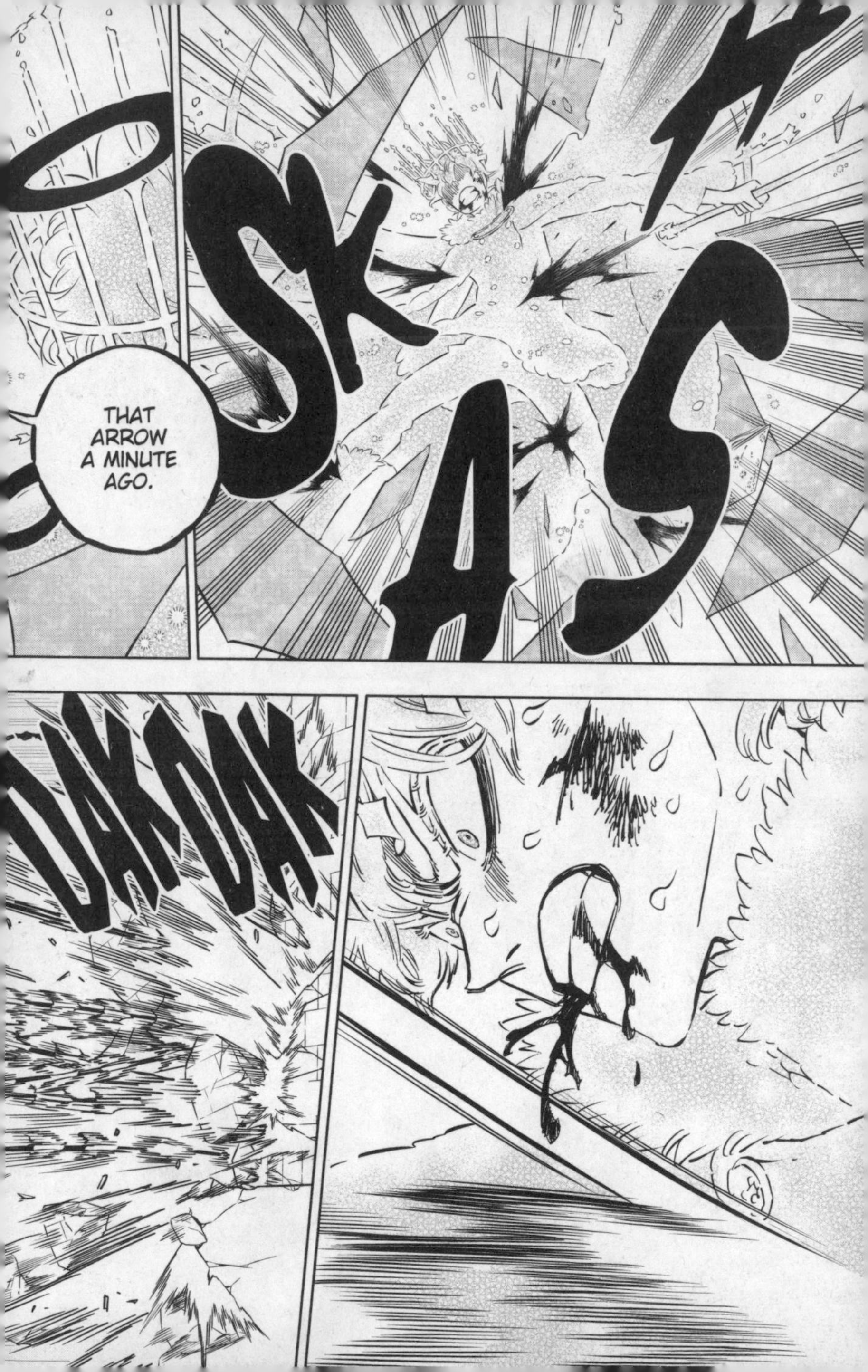
THAT ARROW A MINUTE AGO.

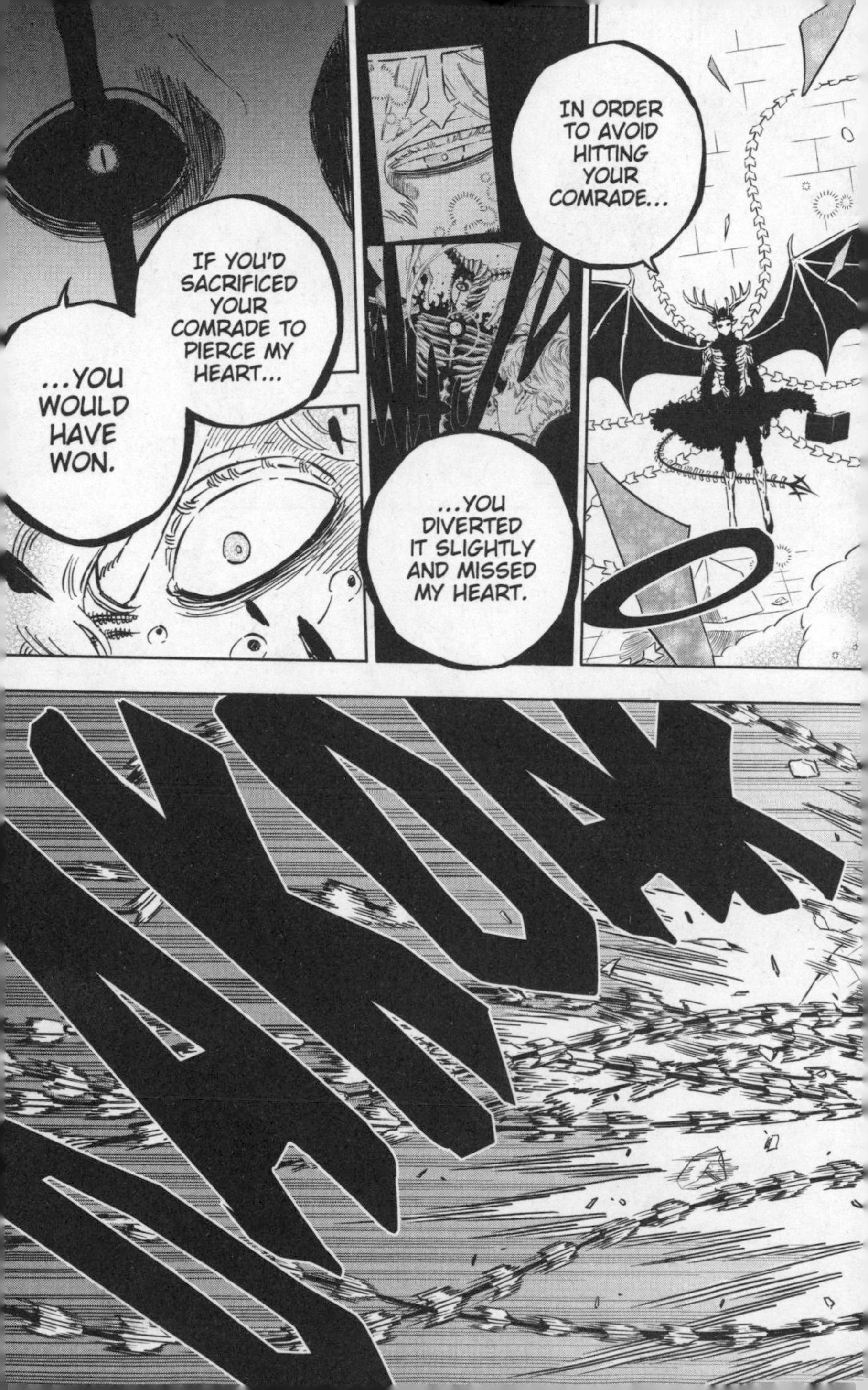
IN ORDER TO AVOID HITTING YOUR COMRADE...
...YOU DIVERTED IT SLIGHTLY AND MISSED MY HEART.
IF YOU'D SACRIFICED YOUR COMRADE TO PIERCE MY HEART...
...YOU WOULD HAVE WON.

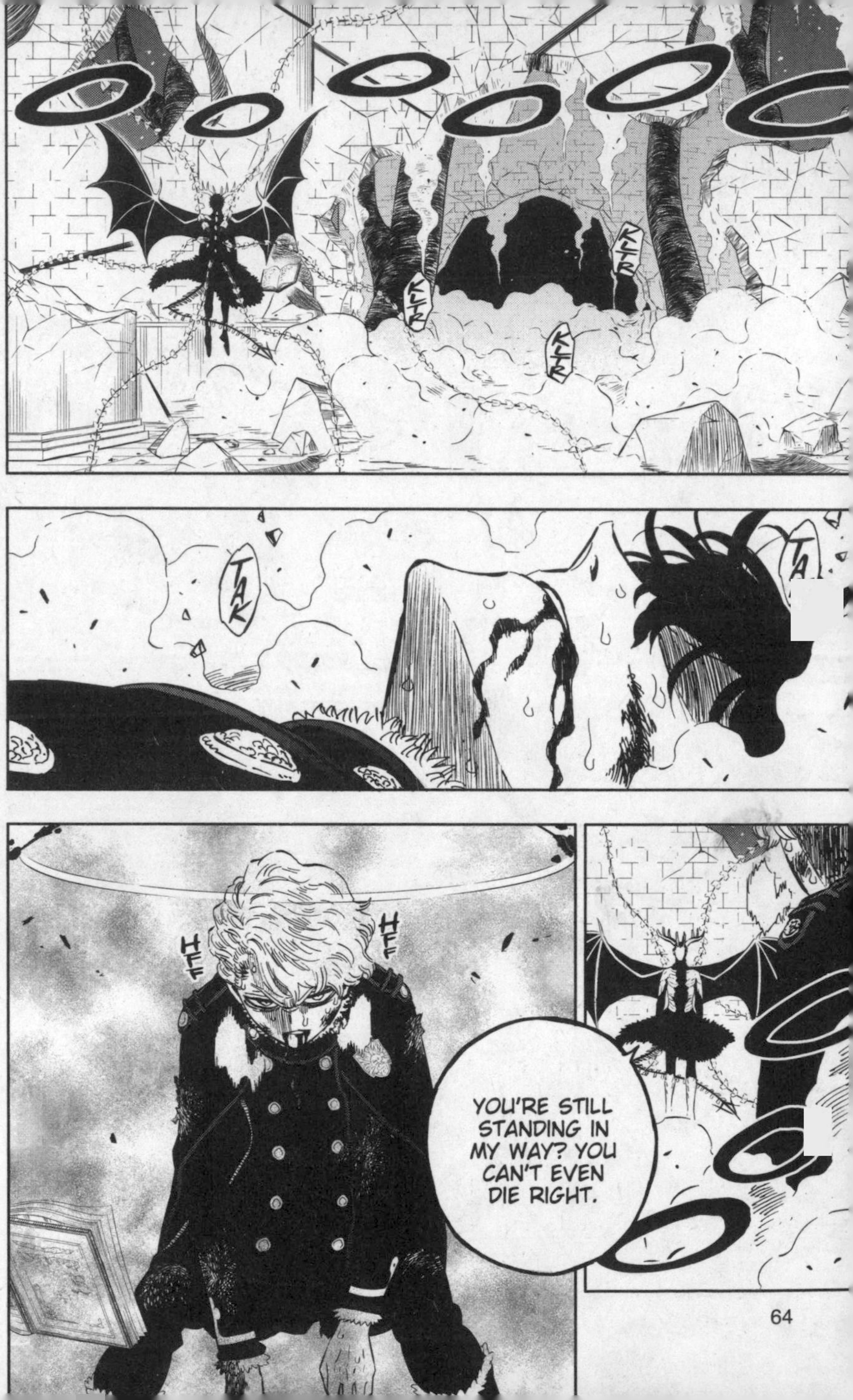
KLTR
KLTR
KLTR
TAK
YOU'RE STILL STANDING IN MY WAY? YOU CAN'T EVEN DIE RIGHT.
HFF
HFF

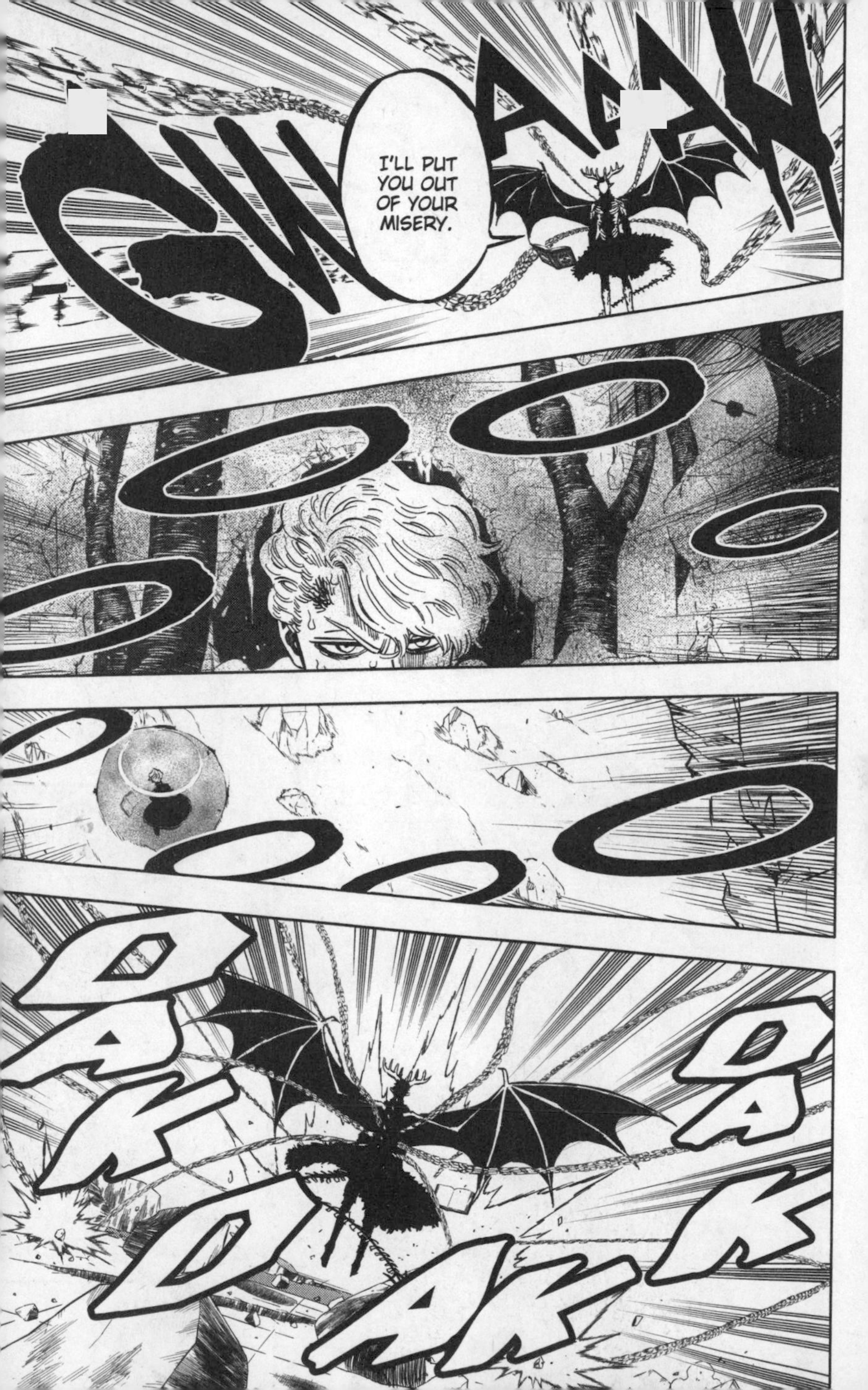
I'LL PUT YOU OUT OF YOUR MISERY.

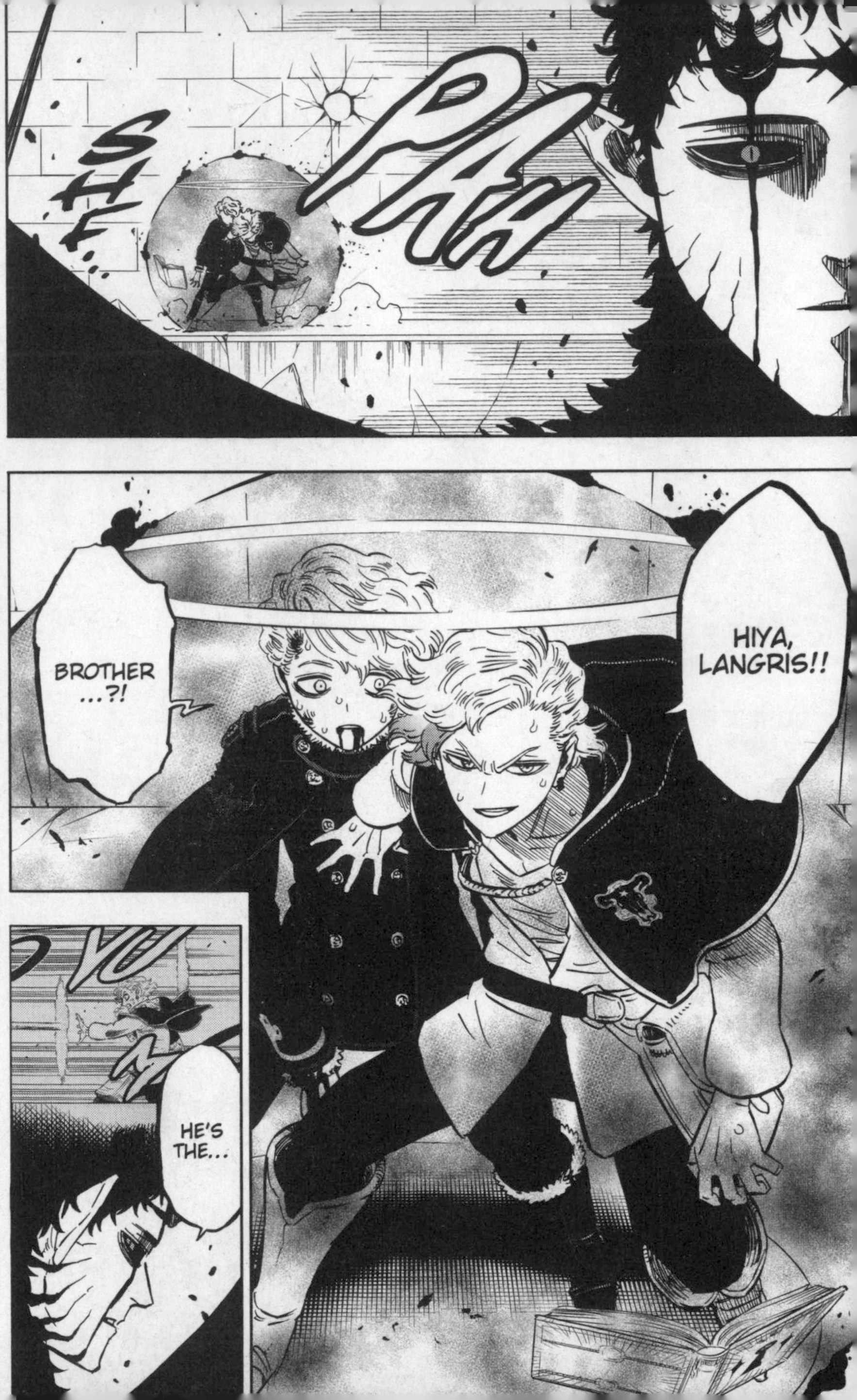
PAH
SHF...
HIYA, LANGRIS!!
BROTHER ...?!
HE'S THE...

NOPE!!

I SAW LANGRIS AND THAT GUY...AND DASHED OUT HERE WITHOUT THINKING.

YOU CAME TO RESCUE ME AGAIN?!

WHAT ARE YOU DOING HERE...?

SORRY.

I CAN'T SEE A GUY LIKE THAT AND JUST WALK AWAY!!

THAT GUY ABDUCTED OUR CAPTAIN.

USING SPATIAL MAGIC!!

SHRZEE

...MISTER YAMI!!

I'M GOING TO TAKE A LITTLE SIDE TRIP...

ZZT

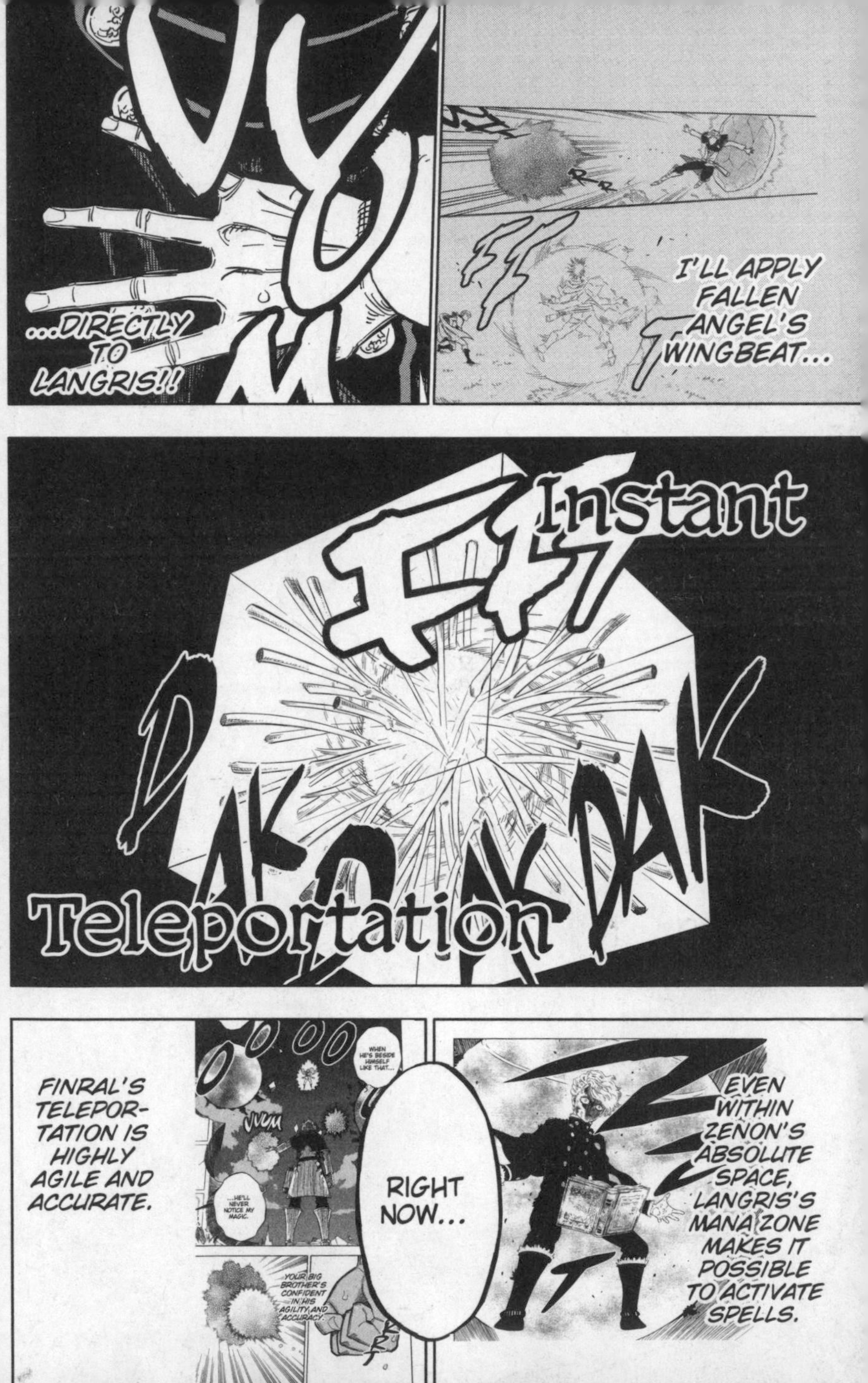
I'LL APPLY FALLEN ANGEL'S WINGBEAT...
...DIRECTLY TO LANGRIS!!
Instant Teleportation
DAK DAK DAK DAK
EVEN WITHIN ZENON'S ABSOLUTE SPACE, LANGRIS'S MANA ZONE MAKES IT POSSIBLE TO ACTIVATE SPELLS.
RIGHT NOW...
WHEN HE'S BESIDE HIMSELF LIKE THAT...
...HE'LL NEVER NOTICE MY MAGIC.
YOUR BIG BROTHER'S CONFIDENT IN HIS AGILITY AND ACCURACY.
FINRAL'S TELEPORTATION IS HIGHLY AGILE AND ACCURATE.

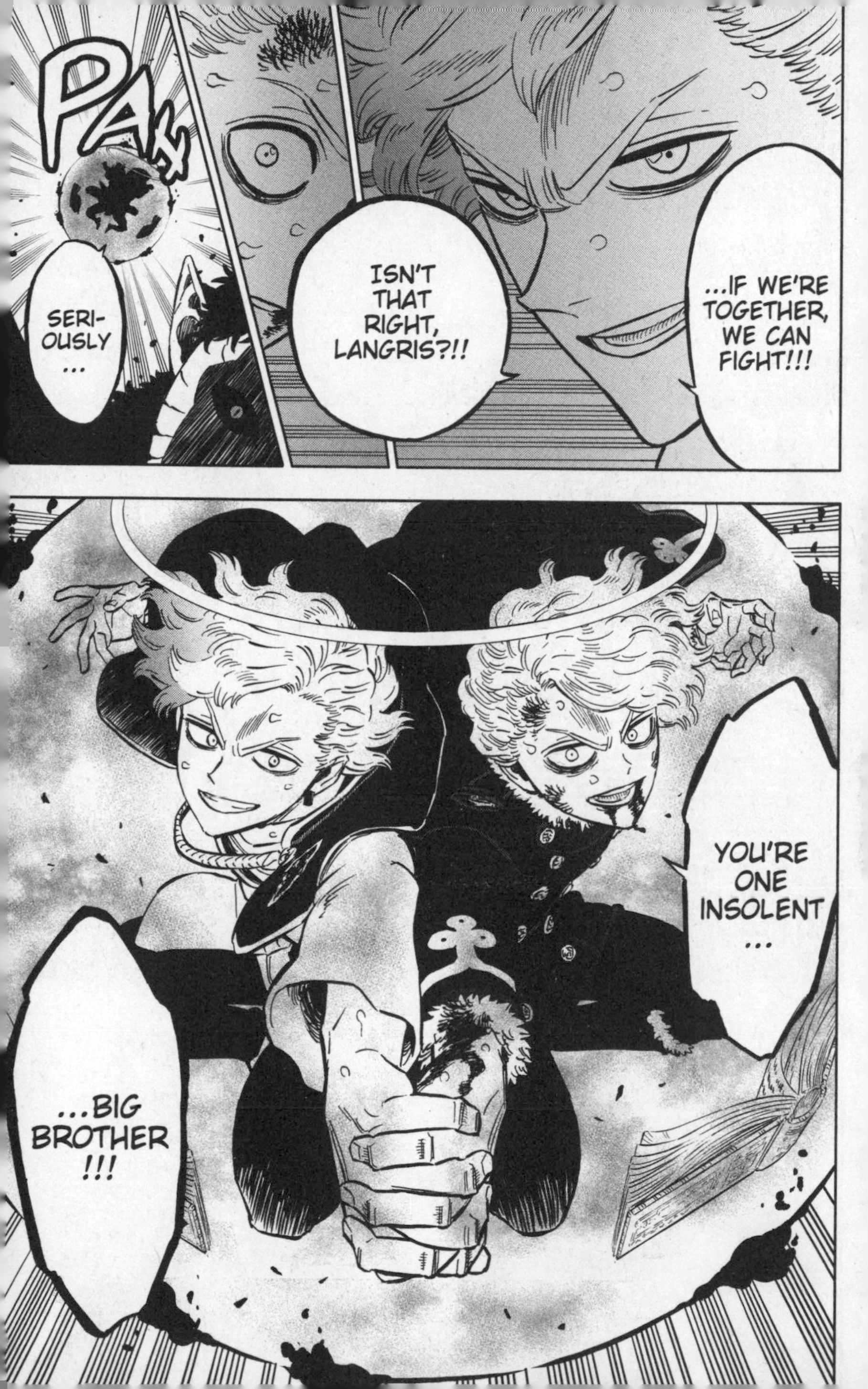
...IF WE'RE TOGETHER, WE CAN FIGHT!!!
ISN'T THAT RIGHT, LANGRIS?!!
PAK
SERI-OUSLY...
YOU'RE ONE INSOLENT...
...BIG BROTHER!!!

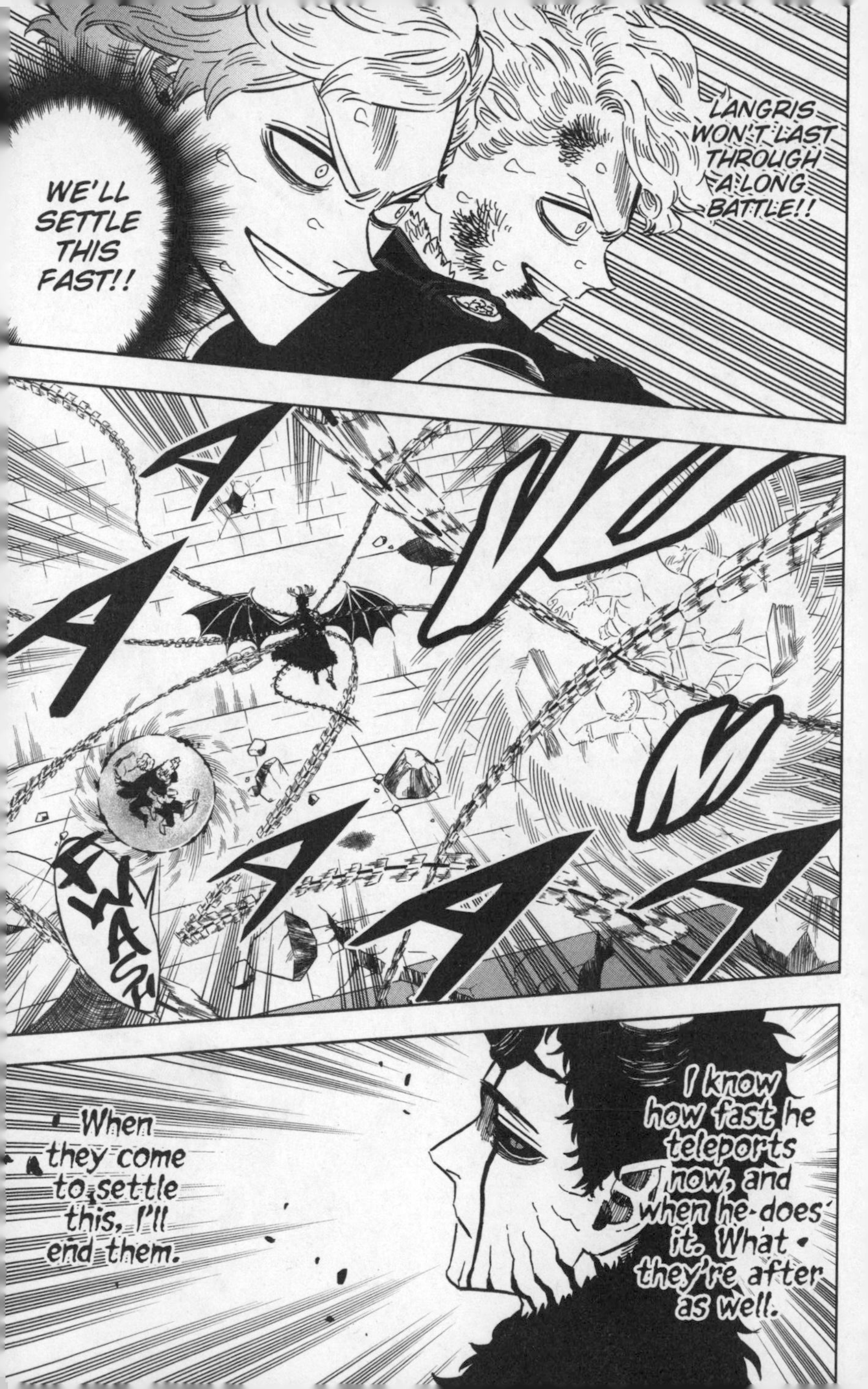
LANGRIS WON'T LAST THROUGH A LONG BATTLE!!
WE'LL SETTLE THIS FAST!!
I know how fast he teleports now, and when he does it. What they're after as well.
When they come to settle this, I'll end them.

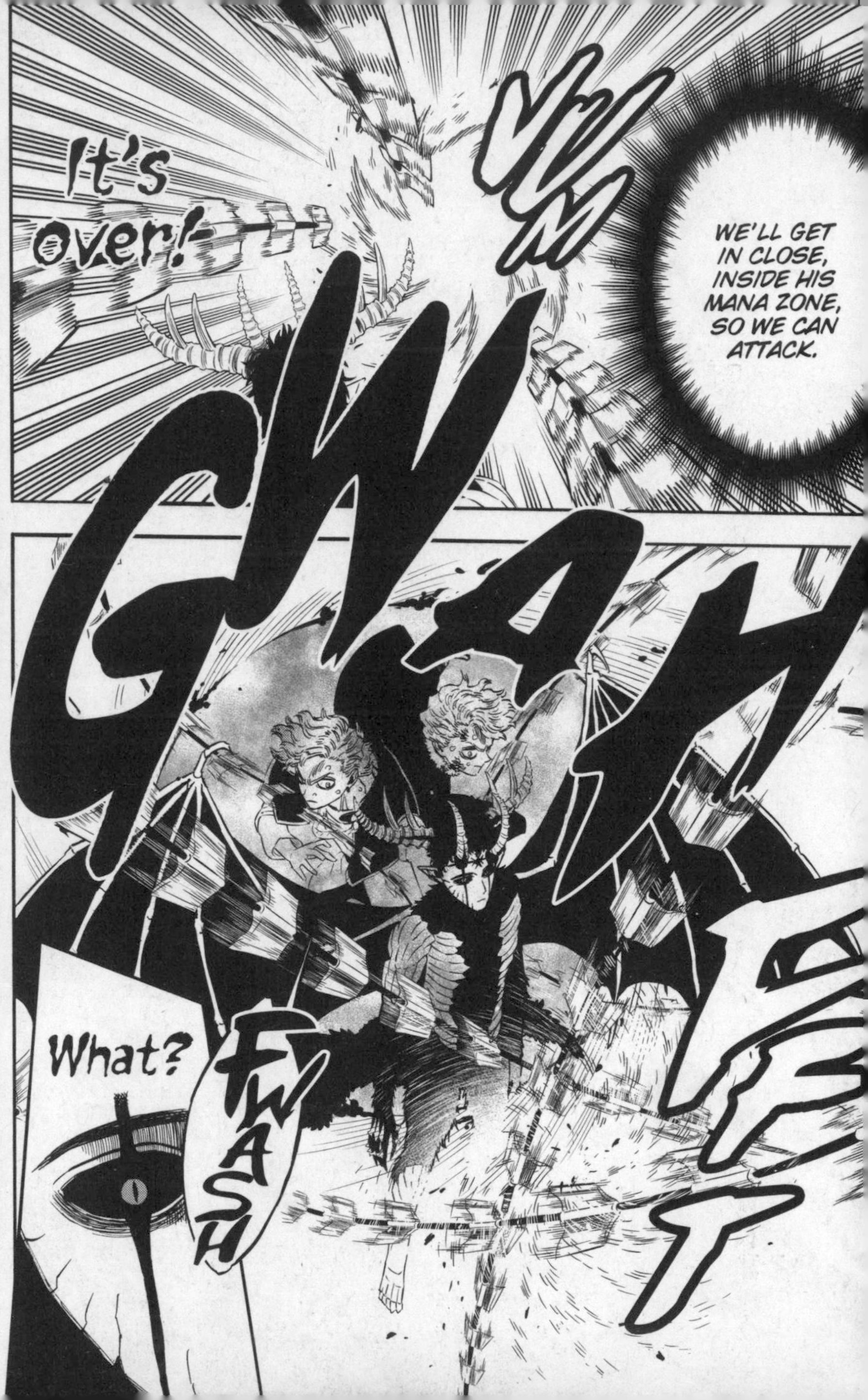
WE'LL GET IN CLOSE, INSIDE HIS MANA ZONE, SO WE CAN ATTACK.
It's over!
FWASH
What?

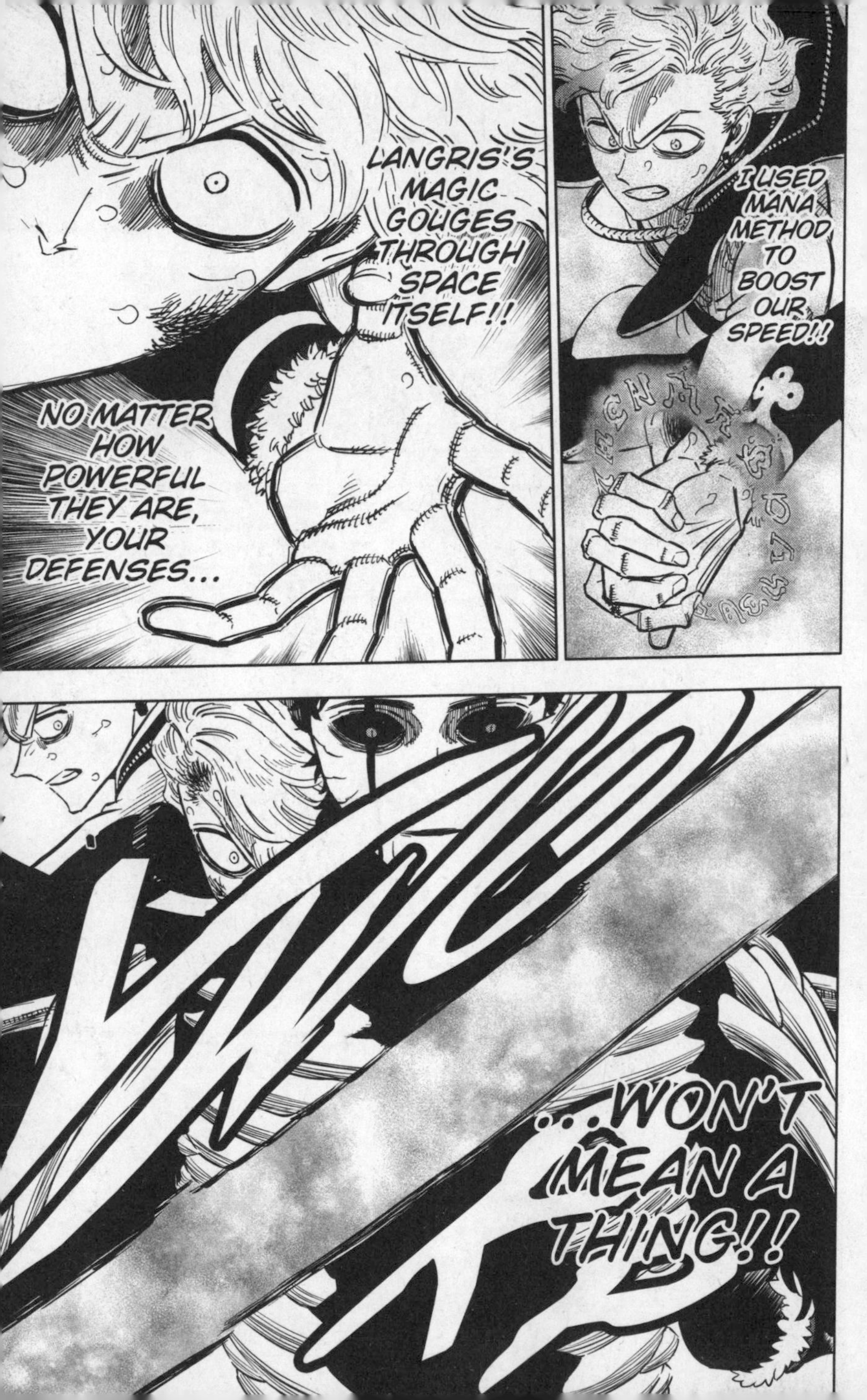
I USED MANA METHOD TO BOOST OUR SPEED!!
LANGRIS'S MAGIC GOUGES THROUGH SPACE ITSELF!!
NO MATTER HOW POWERFUL THEY ARE, YOUR DEFENSES...
...WON'T MEAN A THING!!

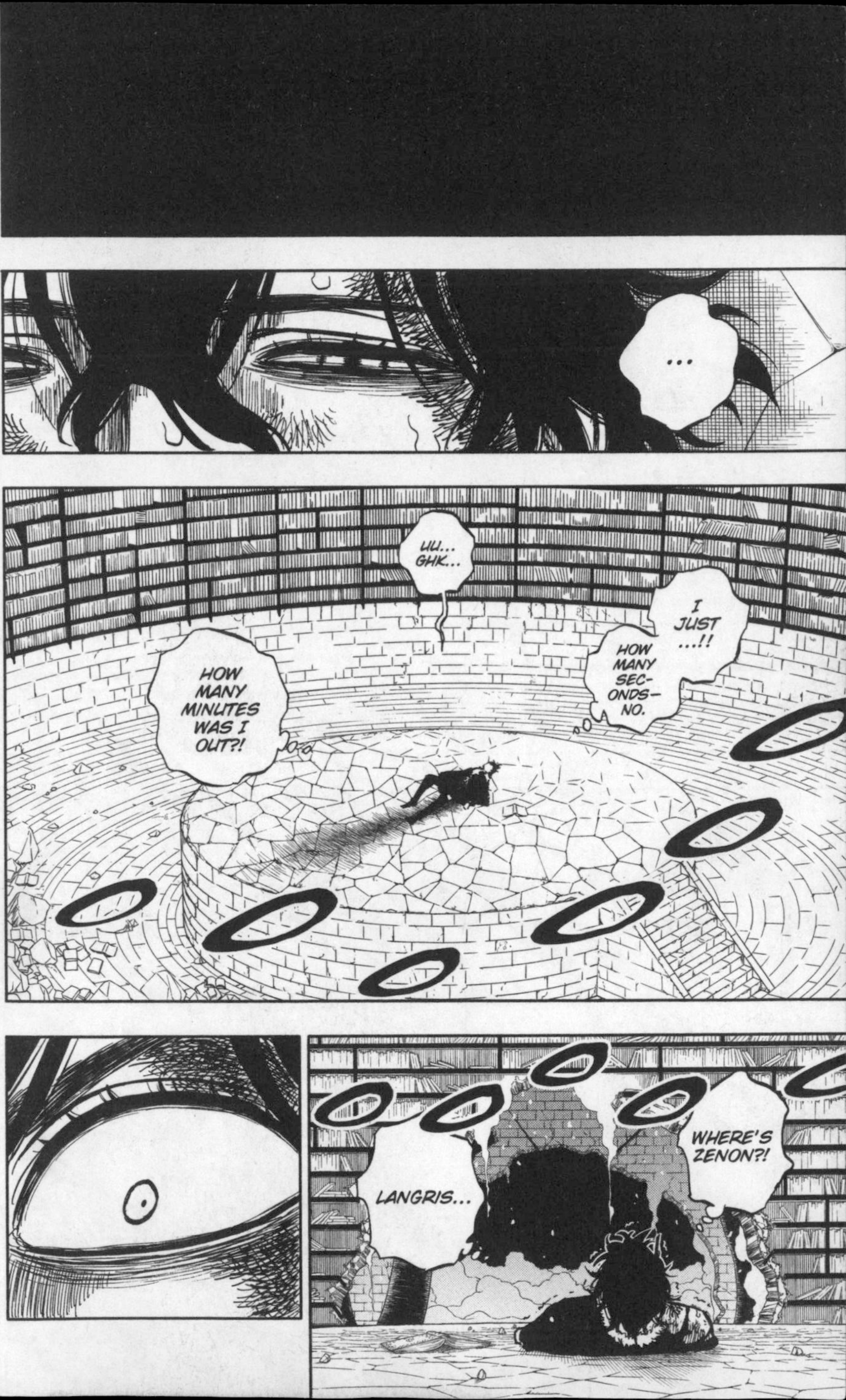
...
UU... GHK...
I JUST ...!!
HOW MANY SEC-ONDS-NO.
HOW MANY MINUTES WAS I OUT?!
WHERE'S ZENON?!
LANGRIS...

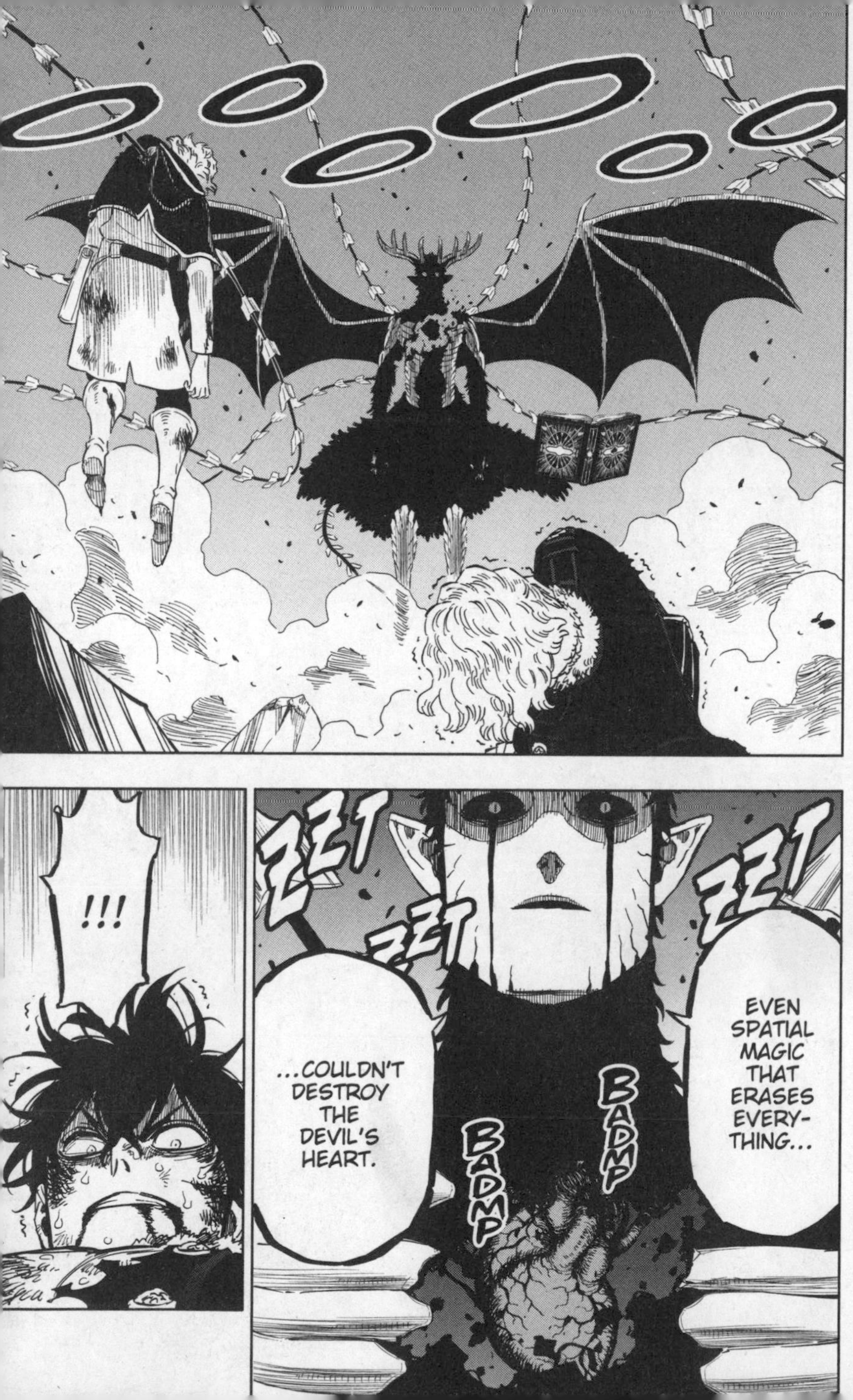
ZZT
EVEN SPATIAL MAGIC THAT ERASES EVERY-THING...
BADMP
ZZT
ZZT
BADMP
...COULDN'T DESTROY THE DEVIL'S HEART.
!!!

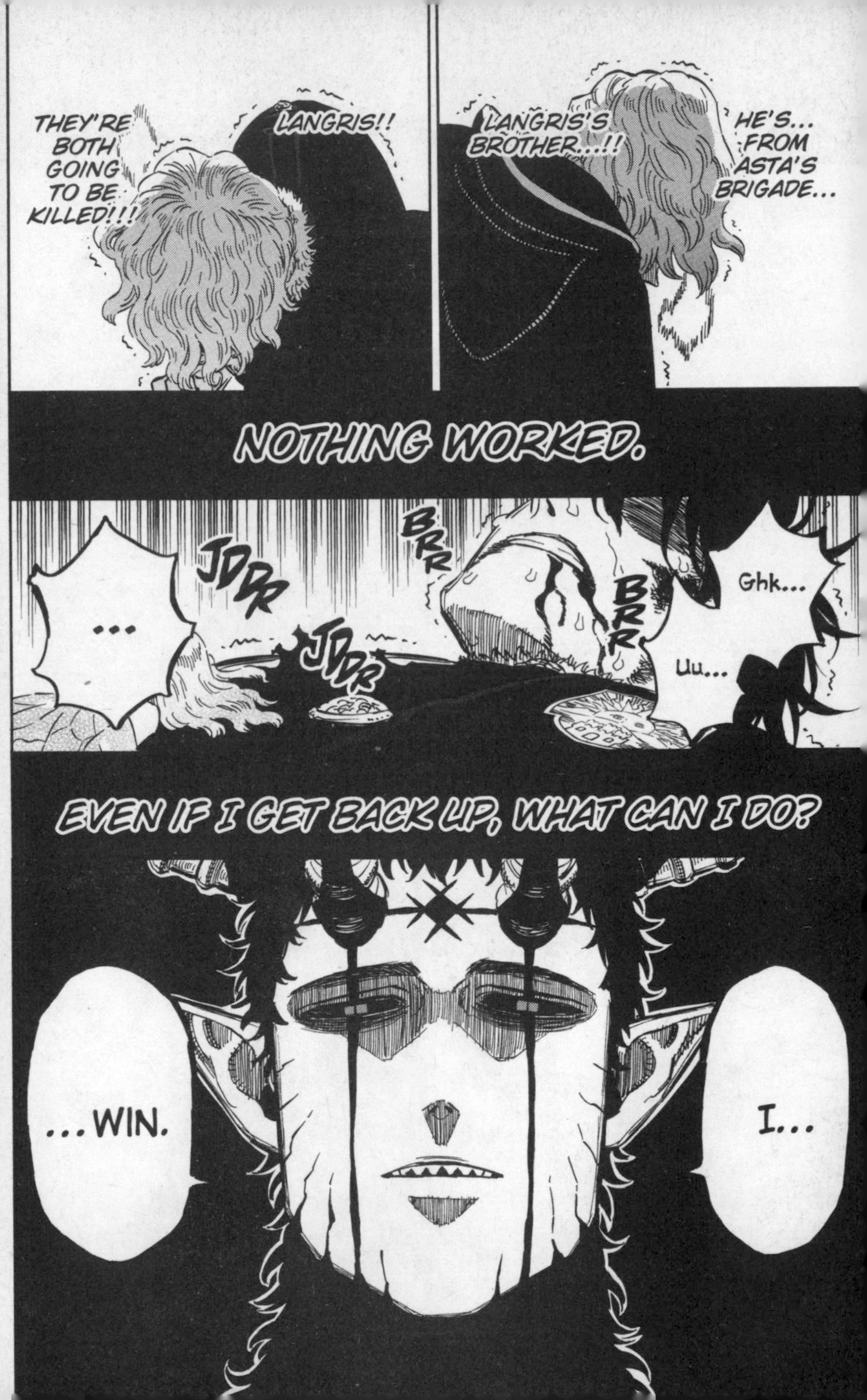
HE'S... FROM ASTA'S BRIGADE...
LANGRIS'S BROTHER...!!
LANGRIS!!
THEY'RE BOTH GOING TO BE KILLED!!!
NOTHING WORKED.
Ghk...
Uu...
BRR
BRR
JDDR
JDDR
...
EVEN IF I GET BACK UP, WHAT CAN I DO?
I...
...WIN.

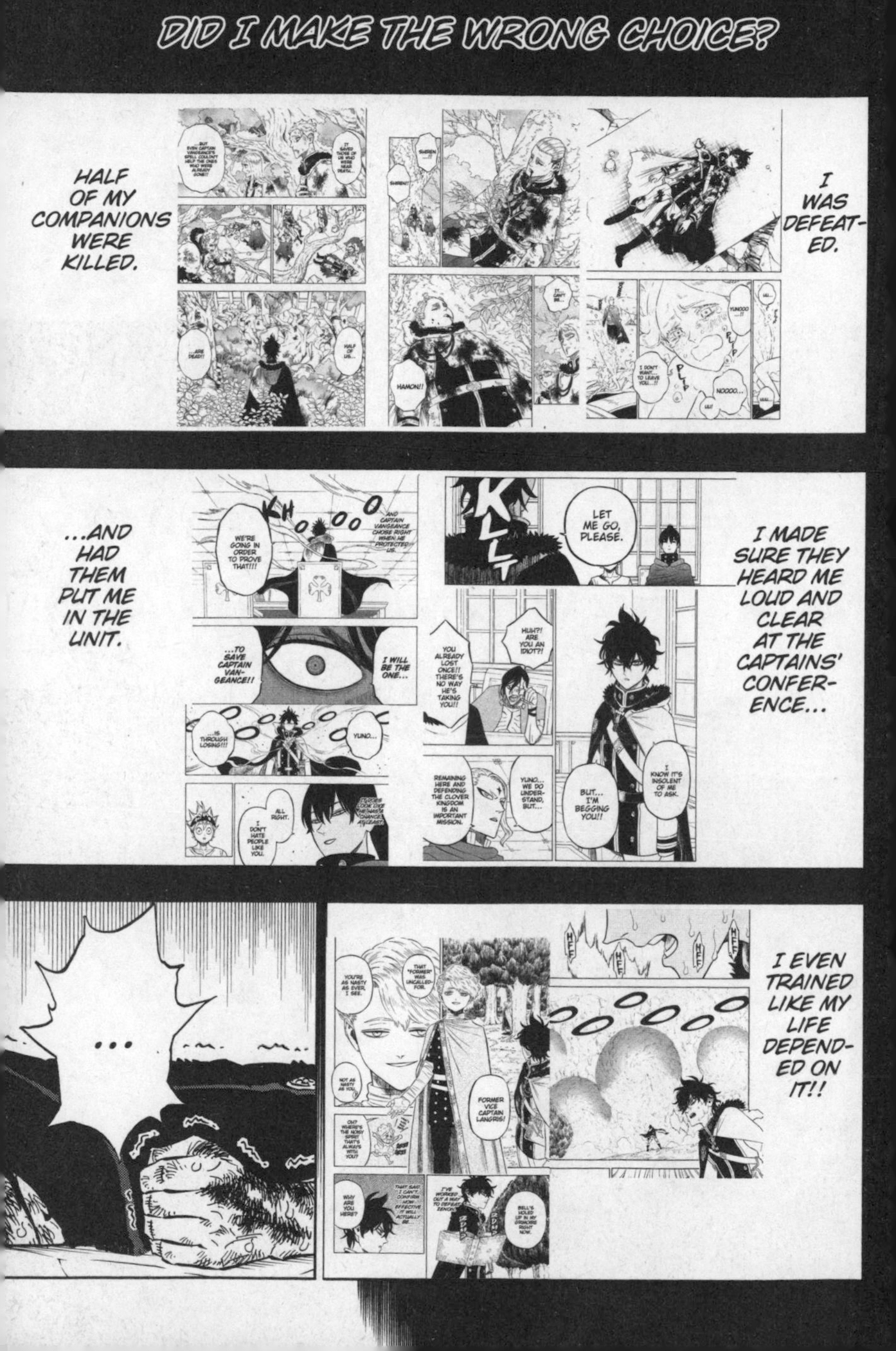
DID I MAKE THE WRONG CHOICE?
I WAS DEFEATED.
HAMON!!
HALF OF MY COMPANIONS WERE KILLED.
I MADE SURE THEY HEARD ME LOUD AND CLEAR AT THE CAPTAINS' CONFERENCE...
LET ME GO, PLEASE.
BUT... I'M BEGGING YOU!!
...AND HAD THEM PUT ME IN THE UNIT.
I WILL BE THE ONE...
...TO SAVE CAPTAIN VAN-GEANCE!!
I EVEN TRAINED LIKE MY LIFE DEPENDED ON IT!!
FORMER VICE CAPTAIN LANGRIS!
...

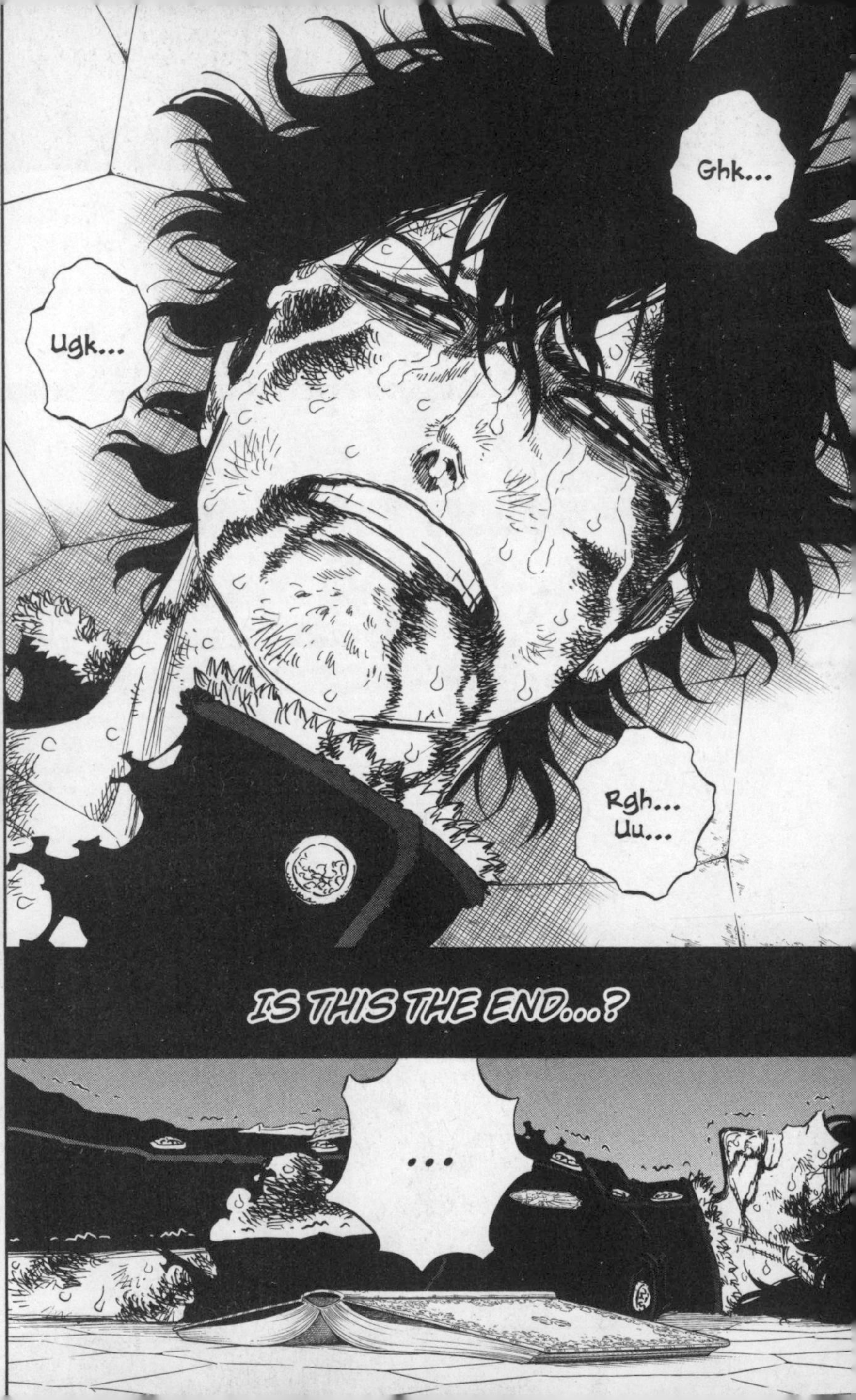
Ghk...
Ugk...
Rgh... Uu...
IS THIS THE END...?
...

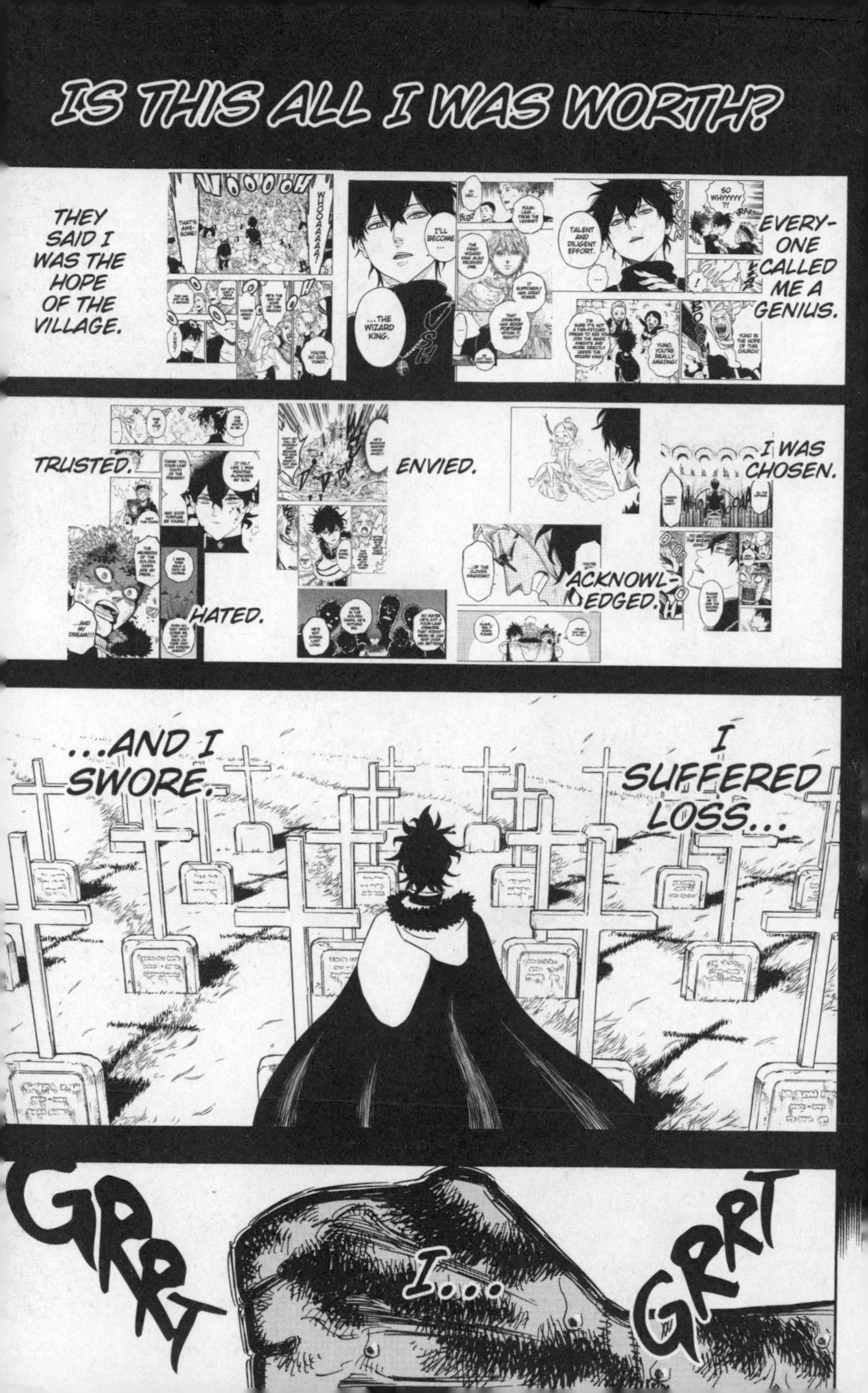
IS THIS ALL I WAS WORTH?
EVERY-ONE CALLED ME A GENIUS.
THEY SAID I WAS THE HOPE OF THE VILLAGE.
I WAS CHOSEN.
ACKNOWL-EDGED.
ENVIED.
HATED.
TRUSTED.
I SUFFERED LOSS...
...AND I SWORE...
GRRT
I...
GRRT

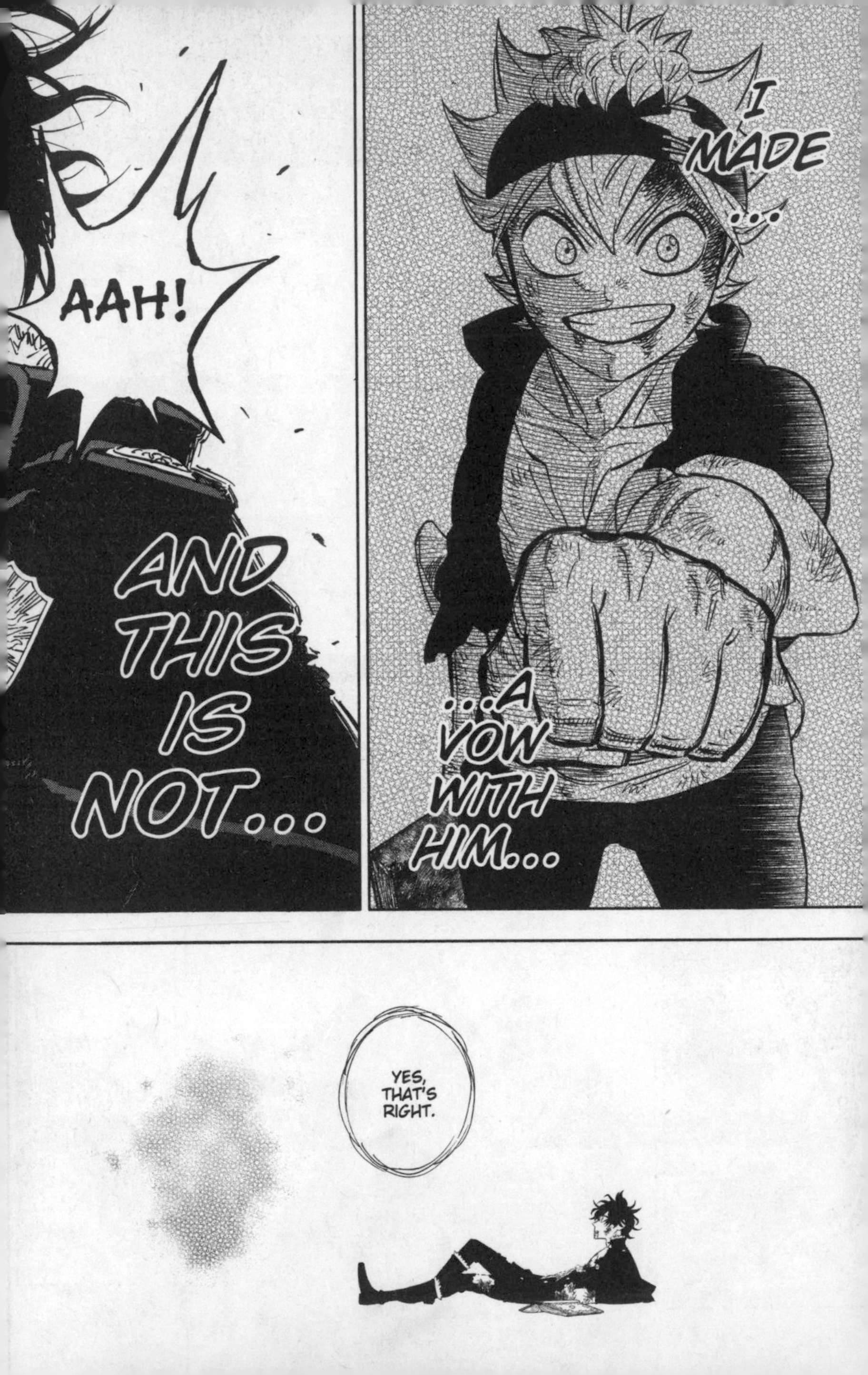
I MADE ...
...A VOW WITH HIM...
AAH!
AND THIS IS NOT...
YES, THAT'S RIGHT.

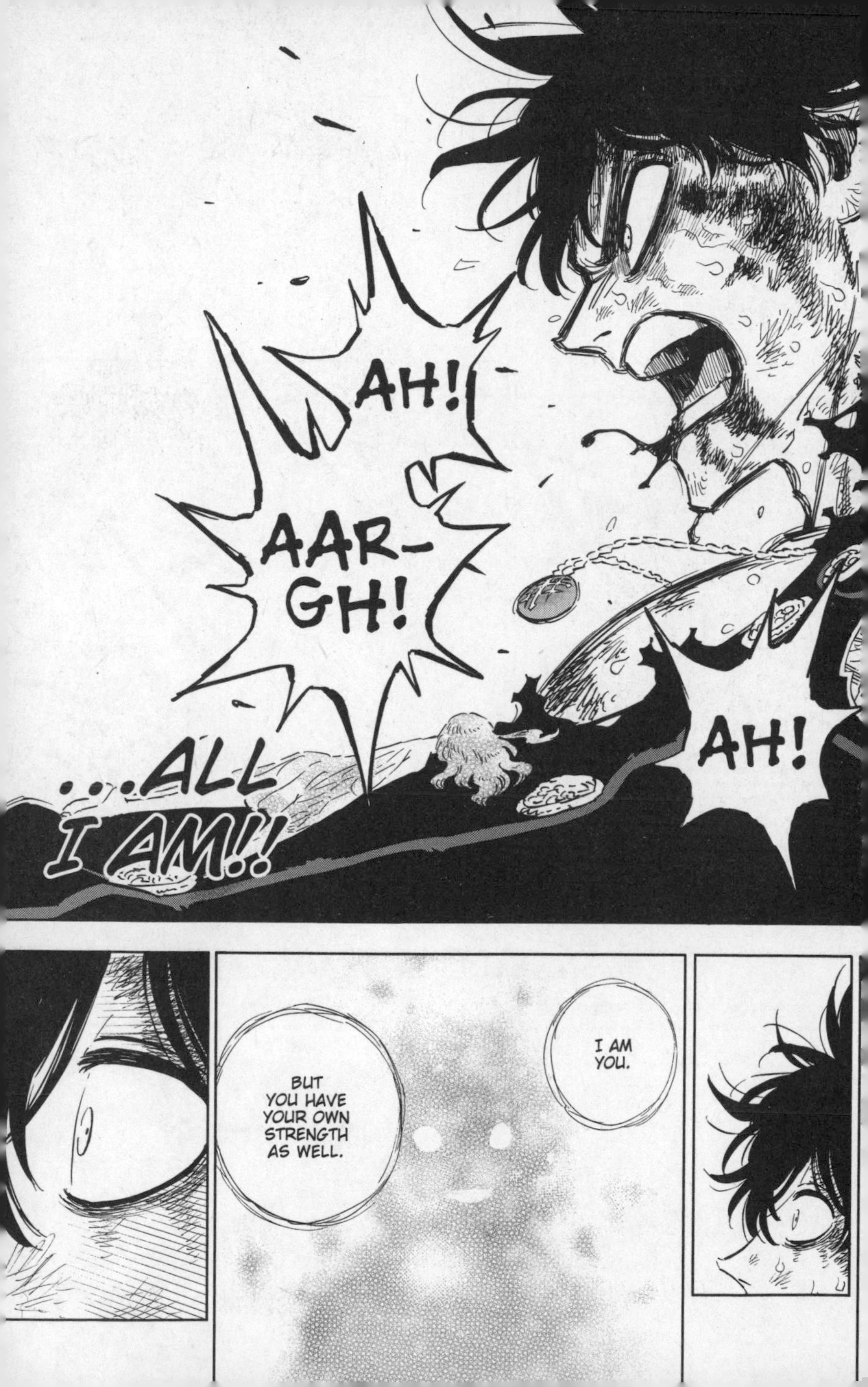
AH!
AAR-GH!
AH!
...ALL I AM!!
I AM YOU.
BUT YOU HAVE YOUR OWN STRENGTH AS WELL.

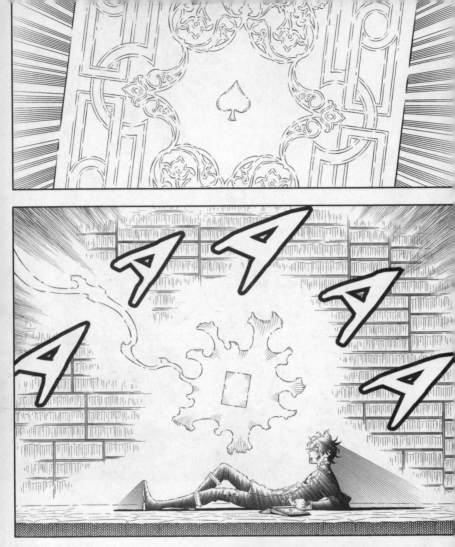

...MOIRE
...!!

A
GRI...

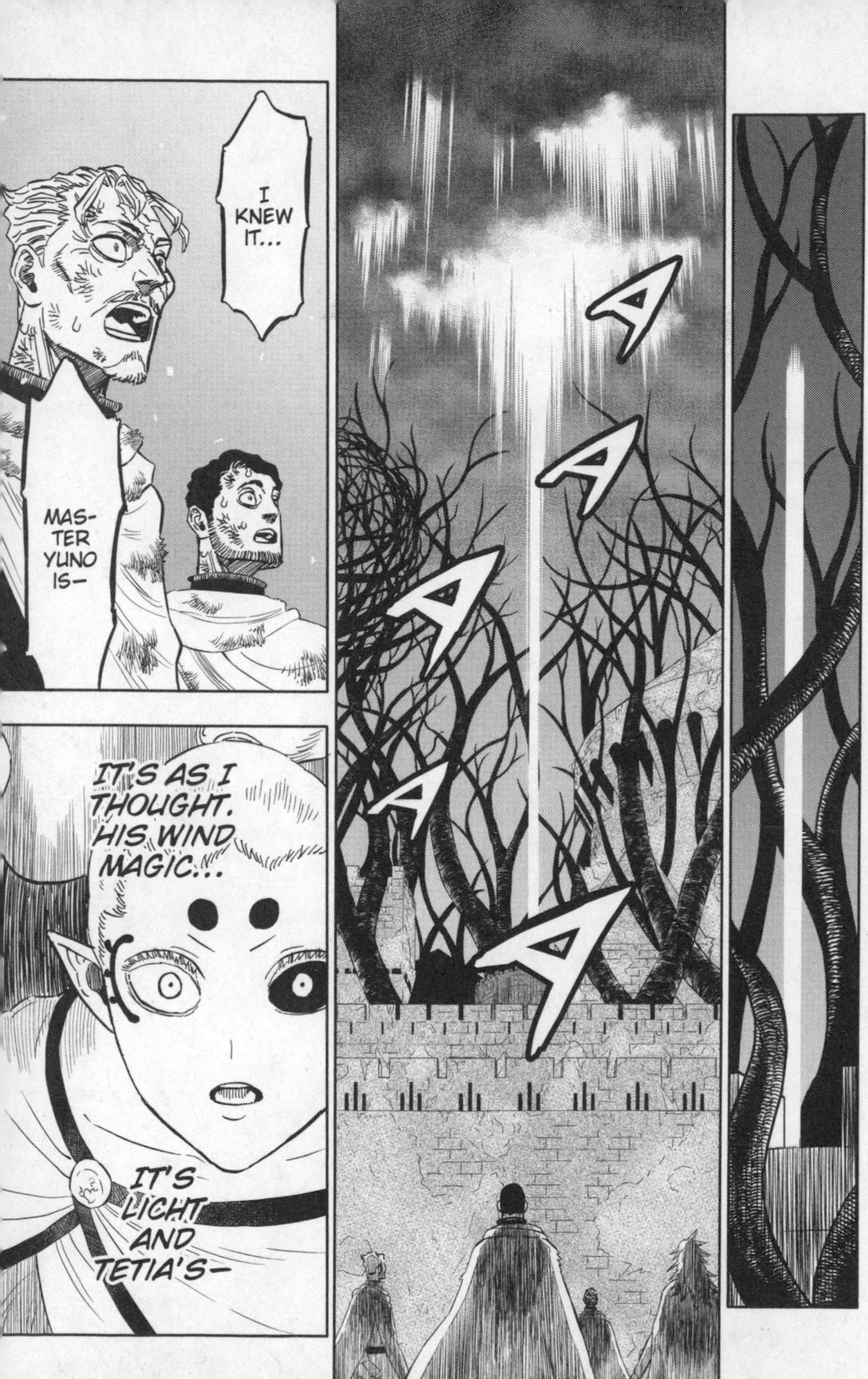

AAAAA
I KNEW IT...
MASTER YUNO IS—
IT'S AS I THOUGHT. HIS WIND MAGIC...
IT'S LICHT AND TETIA'S—

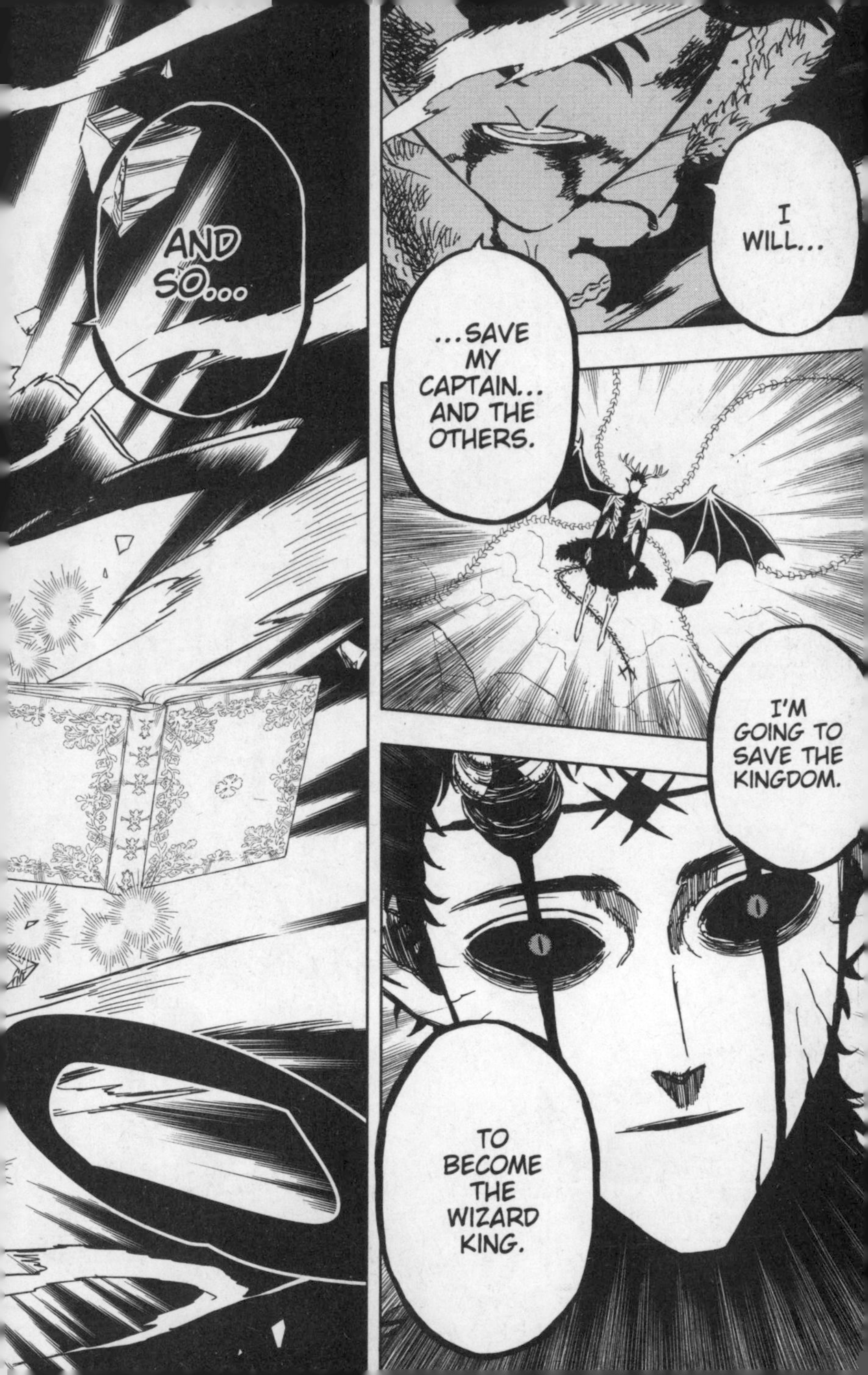
I WILL...
...SAVE MY CAPTAIN... AND THE OTHERS.
I'M GOING TO SAVE THE KINGDOM.
TO BECOME THE WIZARD KING.
AND SO...

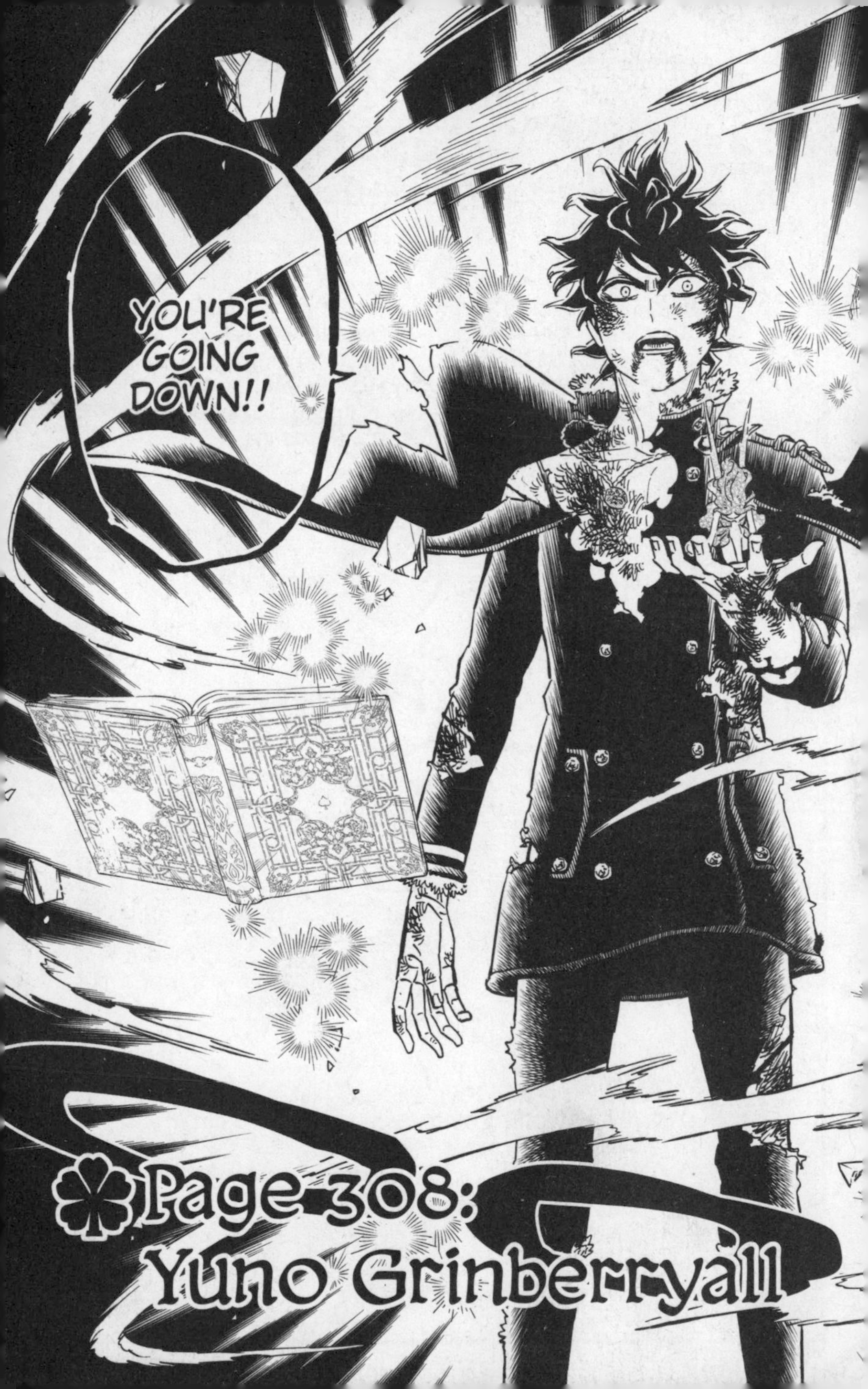
YOU'RE GOING DOWN!!
Page 308: Yuno Grinberryall

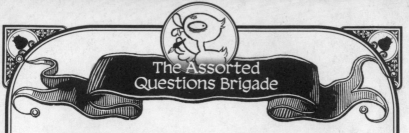

The Assorted Questions Brigade

Q: Tabata sensei, I always look forward to reading *Black Clover*. I had a question--in volume 12, you told us what types of people each of the Black Bulls liked. Could you tell us about the remaining members: Nacht, Nero, Henry, and Zora? Also, while I'm asking, I'd like to know Yuno, Mimosa, Klaus and Leopold's types too. Thank you very much. (*Ransan*)

Zora

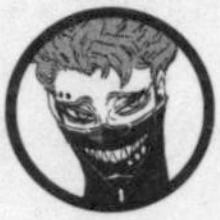

"KEH HEE HEE. A WOMAN WHO FORGIVES ME WHEN I'M NOT A TEAM PLAYER."

Henry

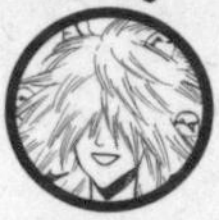

"SOMEBODY WHO'LL TEACH ME THINGS I DON'T KNOW."

Nero

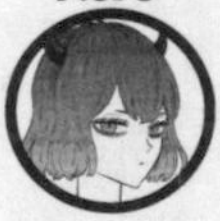

"SOMEONE WHO LOVES LEARNING..."

Nacht

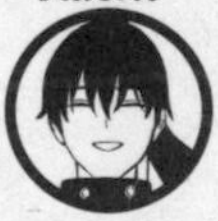

"SOMEONE WHO'S RIGHT."

Yuno

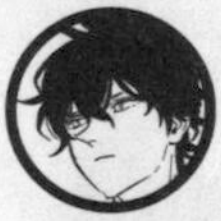

"SOMEONE WHO'S RELAXING TO BE AROUND..."

Mimosa

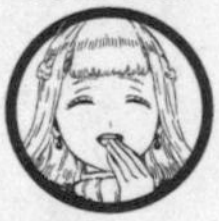

"UM... SOMEONE WHO'S FAITHFUL AND EARNEST."

Klaus

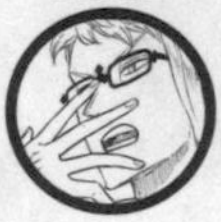

"AN INTELLIGENT WOMAN WHO KNOWS WHAT SHE WANTS!"

Leopold

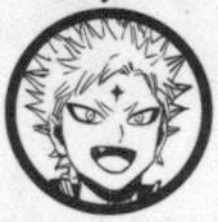

"LET'S SEE! A WOMAN WHO'S FUN TO BE AROUND!"

Q: Hello, Tabata sensei. I have a few questions.

1) Have any women ever been the wizard king?
2) Which wizard king is Julius?

They're kinda weird questions, but I really want to know!! Please tell me!! (*Matcha-mikan*)

A: 1) Yes! 2) He's the 28th wizard king!

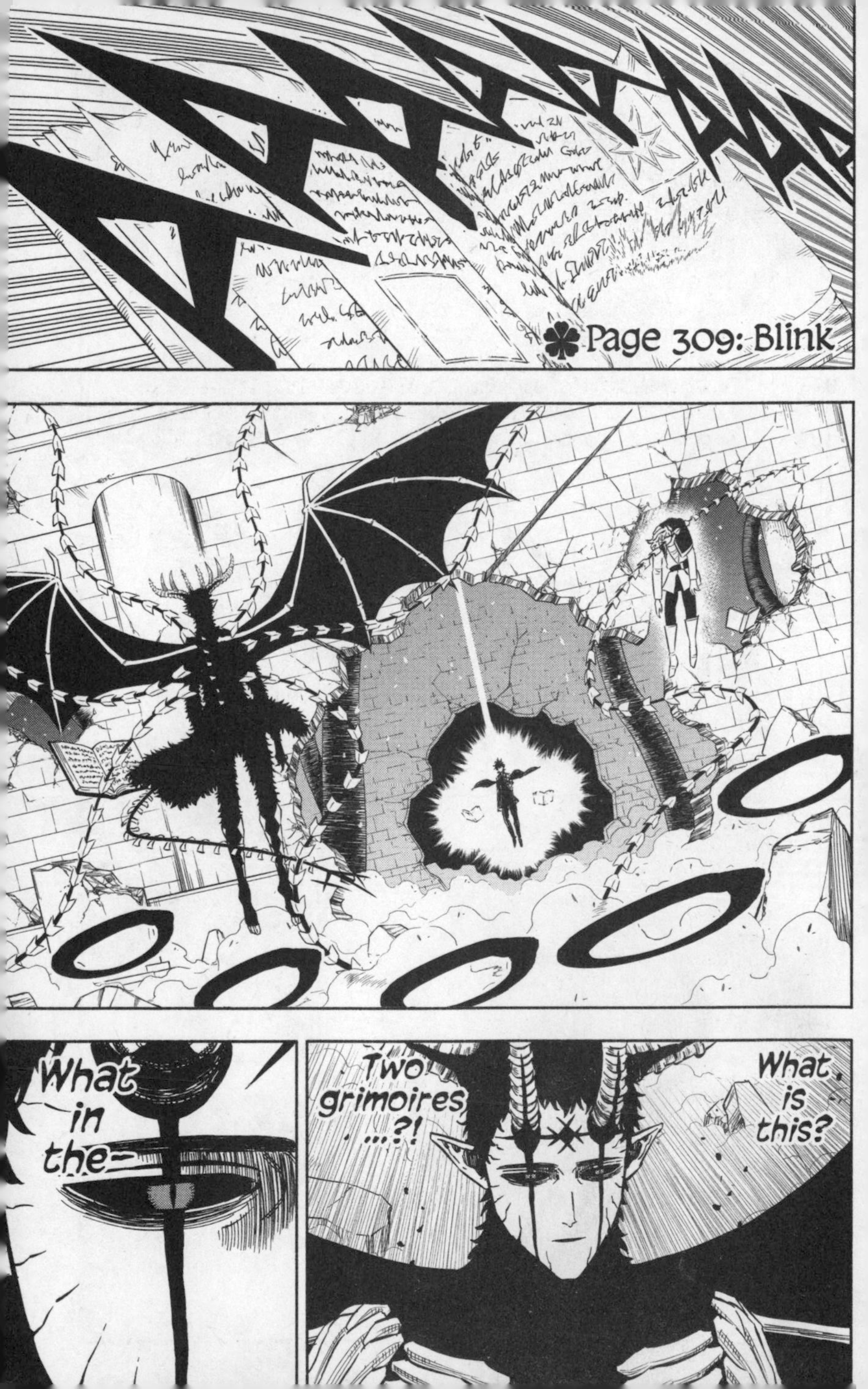
Page 309: Blink
What is this?
Two grimoires ...?!
What in the—

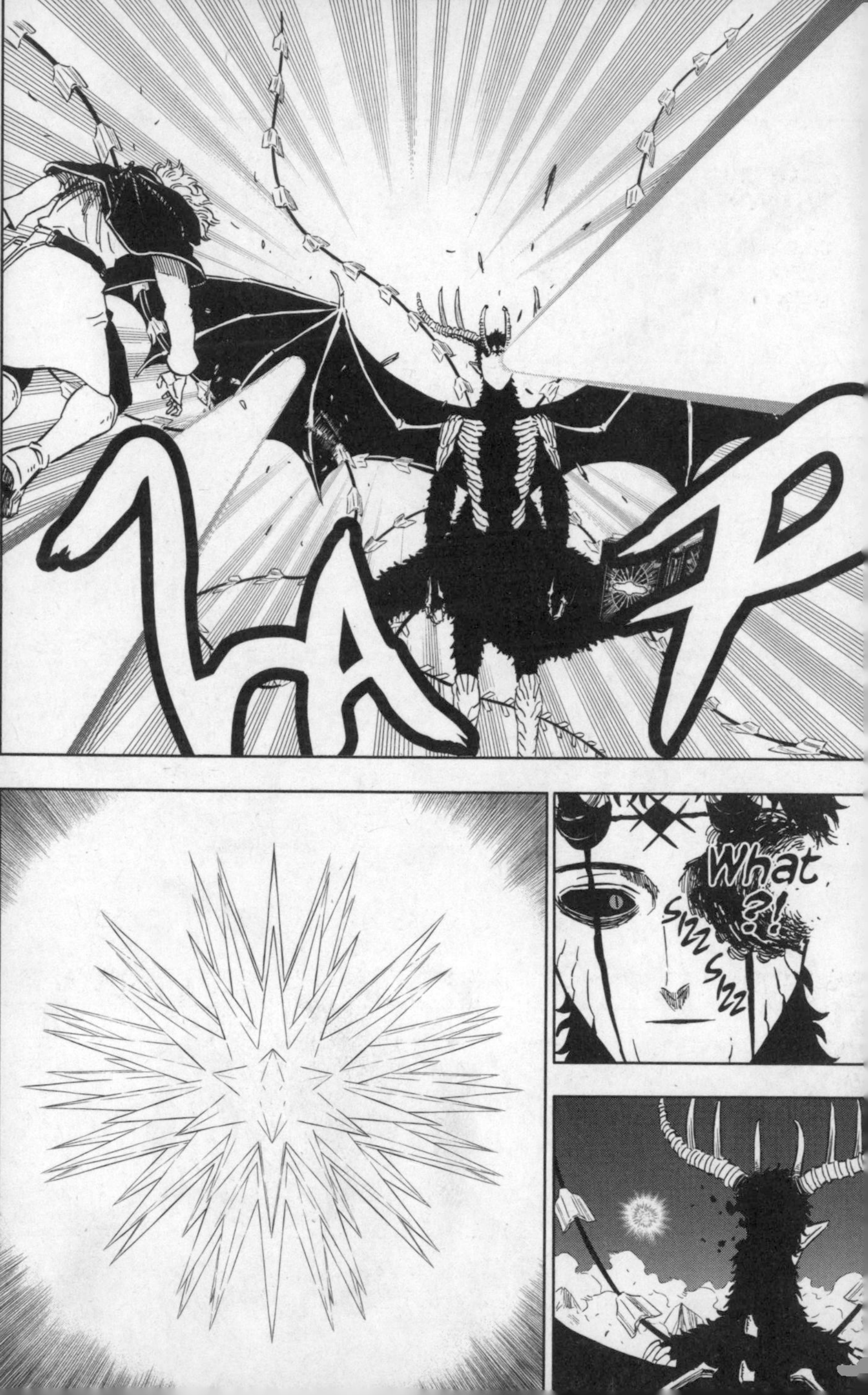
What ?!
SIZZ
SIZZ

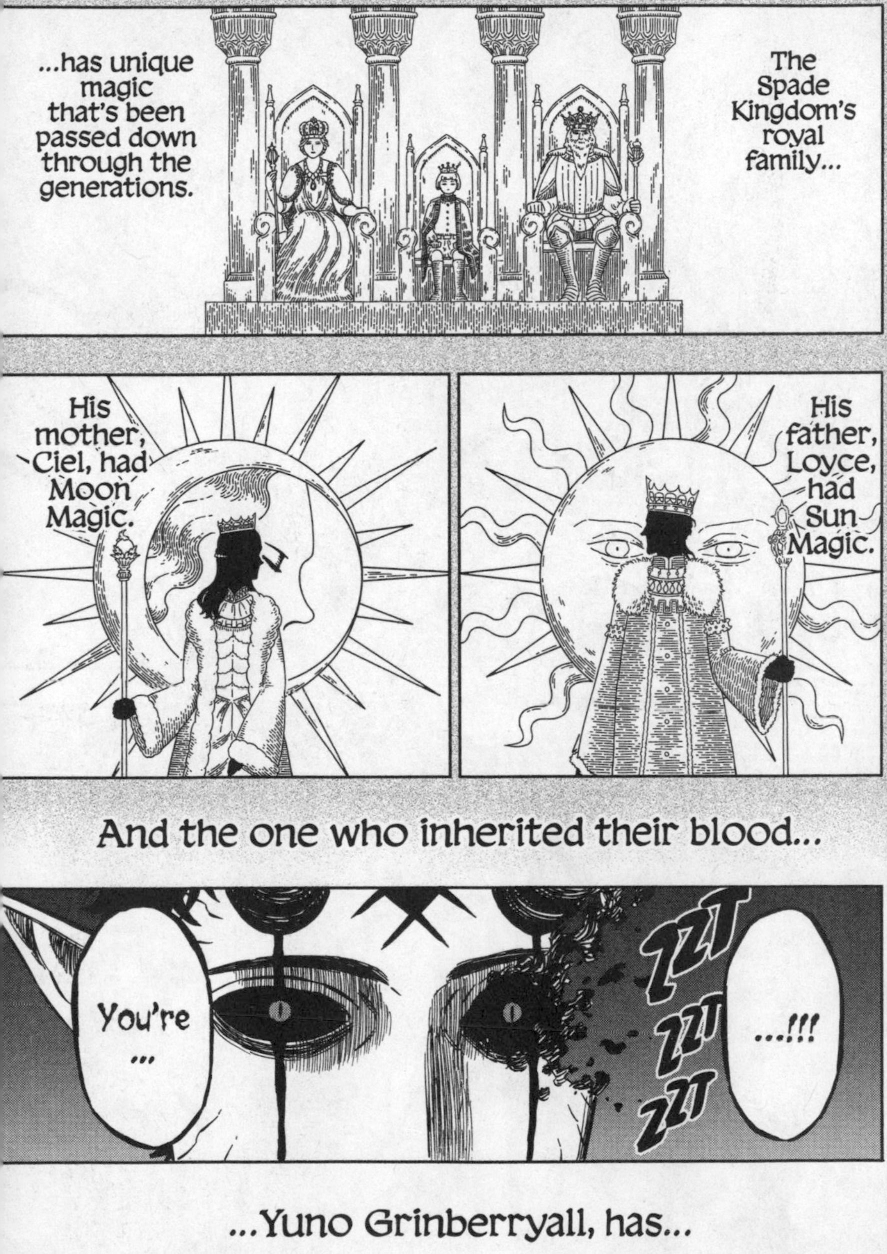
The Spade Kingdom's royal family...
...has unique magic that's been passed down through the generations.
His father, Loyce, had Sun Magic.
His mother, Ciel, had Moon Magic.
And the one who inherited their blood...
...!!!
ZZT
ZZT
ZZT
You're ...
...Yuno Grinberryall, has...

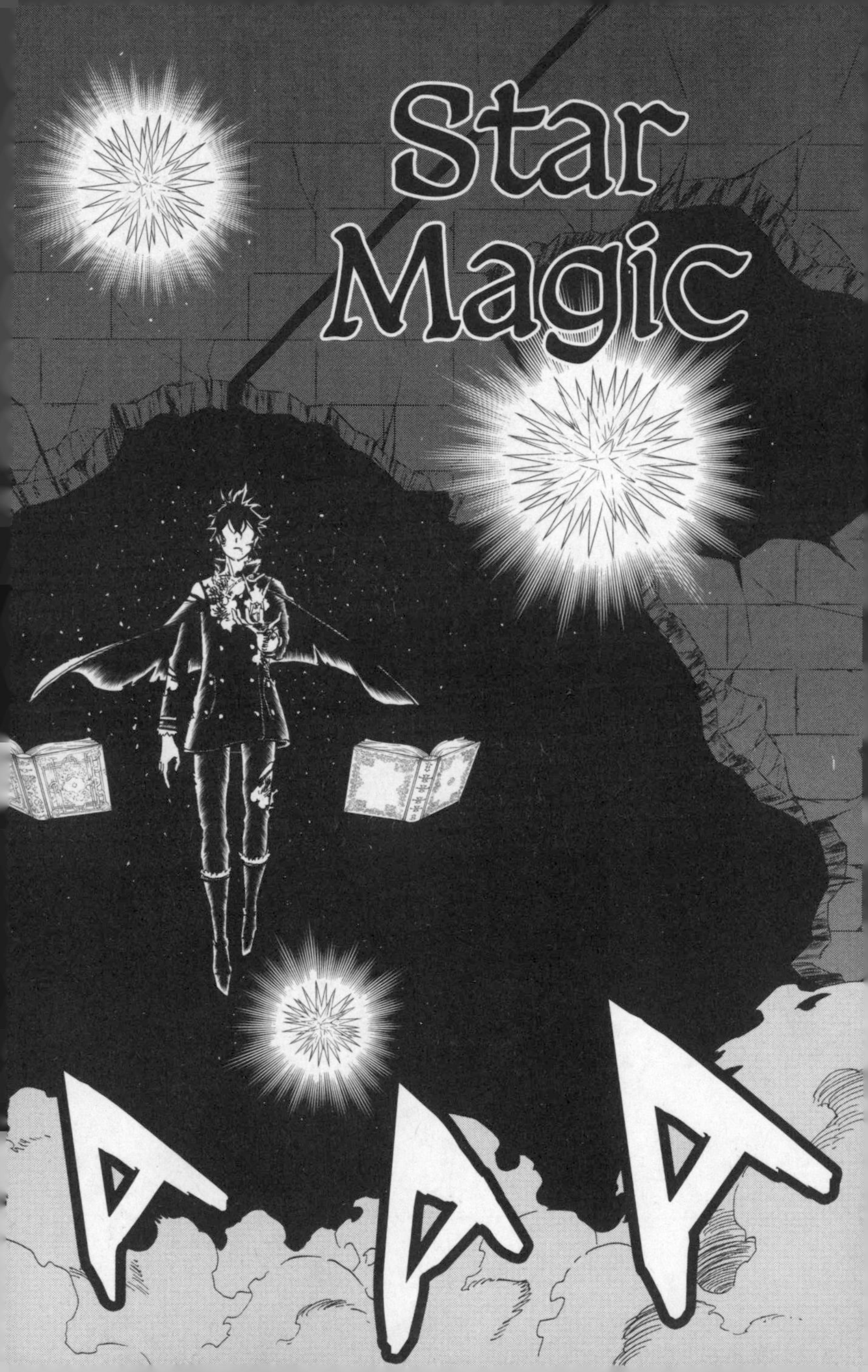
Star Magic

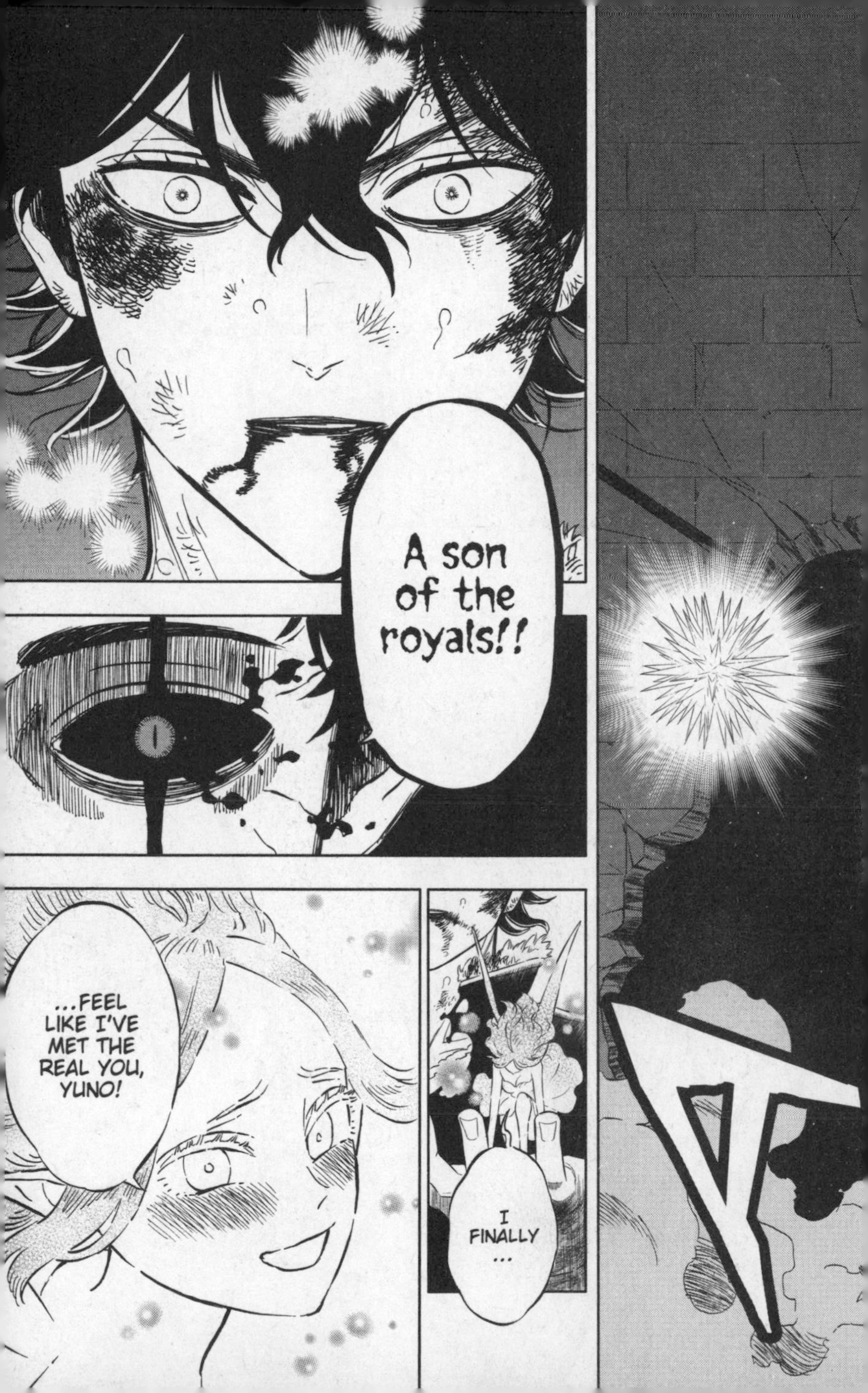
A son of the royals!!
I FINALLY ...
...FEEL LIKE I'VE MET THE REAL YOU, YUNO!

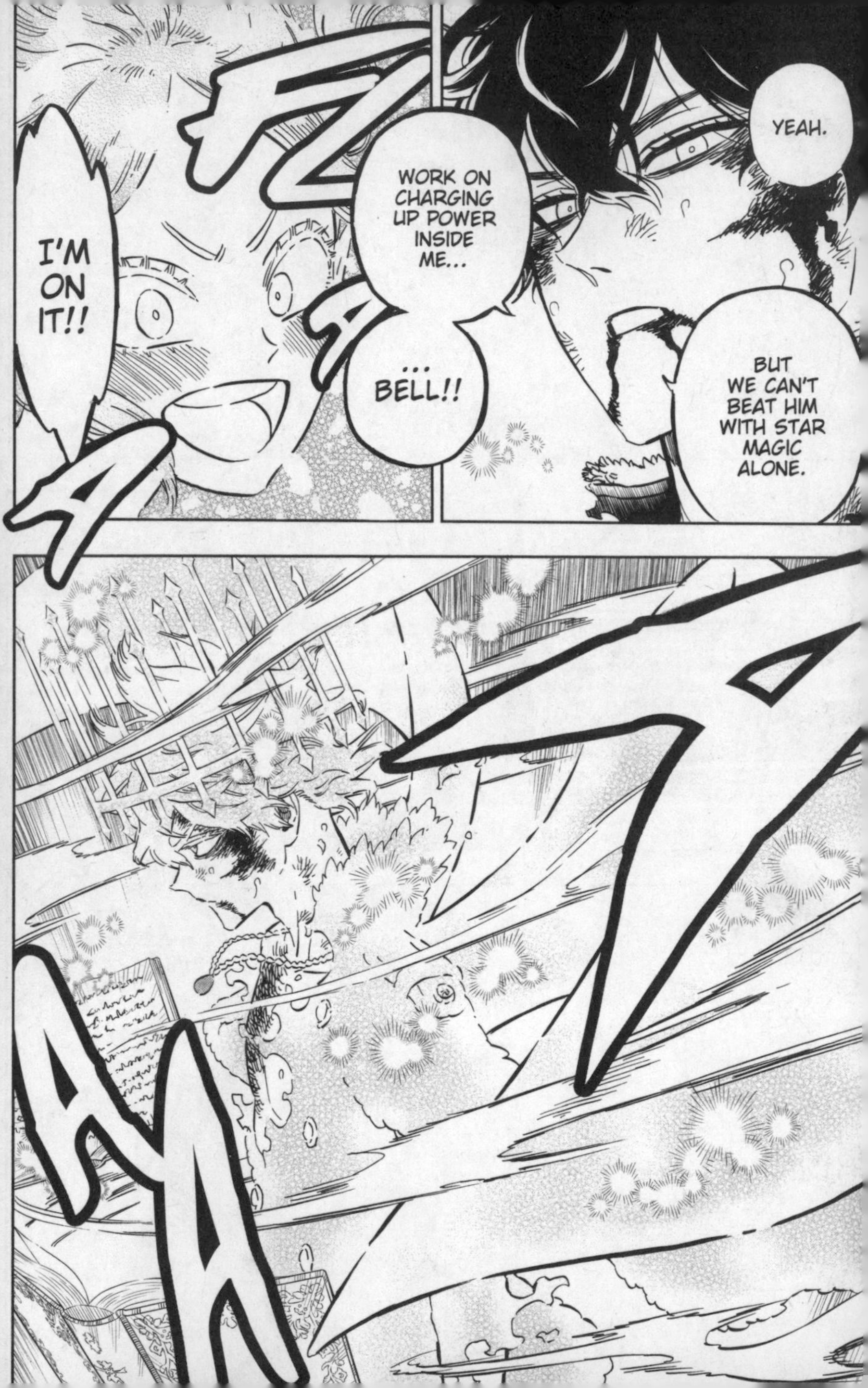
YEAH.
BUT WE CAN'T BEAT HIM WITH STAR MAGIC ALONE.
WORK ON CHARGING UP POWER INSIDE ME...
...BELL!!
I'M ON IT!!

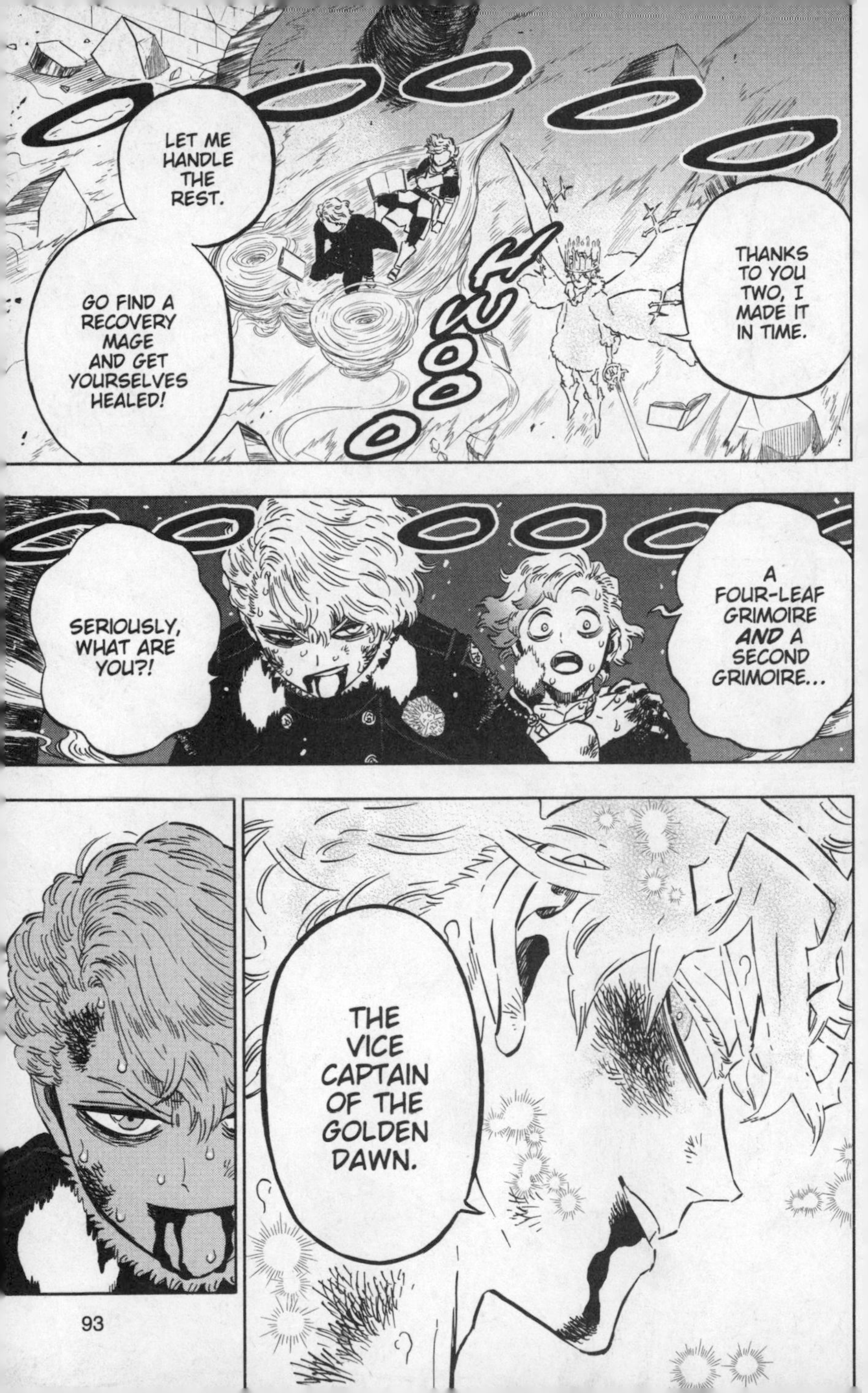
THANKS TO YOU TWO, I MADE IT IN TIME.
HUOOOO
LET ME HANDLE THE REST.
GO FIND A RECOVERY MAGE AND GET YOURSELVES HEALED!
A FOUR-LEAF GRIMOIRE *AND* A SECOND GRIMOIRE...
SERIOUSLY, WHAT ARE YOU?!
THE VICE CAPTAIN OF THE GOLDEN DAWN.

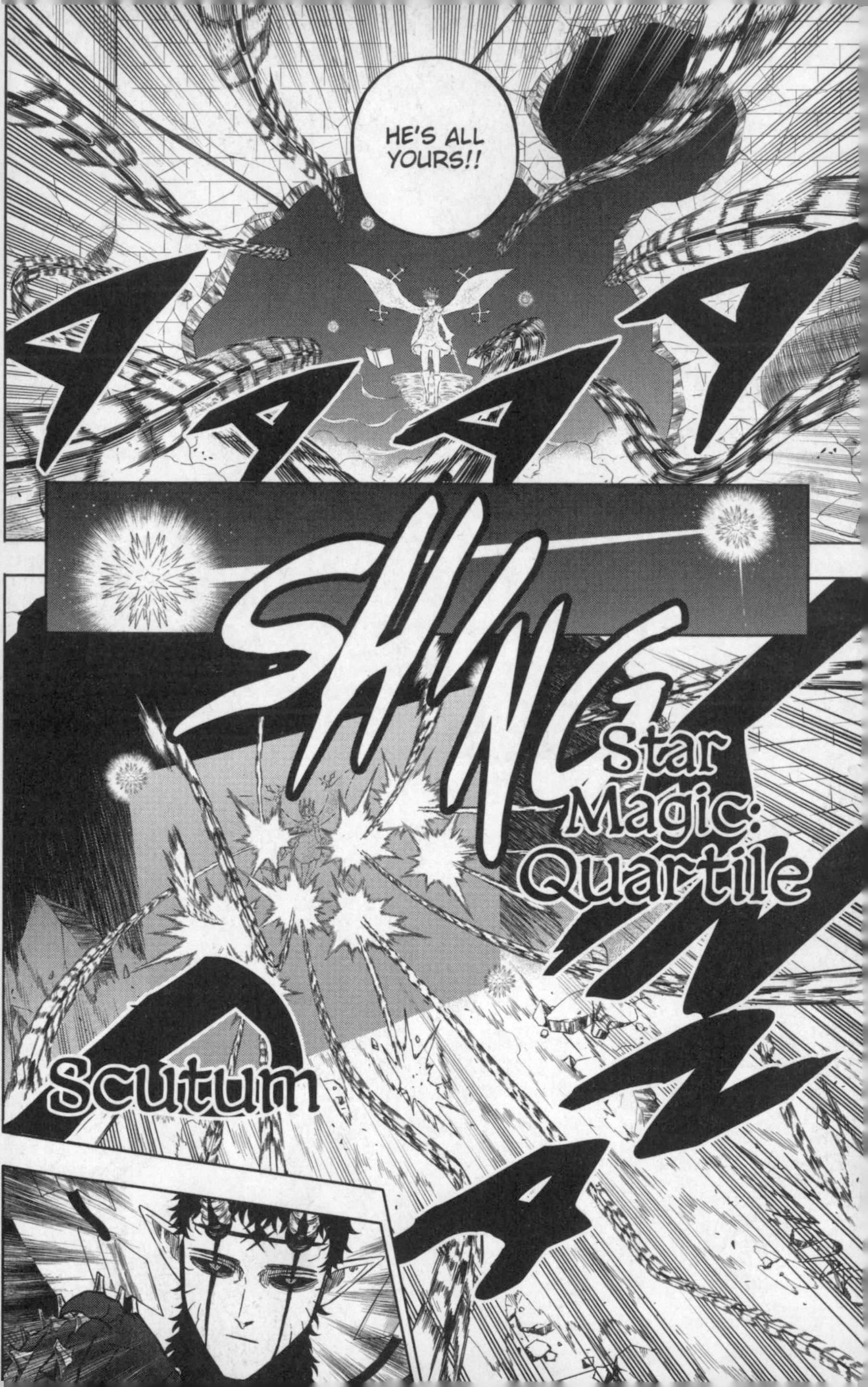
HE'S ALL YOURS!!
SHING
Star Magic: Quartile
Scutum

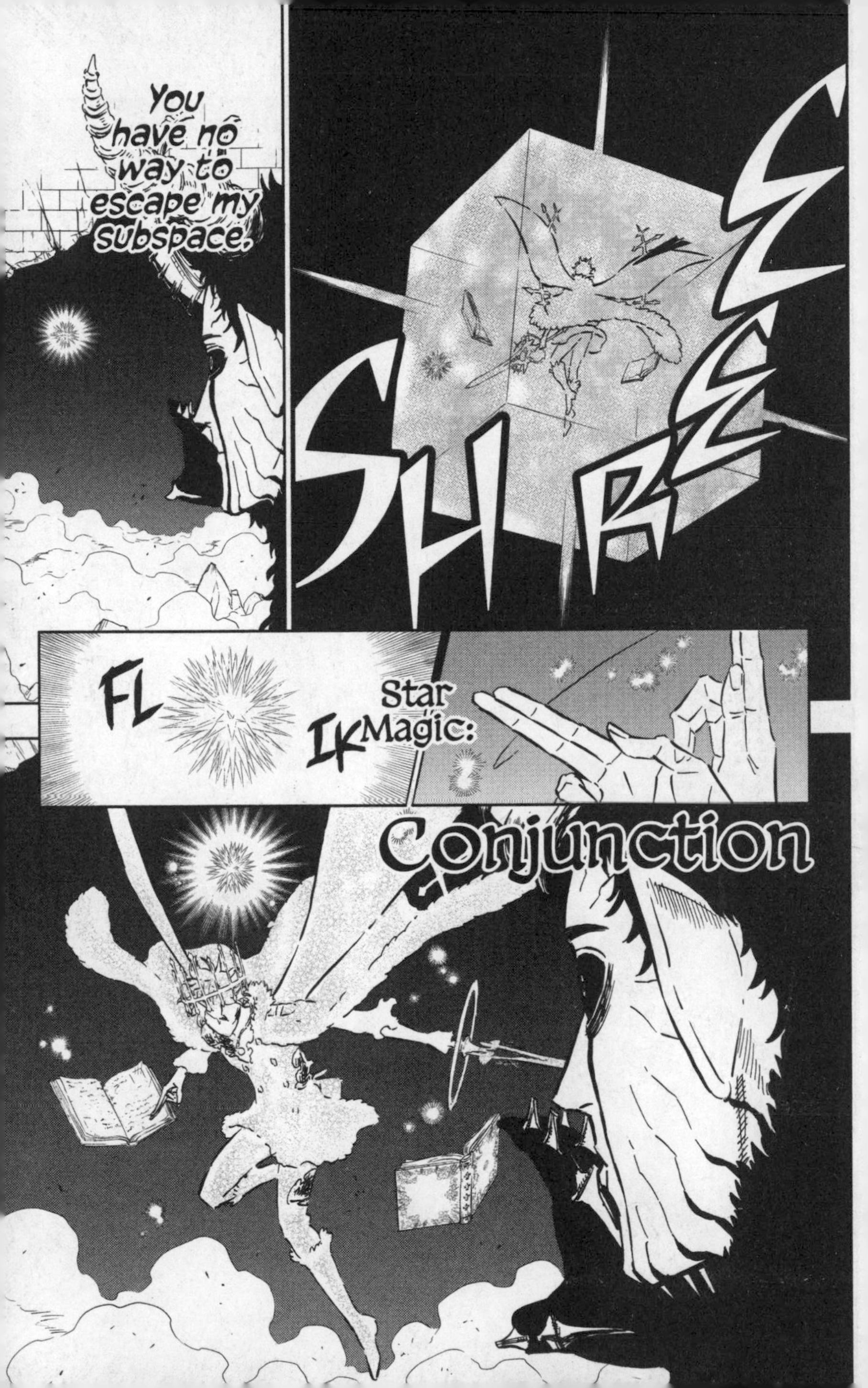
You have no way to escape my subspace.
Star Magic:
FLIK
Conjunction

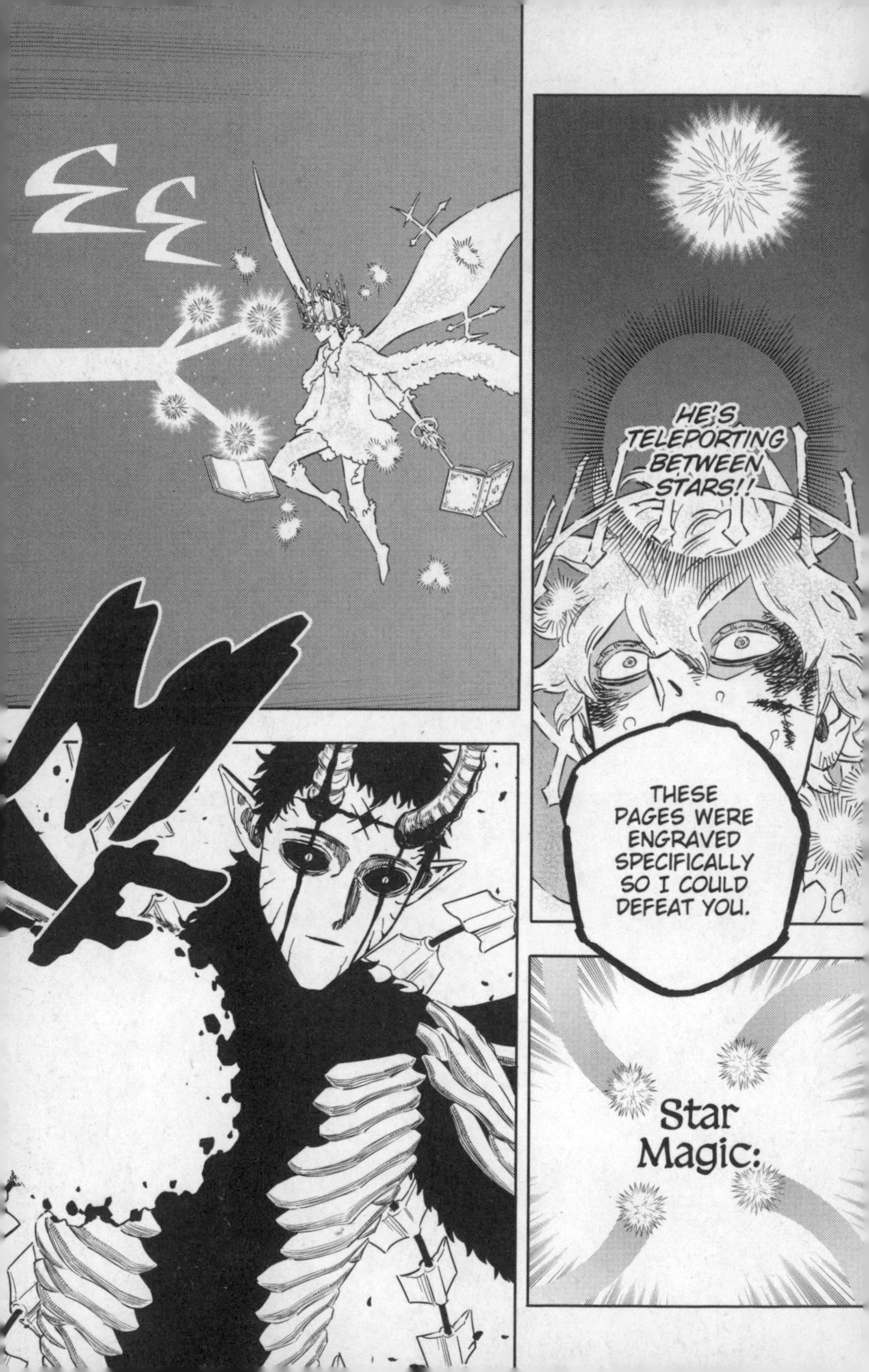
HE'S TELEPORTING BETWEEN STARS!!
THESE PAGES WERE ENGRAVED SPECIFICALLY SO I COULD DEFEAT YOU.
Star Magic:

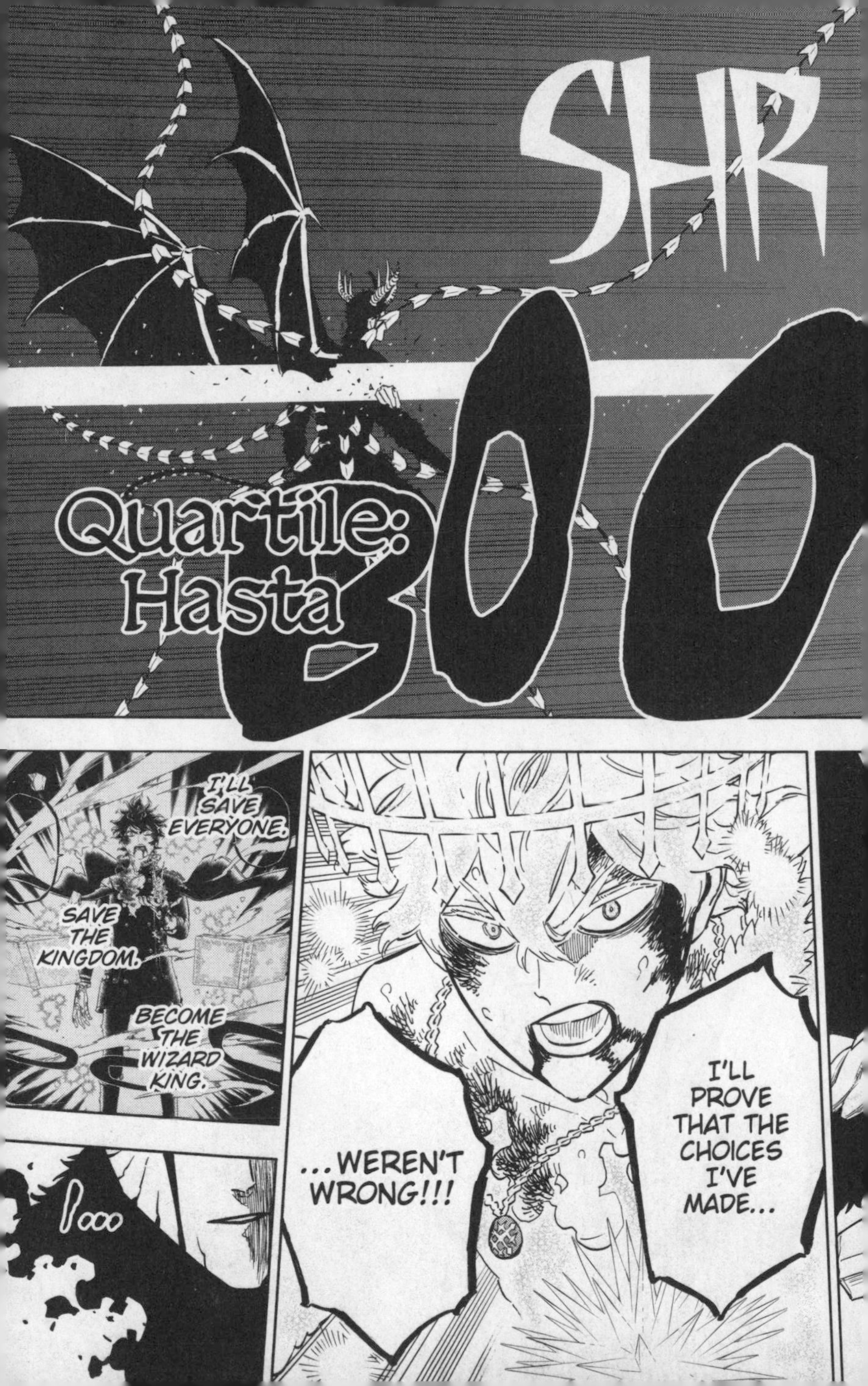
SHR
BOO
Quartile: Hasta
I'LL PROVE THAT THE CHOICES I'VE MADE...
...WEREN'T WRONG!!!
I'LL SAVE EVERYONE.
SAVE THE KINGDOM.
BECOME THE WIZARD KING.
I...

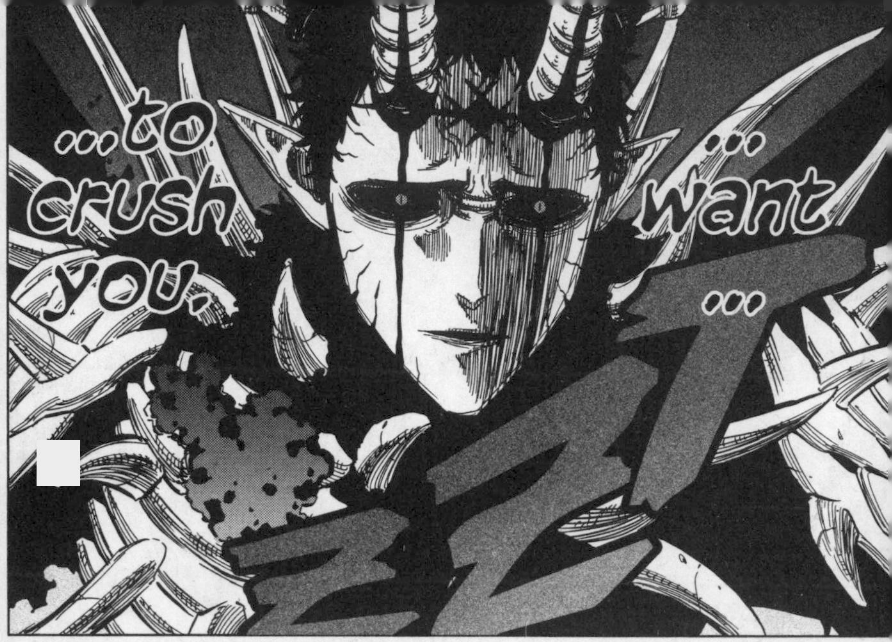
...want...
...to crush you.

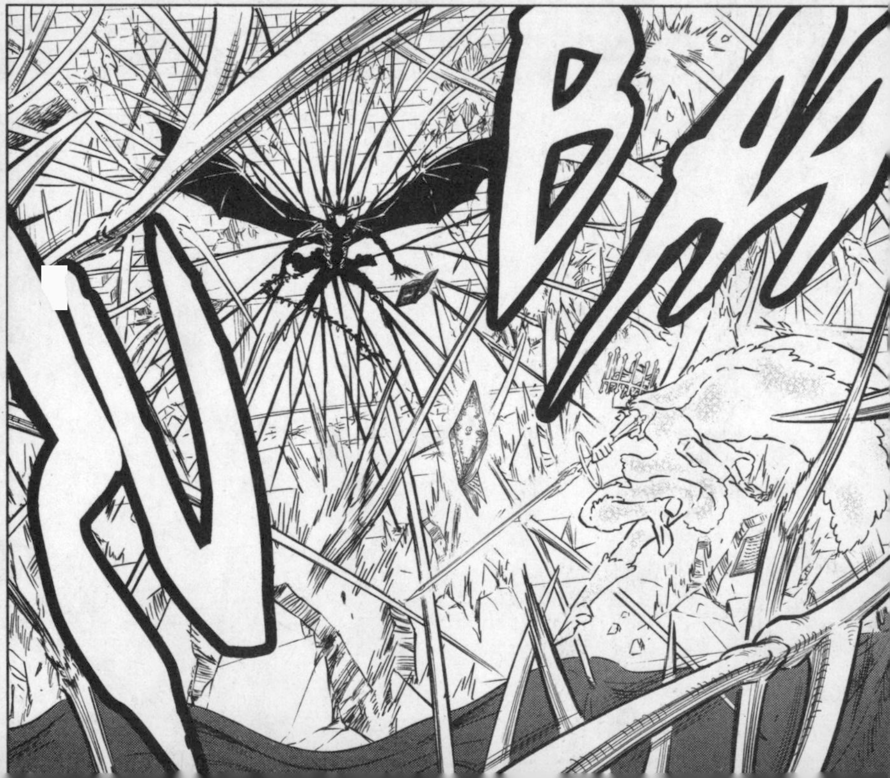

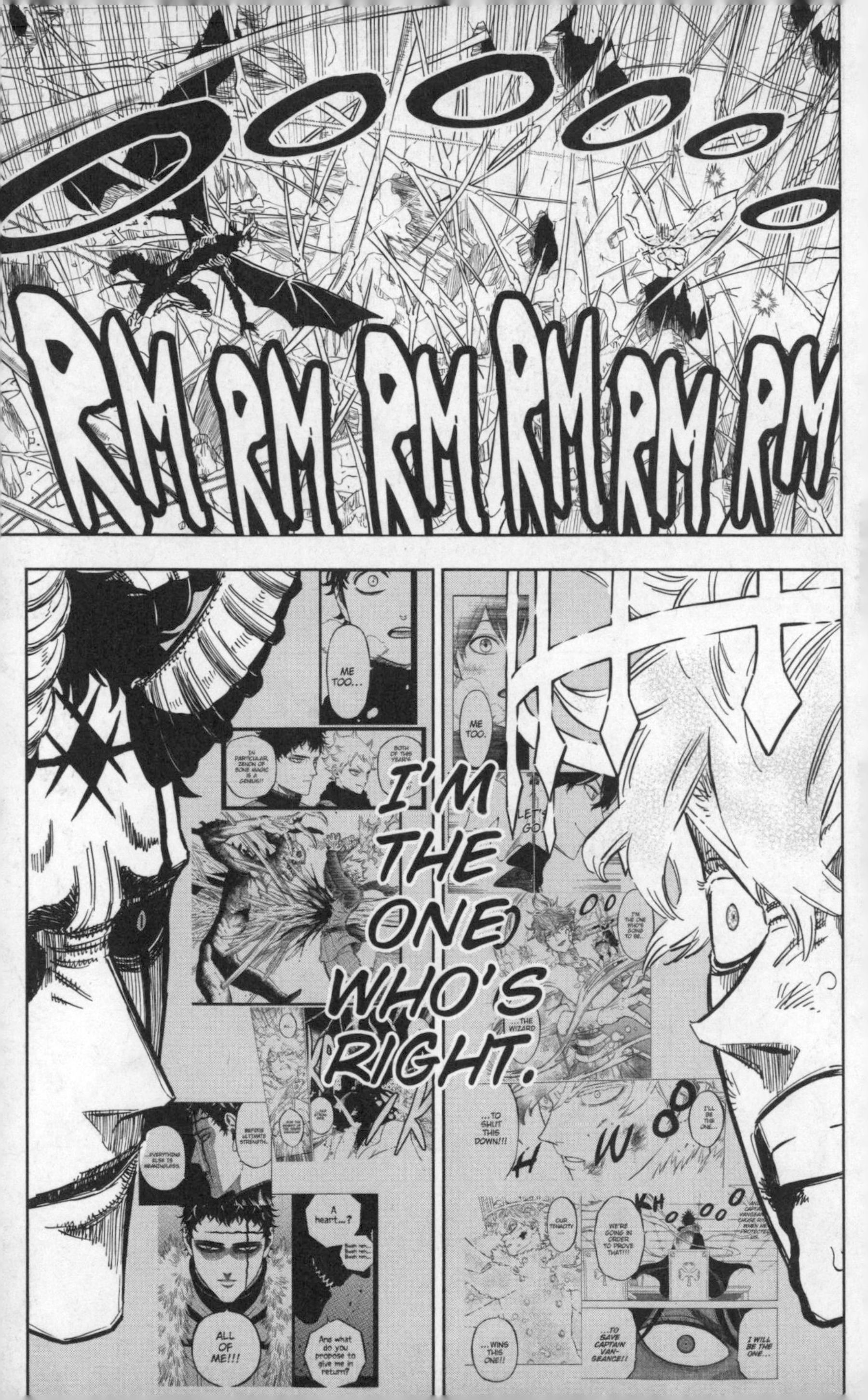
OOOOOOOO
RM RM RM RM RM RM
ME TOO.
LET'S GO
I'M THE ONE WHO'S GOING TO BE...
...THE WIZARD
I'LL BE THE ONE...
...TO SHUT THIS DOWN!!!
WE'RE GOING IN ORDER TO PROVE THAT!!!
OUR TENACITY...
I WILL BE THE ONE...
...TO SAVE CAPTAIN VAN-GEANCE!!
...WINS THIS ONE!!
ME TOO...
IN PARTICULAR, ZENON OF BONE MAGIC IS A GENIUS!!
BEFORE ULTIMATE STRENGTH...
...EVERYTHING ELSE IS MEANINGLESS.
A heart...?
And what do you propose to give me in return?
ALL OF ME!!!
I'M THE ONE WHO'S RIGHT.

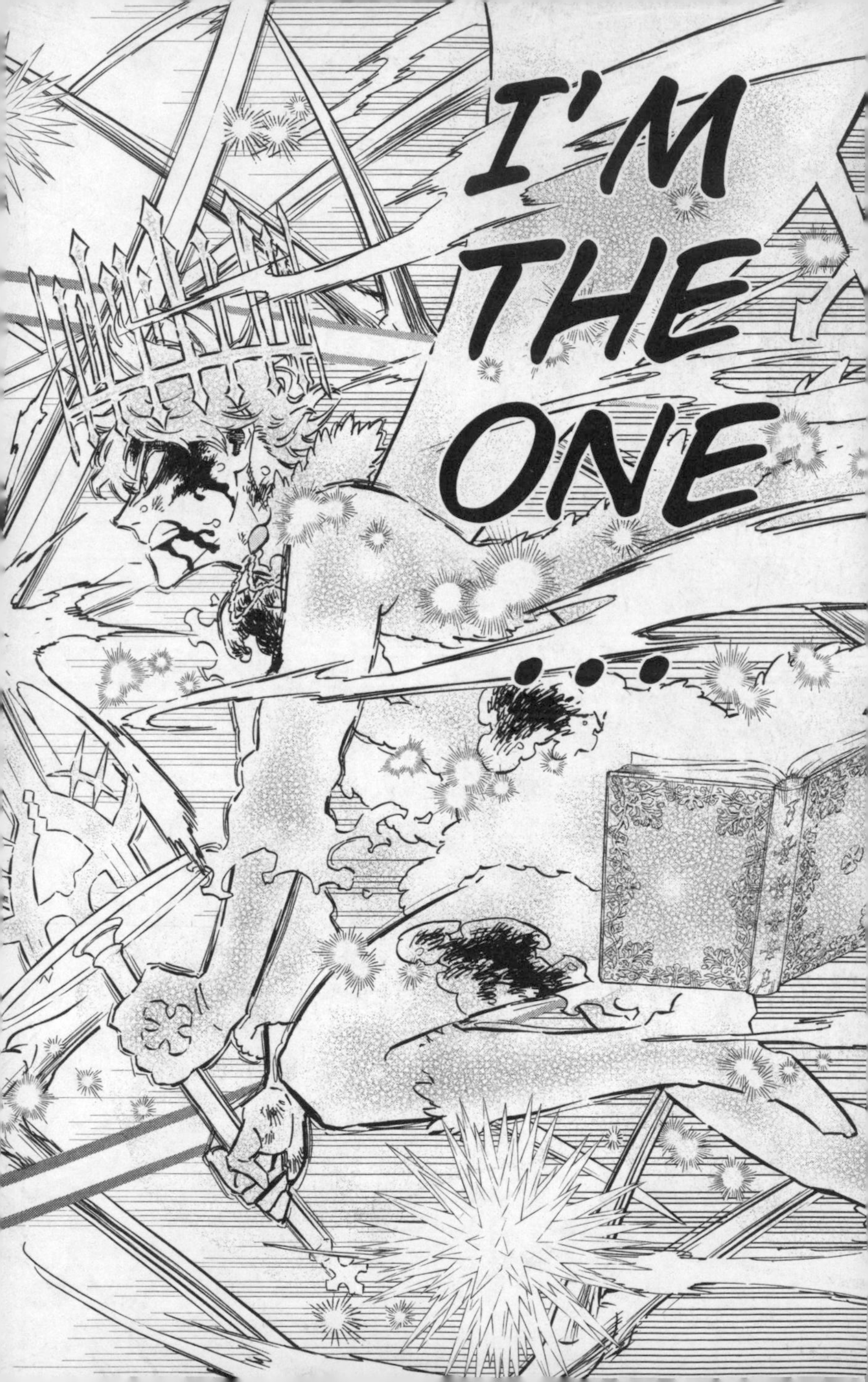
I'M THE ONE...

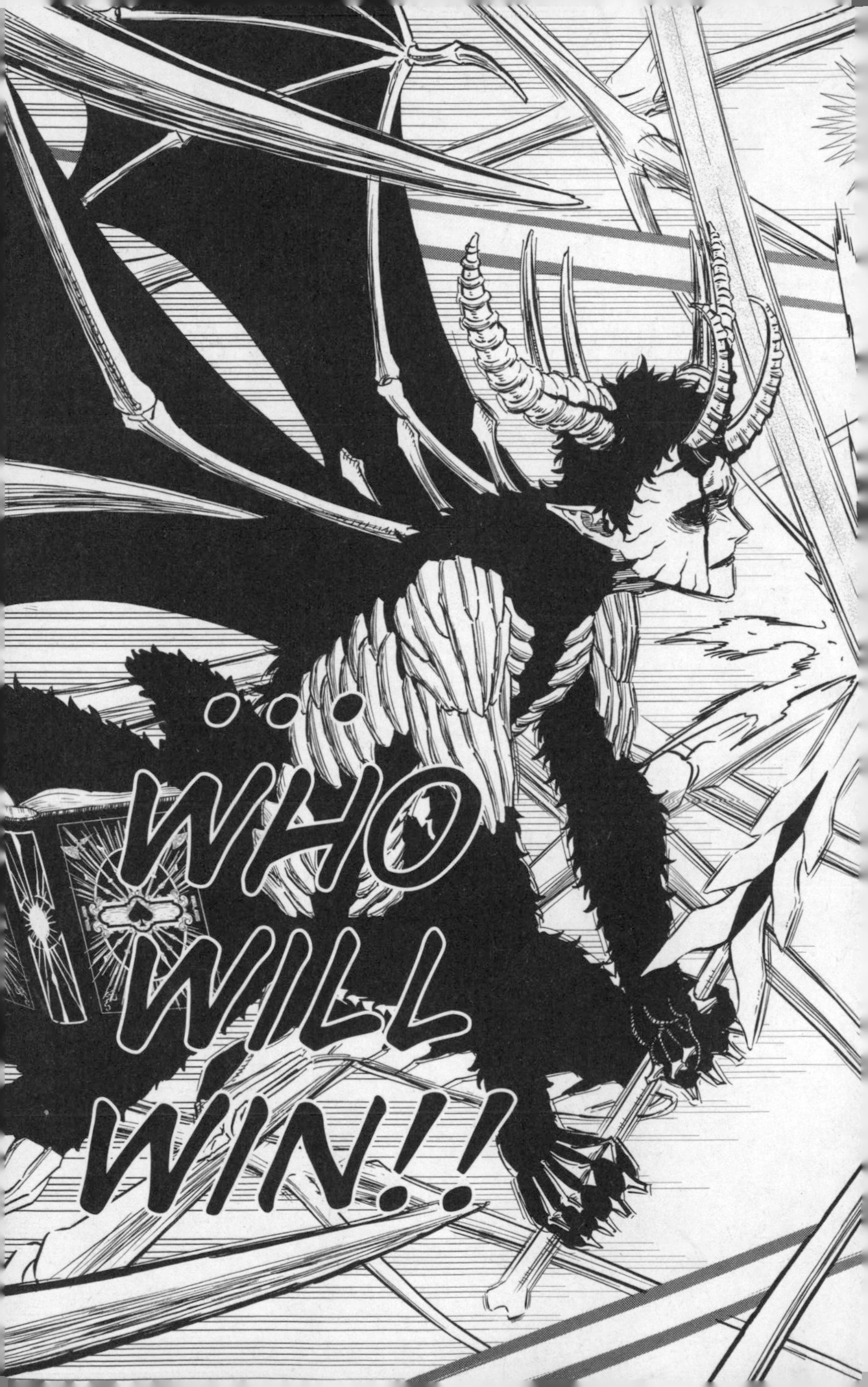
...WHO WILL WIN!!

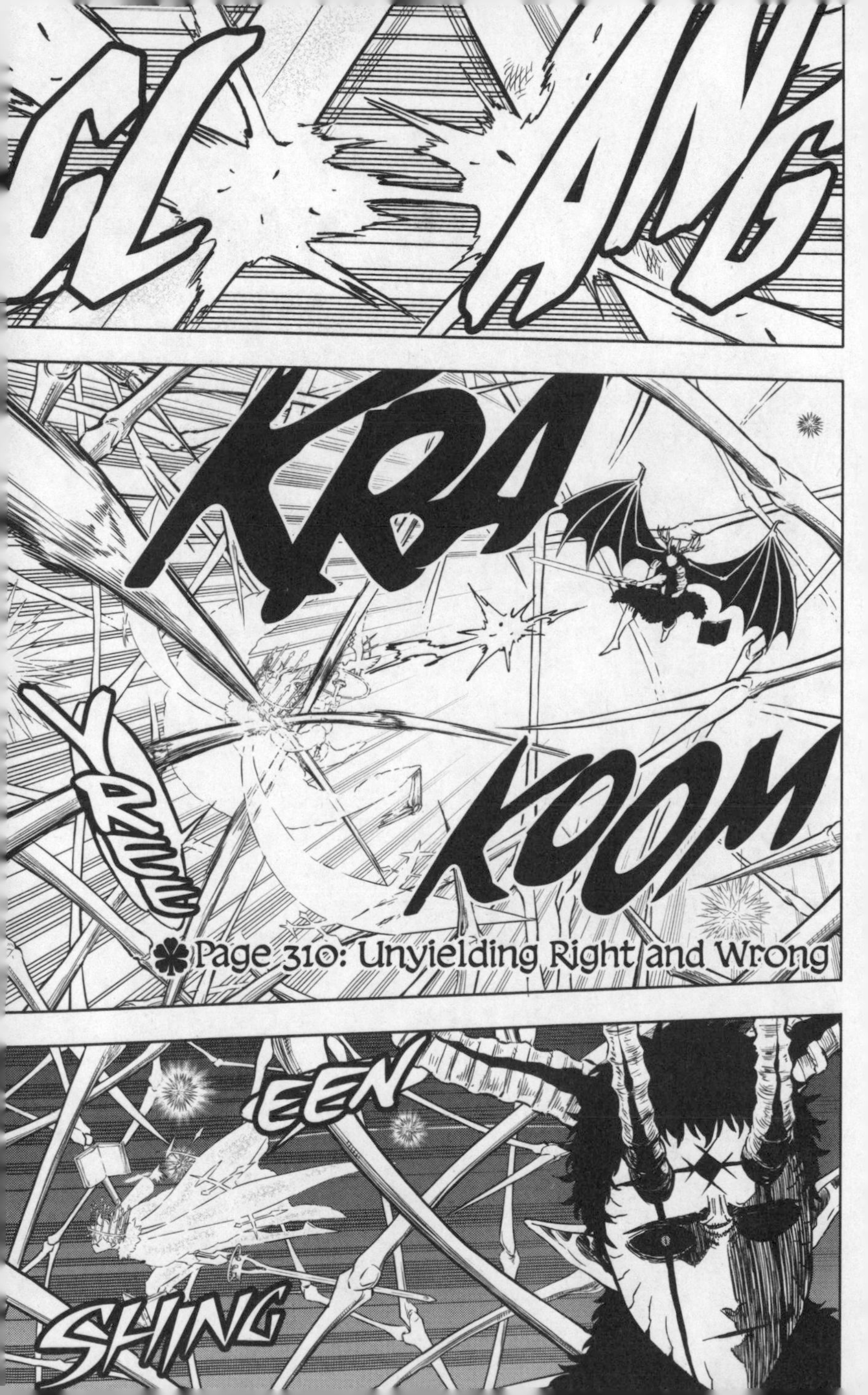
CLANG
KRA
KOOM
Page 310: Unyielding Right and Wrong
EEN
SHING

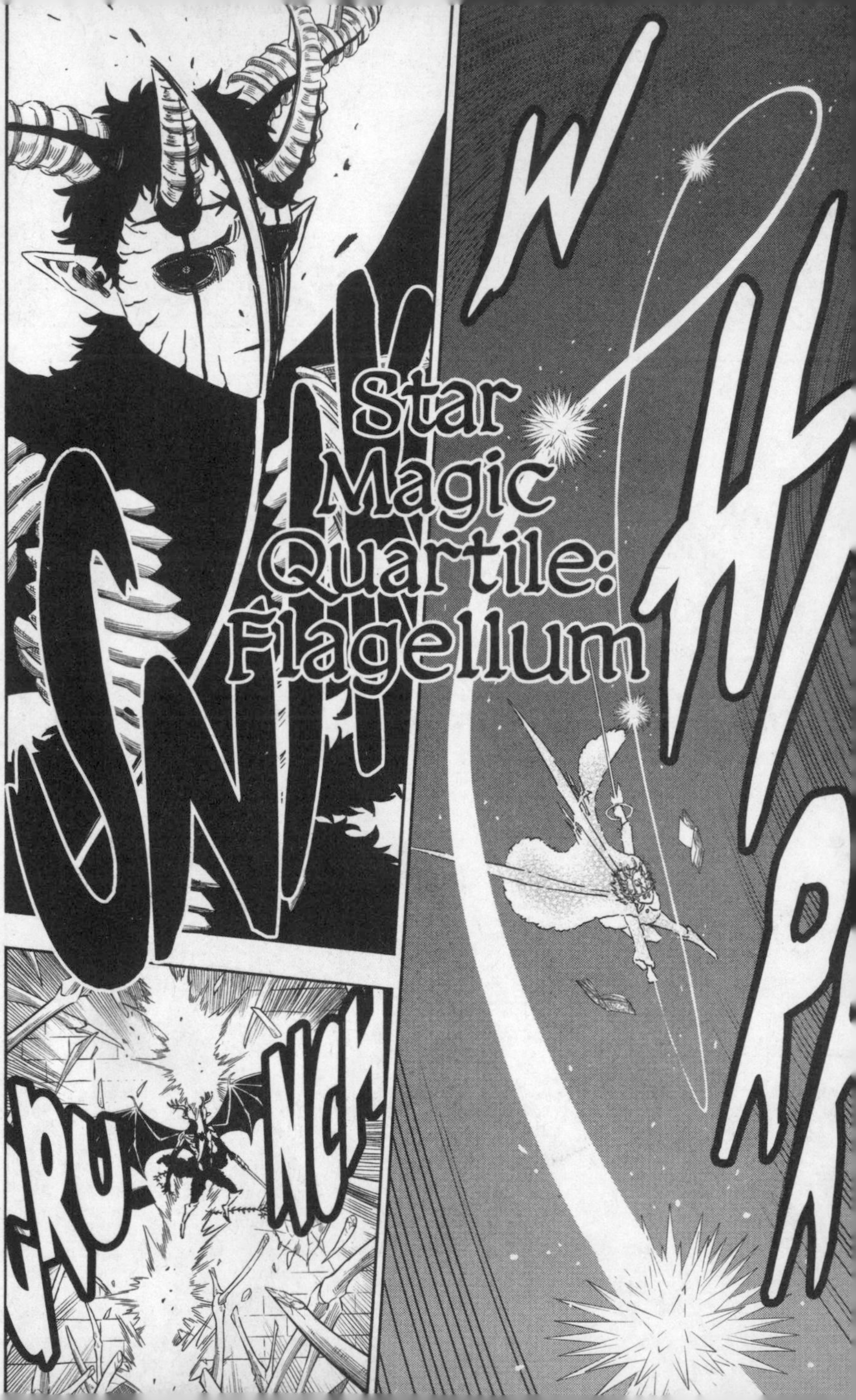
Star Magic Quartile: Flagellum
CRU
NCH

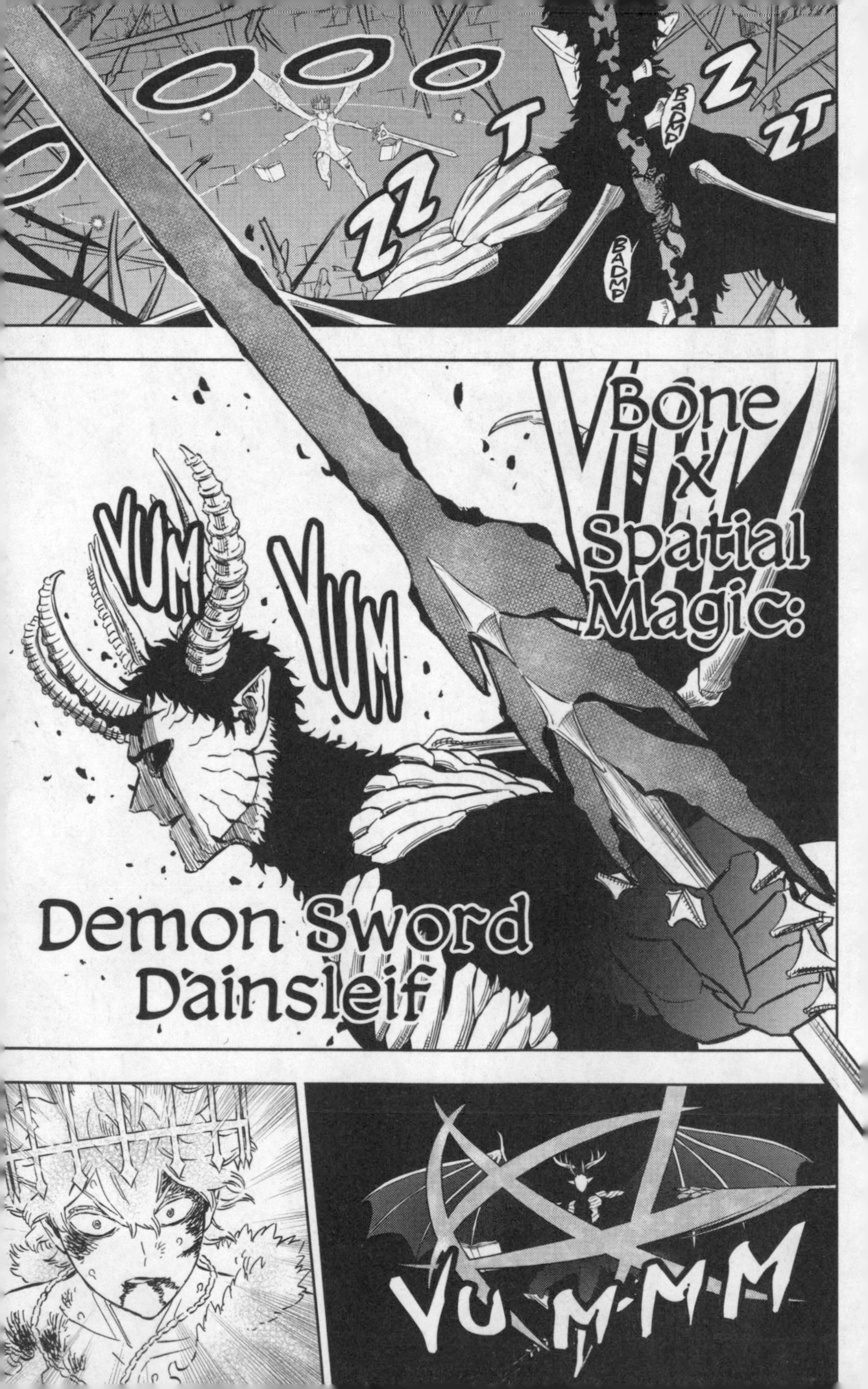

ZZT
BADMP
BADMP
ZZT
OOOO
Bone x Spatial Magic:
VUM VUM
Demon Sword Dainsleif
VUMMMM

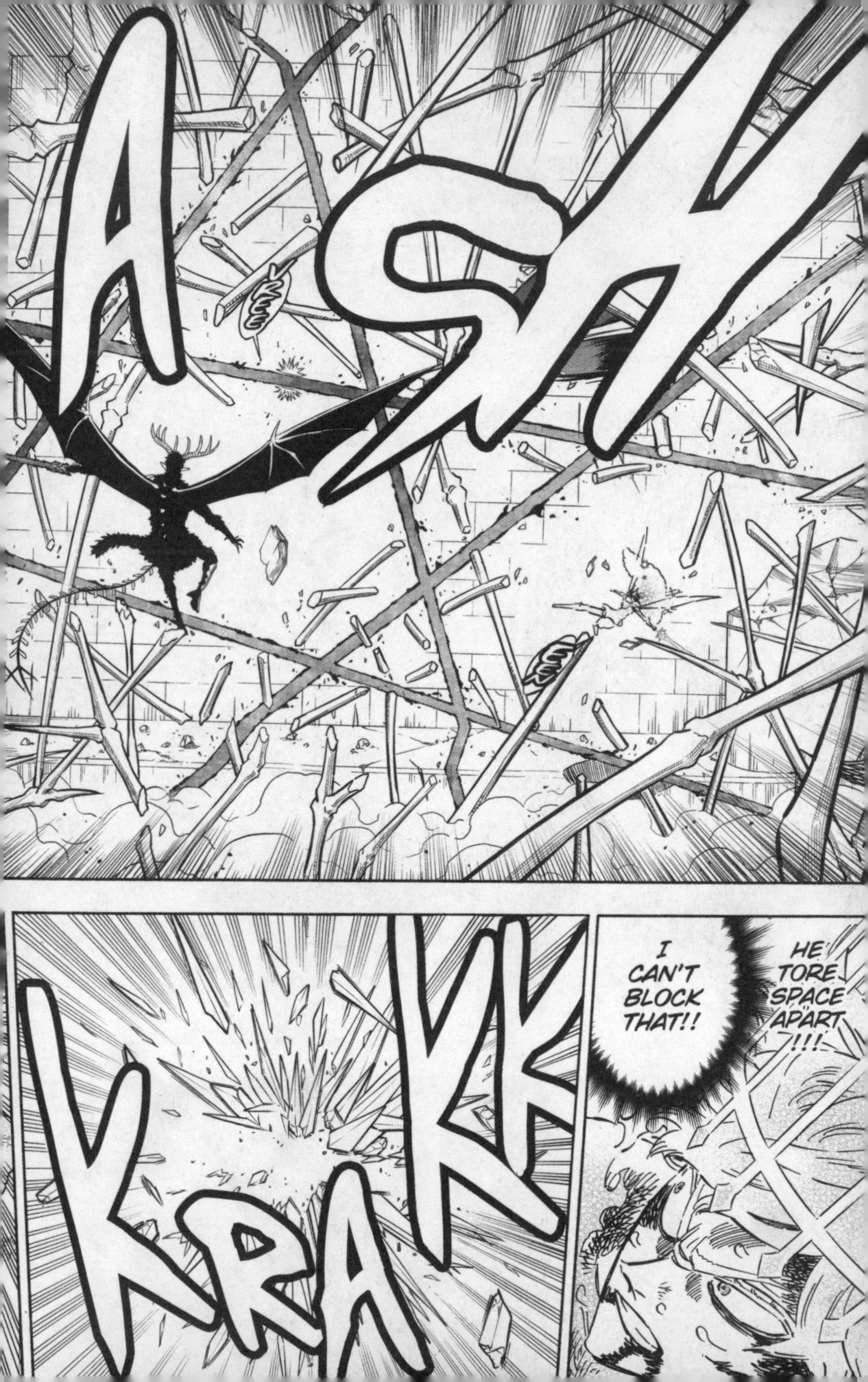
ASH
HE TORE SPACE APART!!!
I CAN'T BLOCK THAT!!
KRAK

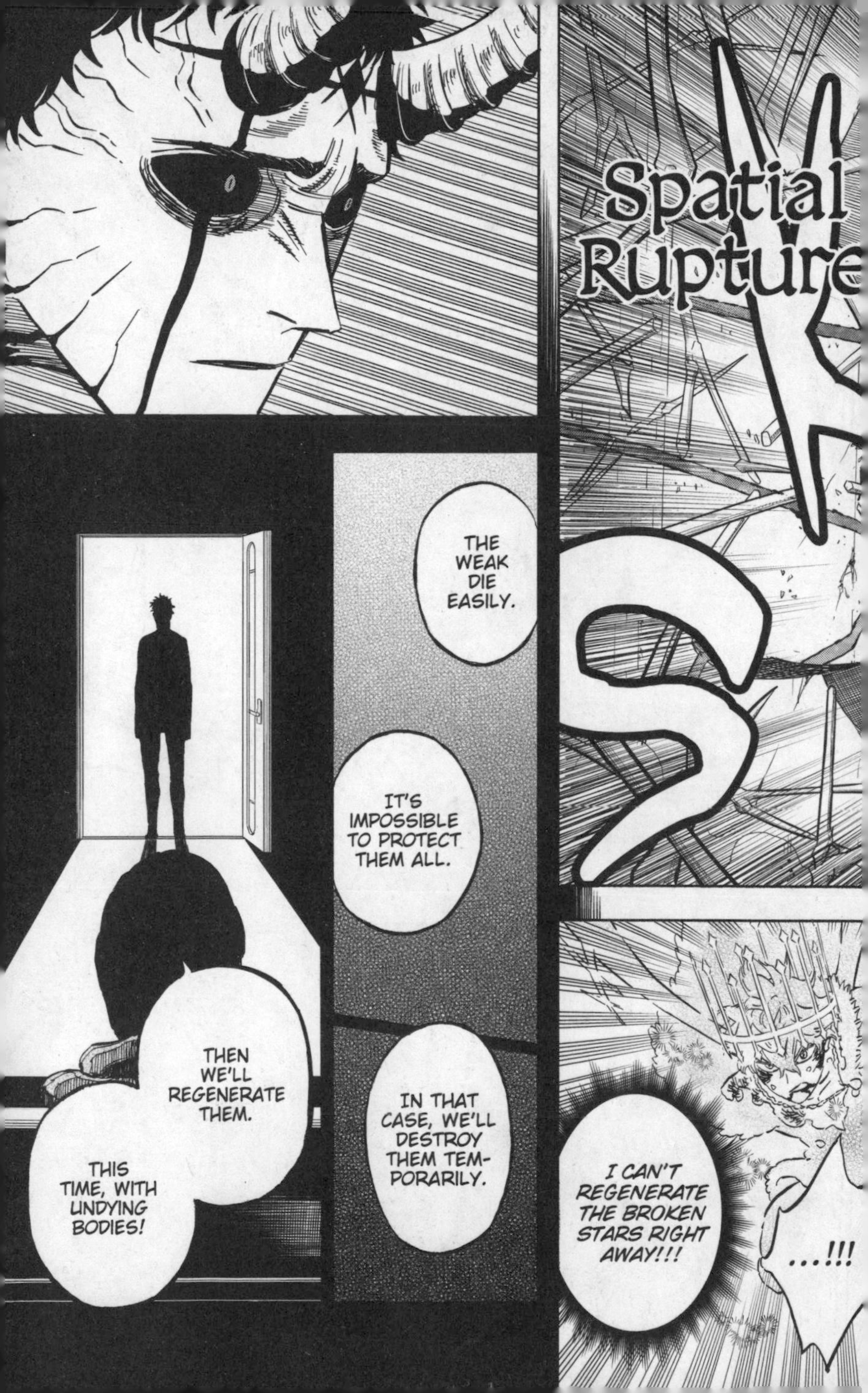
Spatial Rupture
I CAN'T REGENERATE THE BROKEN STARS RIGHT AWAY!!!
...!!!
THE WEAK DIE EASILY.
IT'S IMPOSSIBLE TO PROTECT THEM ALL.
IN THAT CASE, WE'LL DESTROY THEM TEMPORARILY.
THEN WE'LL REGENERATE THEM.
THIS TIME, WITH UNDYING BODIES!

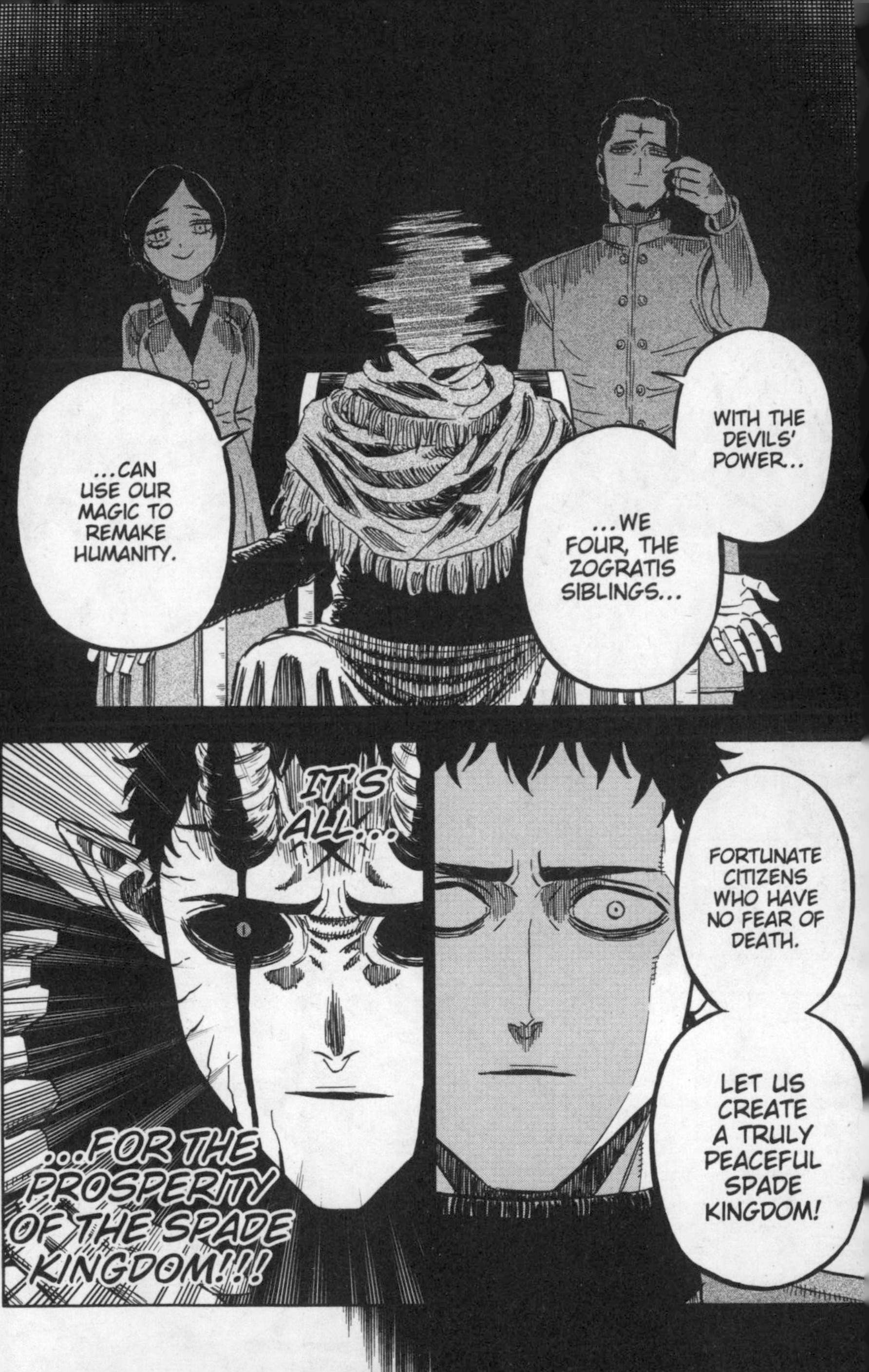
WITH THE DEVILS' POWER..
...WE FOUR, THE ZOGRATIS SIBLINGS...
...CAN USE OUR MAGIC TO REMAKE HUMANITY.
FORTUNATE CITIZENS WHO HAVE NO FEAR OF DEATH.
LET US CREATE A TRULY PEACEFUL SPADE KINGDOM!
IT'S ALL...
...FOR THE PROSPERITY OF THE SPADE KINGDOM!!!

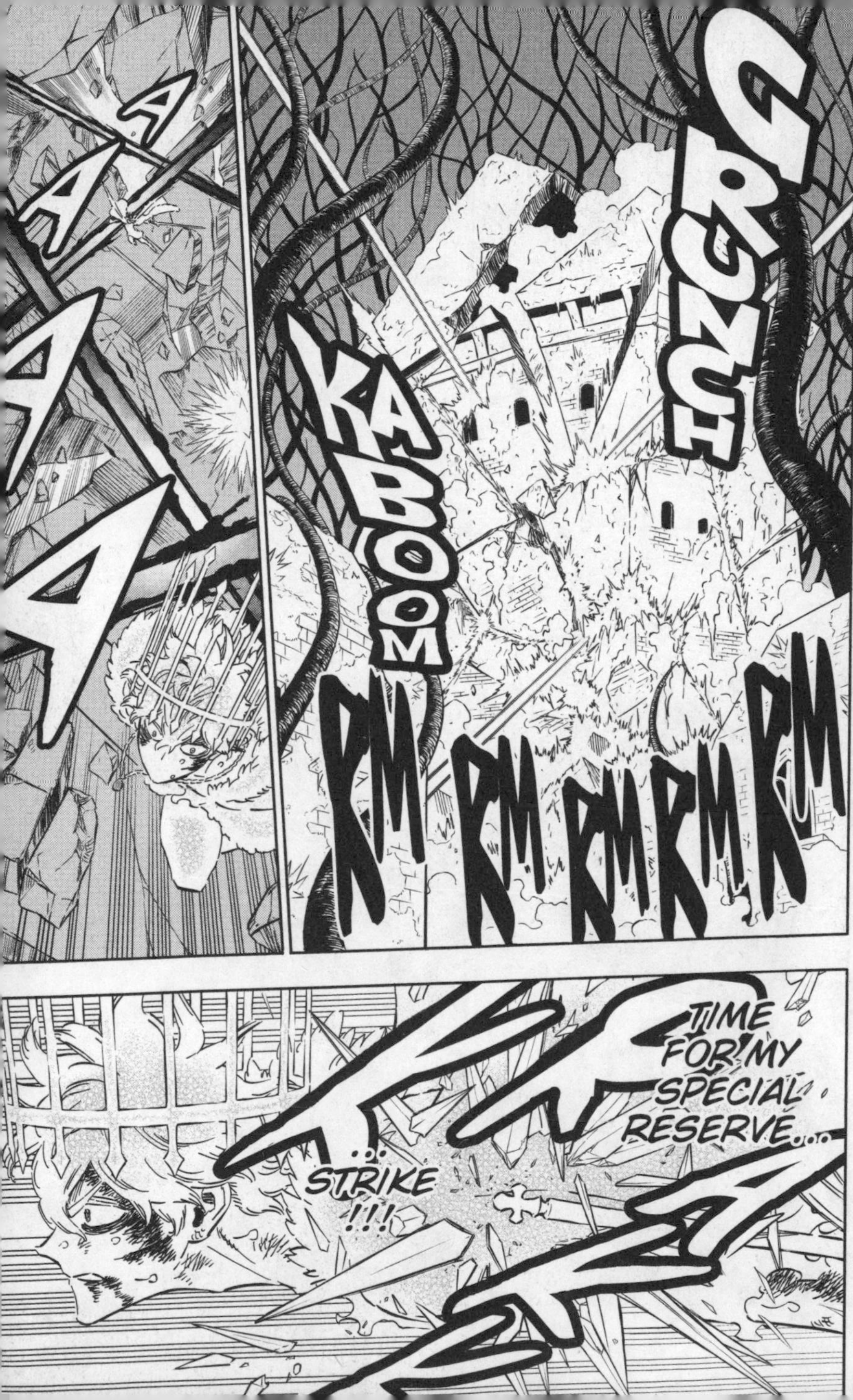
CRUNCH
KABOOM
RM RM RM RM RM RM
AAAAA
TIME FOR MY SPECIAL RESERVE...
...STRIKE!!!

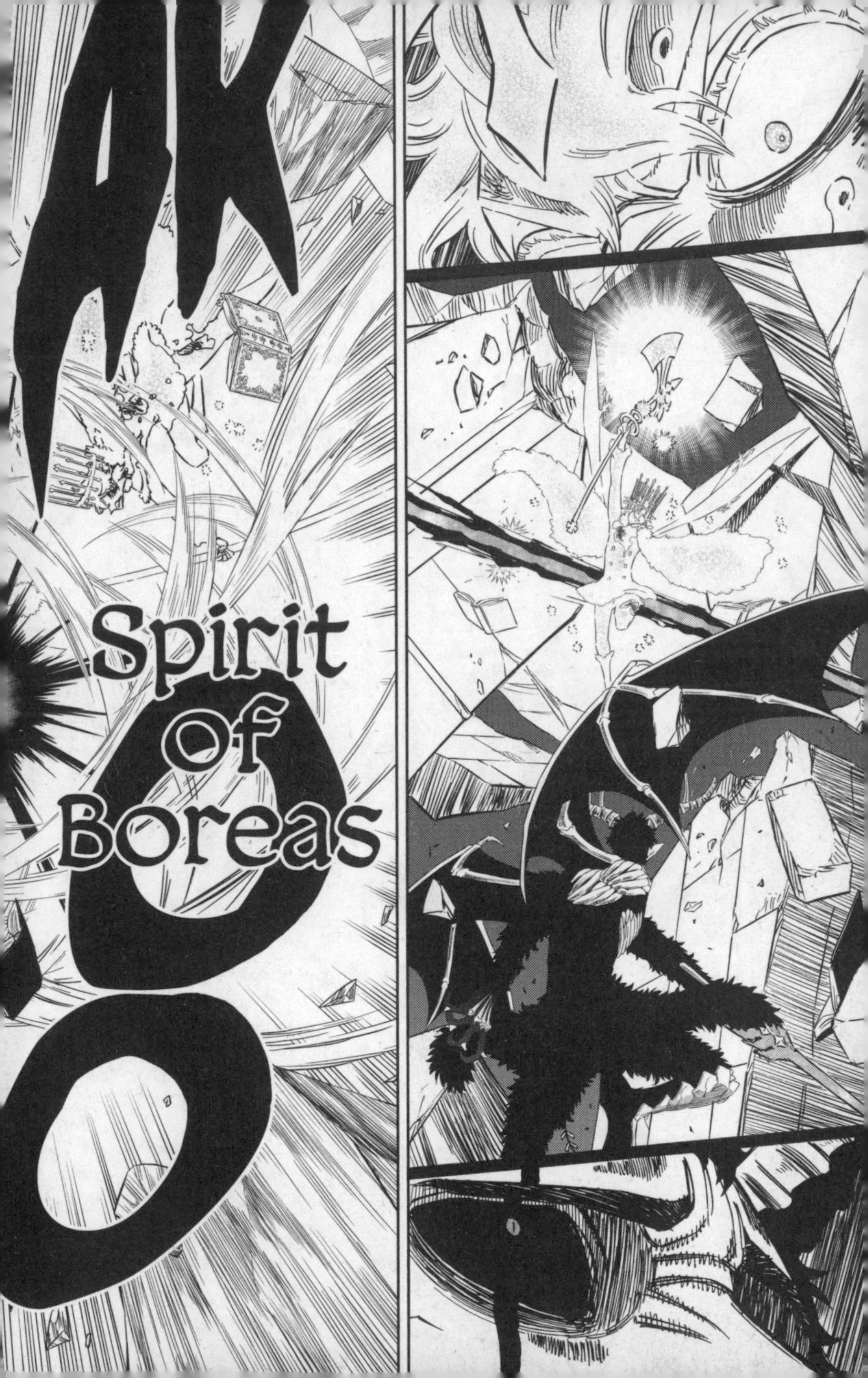
Spirit Of Boreas

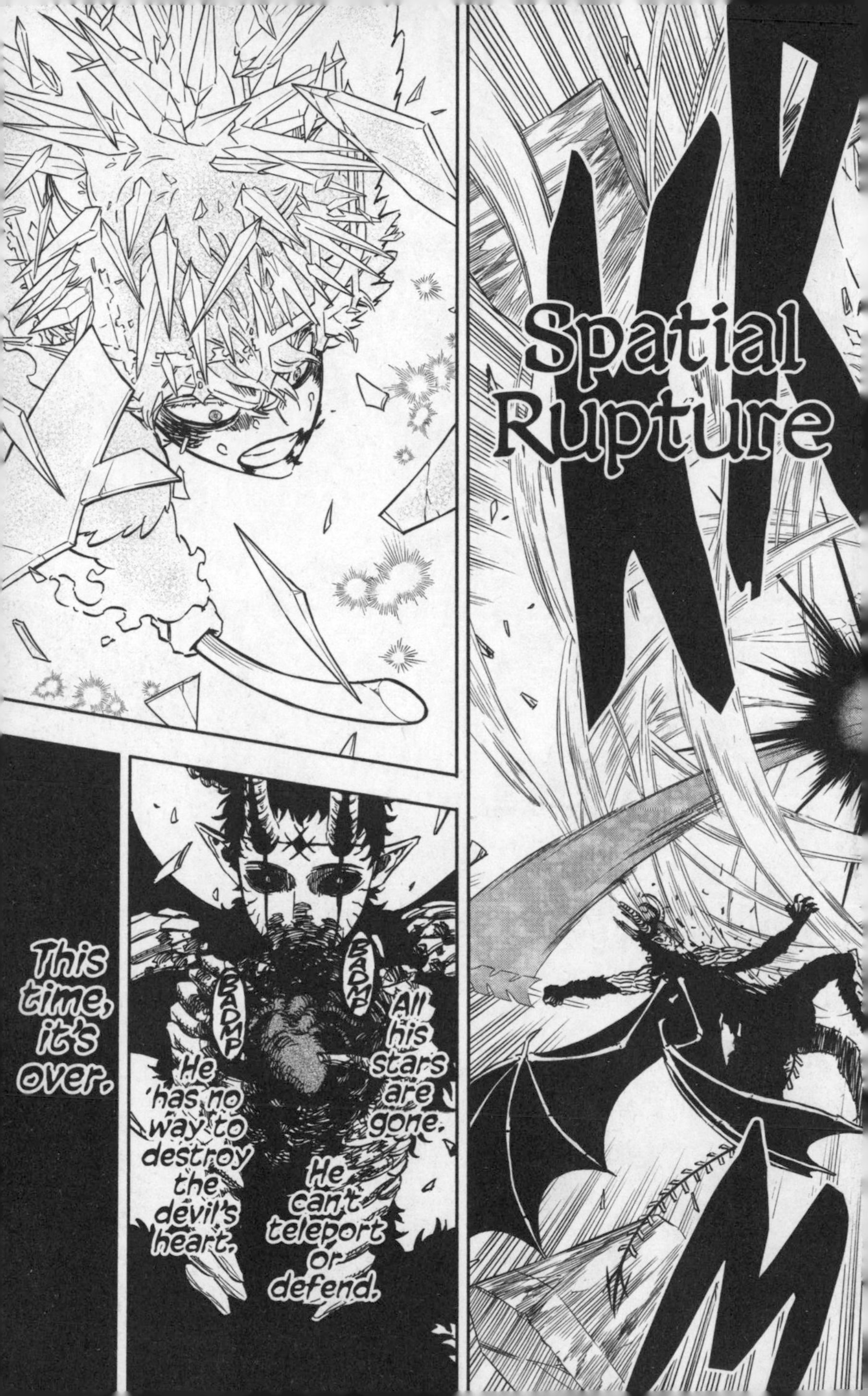
Spatial Rupture
BADMP
BADMP
All his stars are gone.
He can't teleport or defend.
He has no way to destroy the devil's heart.
This time, it's over.

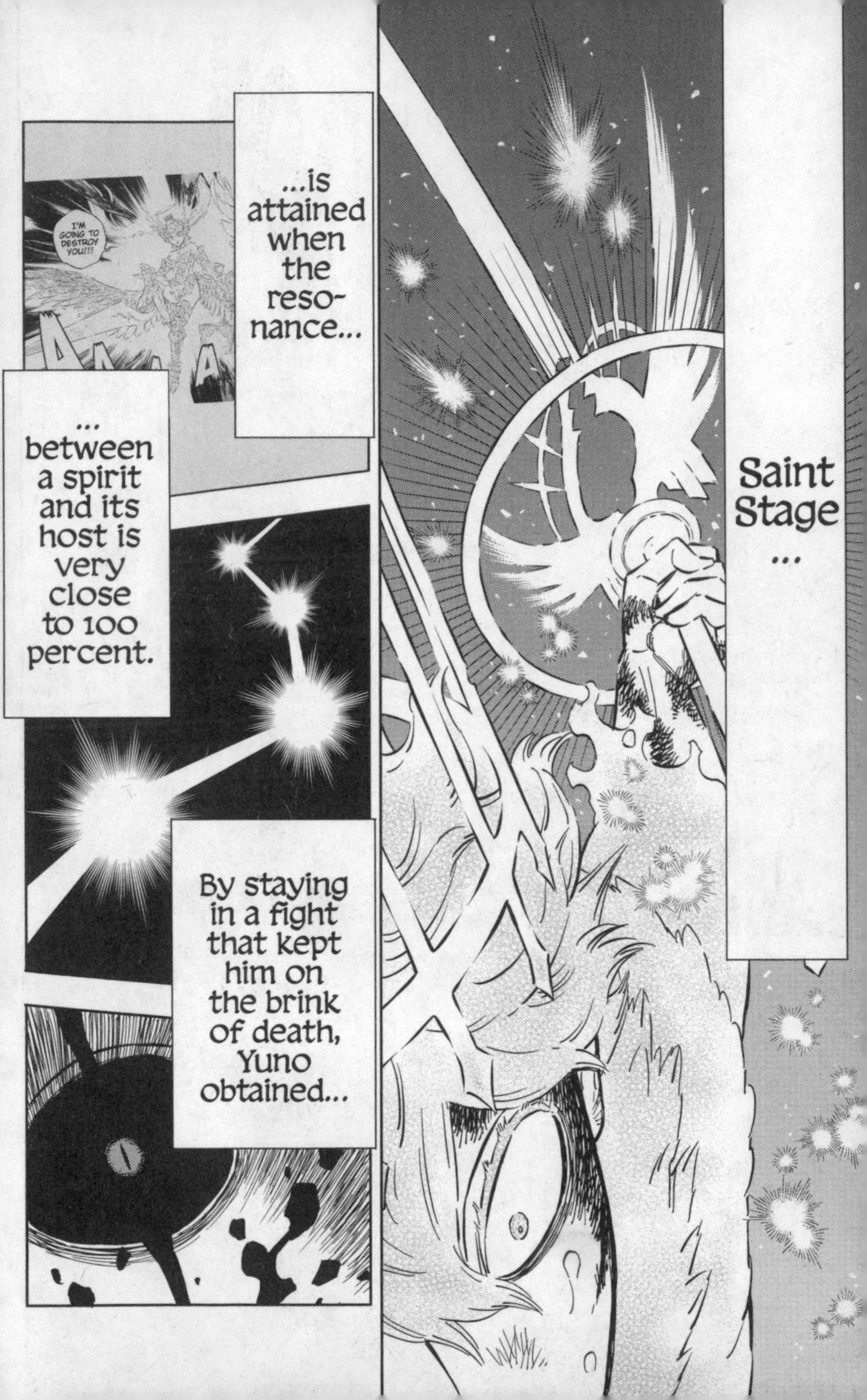
Saint Stage...
...is attained when the resonance...
I'M GOING TO DESTROY YOU!!!
...between a spirit and its host is very close to 100 percent.
By staying in a fight that kept him on the brink of death, Yuno obtained...

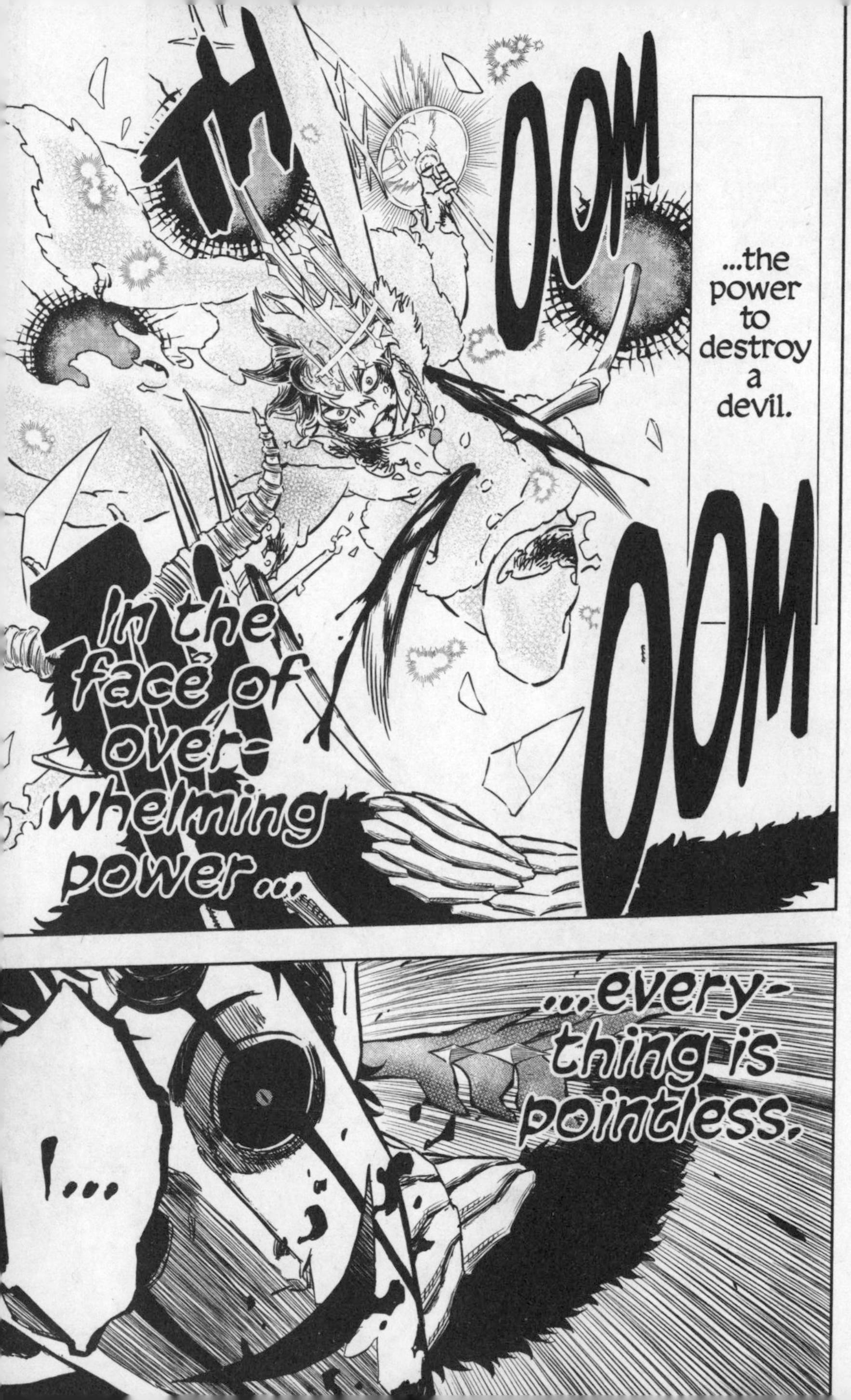
...the power to destroy a devil.
THOOM
OOM
In the face of over-whelming power...
...every-thing is pointless.
I...

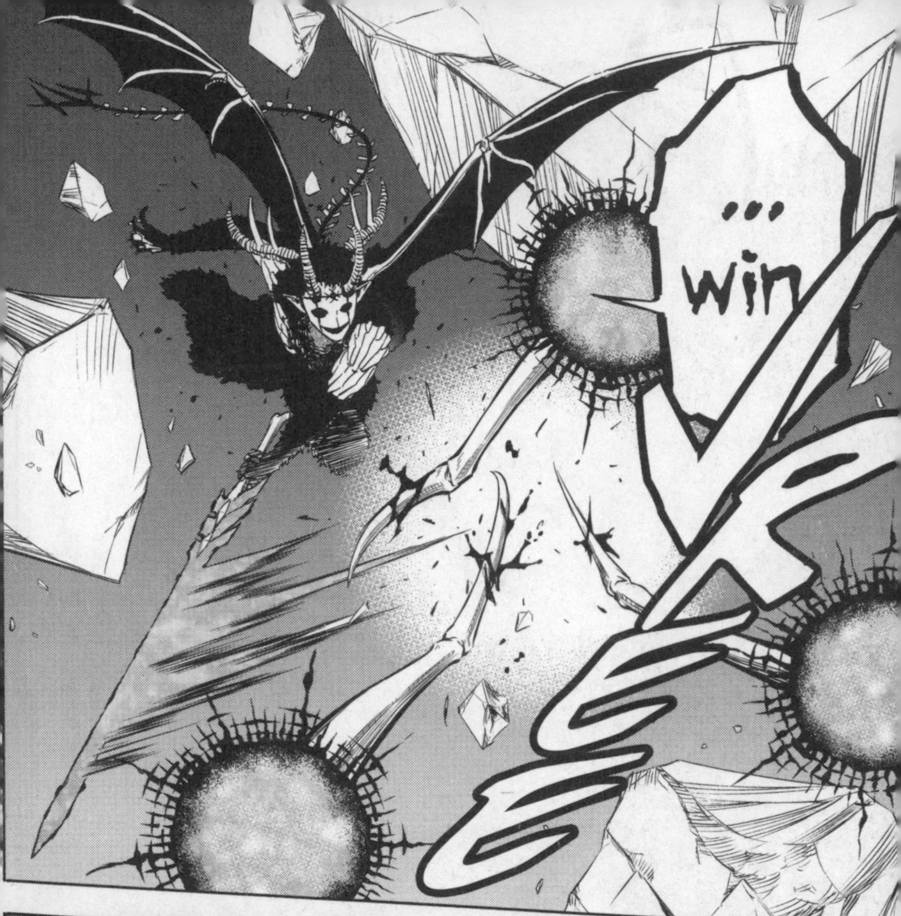
...win
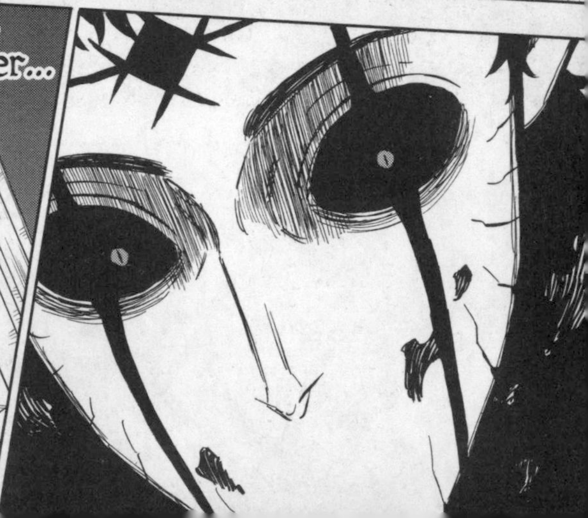
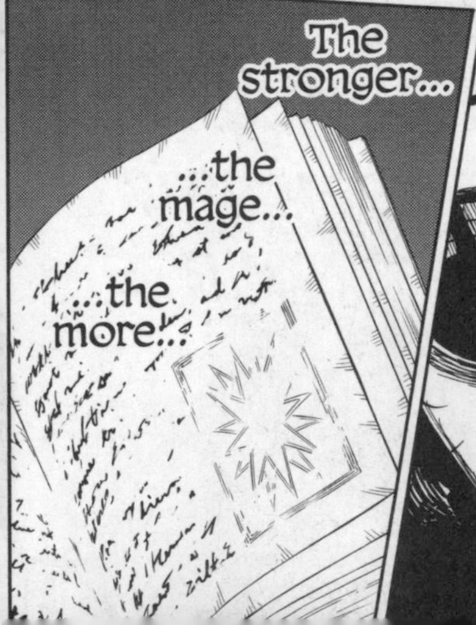
The stronger...
...the mage...
...the more...

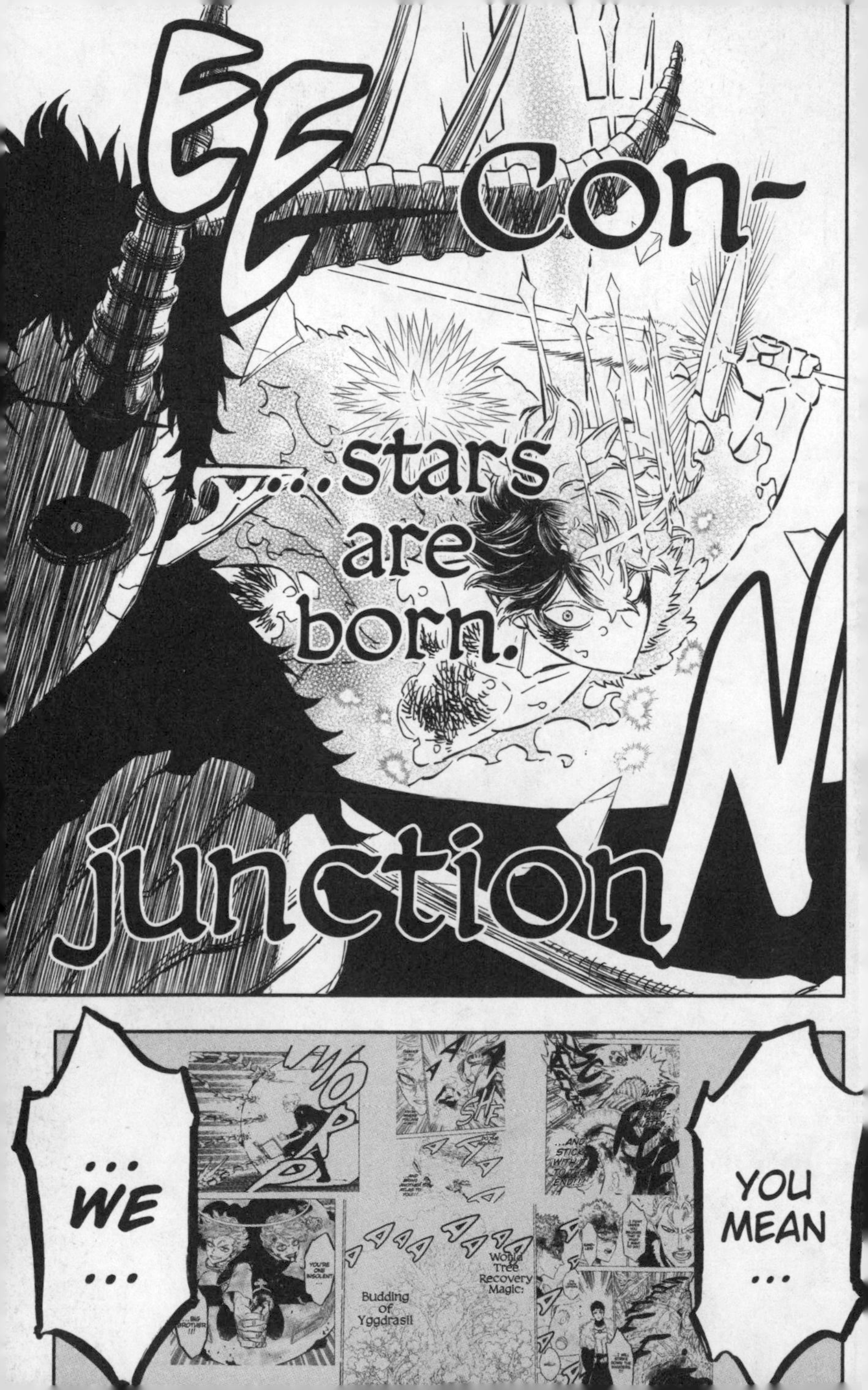
C-Con-
junction
...stars are born.
YOU MEAN ...
... WE ...
World Tree Recovery Magic:
Budding of Yggdrasil
YOU'RE ONE INSOLENT ...
BIG BROTHER!!

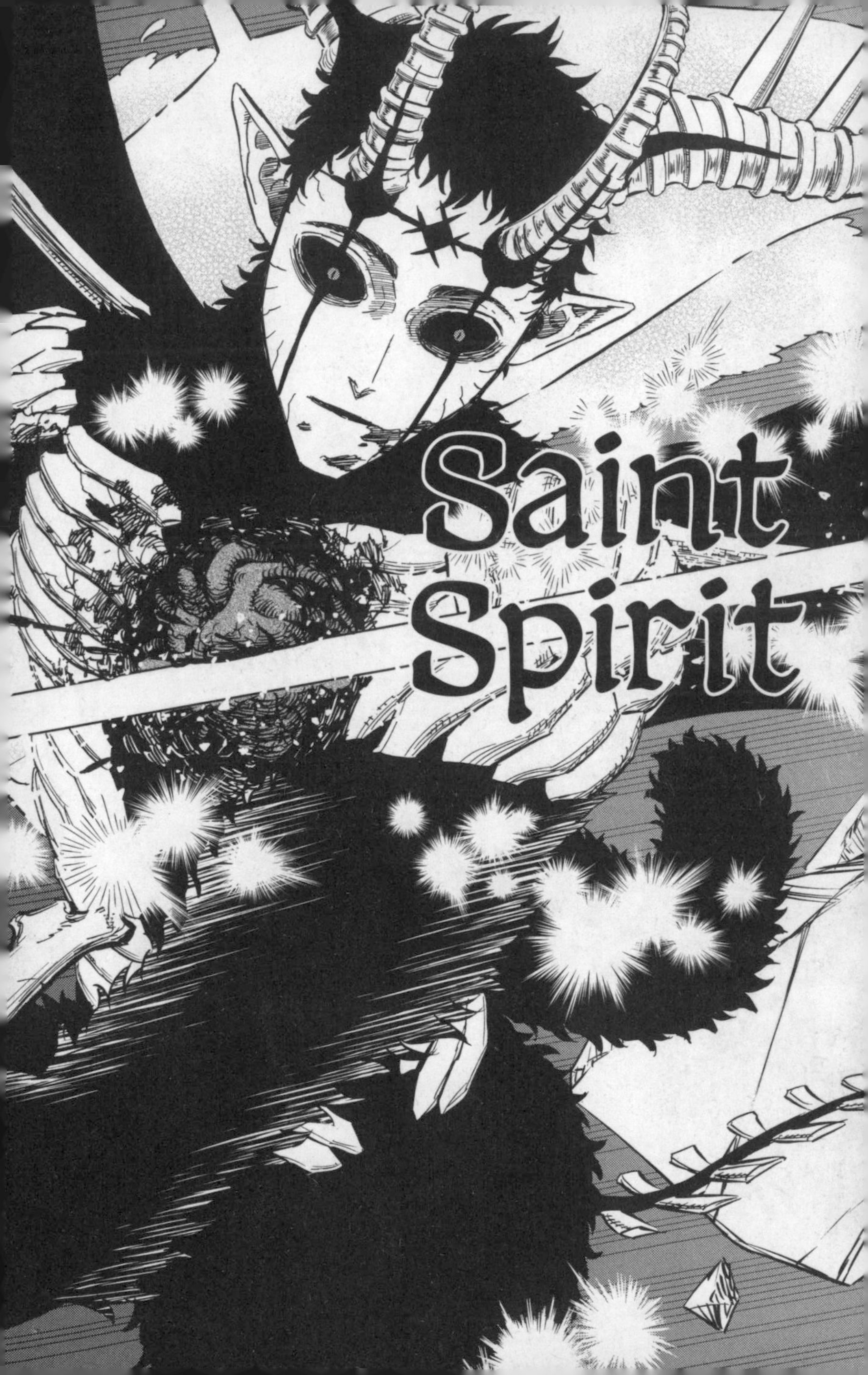
Saint Spirit

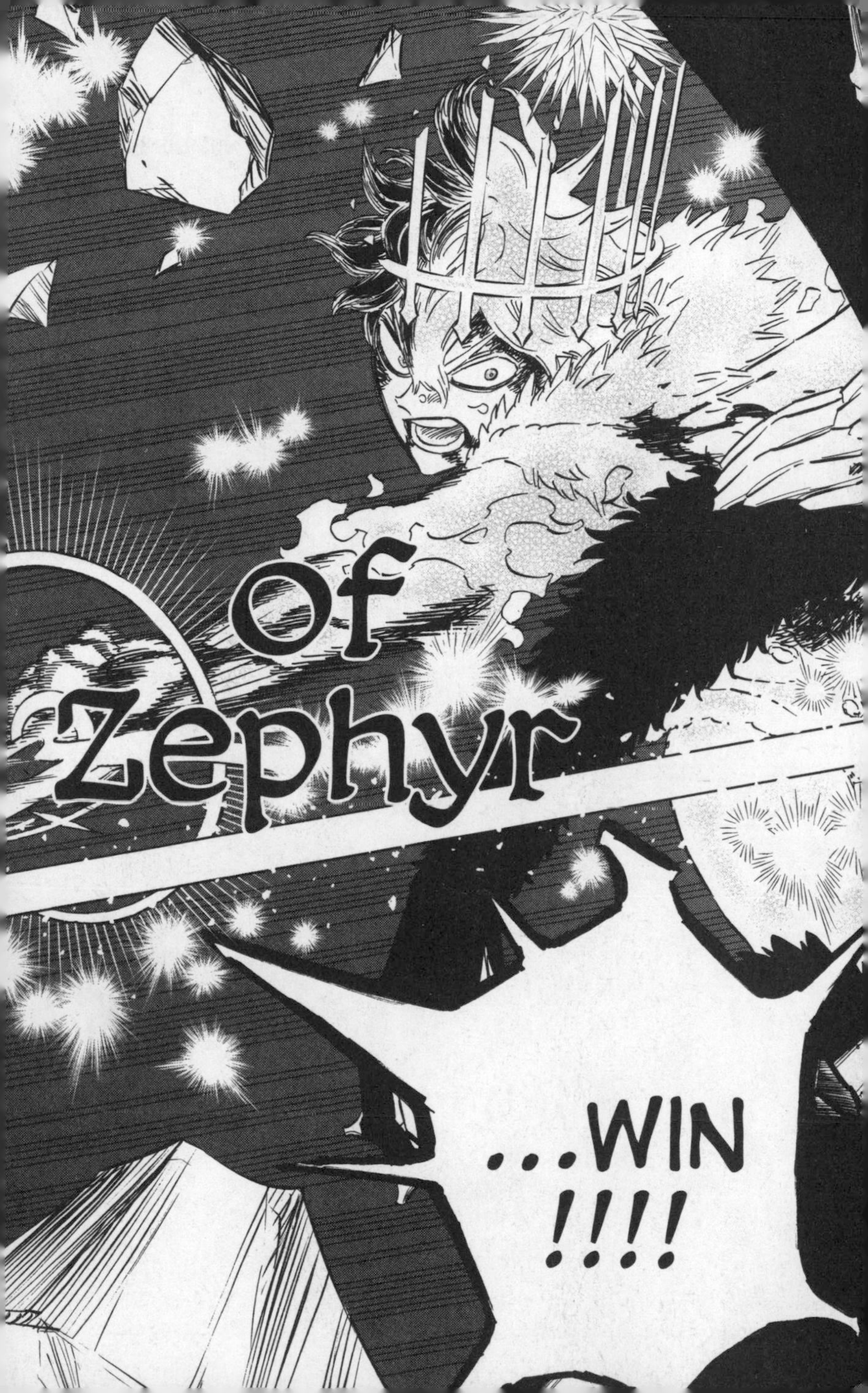
of
Zephyr
...WIN
!!!!

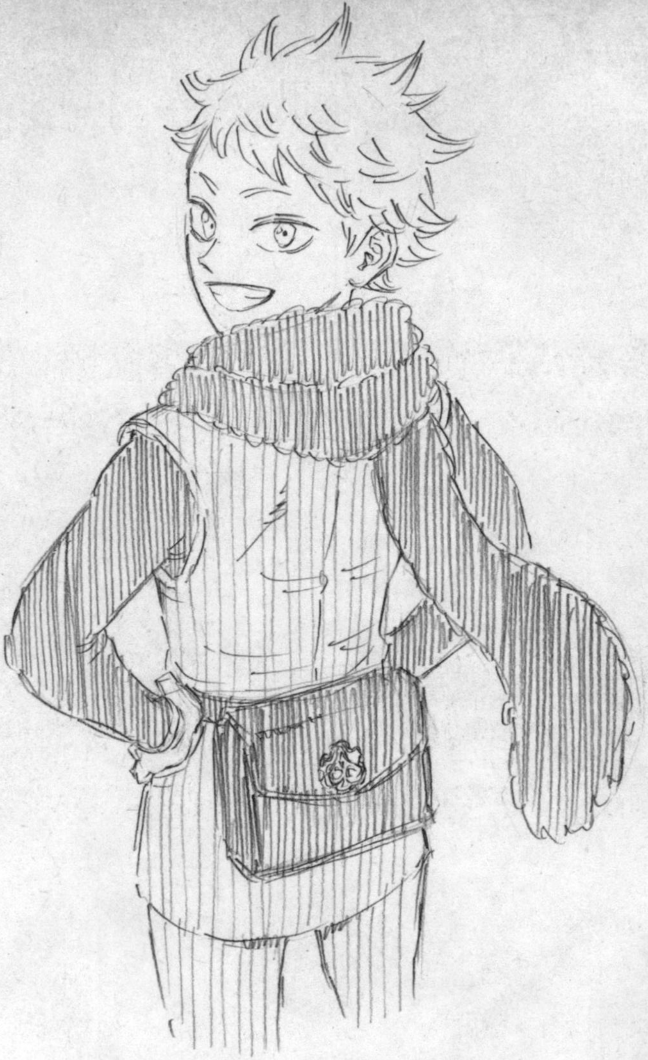

Allen Fiarain

Age at death: 17 Height: 168 cm
Birthday: April 10
Sign: Aries Blood Type: O
Likes: Hot daztato soup and bread

Character Profile

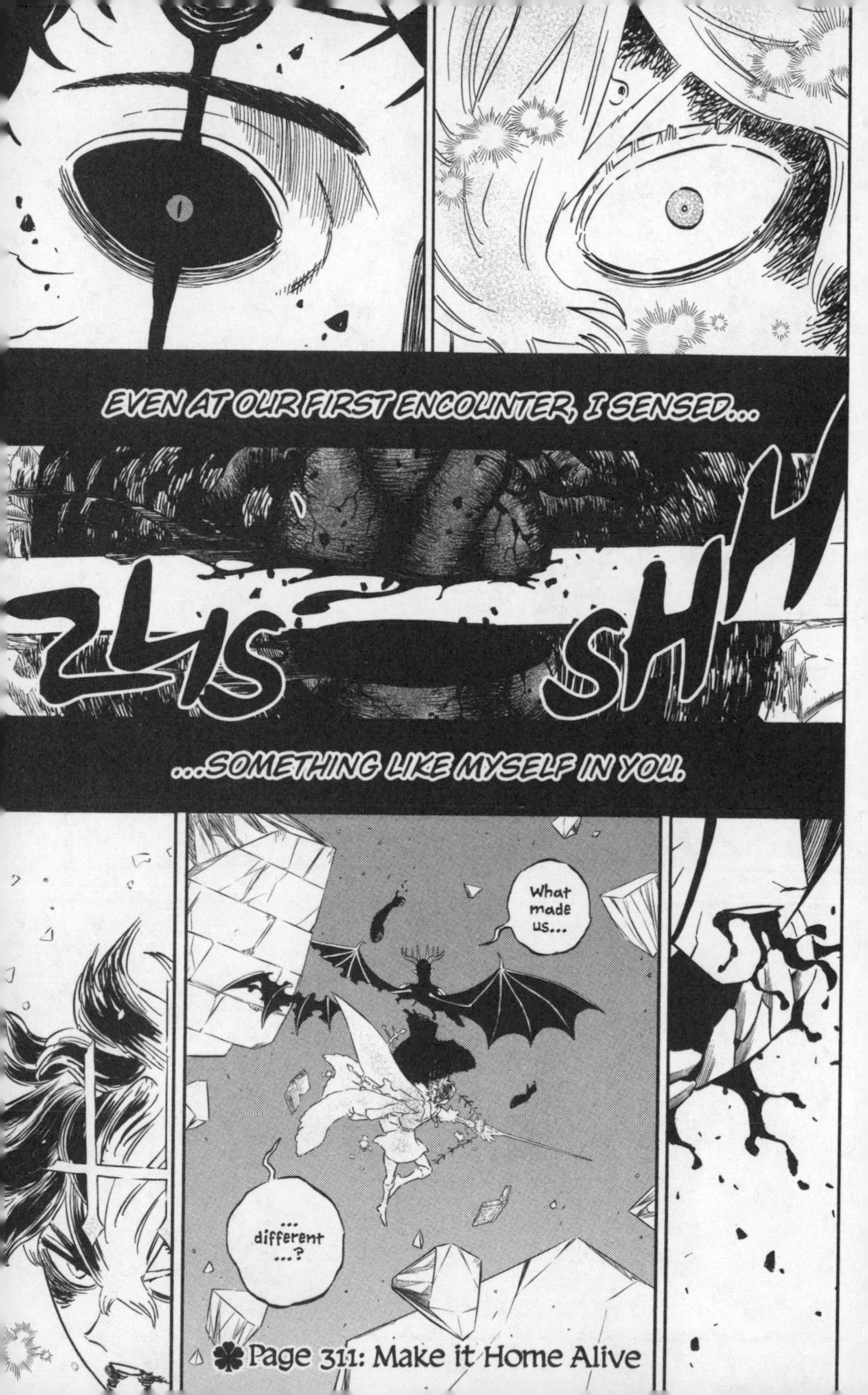
EVEN AT OUR FIRST ENCOUNTER, I SENSED...
...SOMETHING LIKE MYSELF IN YOU.
What made us...
...different...?

Page 311: Make it Home Alive

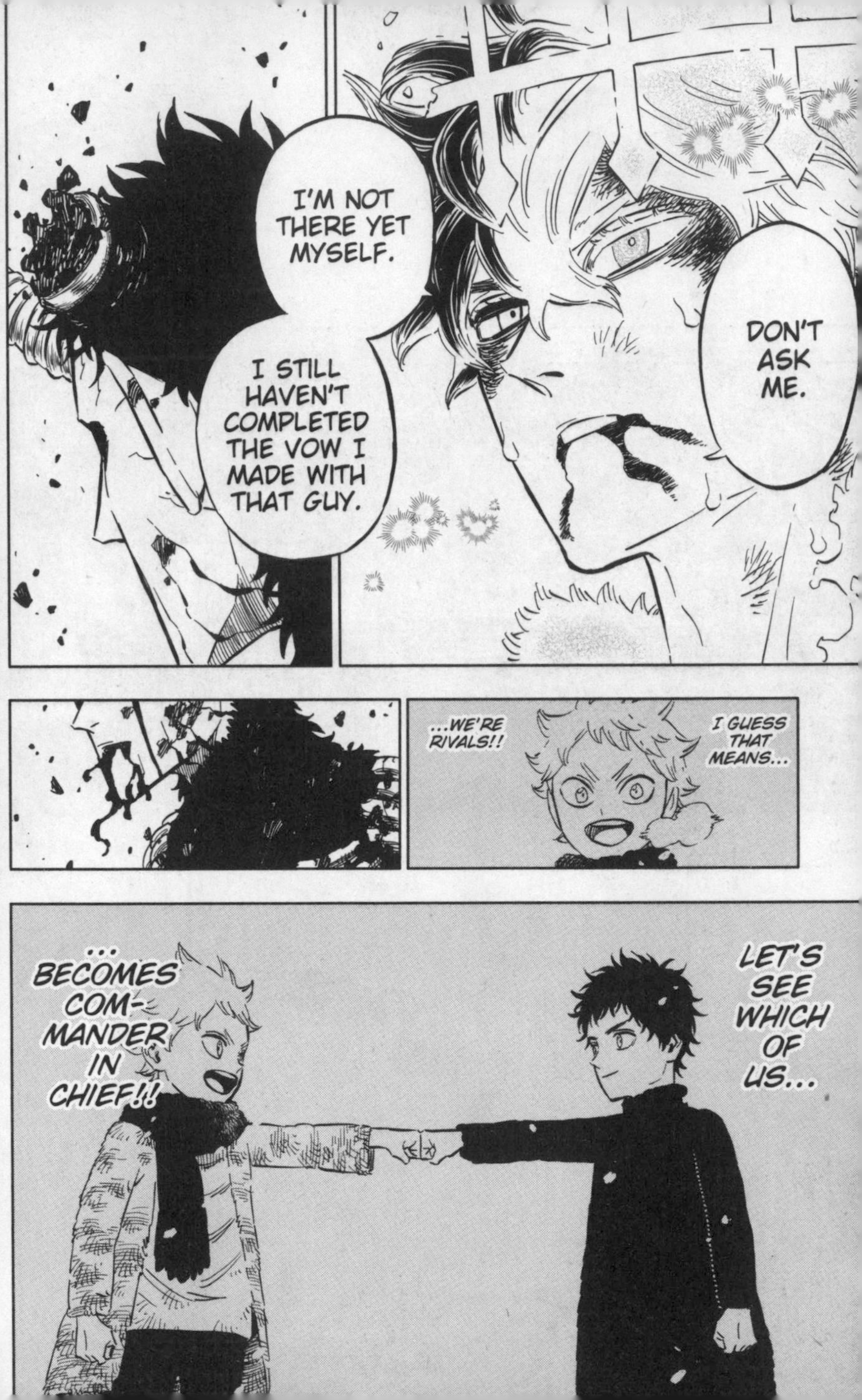
DON'T ASK ME.
I'M NOT THERE YET MYSELF.
I STILL HAVEN'T COMPLETED THE VOW I MADE WITH THAT GUY.
I GUESS THAT MEANS...
...WE'RE RIVALS!!
LET'S SEE WHICH OF US...
...BECOMES COMMANDER IN CHIEF!!

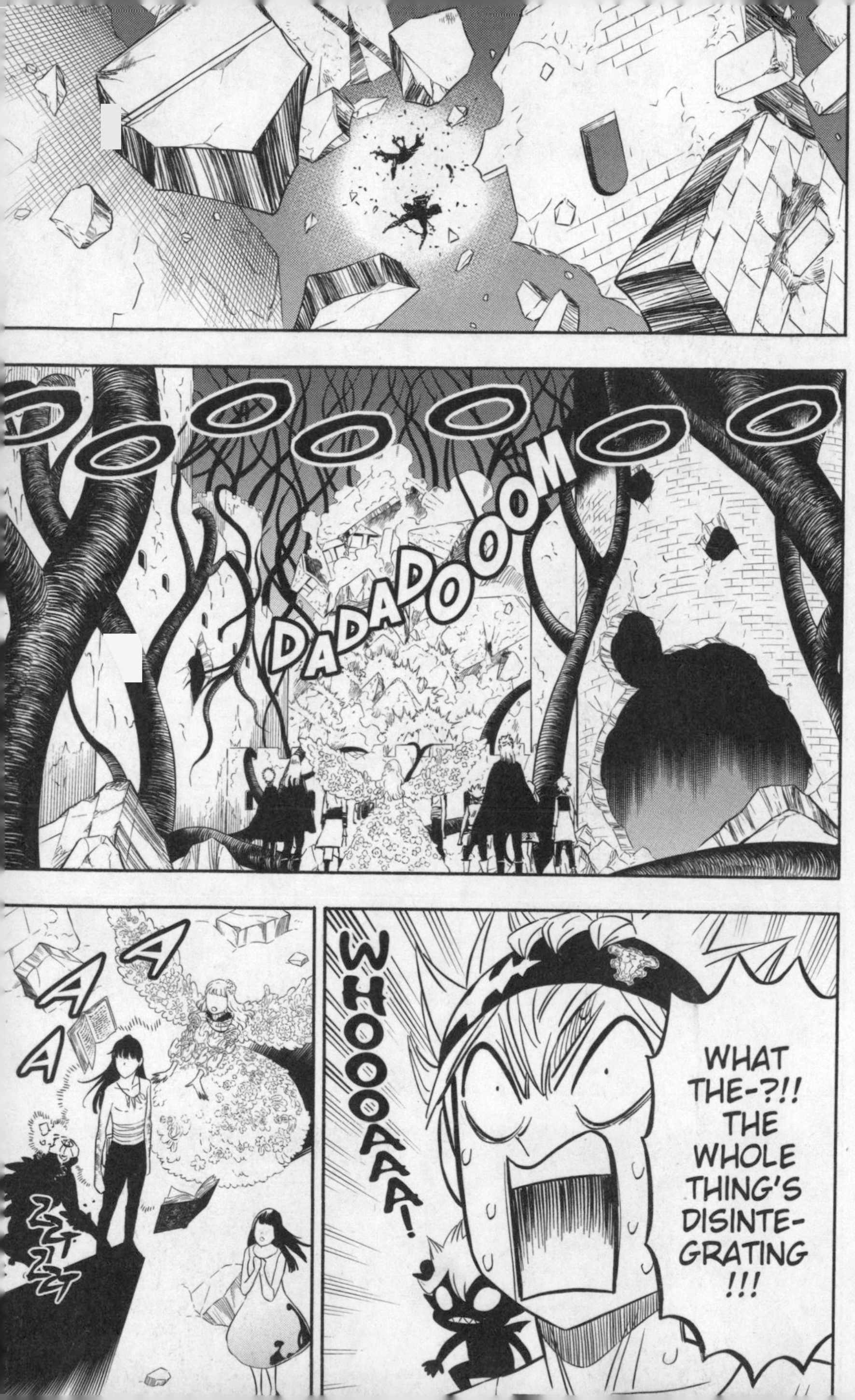
DOOOOOOOO
DADADOOOOM
WHOOOAAA!
WHAT THE-?!! THE WHOLE THING'S DISINTE-GRATING!!!
AAAA
ZZZ ZZZ

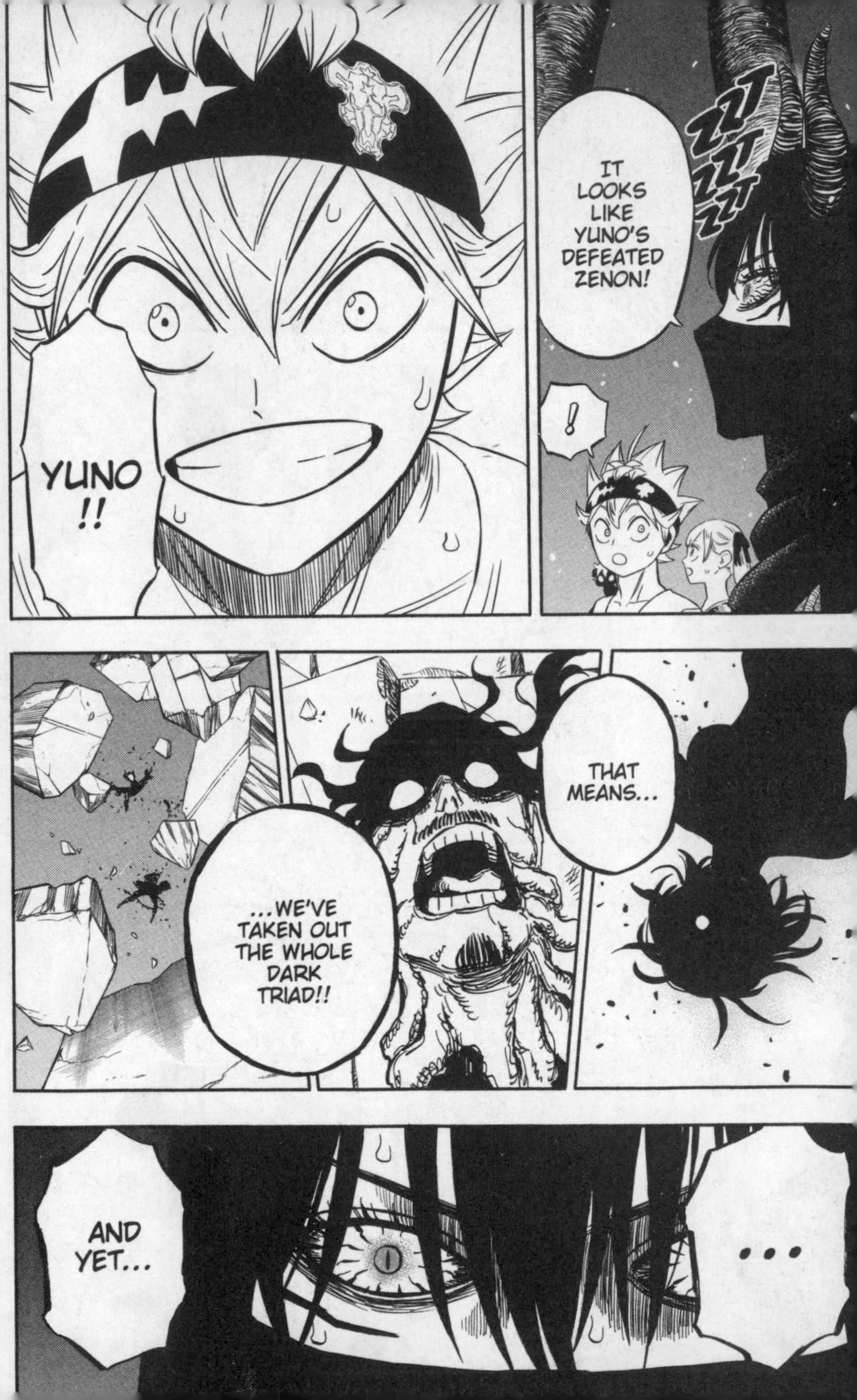
ZZT ZZT ZZT
IT LOOKS LIKE YUNO'S DEFEATED ZENON!
!
YUNO!!
THAT MEANS...
...WE'VE TAKEN OUT THE WHOLE DARK TRIAD!!
...
AND YET...

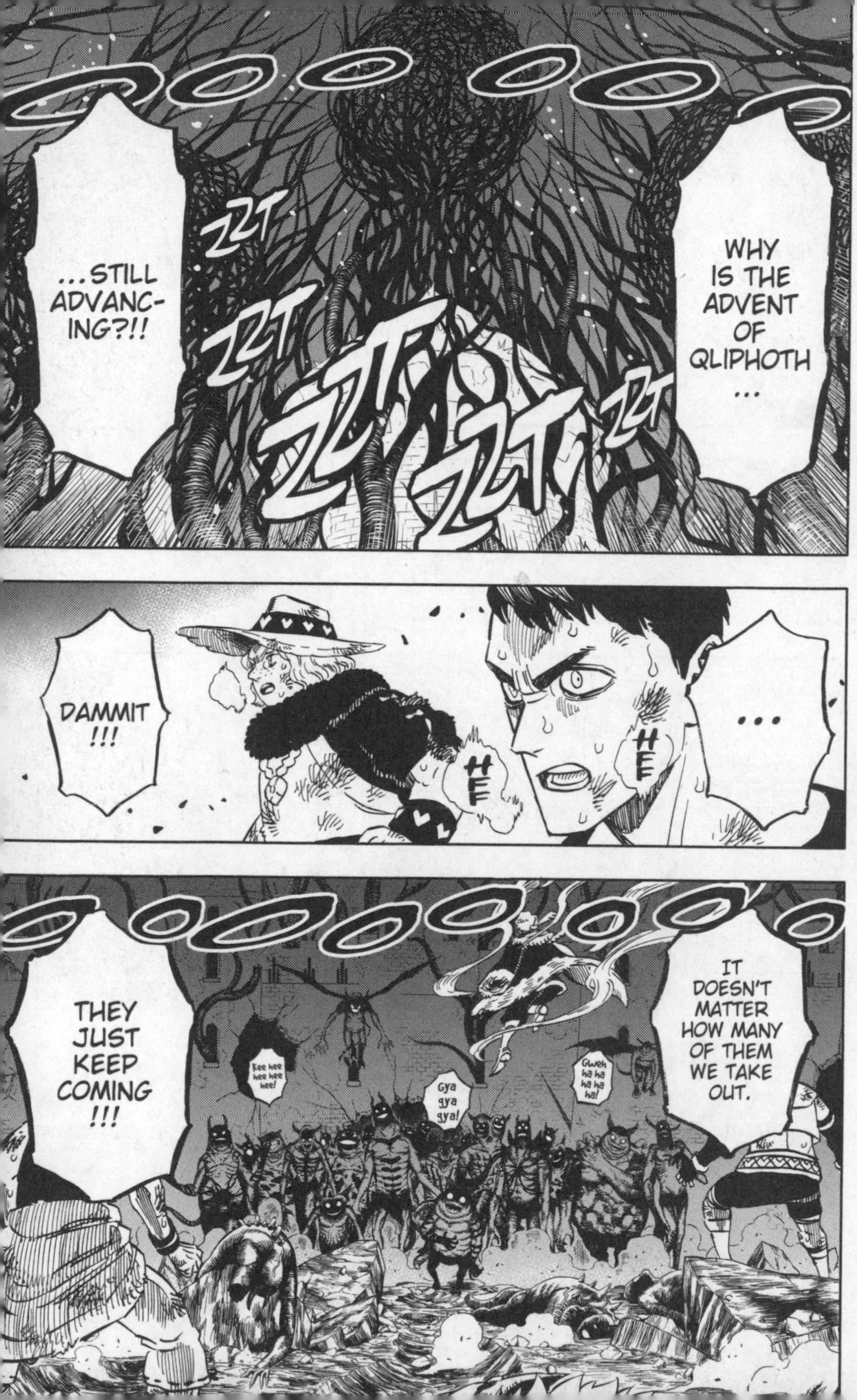
WHY IS THE ADVENT OF QLIPHOTH...
...STILL ADVANCING?!!
ZZT
ZZT
ZZT
ZZT
ZZT
ZZT
...
HEF
HEF
DAMMIT!!!
IT DOESN'T MATTER HOW MANY OF THEM WE TAKE OUT.
Gweh ha ha ha ha ha!
Gya gya gya!
Kee hee hee hee hee!
THEY JUST KEEP COMING!!!

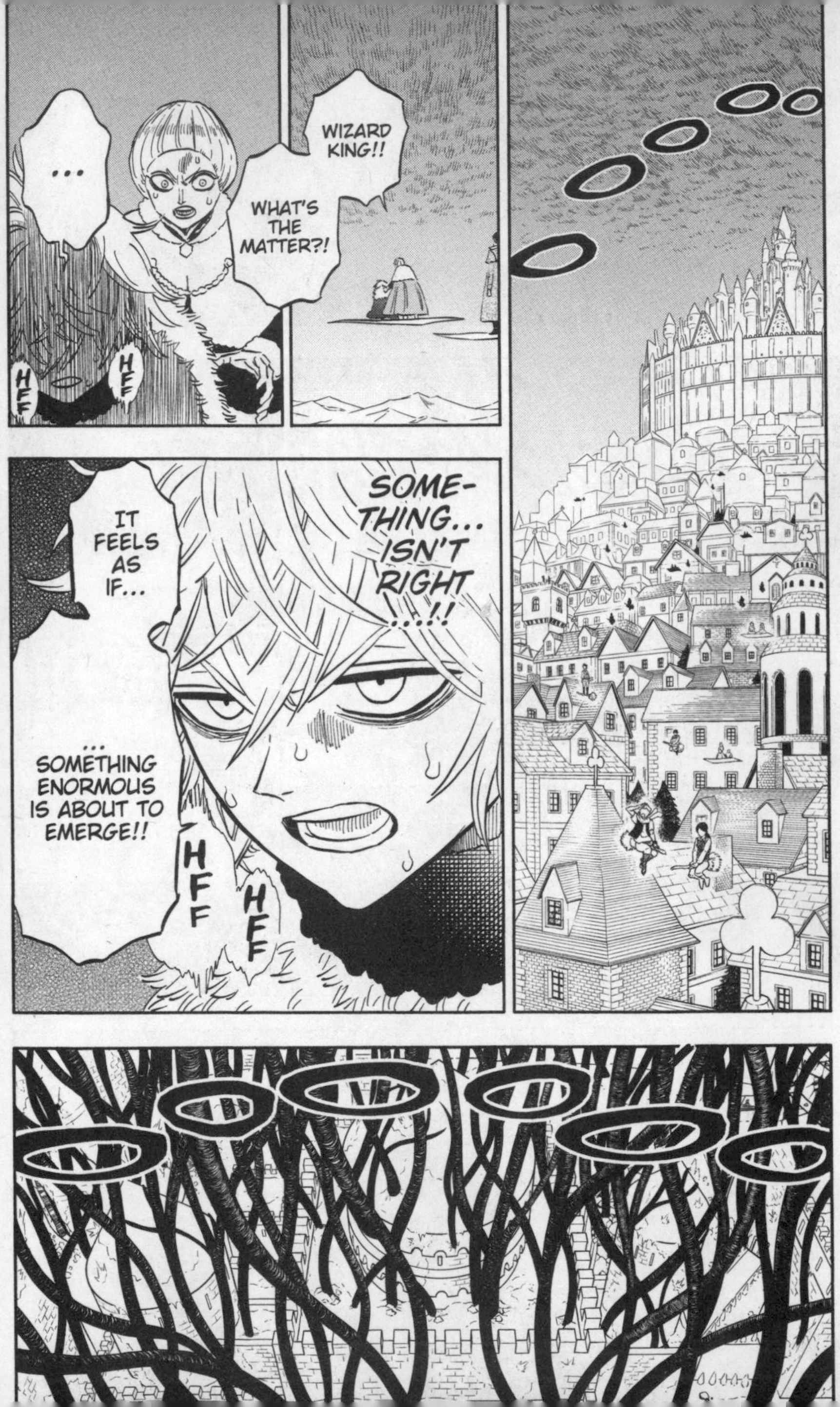
WIZARD KING!!
WHAT'S THE MATTER?!
...
HFF
HFF
SOMETHING... ISN'T RIGHT ...!!
IT FEELS AS IF...
... SOMETHING ENORMOUS IS ABOUT TO EMERGE!!
HFF
HFF

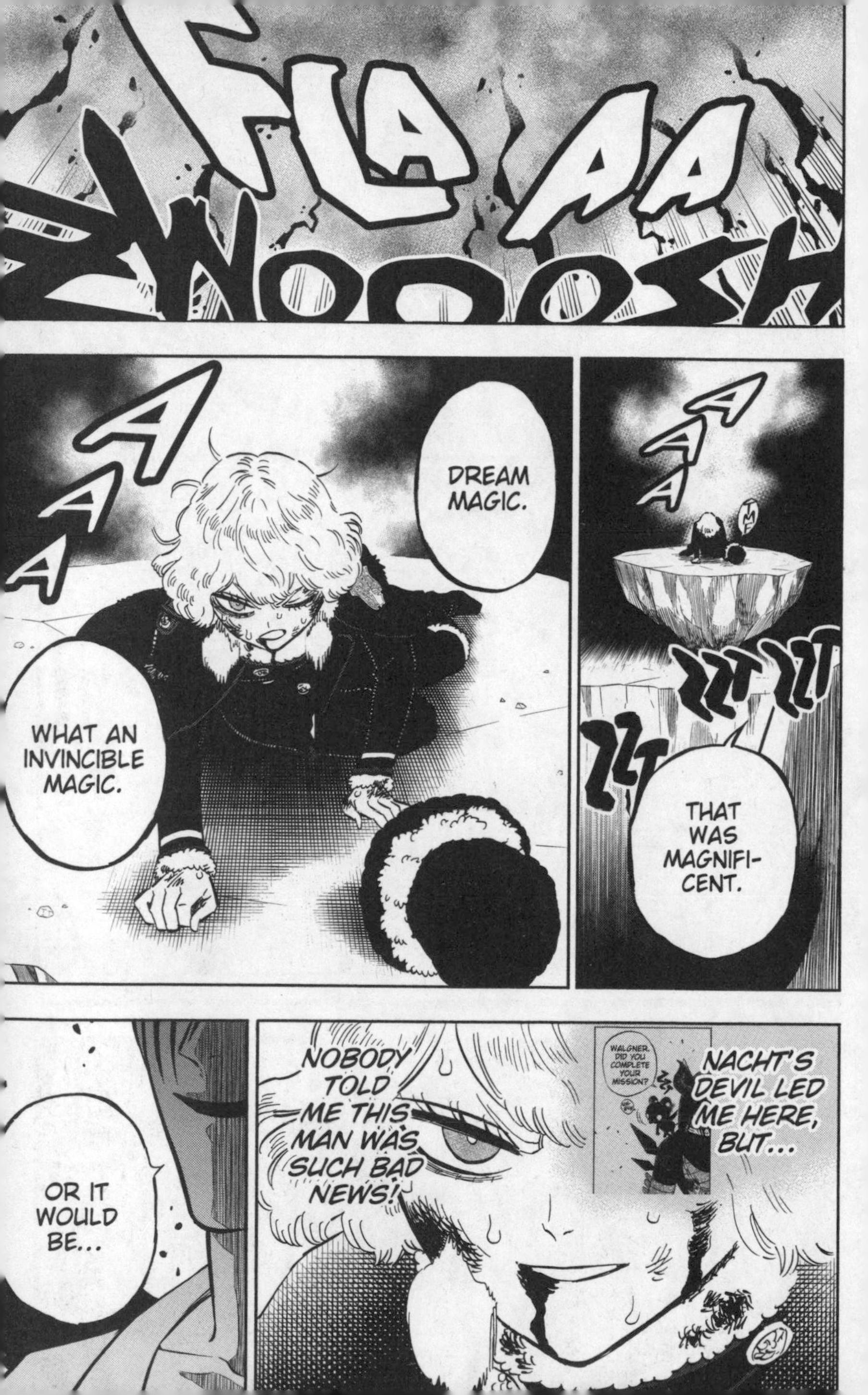
FLAAA
WHOOOSH
AAA
THAT WAS MAGNIFICENT.
DREAM MAGIC.
WHAT AN INVINCIBLE MAGIC.
AAA
NACHT'S DEVIL LED ME HERE, BUT...
WALGNER, DID YOU COMPLETE YOUR MISSION?
NOBODY TOLD ME THIS MAN WAS SUCH BAD NEWS!
OR IT WOULD BE...

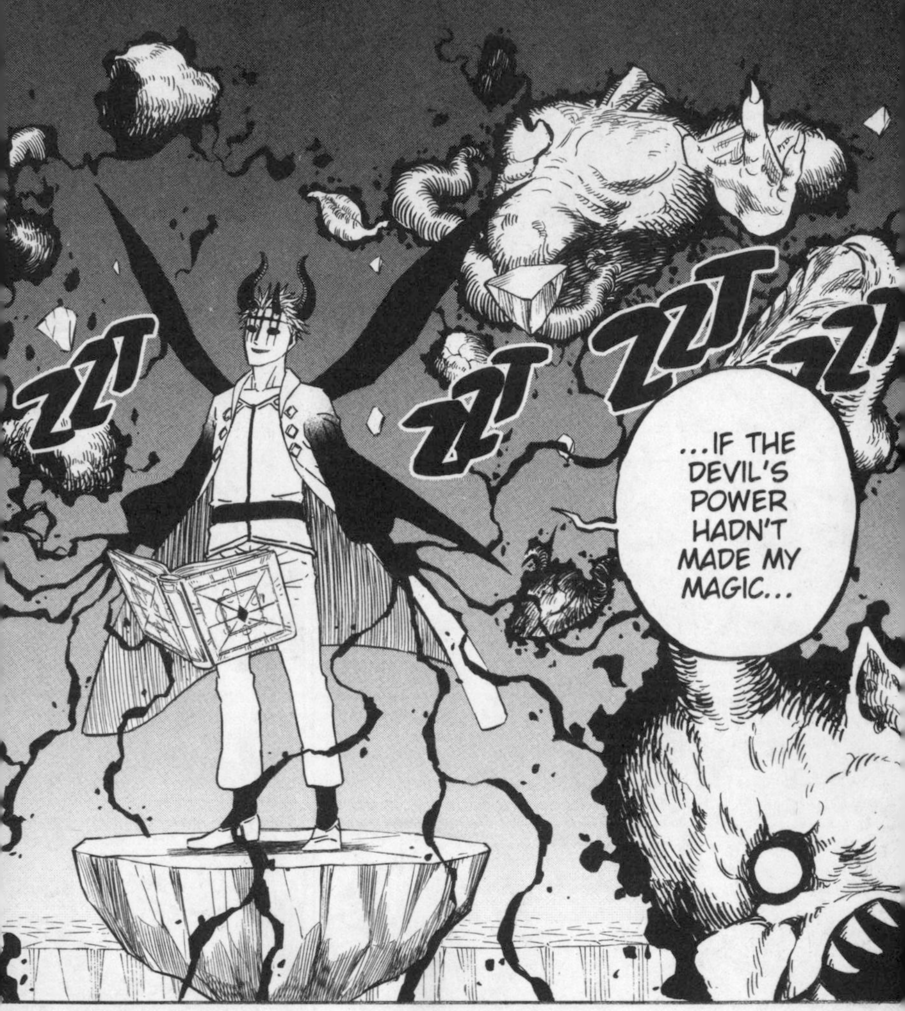
ZZT ZZT ZZT ZZT
...IF THE DEVIL'S POWER HADN'T MADE MY MAGIC...
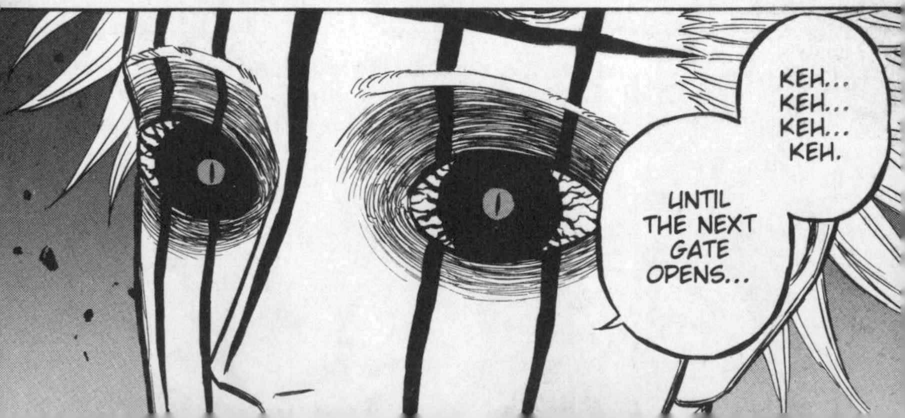
KEH... KEH... KEH... KEH.
UNTIL THE NEXT GATE OPENS...

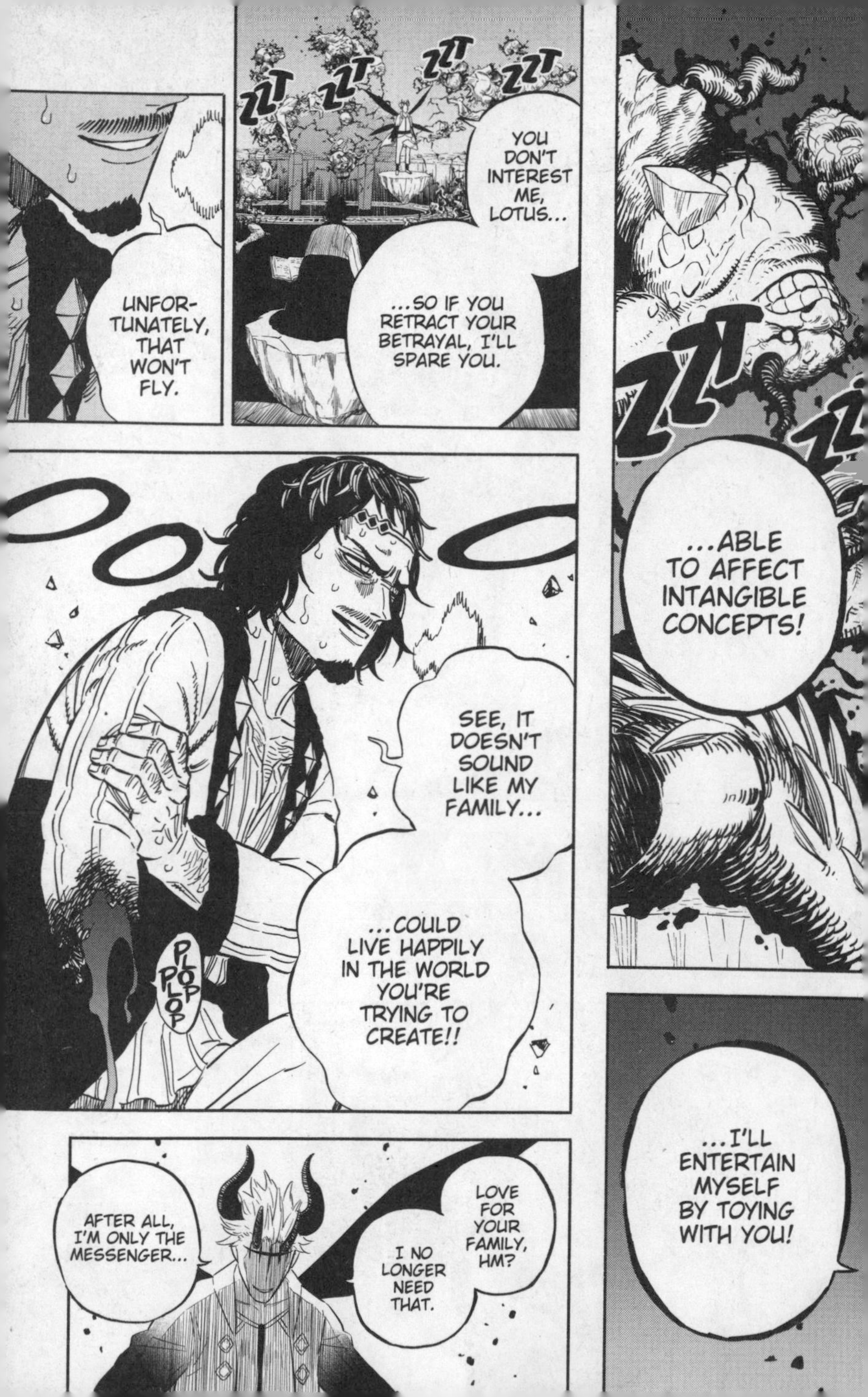
ZZZT
ZZZT
...ABLE TO AFFECT INTANGIBLE CONCEPTS!
ZZZT ZZZT ZZZT ZZZT
YOU DON'T INTEREST ME, LOTUS...
...SO IF YOU RETRACT YOUR BETRAYAL, I'LL SPARE YOU.
UNFORTUNATELY, THAT WON'T FLY.
SEE, IT DOESN'T SOUND LIKE MY FAMILY...
...COULD LIVE HAPPILY IN THE WORLD YOU'RE TRYING TO CREATE!!
PLOP PLOP
...I'LL ENTERTAIN MYSELF BY TOYING WITH YOU!
LOVE FOR YOUR FAMILY, HM?
I NO LONGER NEED THAT.
AFTER ALL, I'M ONLY THE MESSENGER...

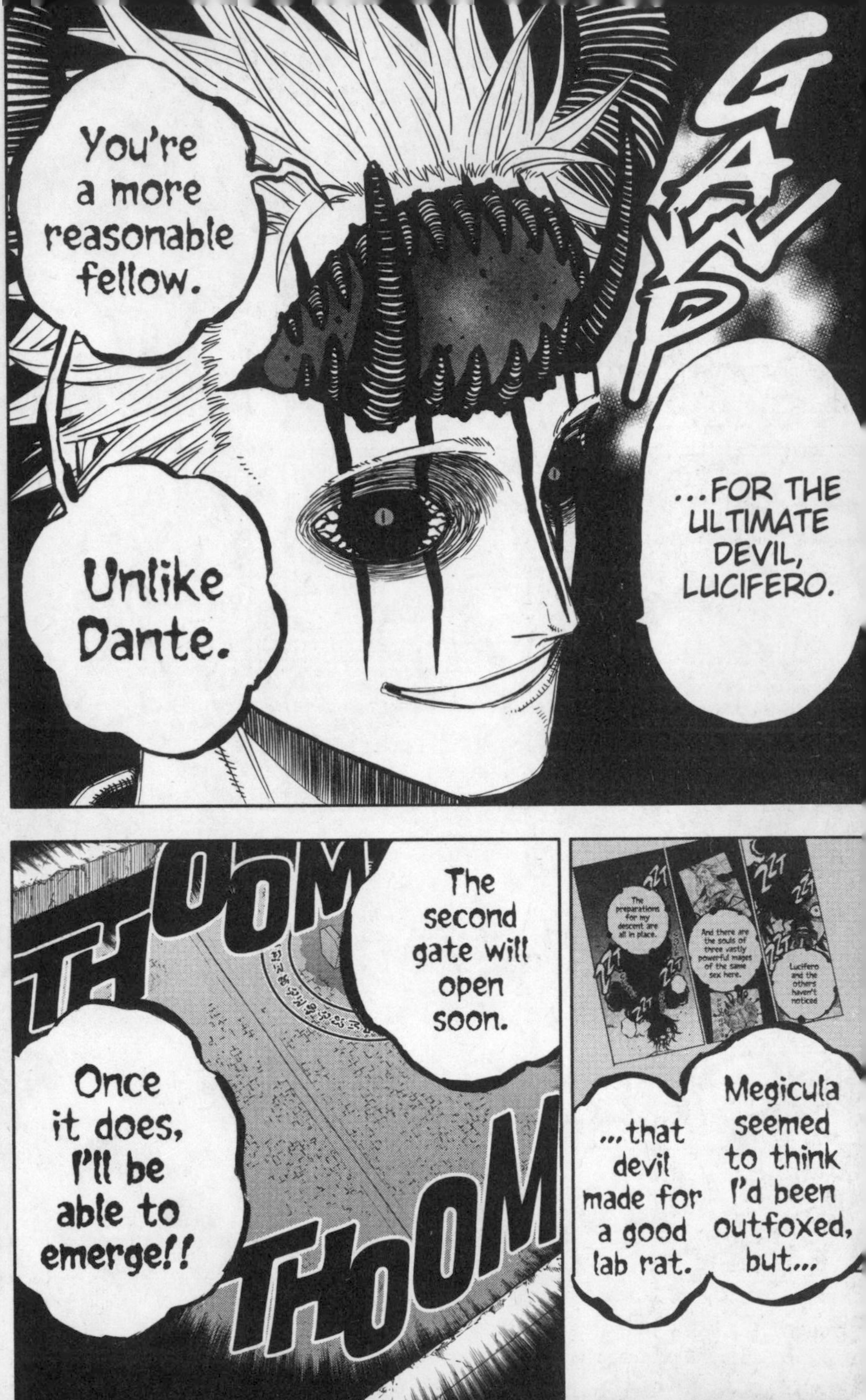
GAWP
...FOR THE ULTIMATE DEVIL, LUCIFERO.
You're a more reasonable fellow.
Unlike Dante.
The preparations for my descent are all in place.
And there are the souls of three vastly powerful mages of the same sex here.
Lucifero and the others haven't noticed
Megicula seemed to think I'd been outfoxed, but...
...that devil made for a good lab rat.
THOOM
The second gate will open soon.
Once it does, I'll be able to emerge!!
THOOM

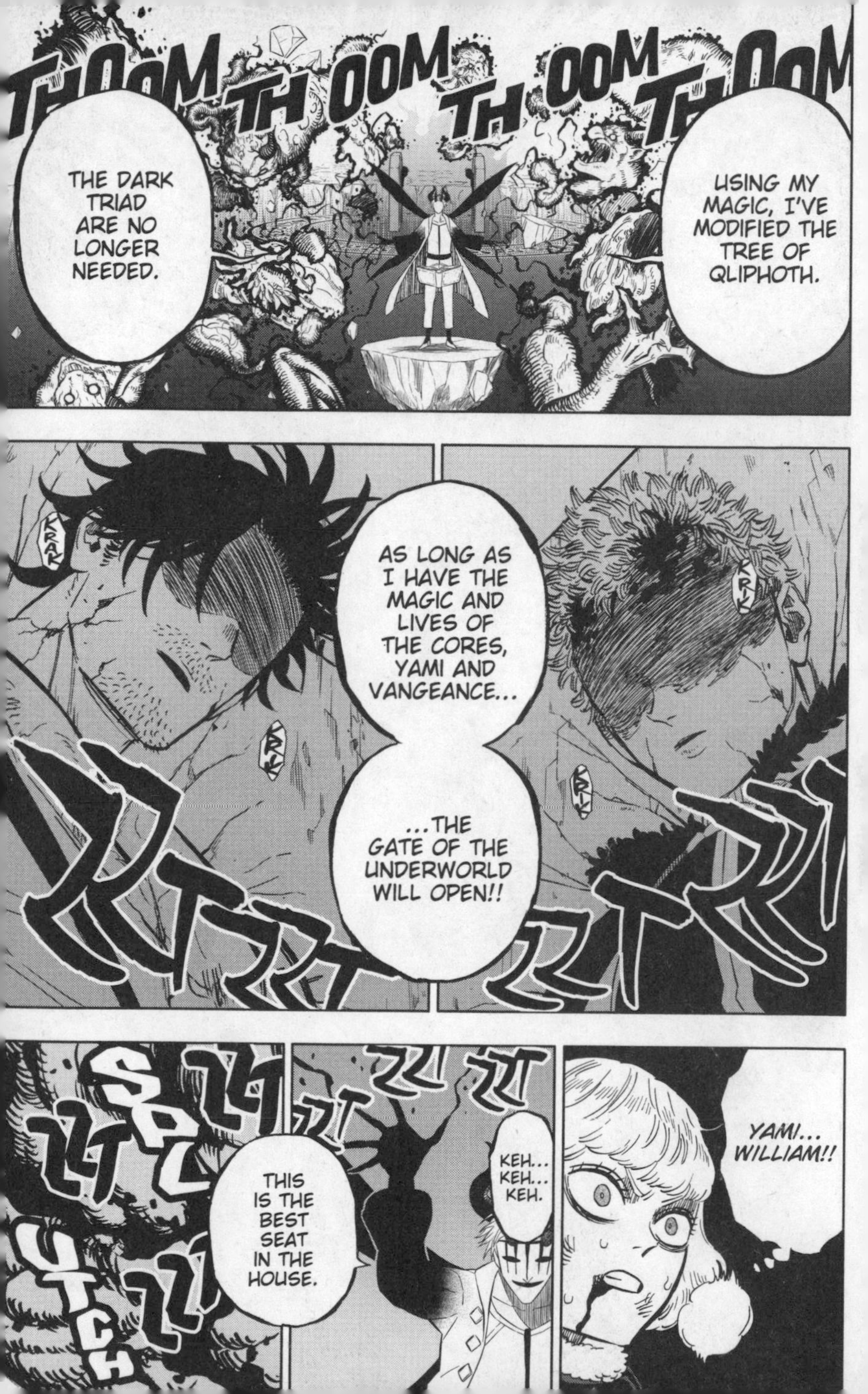
THOOM THOOM THOOM THOOM
USING MY MAGIC, I'VE MODIFIED THE TREE OF QLIPHOTH.
THE DARK TRIAD ARE NO LONGER NEEDED.
KRIK
KRIK
AS LONG AS I HAVE THE MAGIC AND LIVES OF THE CORES, YAMI AND VANGEANCE...
...THE GATE OF THE UNDERWORLD WILL OPEN!!
KRAK
KRIK
YAMI... WILLIAM!!
KEH... KEH... KEH.
THIS IS THE BEST SEAT IN THE HOUSE.
SPLUTCH

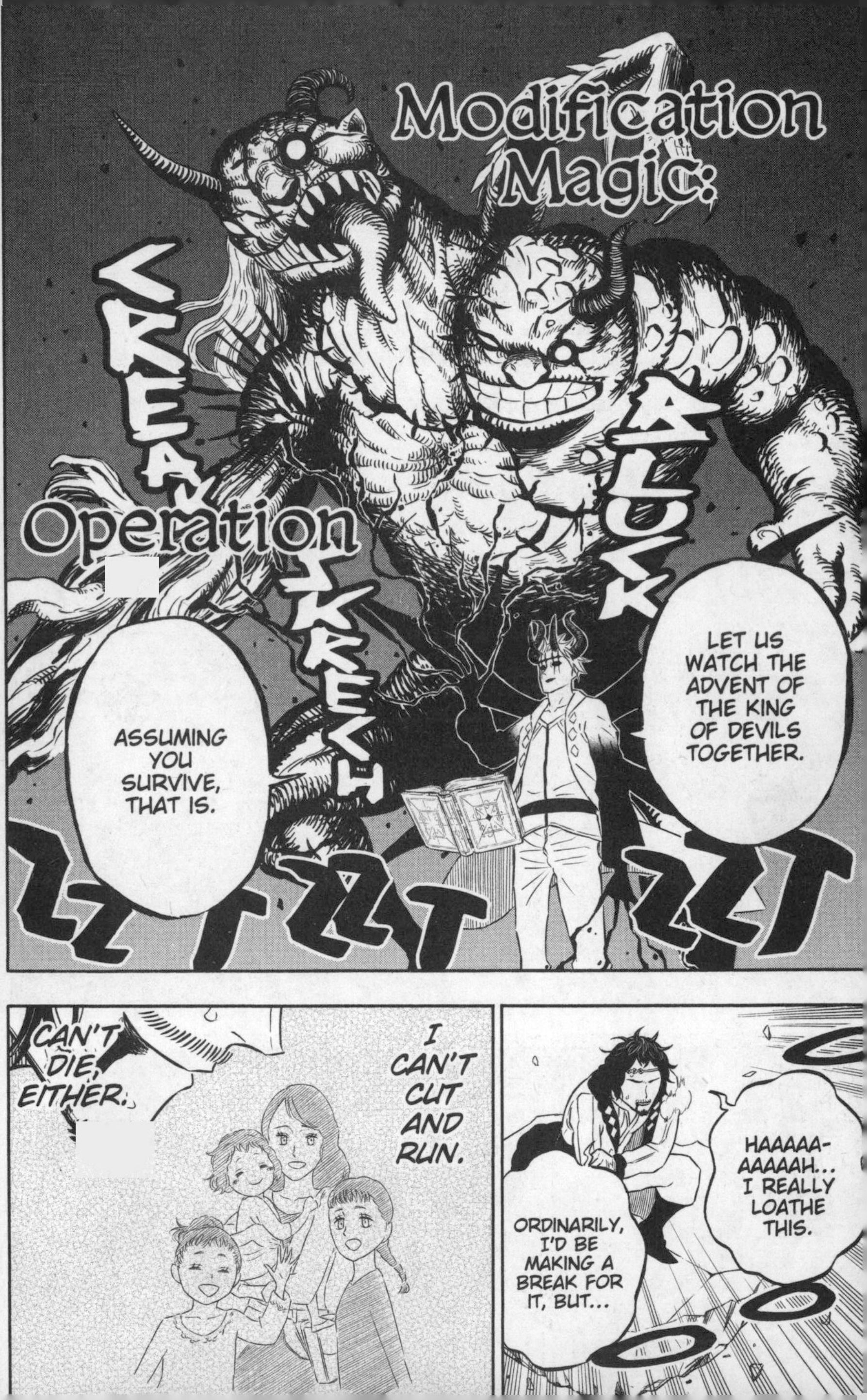
Modification Magic:
Operation
SKRECH
LET US WATCH THE ADVENT OF THE KING OF DEVILS TOGETHER.
ASSUMING YOU SURVIVE, THAT IS.
ZZT ZZT ZZT
HAAAAA-AAAAAH... I REALLY LOATHE THIS.
ORDINARILY, I'D BE MAKING A BREAK FOR IT, BUT...
I CAN'T CUT AND RUN.
CAN'T DIE, EITHER.

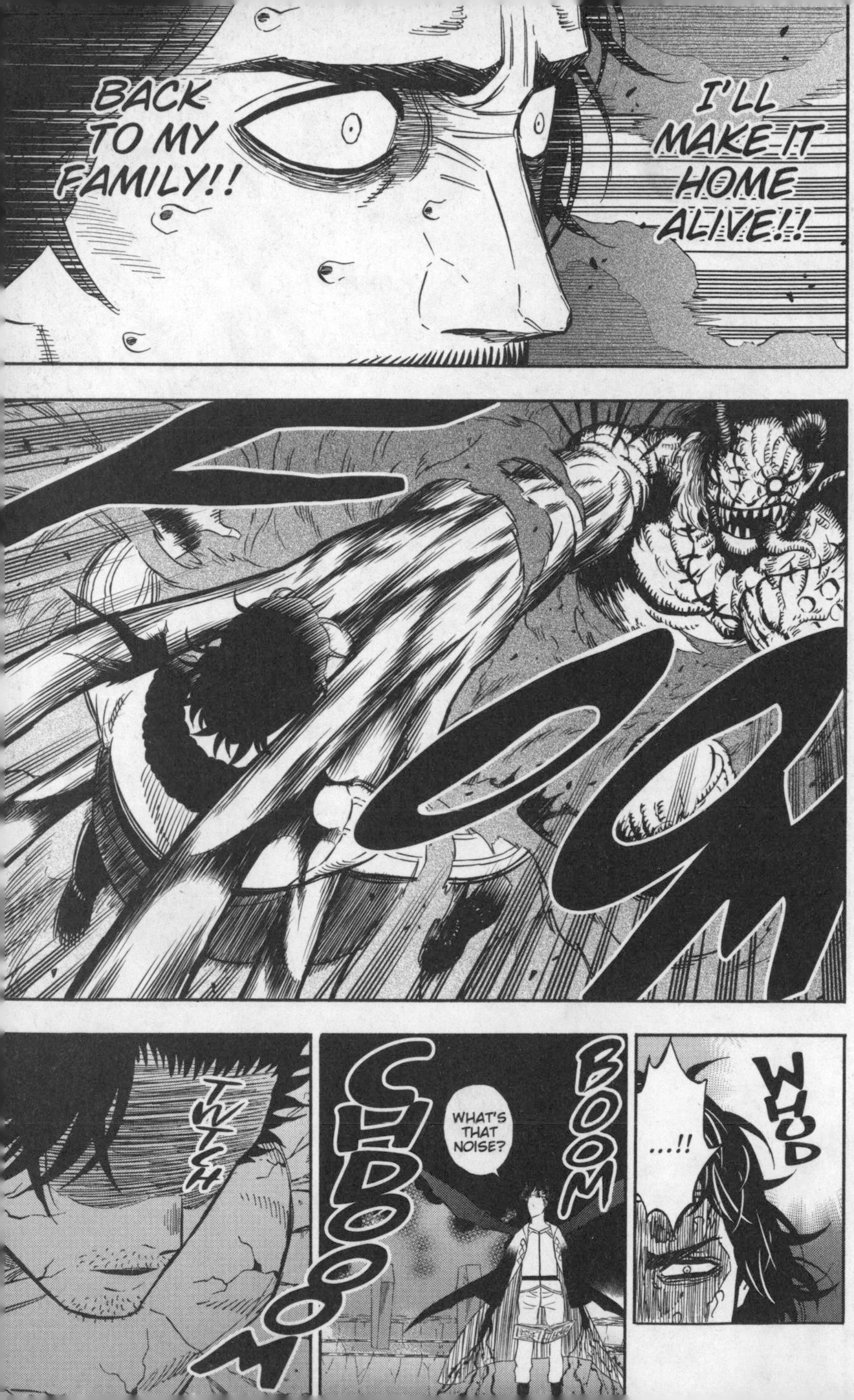
I'LL MAKE IT HOME ALIVE!!
BACK TO MY FAMILY!!
WHUD
...!!
BOOM
WHAT'S THAT NOISE?
CHDOOOOM
TWITCH

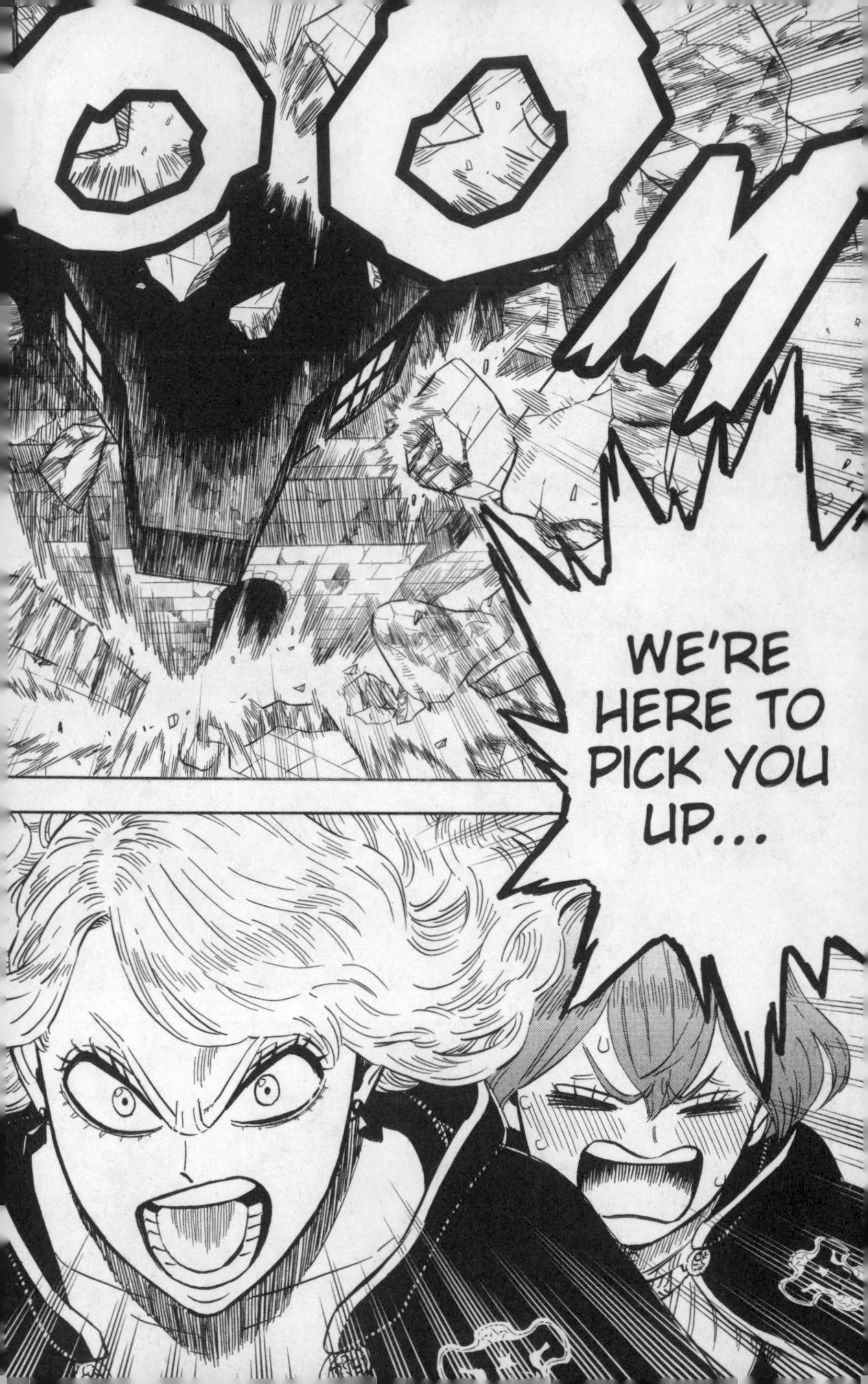
OOM
WE'RE HERE TO PICK YOU UP...

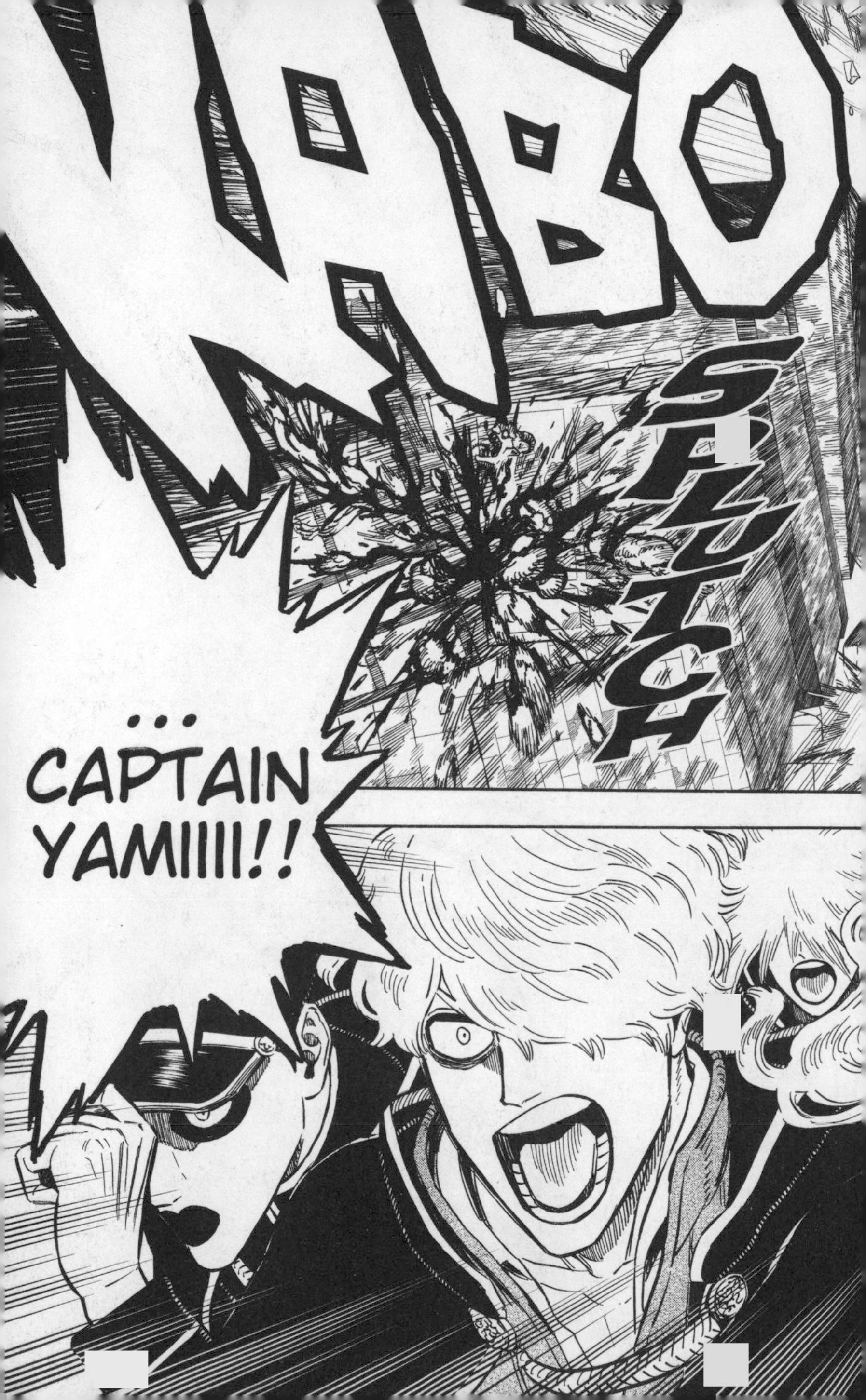
...CAPTAIN YAMIIIII!!

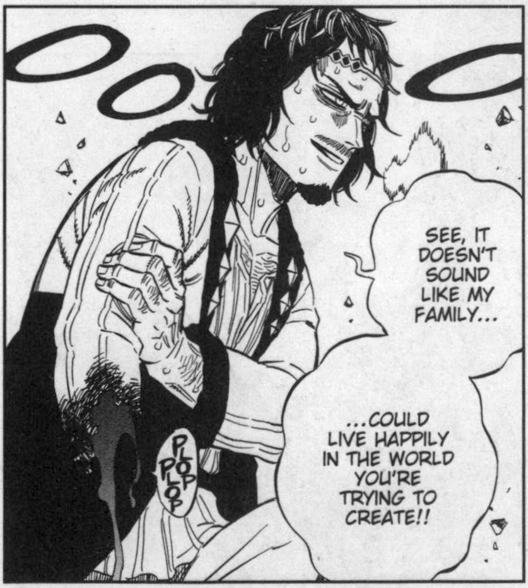
SEE, IT DOESN'T SOUND LIKE MY FAMILY...
...COULD LIVE HAPPILY IN THE WORLD YOU'RE TRYING TO CREATE!!
PLOP PLOP

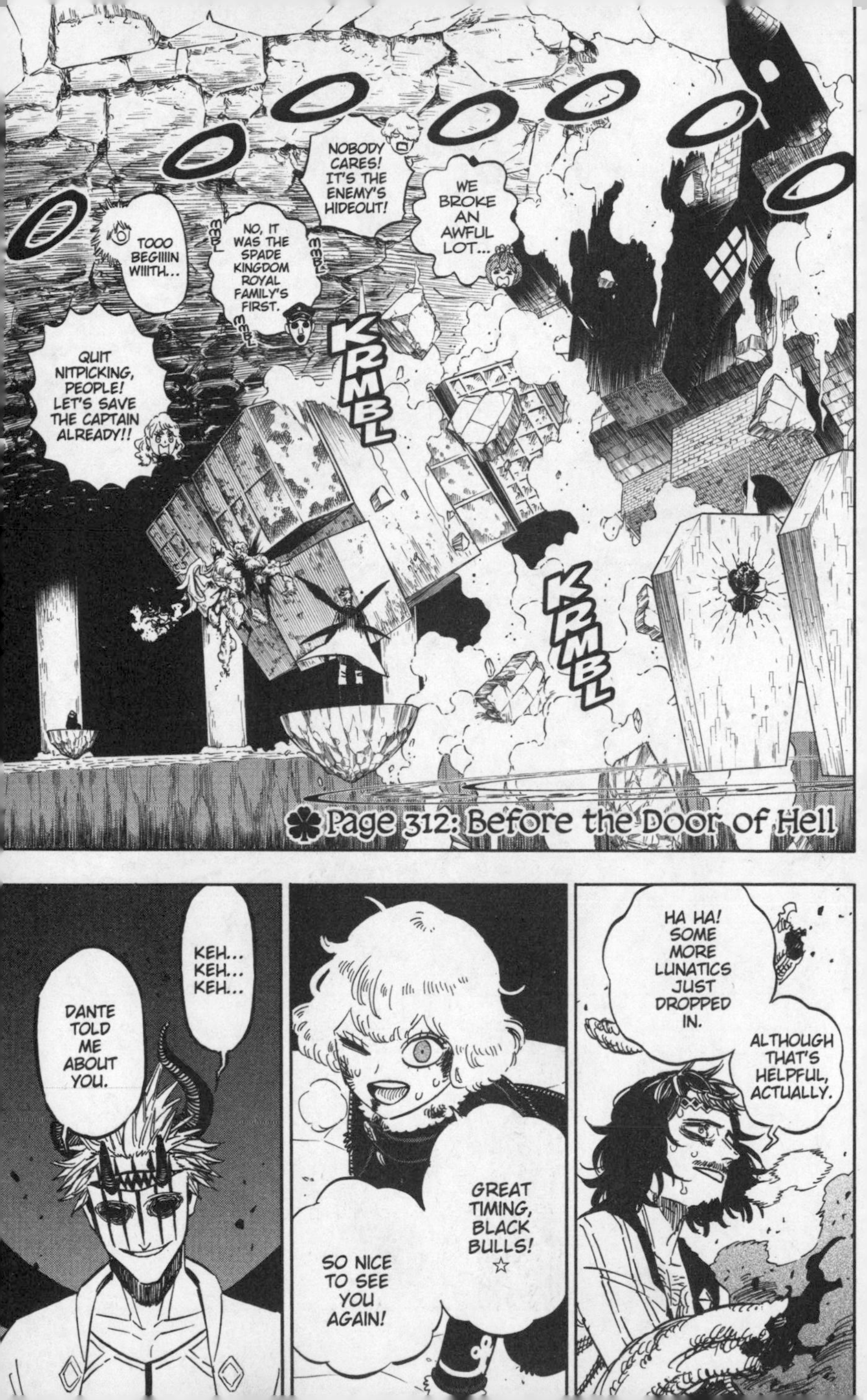
OOOOOOOOO
WE BROKE AN AWFUL LOT...
NOBODY CARES! IT'S THE ENEMY'S HIDEOUT!
MMBL
NO, IT WAS THE SPADE KINGDOM ROYAL FAMILY'S FIRST.
MMBL
TOOO BEGIIIIN WIIITH...
MMBL
QUIT NITPICKING, PEOPLE! LET'S SAVE THE CAPTAIN ALREADY!!
KRMBL
KRMBL
Page 312: Before the Door of Hell
HA HA! SOME MORE LUNATICS JUST DROPPED IN.
ALTHOUGH THAT'S HELPFUL, ACTUALLY.
GREAT TIMING, BLACK BULLS! ☆
SO NICE TO SEE YOU AGAIN!
KEH... KEH... KEH...
DANTE TOLD ME ABOUT YOU.

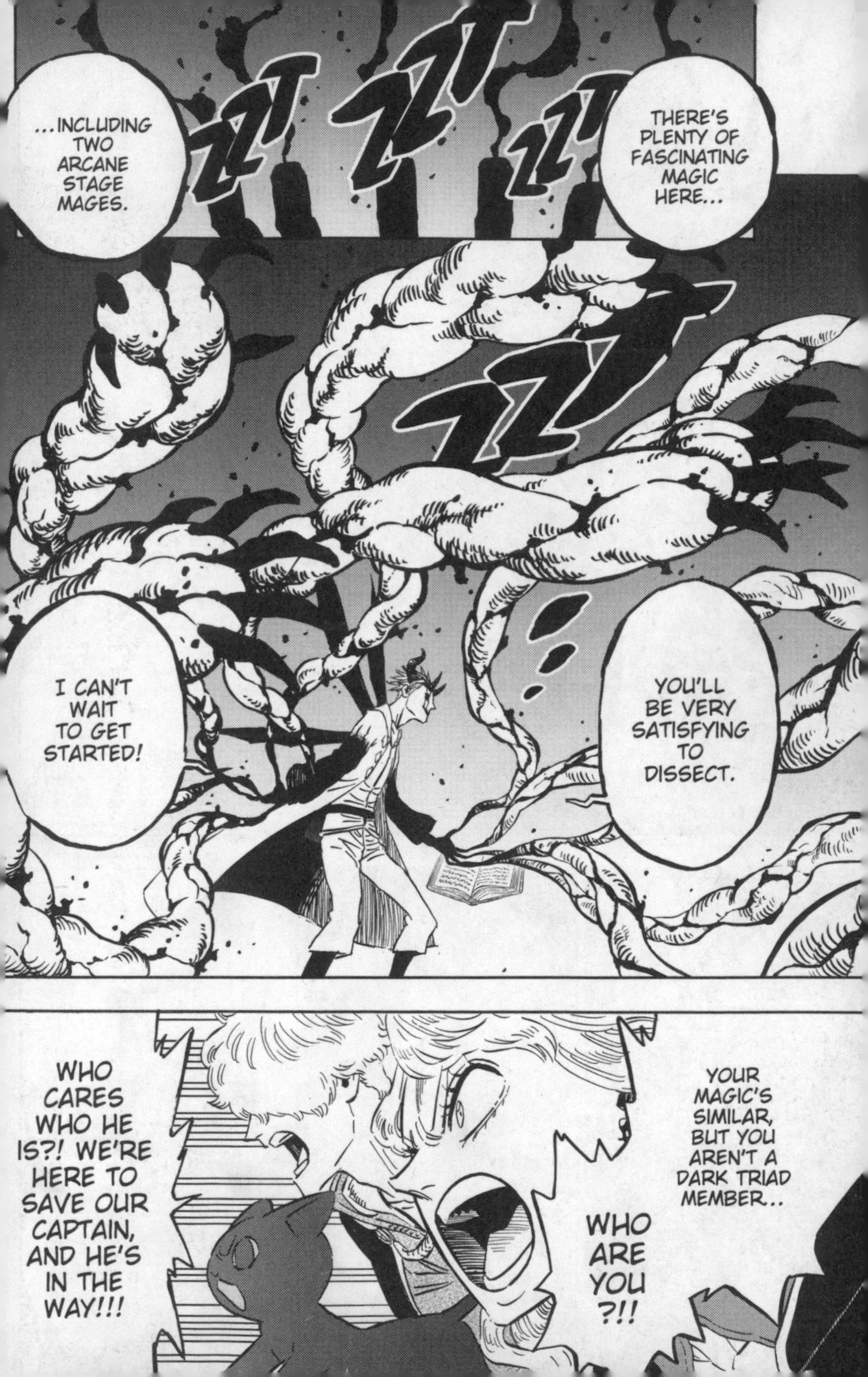
THERE'S PLENTY OF FASCINATING MAGIC HERE...
...INCLUDING TWO ARCANE STAGE MAGES.
YOU'LL BE VERY SATISFYING TO DISSECT.
I CAN'T WAIT TO GET STARTED!
YOUR MAGIC'S SIMILAR, BUT YOU AREN'T A DARK TRIAD MEMBER...
WHO ARE YOU ?!!
WHO CARES WHO HE IS?! WE'RE HERE TO SAVE OUR CAPTAIN, AND HE'S IN THE WAY!!!

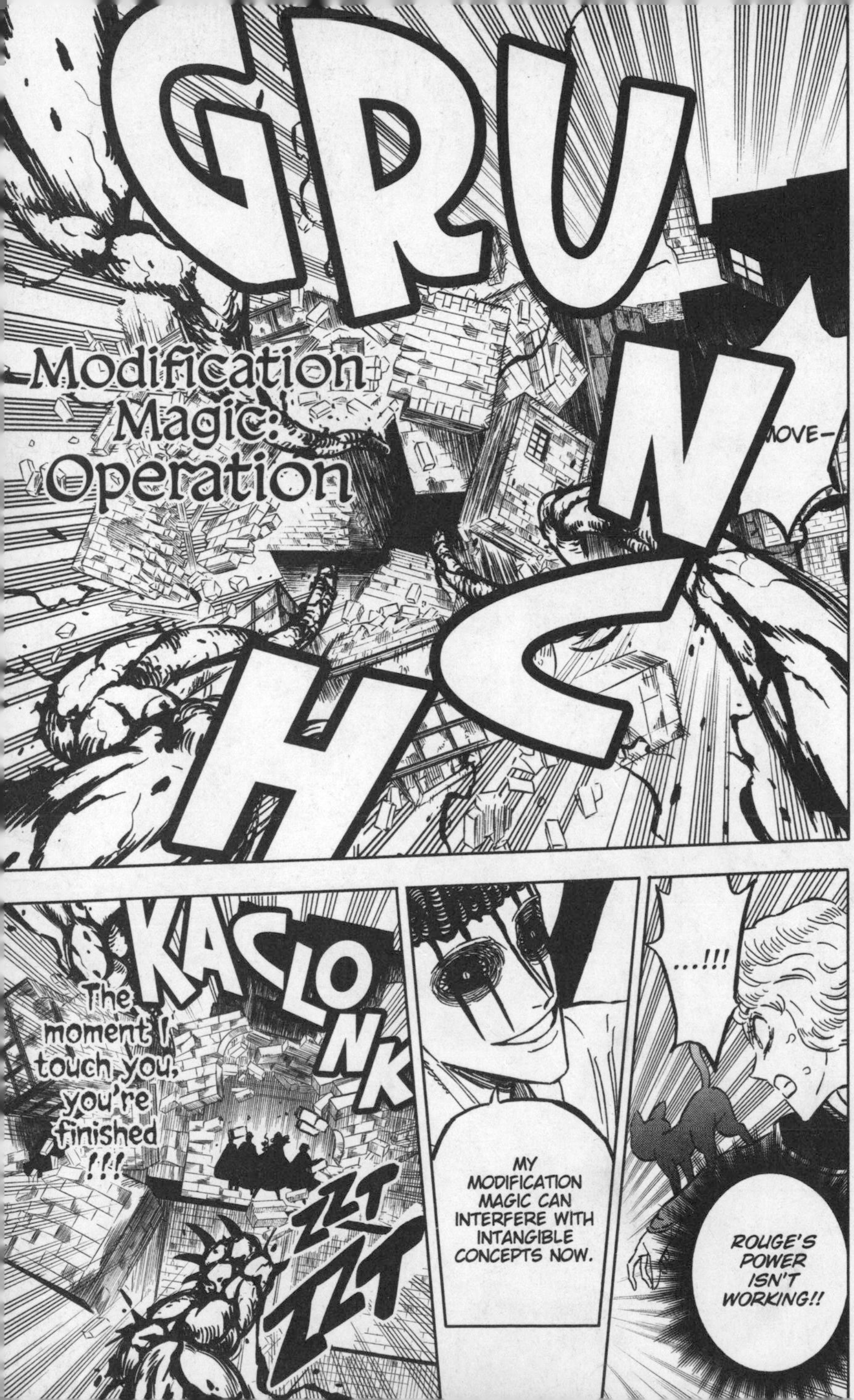
GRU-NCH
MOVE–
Modification Magic: Operation
...!!!
ROUGE'S POWER ISN'T WORKING!!
MY MODIFICATION MAGIC CAN INTERFERE WITH INTANGIBLE CONCEPTS NOW.
KACLONK
The moment I touch you, you're finished!!!
ZZZT
ZZZT

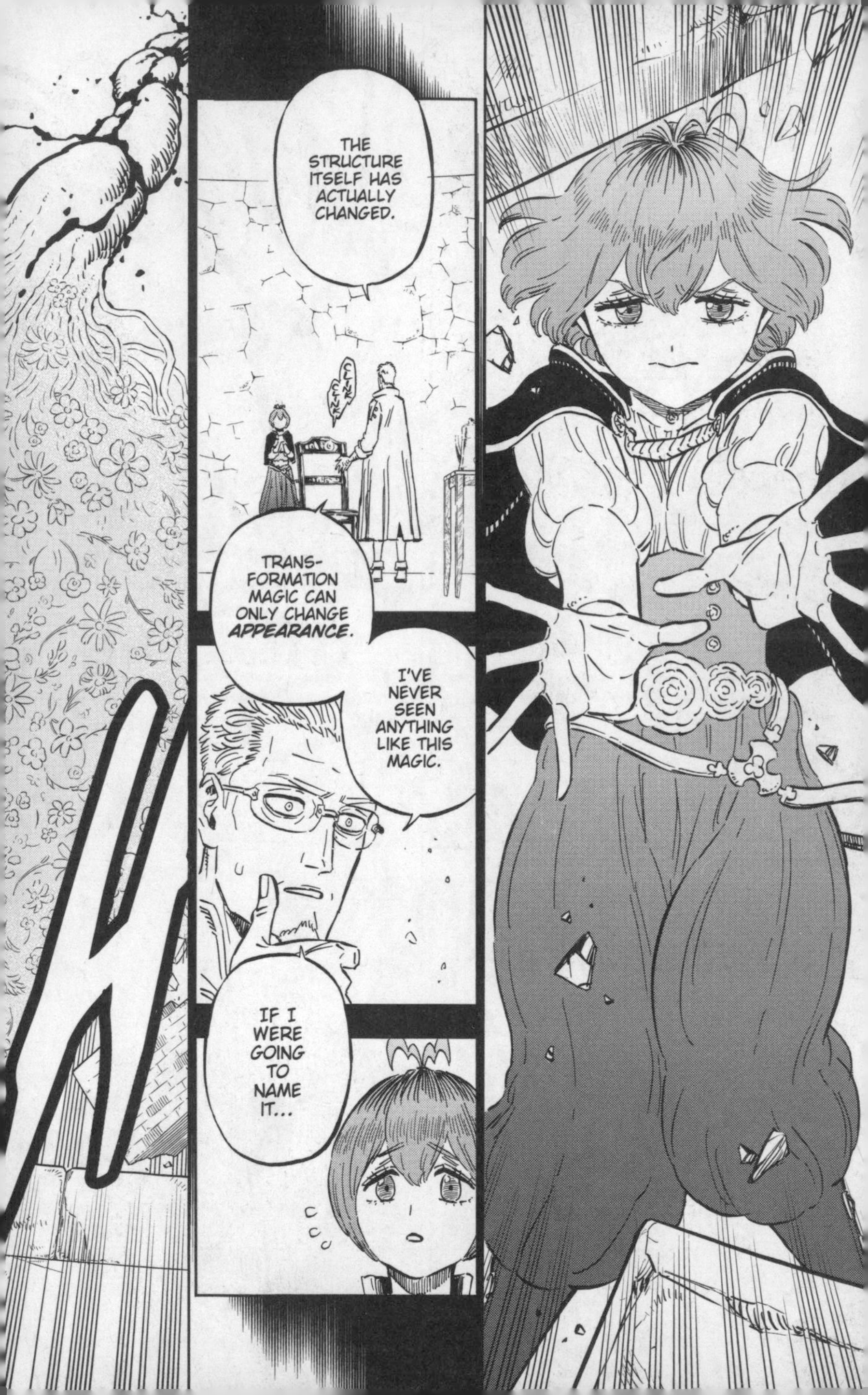
THE STRUCTURE ITSELF HAS ACTUALLY CHANGED.
CLINK CLINK
TRANS-FORMATION MAGIC CAN ONLY CHANGE *APPEARANCE*.
I'VE NEVER SEEN ANYTHING LIKE THIS MAGIC.
IF I WERE GOING TO NAME IT...

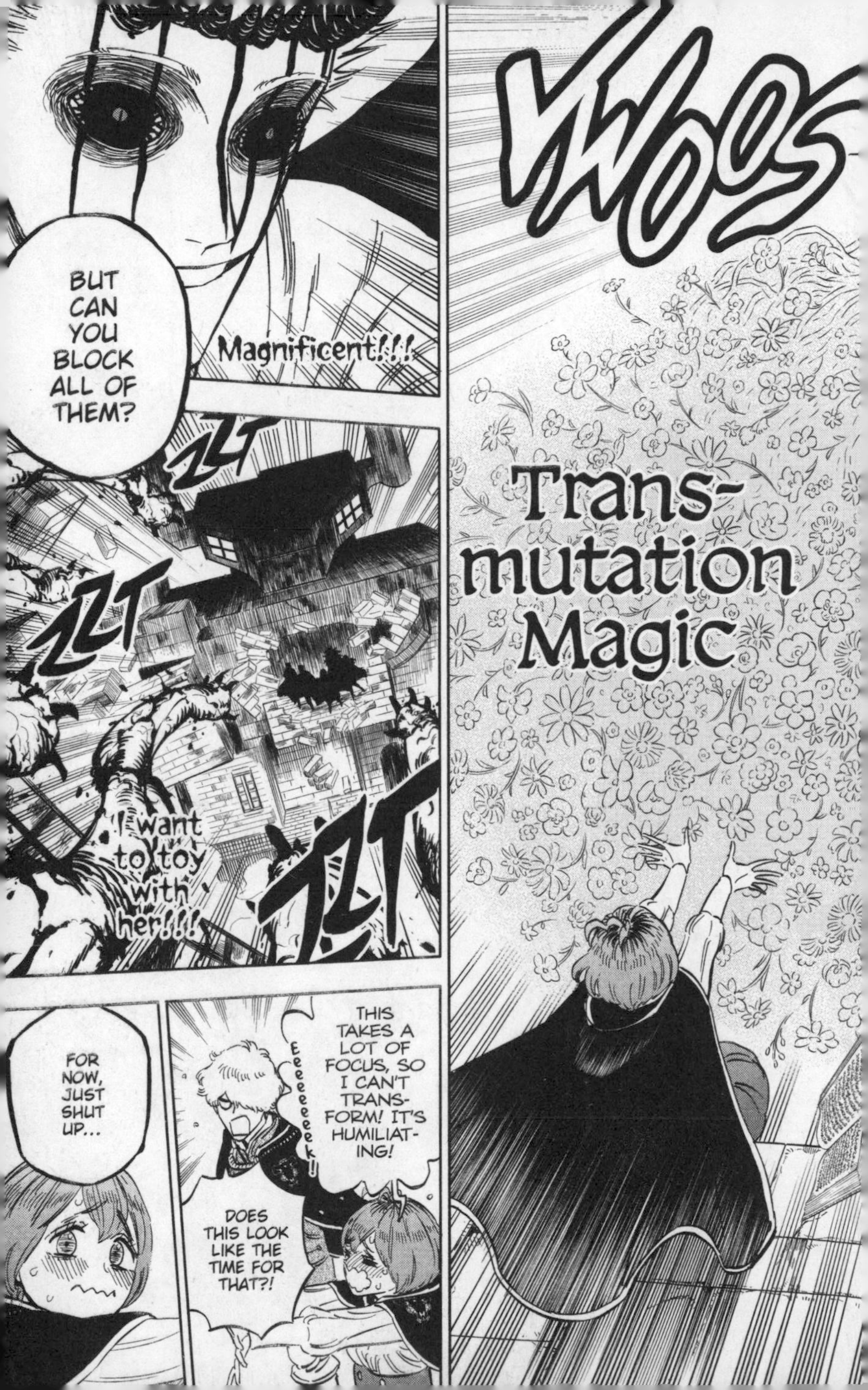
WHOOS
Transmutation Magic
Magnificent!!!
BUT CAN YOU BLOCK ALL OF THEM?
ZZT
ZZT
ZZT
I want to toy with her!!!
Eeeeeeek!
THIS TAKES A LOT OF FOCUS, SO I CAN'T TRANSFORM! IT'S HUMILIATING!
DOES THIS LOOK LIKE THE TIME FOR THAT?!
FOR NOW, JUST SHUT UP...

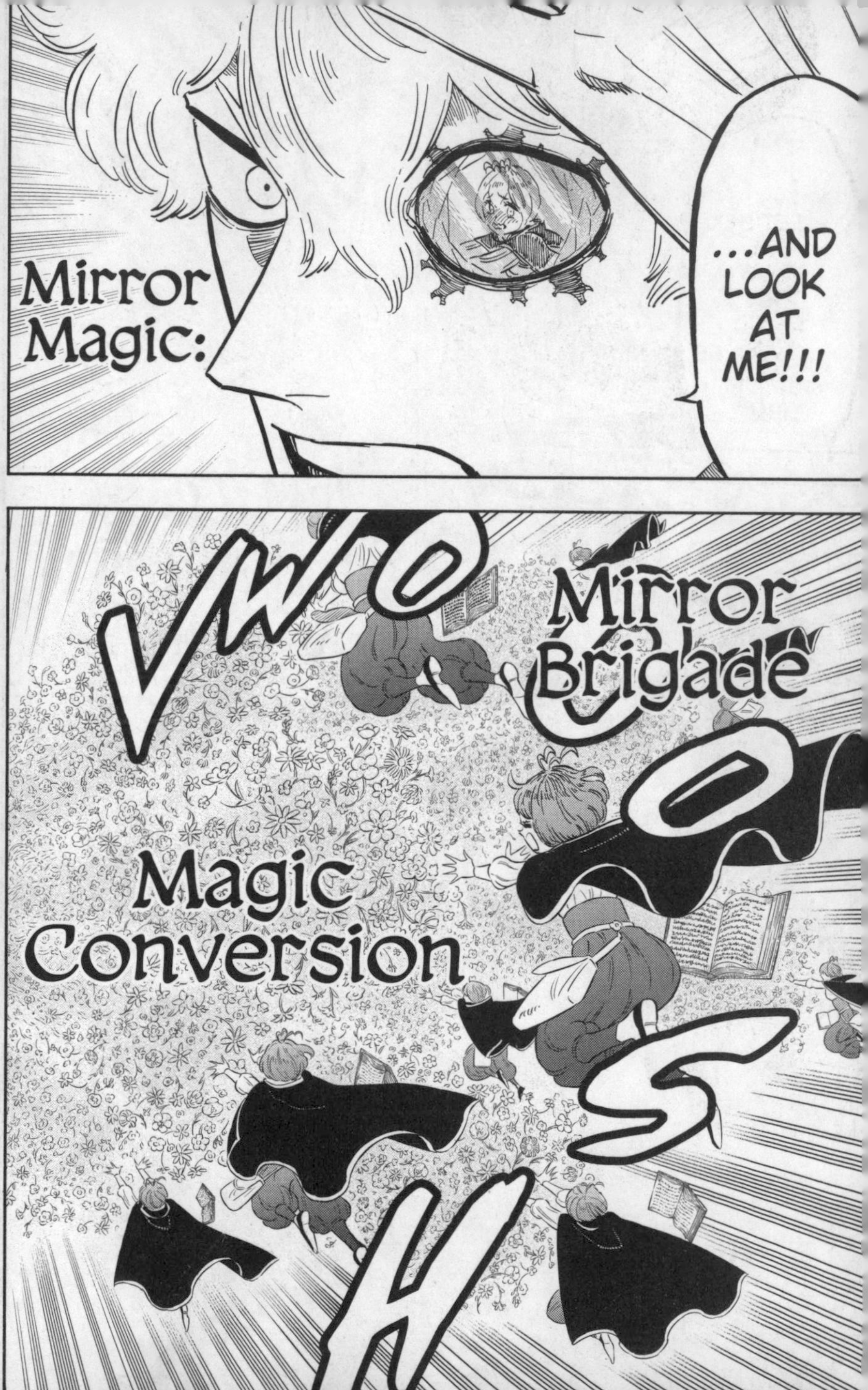
...AND LOOK AT ME!!!
Mirror Magic:
Mirror Brigade
Magic Conversion
VWOOSH

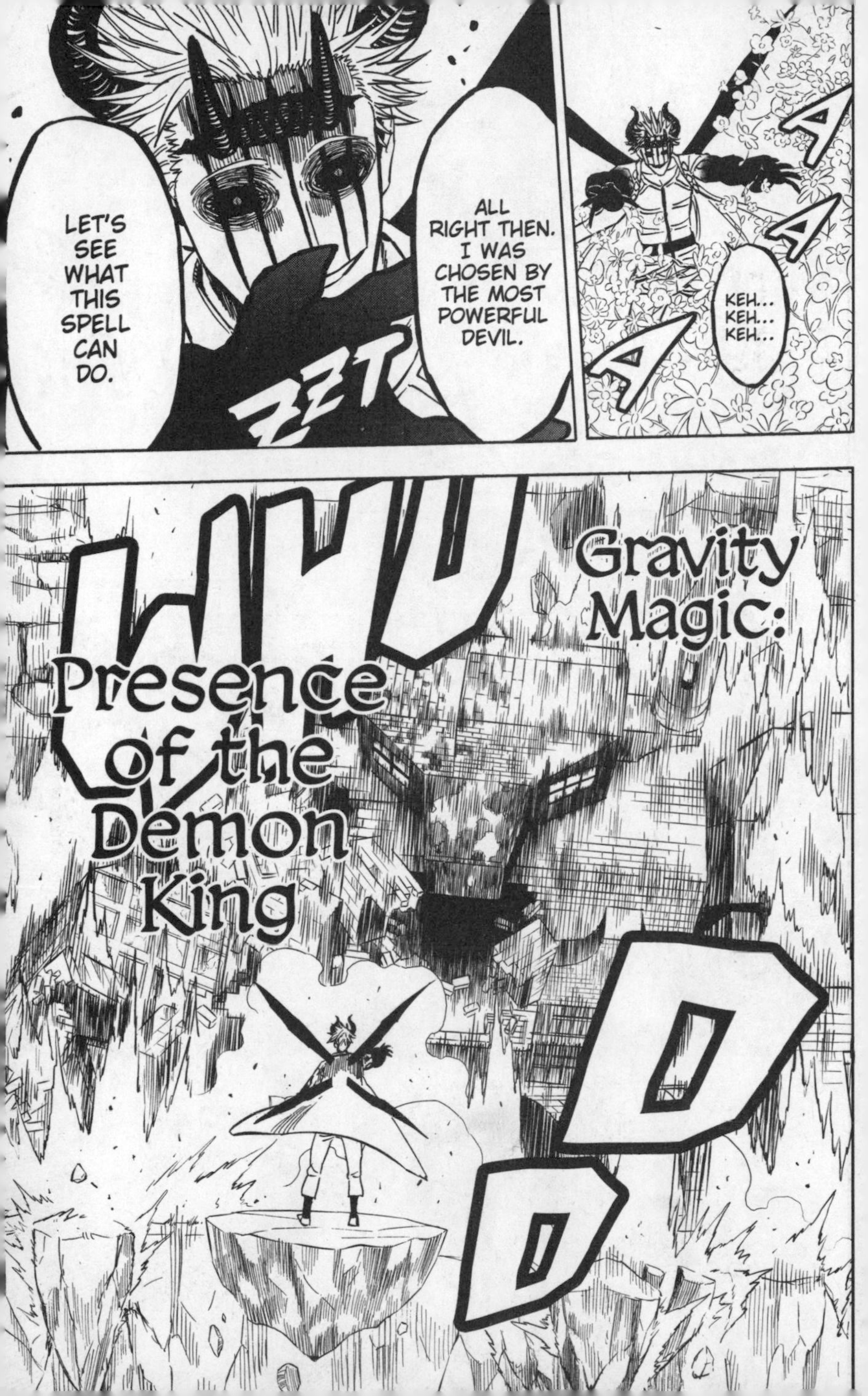

A A A
KEH... KEH... KEH...
ALL RIGHT THEN. I WAS CHOSEN BY THE MOST POWERFUL DEVIL.
LET'S SEE WHAT THIS SPELL CAN DO.
ZZZT
Gravity Magic:
Presence of the Demon King
D D

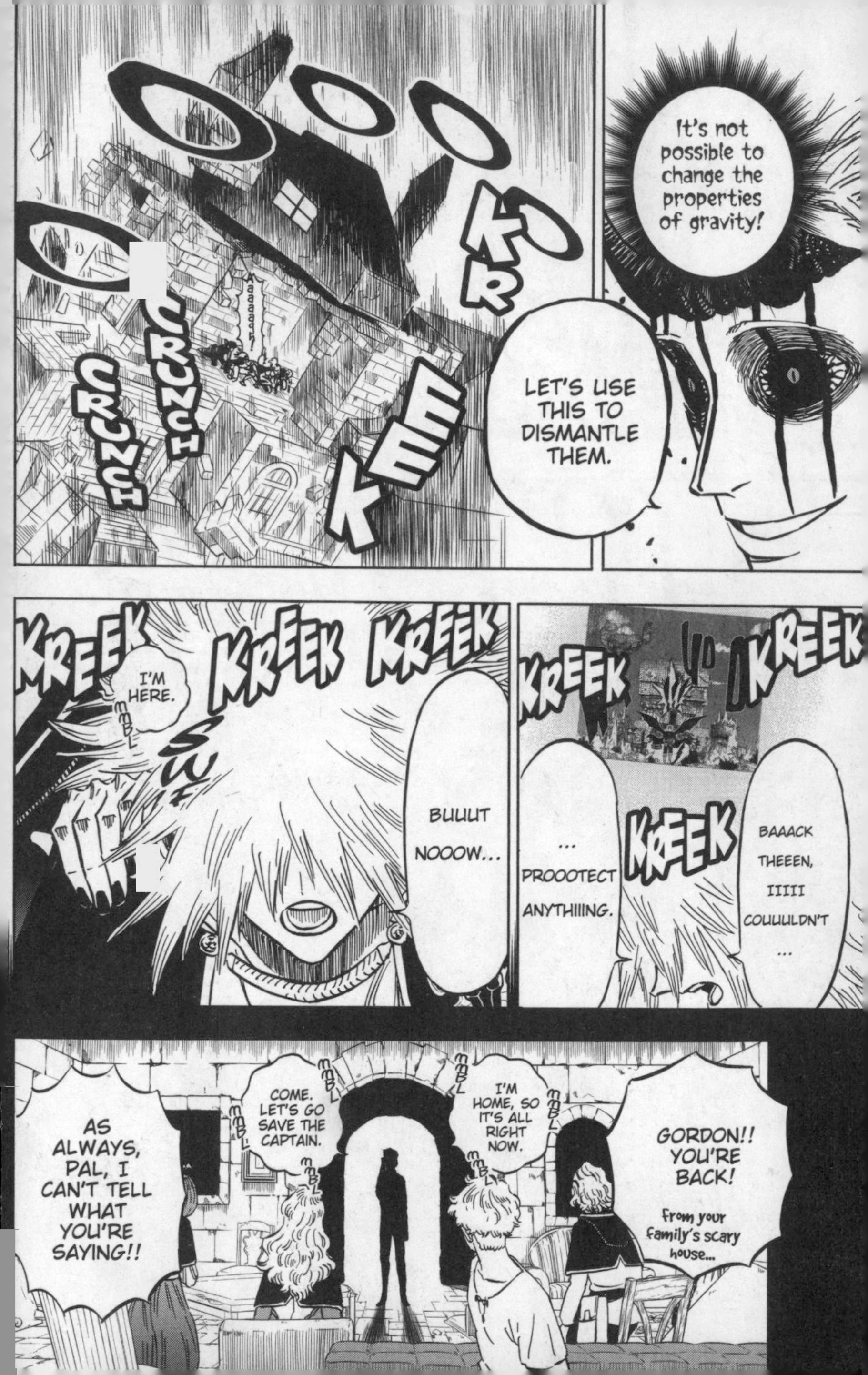
It's not possible to change the properties of gravity!
LET'S USE THIS TO DISMANTLE THEM.
KR
EEK
CRUNCH
CRUNCH
KREEK
KREEK
BAAACK THEEEN, IIIII COUUULDN'T ...
KREEK
... PROOOTECT ANYTHIIING.
KREEK
KREEK
BUUUT NOOOW...
KREEK
I'M HERE.
MMBL
SWF
GORDON!! YOU'RE BACK!
From your family's scary house...
MMBL
I'M HOME, SO IT'S ALL RIGHT NOW.
MMBL
MMBL
COME. LET'S GO SAVE THE CAPTAIN.
MMBL
AS ALWAYS, PAL, I CAN'T TELL WHAT YOU'RE SAYING!!

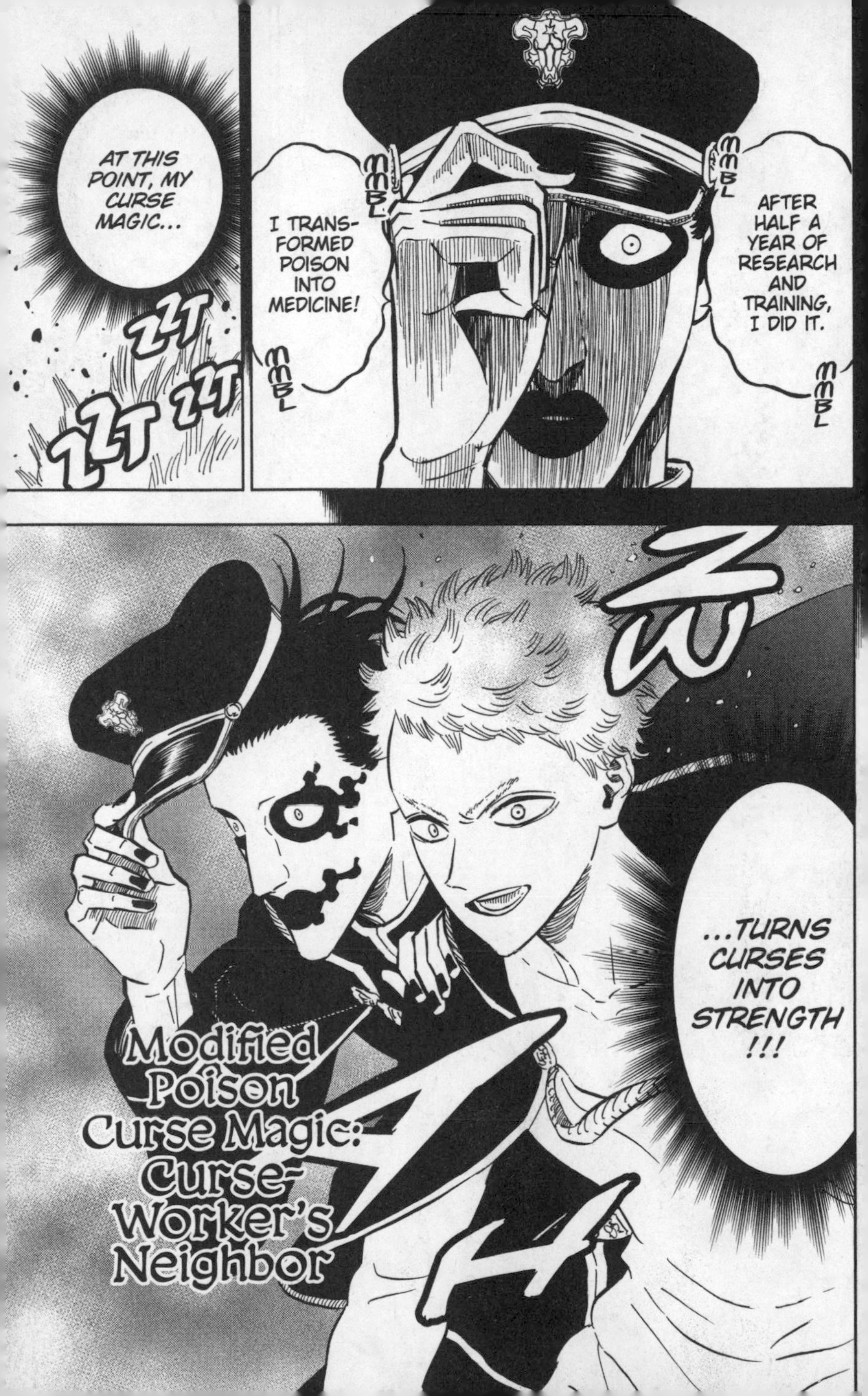
MMBL
AFTER HALF A YEAR OF RESEARCH AND TRAINING, I DID IT.
MMBL
MMBL
I TRANS-FORMED POISON INTO MEDICINE!
MMBL
AT THIS POINT, MY CURSE MAGIC...
ZZT
ZZT ZZT
ZU
...TURNS CURSES INTO STRENGTH!!!
Modified Poison Curse Magic: Curse-Worker's Neighbor

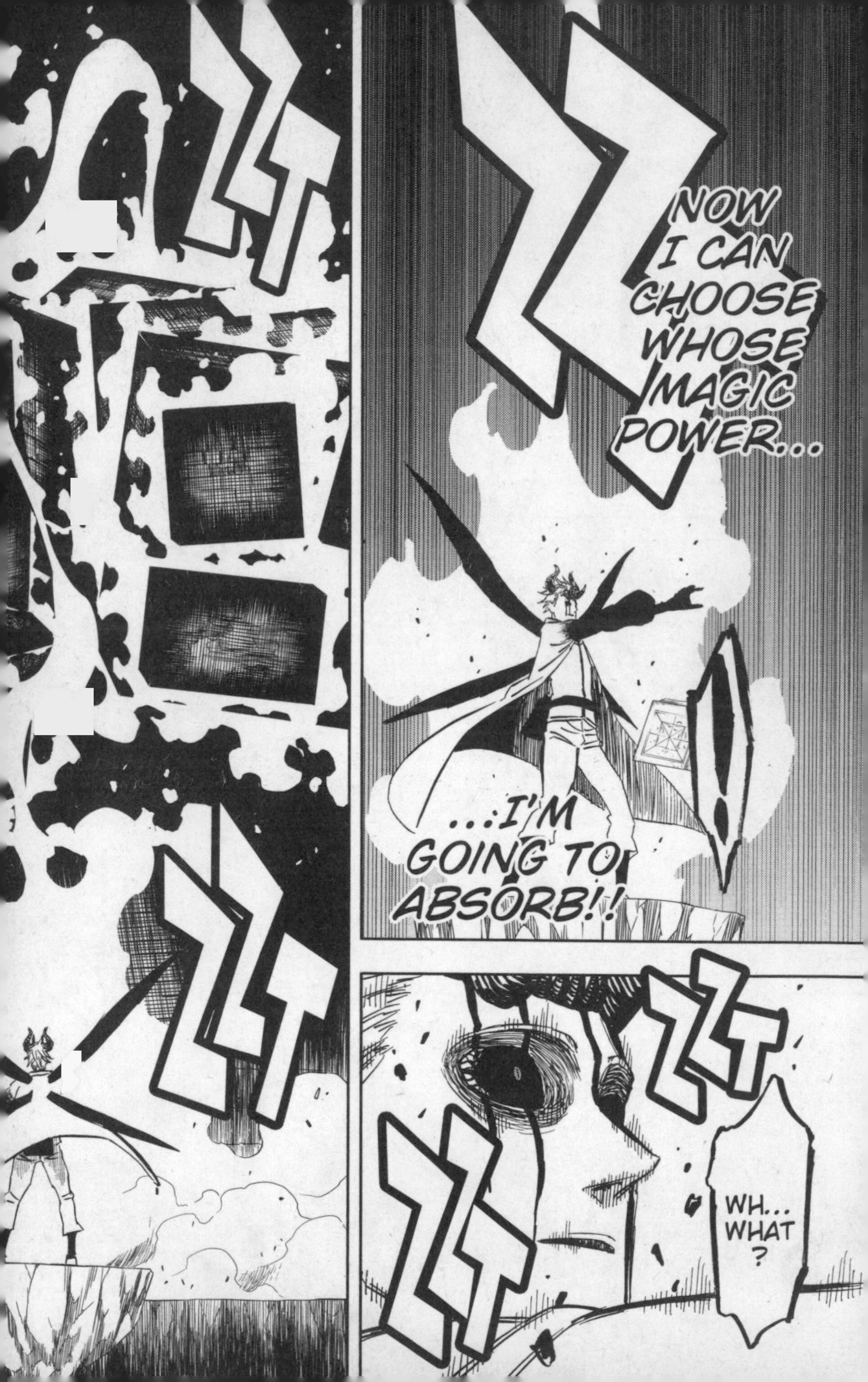
NOW I CAN CHOOSE WHOSE MAGIC POWER...
...I'M GOING TO ABSORB!!
!
ZZT
ZZT
WH... WHAT?

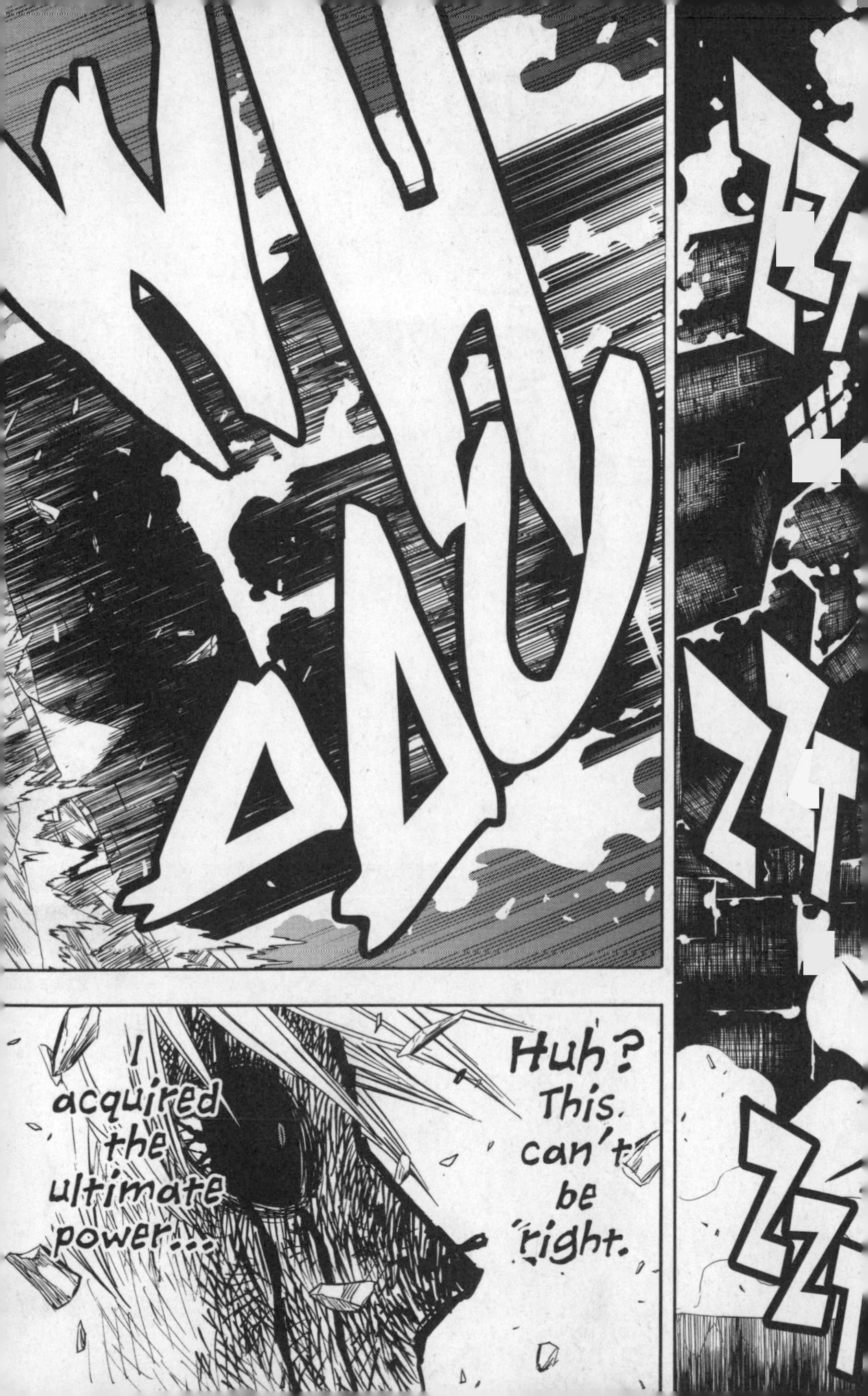
Huh? This can't be right.
I acquired the ultimate power...

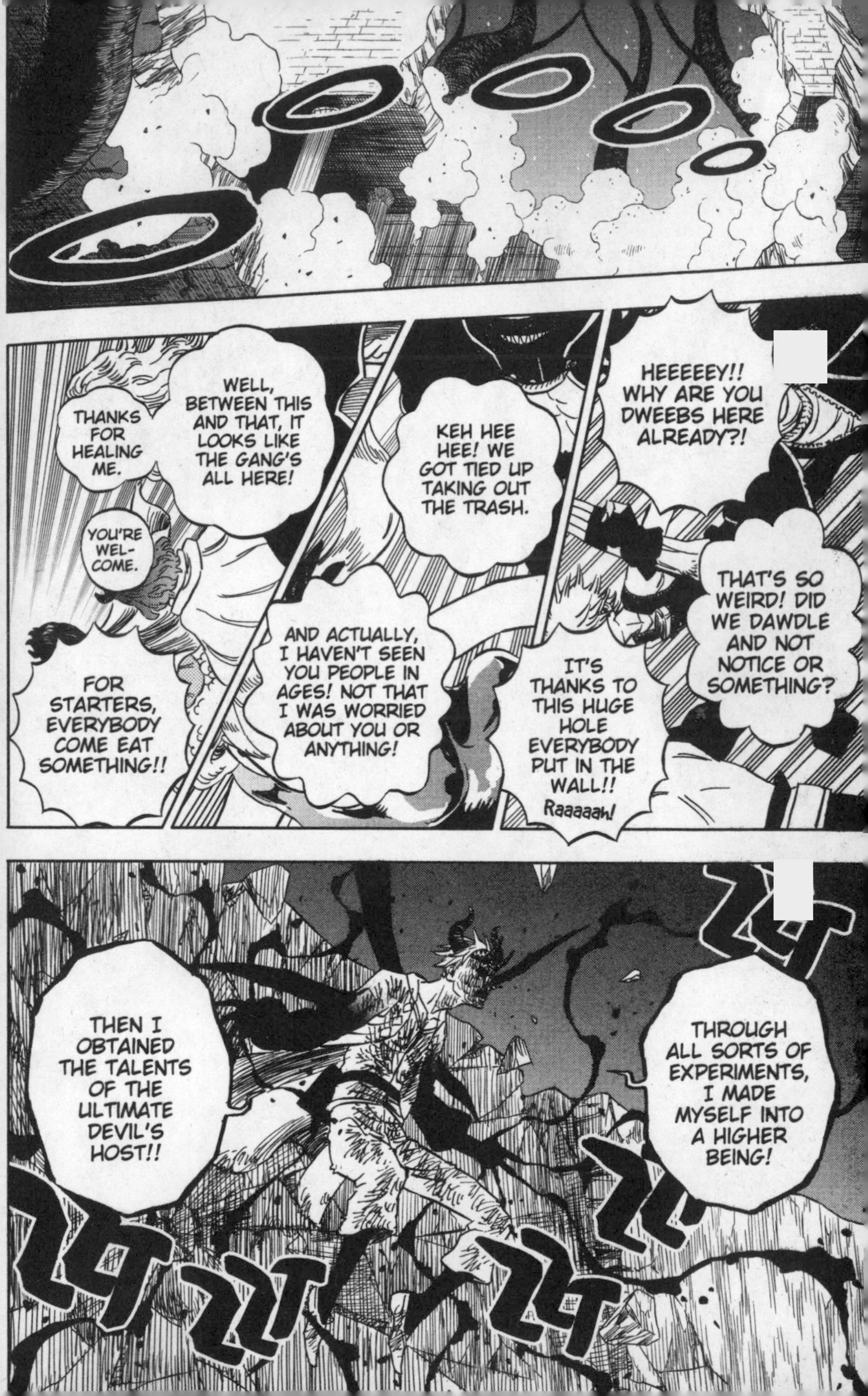
HEEEEEY!! WHY ARE YOU DWEEBS HERE ALREADY?!
THAT'S SO WEIRD! DID WE DAWDLE AND NOT NOTICE OR SOMETHING?
IT'S THANKS TO THIS HUGE HOLE EVERYBODY PUT IN THE WALL!!
Raaaaah!
KEH HEE HEE! WE GOT TIED UP TAKING OUT THE TRASH.
AND ACTUALLY, I HAVEN'T SEEN YOU PEOPLE IN AGES! NOT THAT I WAS WORRIED ABOUT YOU OR ANYTHING!
WELL, BETWEEN THIS AND THAT, IT LOOKS LIKE THE GANG'S ALL HERE!
THANKS FOR HEALING ME.
YOU'RE WEL-COME.
FOR STARTERS, EVERYBODY COME EAT SOMETHING!!
THROUGH ALL SORTS OF EXPERIMENTS, I MADE MYSELF INTO A HIGHER BEING!
THEN I OBTAINED THE TALENTS OF THE ULTIMATE DEVIL'S HOST!!

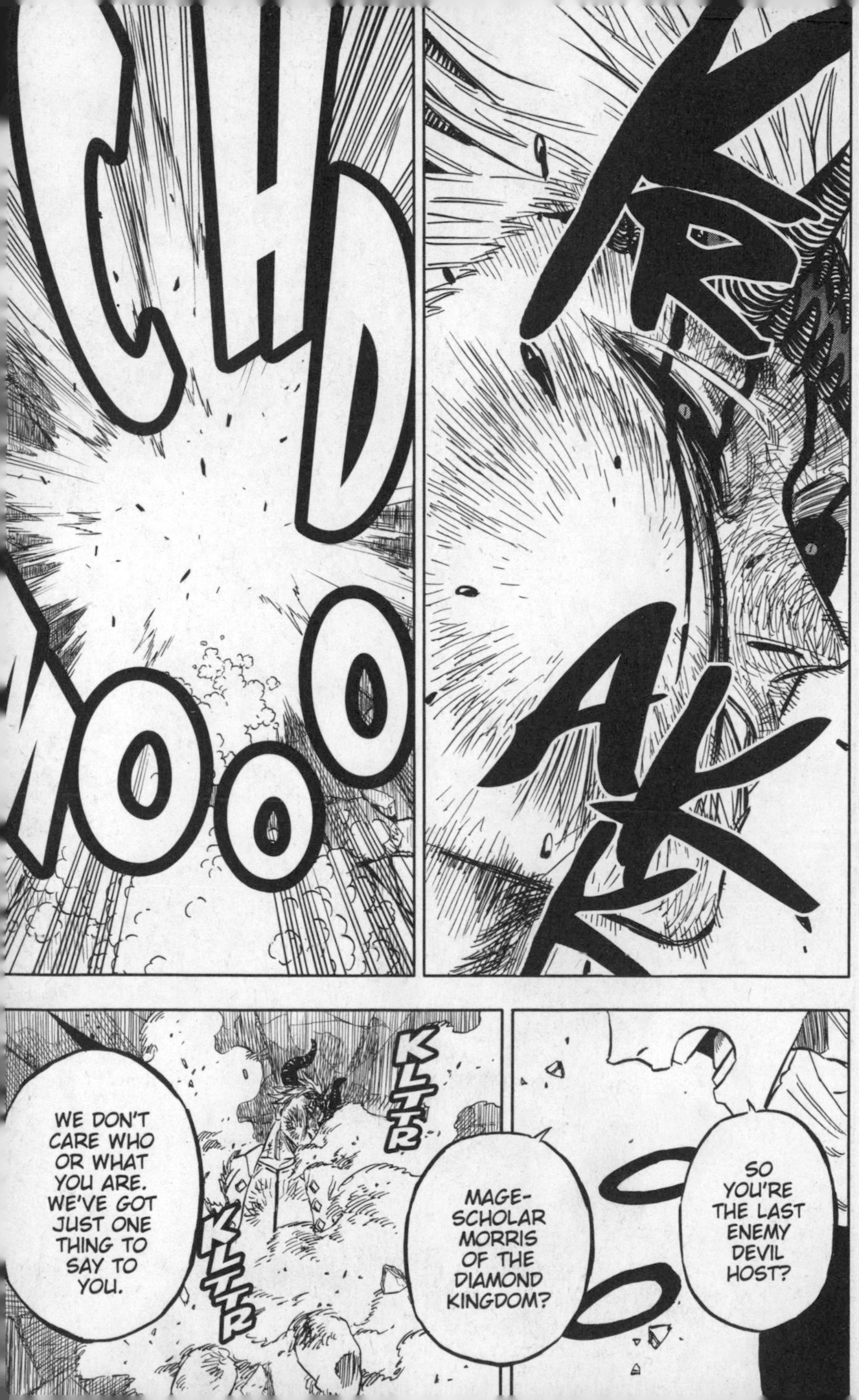
SO YOU'RE THE LAST ENEMY DEVIL HOST?
MAGE-SCHOLAR MORRIS OF THE DIAMOND KINGDOM?
KLTTR
KLTTR
WE DON'T CARE WHO OR WHAT YOU ARE. WE'VE GOT JUST ONE THING TO SAY TO YOU.

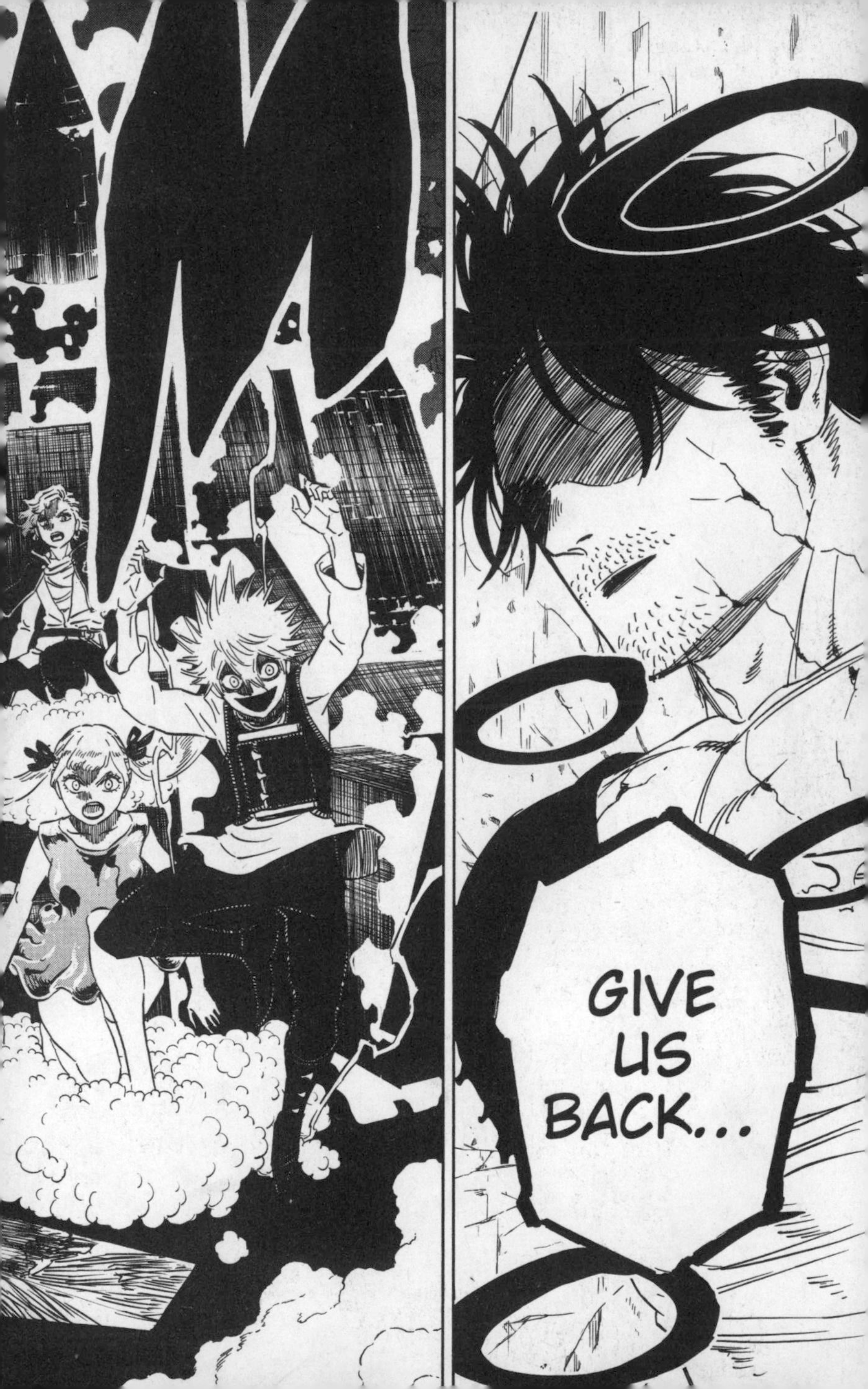
GIVE US BACK...

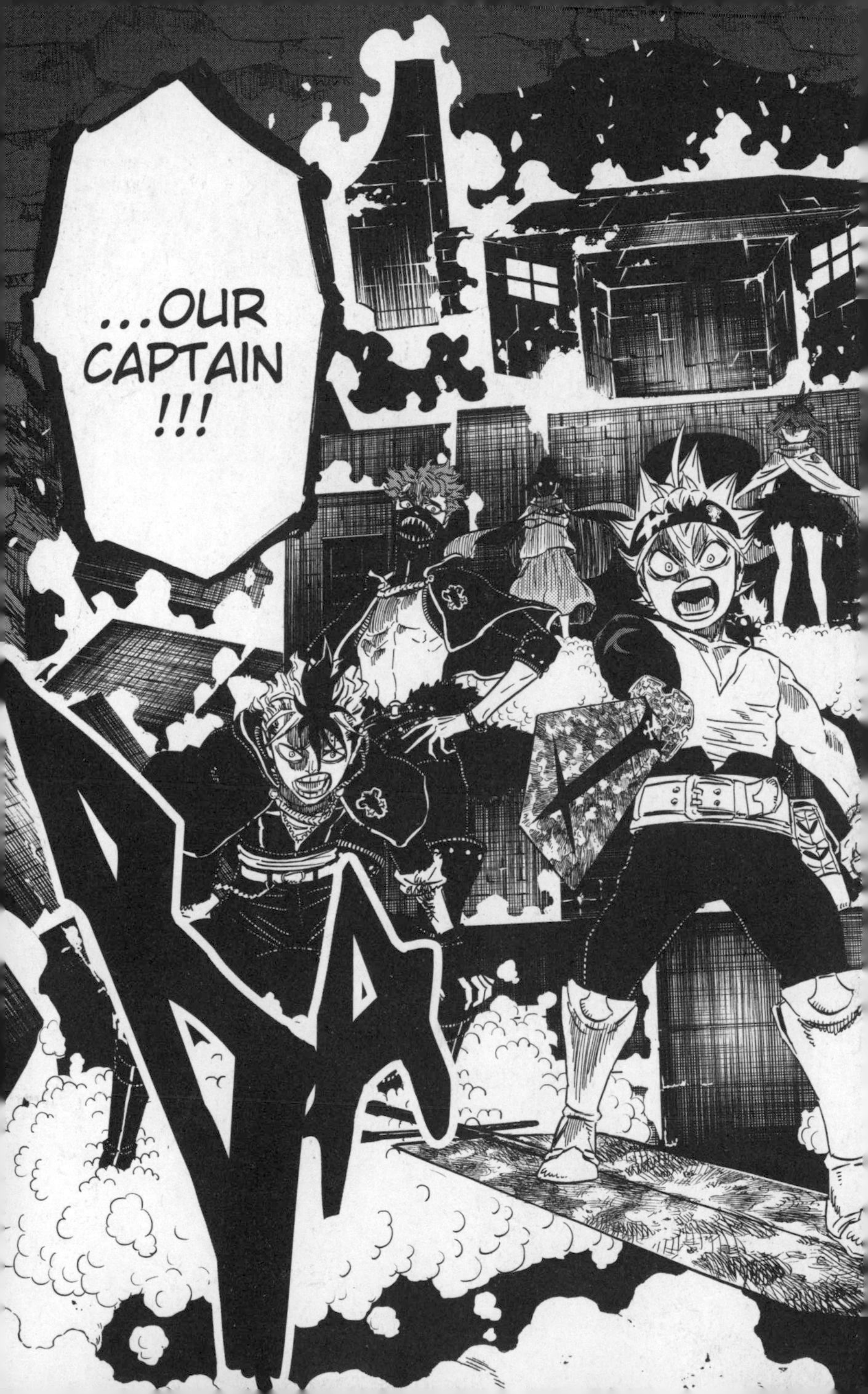
...OUR CAPTAIN !!!

This is super-arbitrary and sudden, so I'm really sorry, but the Assorted Questions Brigade pages will end with this volume.

I've been getting more questions I just can't answer about what's going to happen next in the story, for example, and I started feeling bad that people were sending in postcards for nothing... I'm sorry!!!

We're still accepting submissions for fan art, so do keep sending in your artwork!!!

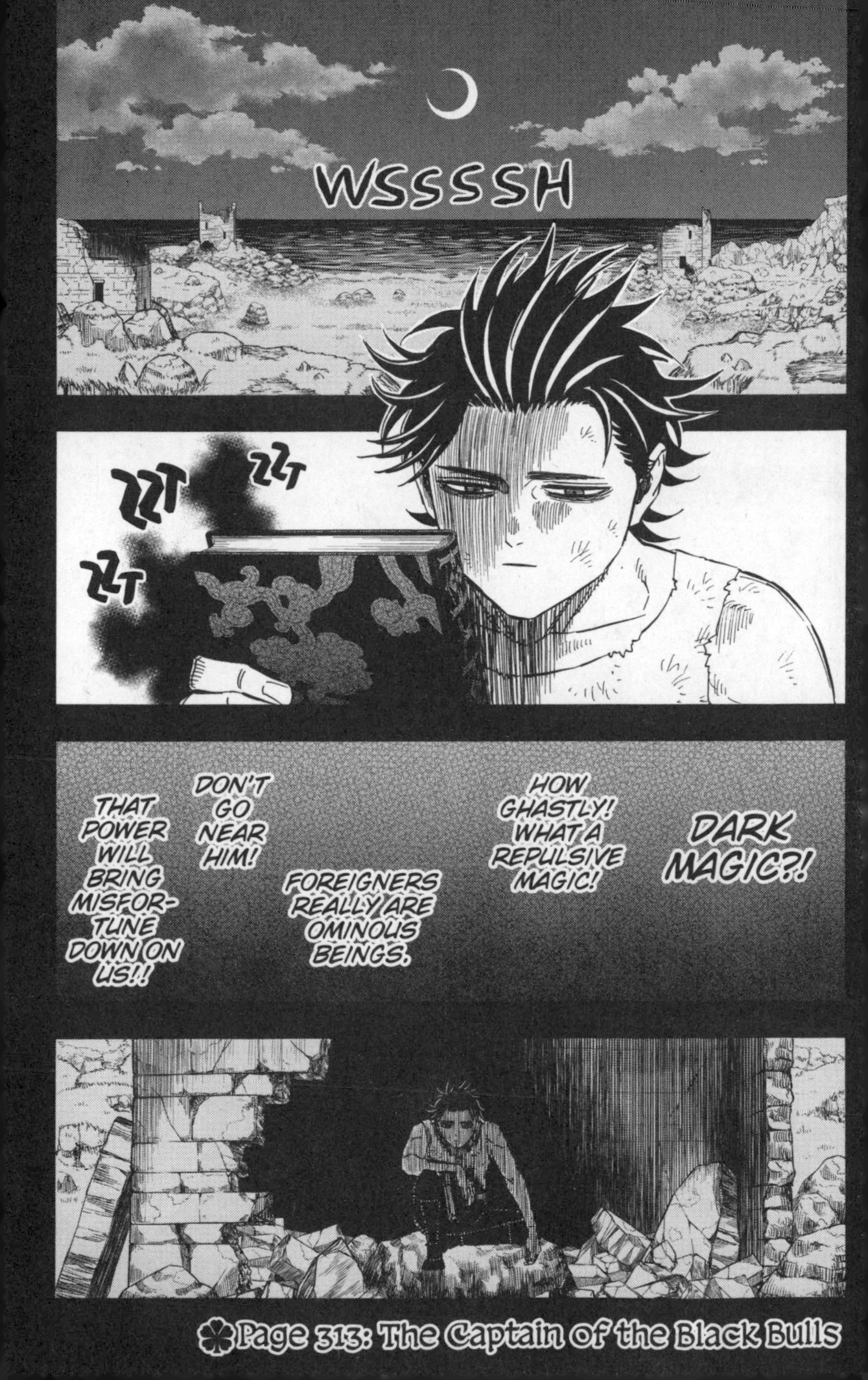
WSSSSH
ZZT
ZZT
ZZT
DARK MAGIC?!
HOW GHASTLY! WHAT A REPULSIVE MAGIC!
FOREIGNERS REALLY ARE OMINOUS BEINGS.
DON'T GO NEAR HIM!
THAT POWER WILL BRING MISFOR-TUNE DOWN ON US!!

Page 313: The Captain of the Black Bulls

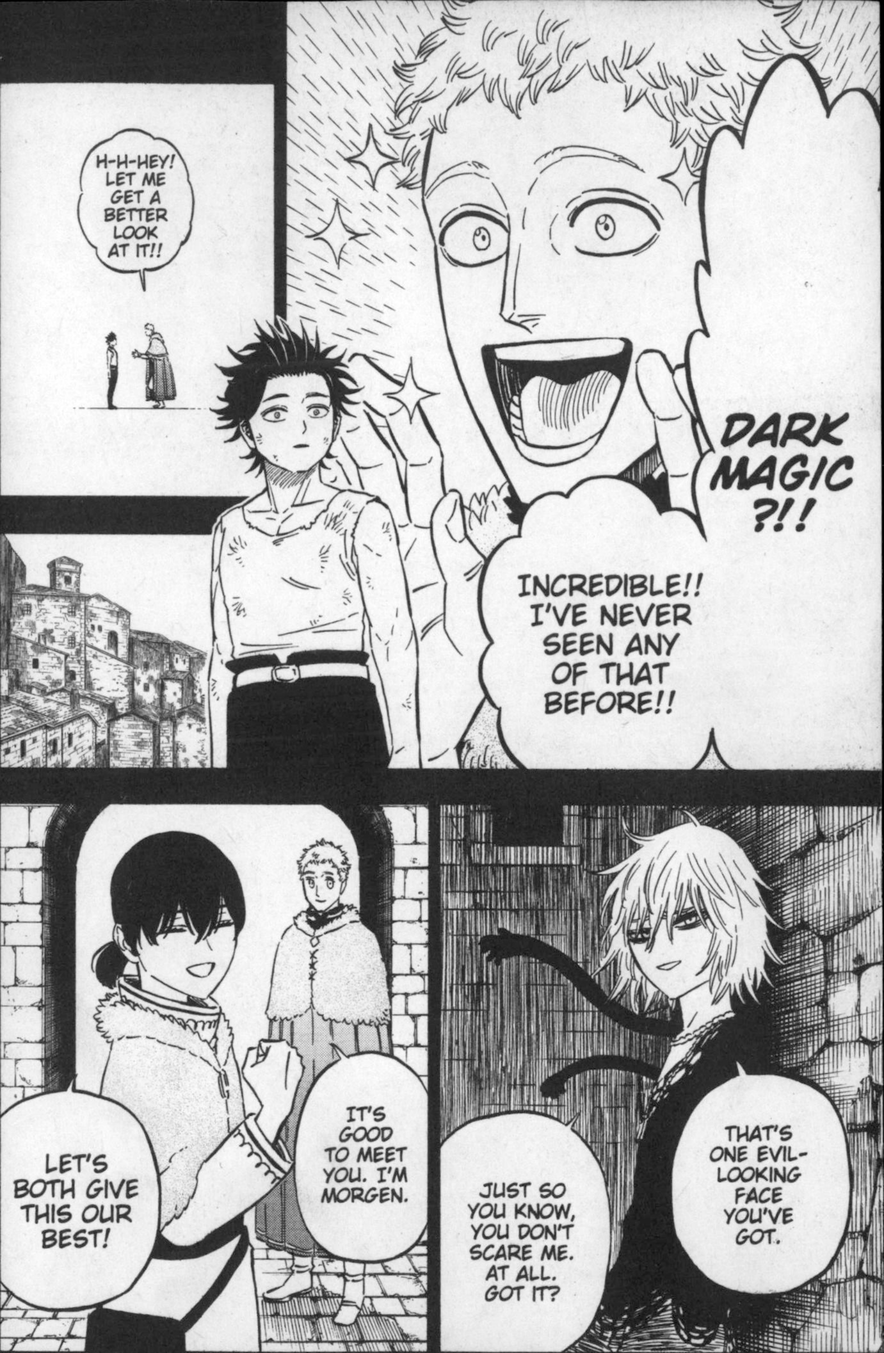
DARK MAGIC?!!
INCREDIBLE!! I'VE NEVER SEEN ANY OF THAT BEFORE!!
H-H-HEY! LET ME GET A BETTER LOOK AT IT!!
THAT'S ONE EVIL-LOOKING FACE YOU'VE GOT.
JUST SO YOU KNOW, YOU DON'T SCARE ME. AT ALL. GOT IT?
IT'S GOOD TO MEET YOU. I'M MORGEN.
LET'S BOTH GIVE THIS OUR BEST!

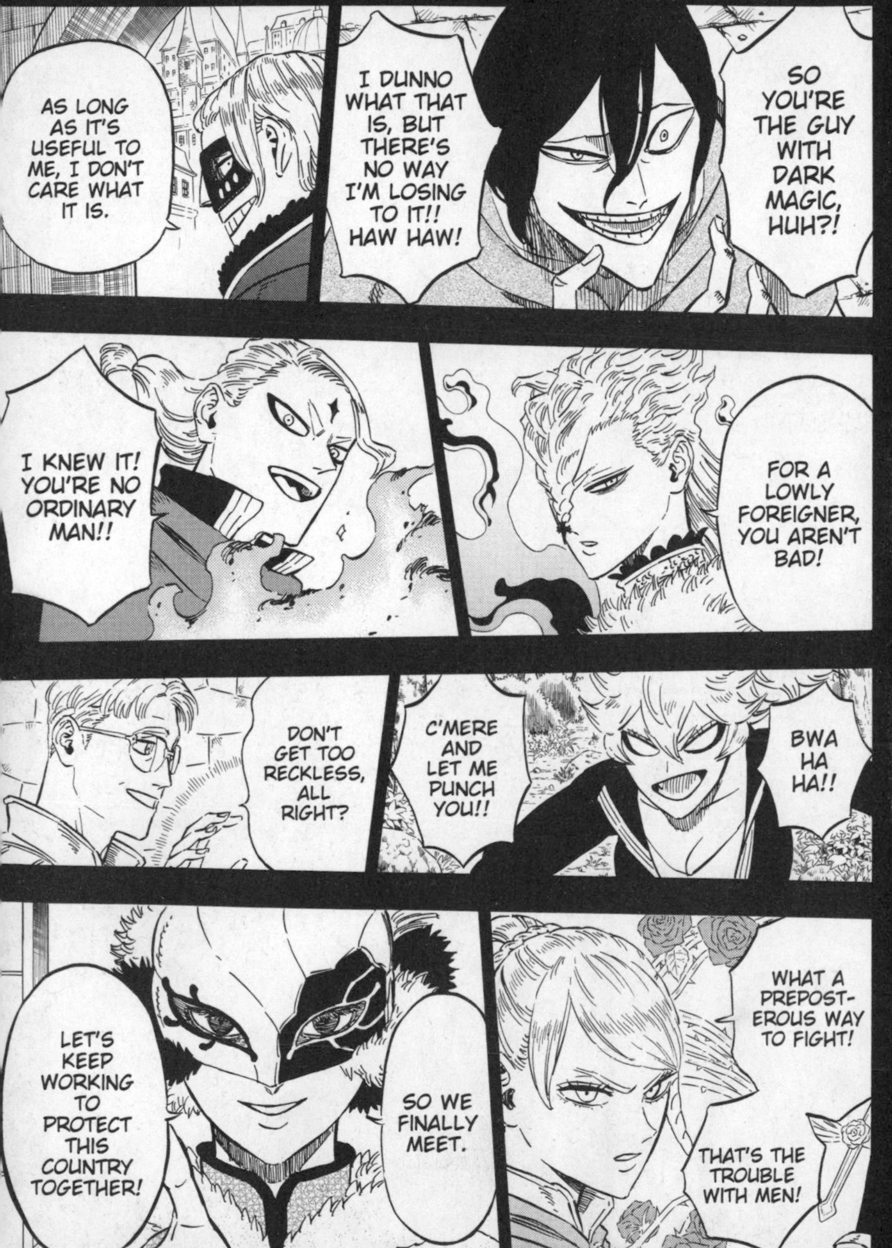
SO YOU'RE THE GUY WITH DARK MAGIC, HUH?!
I DUNNO WHAT THAT IS, BUT THERE'S NO WAY I'M LOSING TO IT!! HAW HAW!
AS LONG AS IT'S USEFUL TO ME, I DON'T CARE WHAT IT IS.
FOR A LOWLY FOREIGNER, YOU AREN'T BAD!
I KNEW IT! YOU'RE NO ORDINARY MAN!!
BWA HA HA!!
C'MERE AND LET ME PUNCH YOU!!
DON'T GET TOO RECKLESS, ALL RIGHT?
WHAT A PREPOST-EROUS WAY TO FIGHT!
THAT'S THE TROUBLE WITH MEN!
SO WE FINALLY MEET.
LET'S KEEP WORKING TO PROTECT THIS COUNTRY TOGETHER!

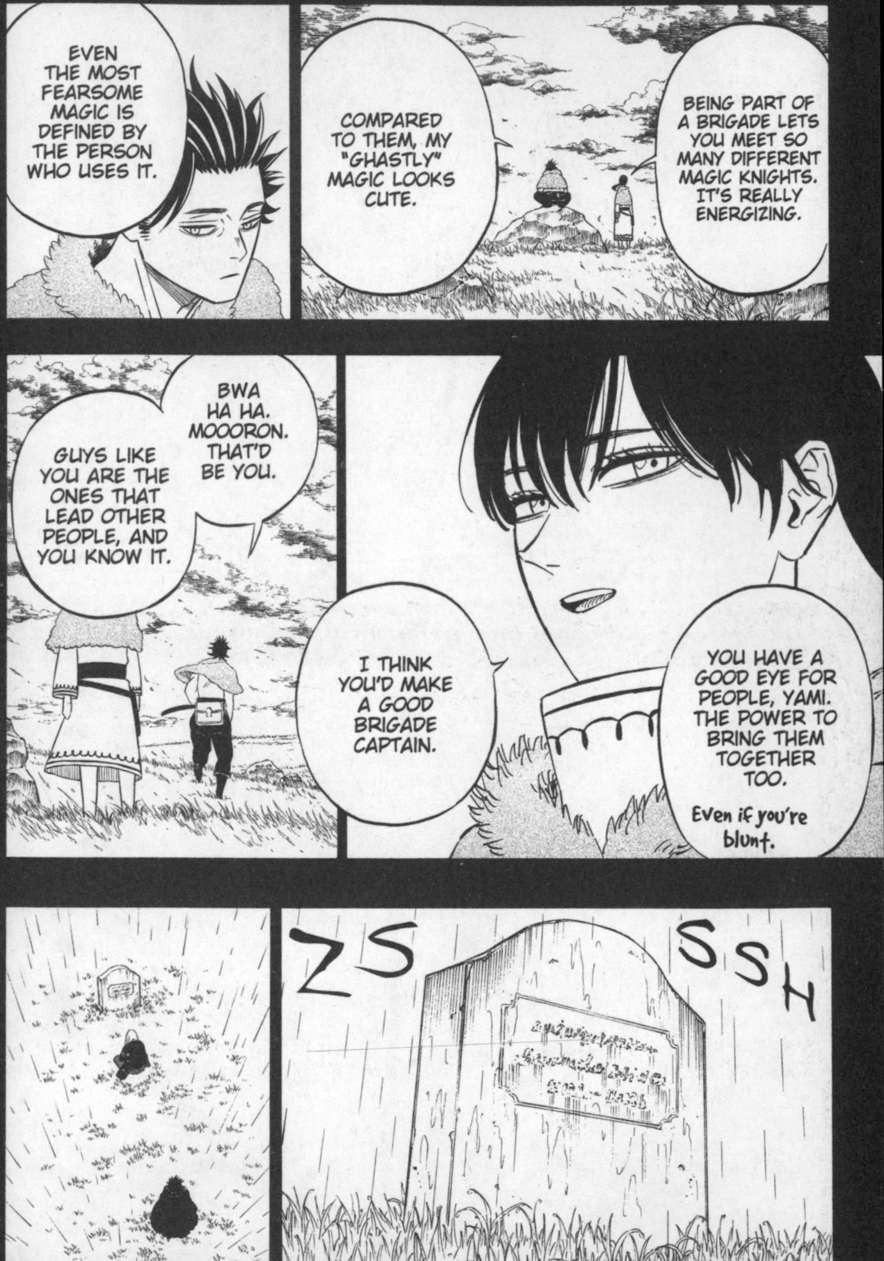
BEING PART OF A BRIGADE LETS YOU MEET SO MANY DIFFERENT MAGIC KNIGHTS. IT'S REALLY ENERGIZING.
COMPARED TO THEM, MY "GHASTLY" MAGIC LOOKS CUTE.
EVEN THE MOST FEARSOME MAGIC IS DEFINED BY THE PERSON WHO USES IT.
YOU HAVE A GOOD EYE FOR PEOPLE, YAMI. THE POWER TO BRING THEM TOGETHER TOO.
Even if you're blunt.
I THINK YOU'D MAKE A GOOD BRIGADE CAPTAIN.
BWA HA HA. MOOORON. THAT'D BE YOU.
GUYS LIKE YOU ARE THE ONES THAT LEAD OTHER PEOPLE, AND YOU KNOW IT.
ZS SSH

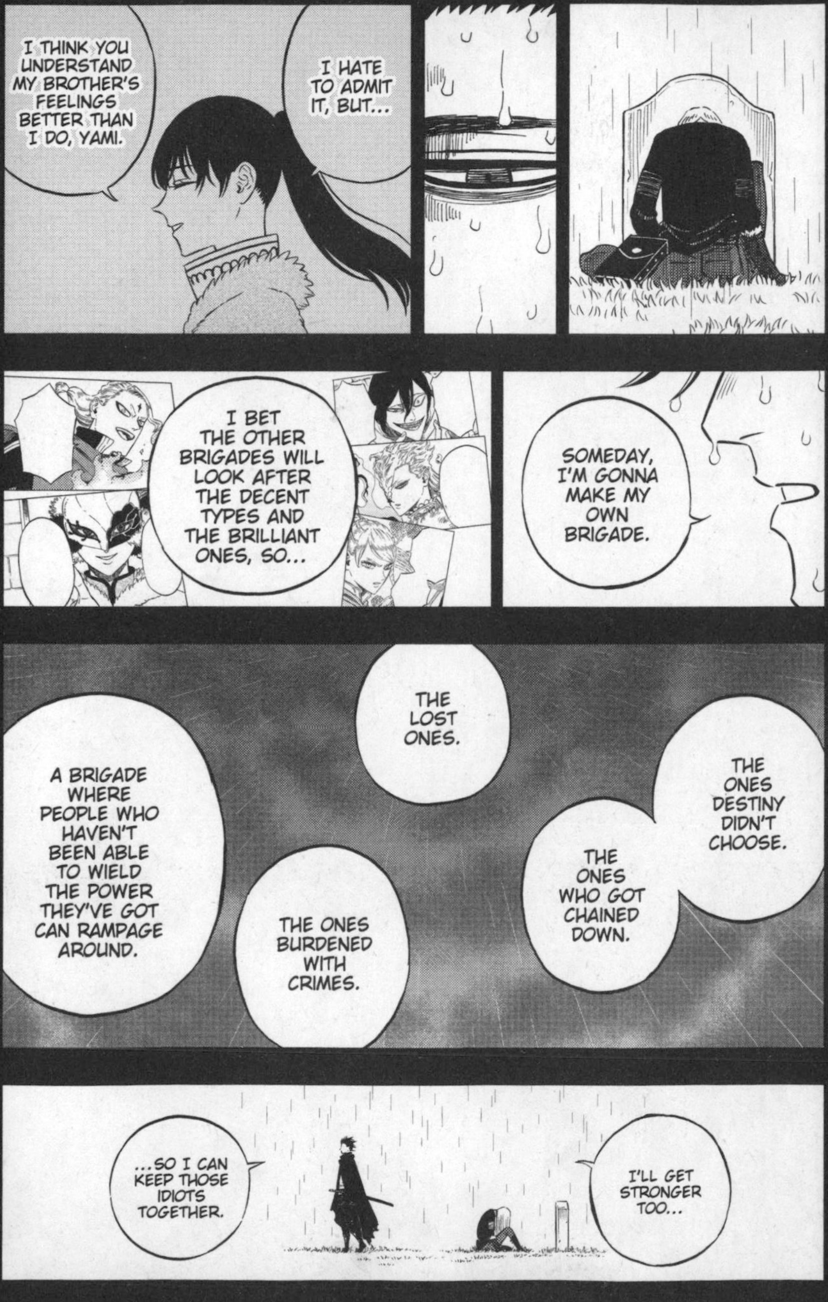
I HATE TO ADMIT IT, BUT...
I THINK YOU UNDERSTAND MY BROTHER'S FEELINGS BETTER THAN I DO, YAMI.
SOMEDAY, I'M GONNA MAKE MY OWN BRIGADE.
I BET THE OTHER BRIGADES WILL LOOK AFTER THE DECENT TYPES AND THE BRILLIANT ONES, SO...
THE LOST ONES.
THE ONES DESTINY DIDN'T CHOOSE.
THE ONES WHO GOT CHAINED DOWN.
THE ONES BURDENED WITH CRIMES.
A BRIGADE WHERE PEOPLE WHO HAVEN'T BEEN ABLE TO WIELD THE POWER THEY'VE GOT CAN RAMPAGE AROUND.
I'LL GET STRONGER TOO...
...SO I CAN KEEP THOSE IDIOTS TOGETHER.

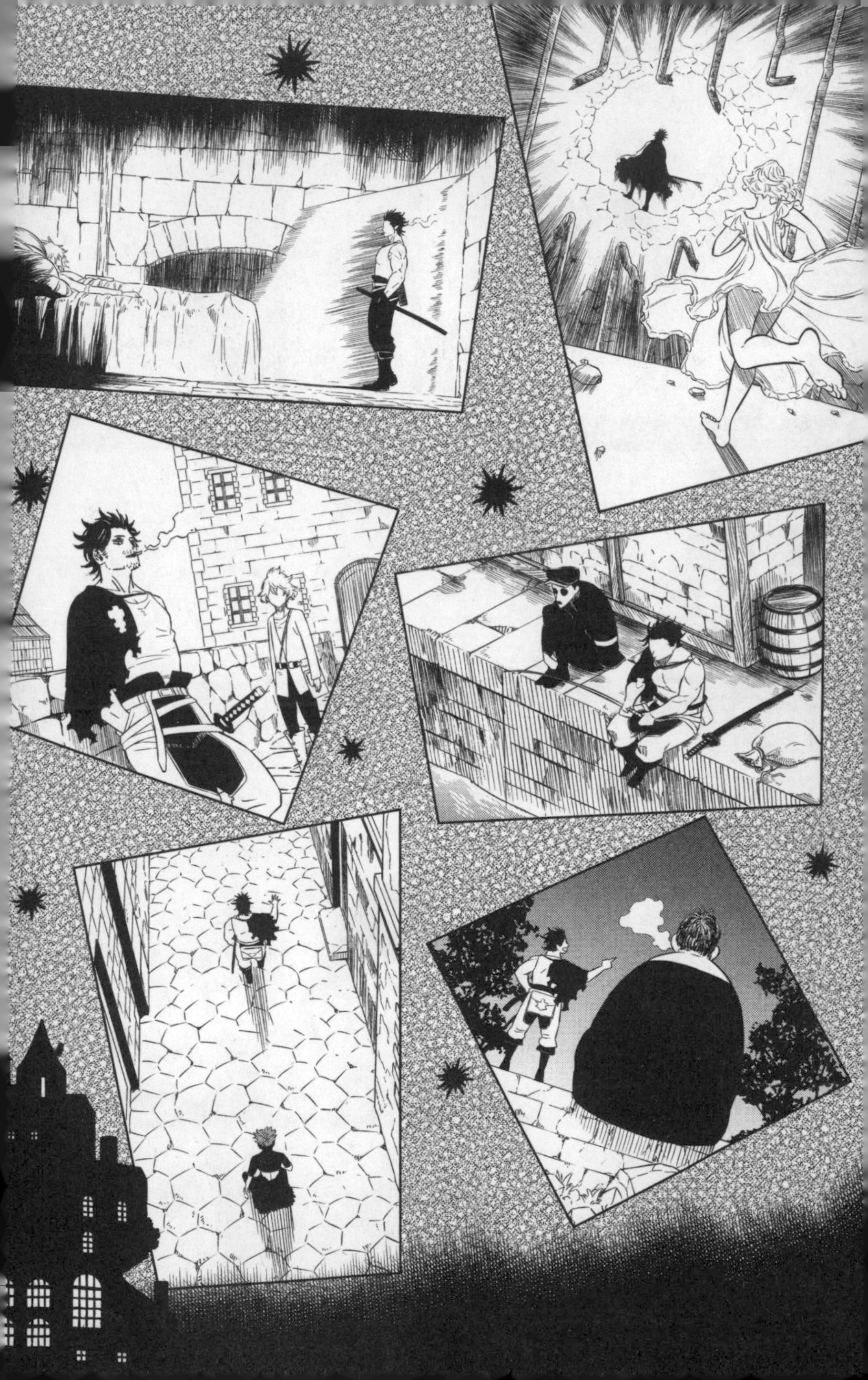

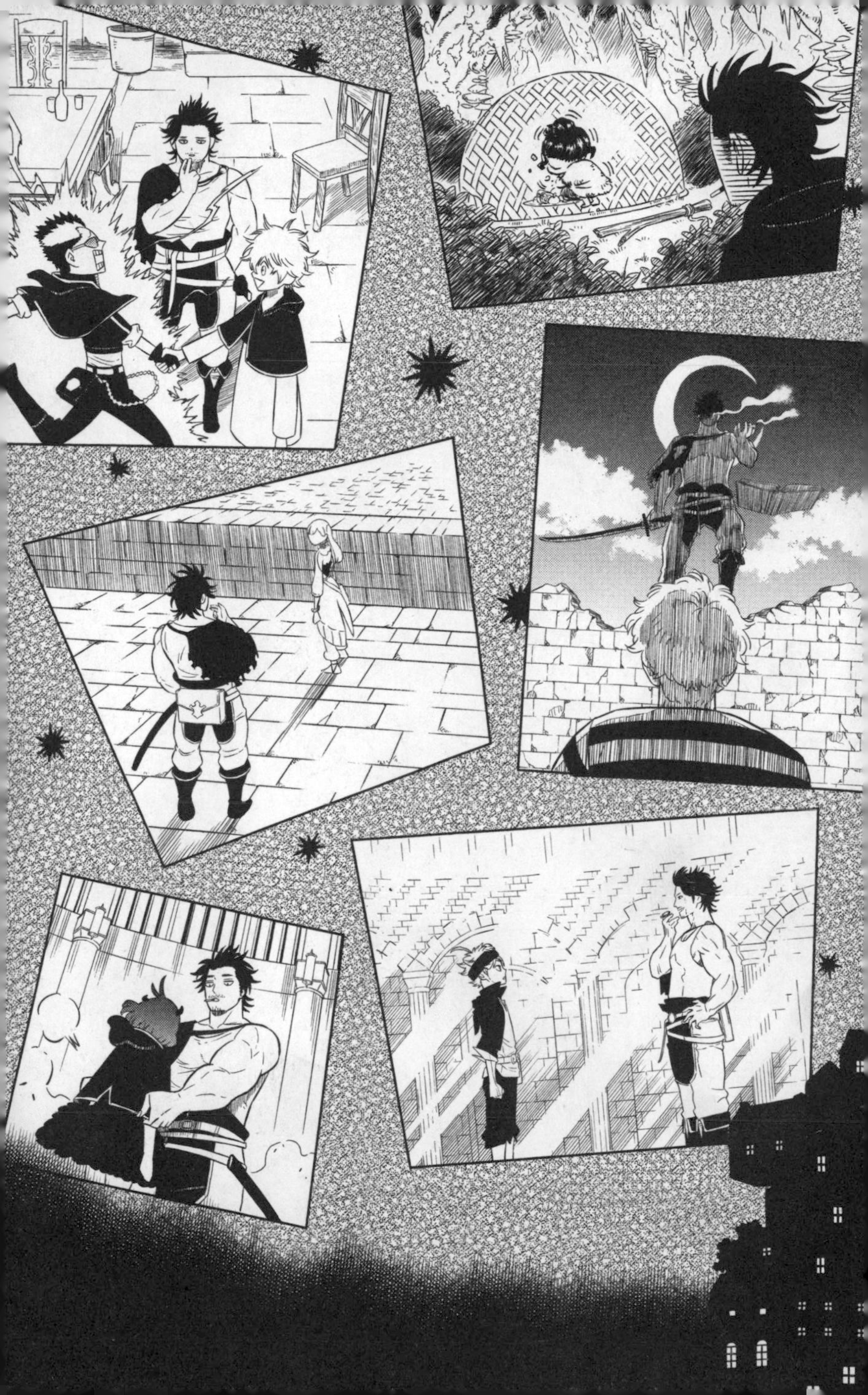

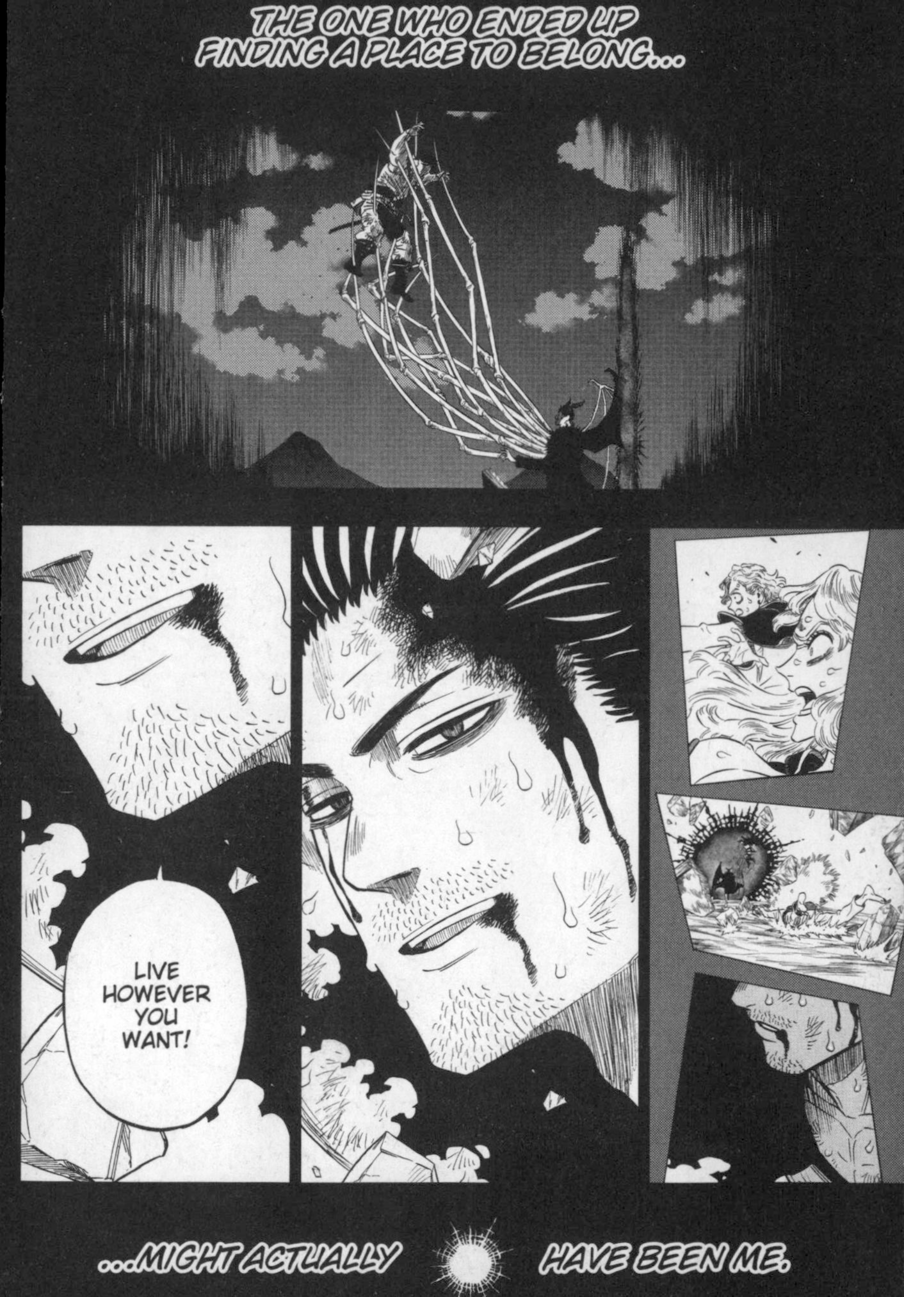
THE ONE WHO ENDED UP FINDING A PLACE TO BELONG...
LIVE HOWEVER YOU WANT!
...MIGHT ACTUALLY HAVE BEEN ME.

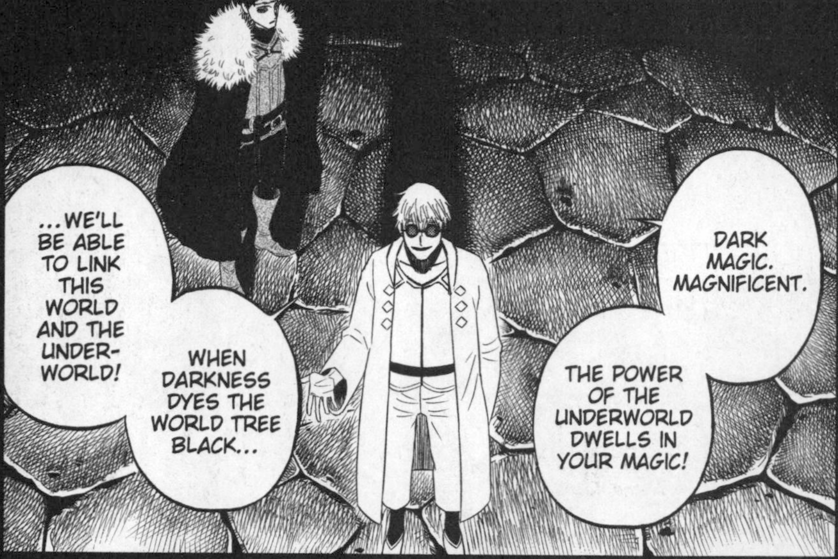
DARK MAGIC. MAGNIFICENT.
THE POWER OF THE UNDERWORLD DWELLS IN YOUR MAGIC!
WHEN DARKNESS DYES THE WORLD TREE BLACK...
...WE'LL BE ABLE TO LINK THIS WORLD AND THE UNDER-WORLD!

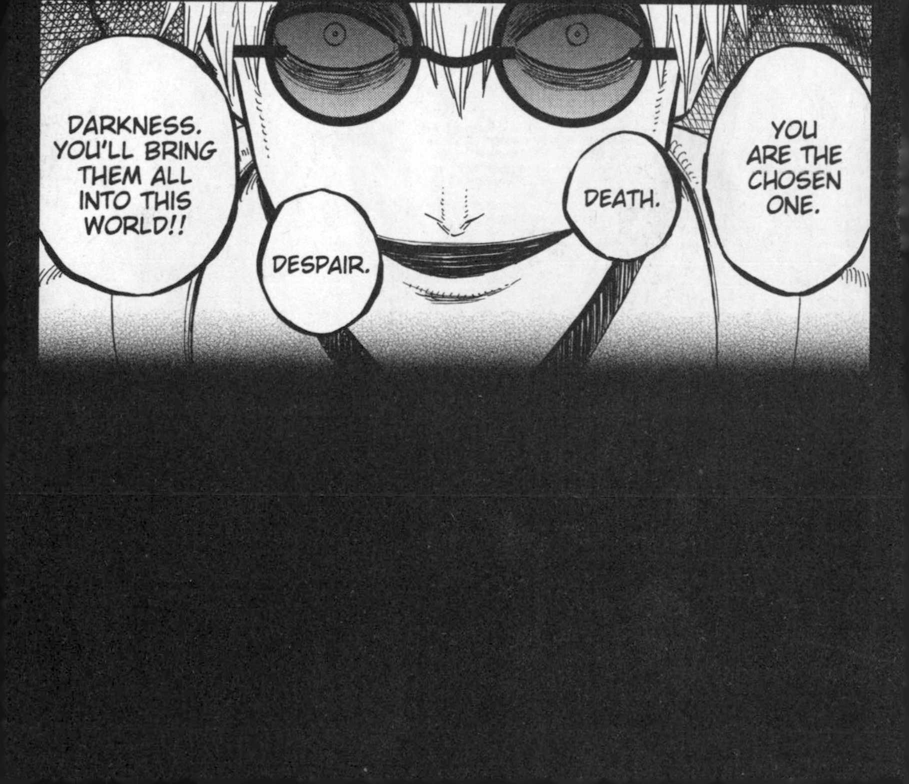
YOU ARE THE CHOSEN ONE.
DEATH.
DESPAIR.
DARKNESS. YOU'LL BRING THEM ALL INTO THIS WORLD!!

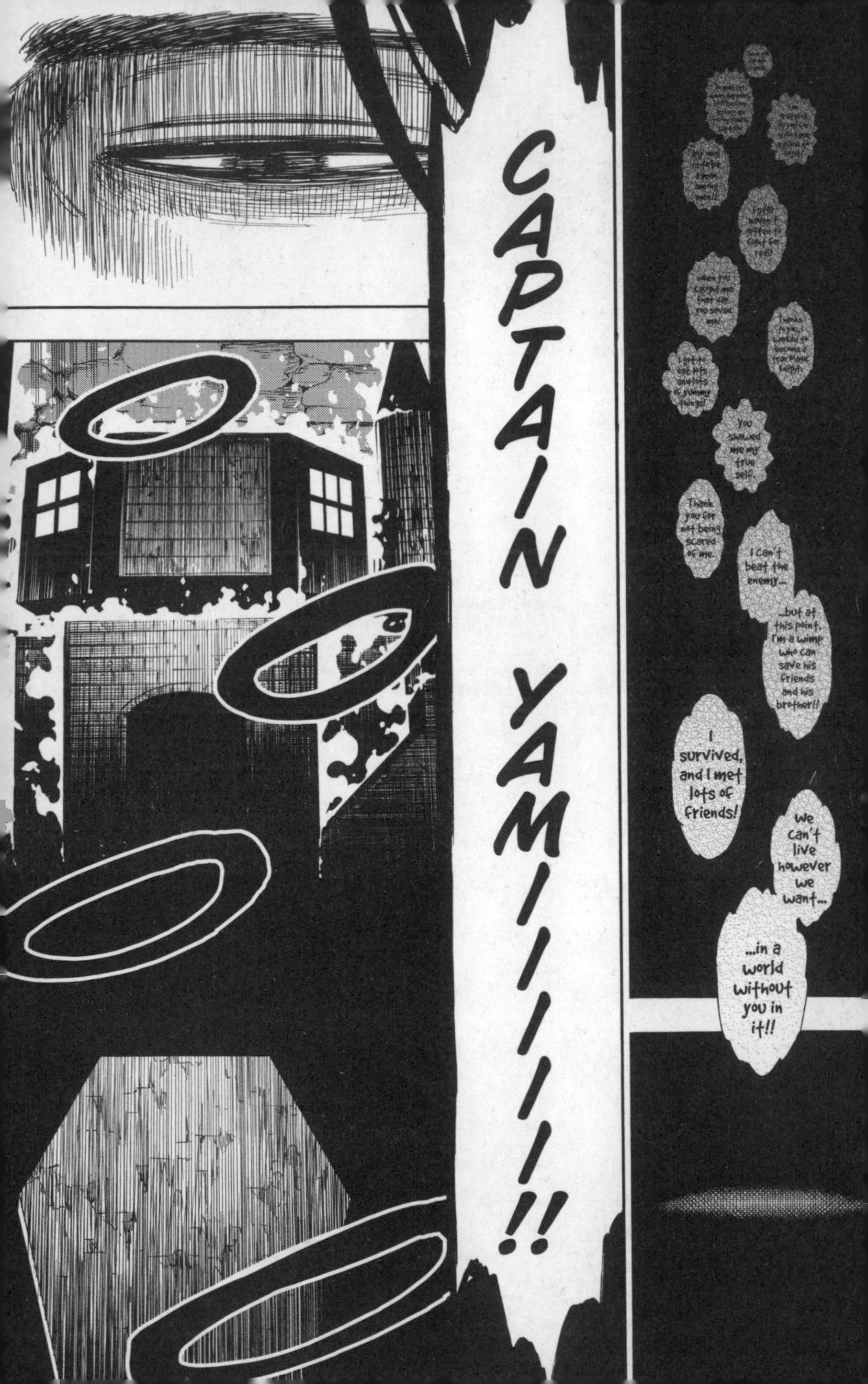
When you caught me that day, you saved me!
Thanks to you, I worked to become a true Magic Knight.
I got to eat lots and lots of yummy things!
You showed me my true self.
Thank you for not being scared of me.
I can't beat the enemy...
...but at this point, I'm a wimp who can save his friends and his brother!!
I survived, and I met lots of friends!
We can't live however we want...
...in a world without you in it!!
CAPTAIN YAMIIIIIII!!

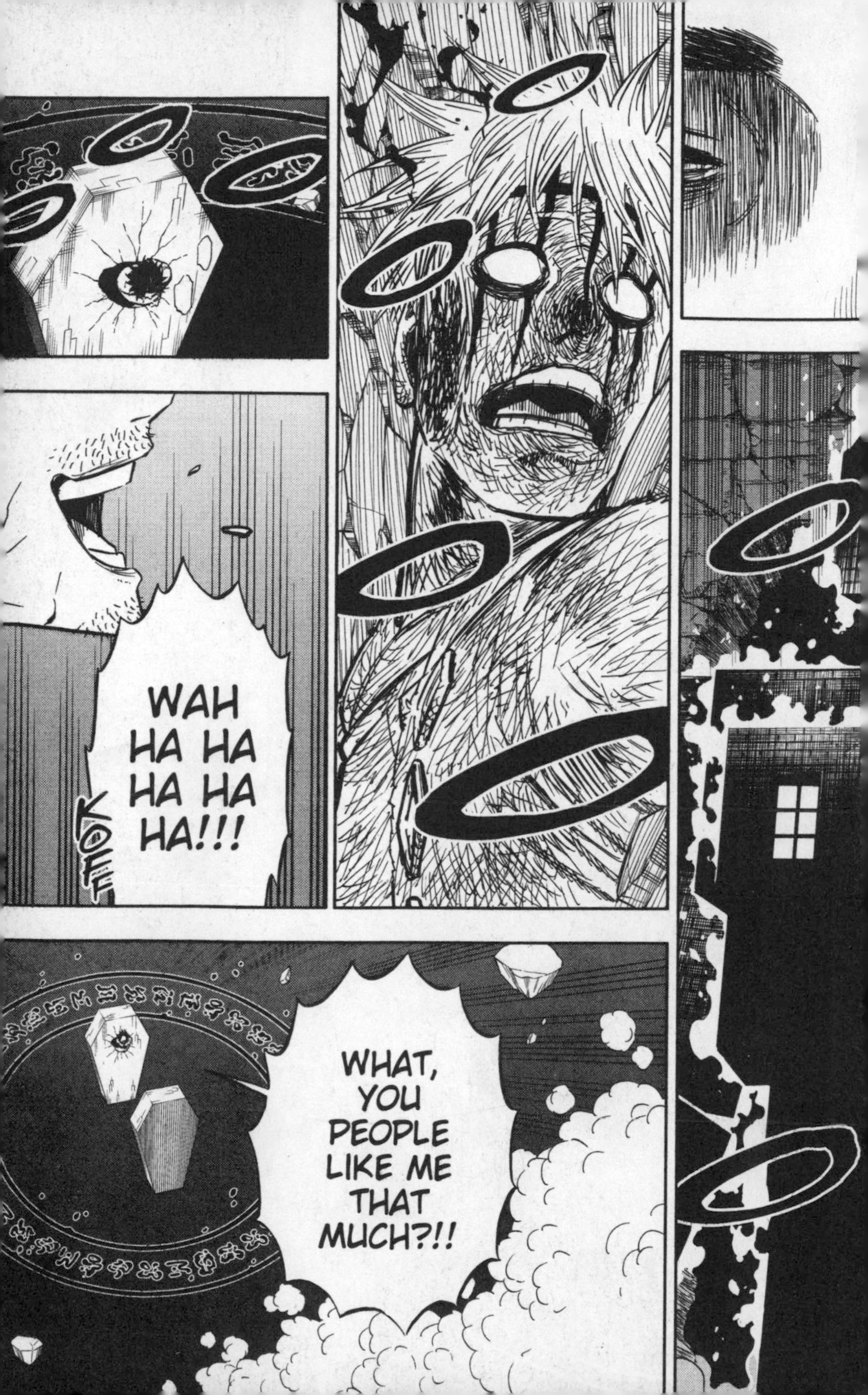
WAH HA HA HA HA HA!!!
KOFF
WHAT, YOU PEOPLE LIKE ME THAT MUCH?!!

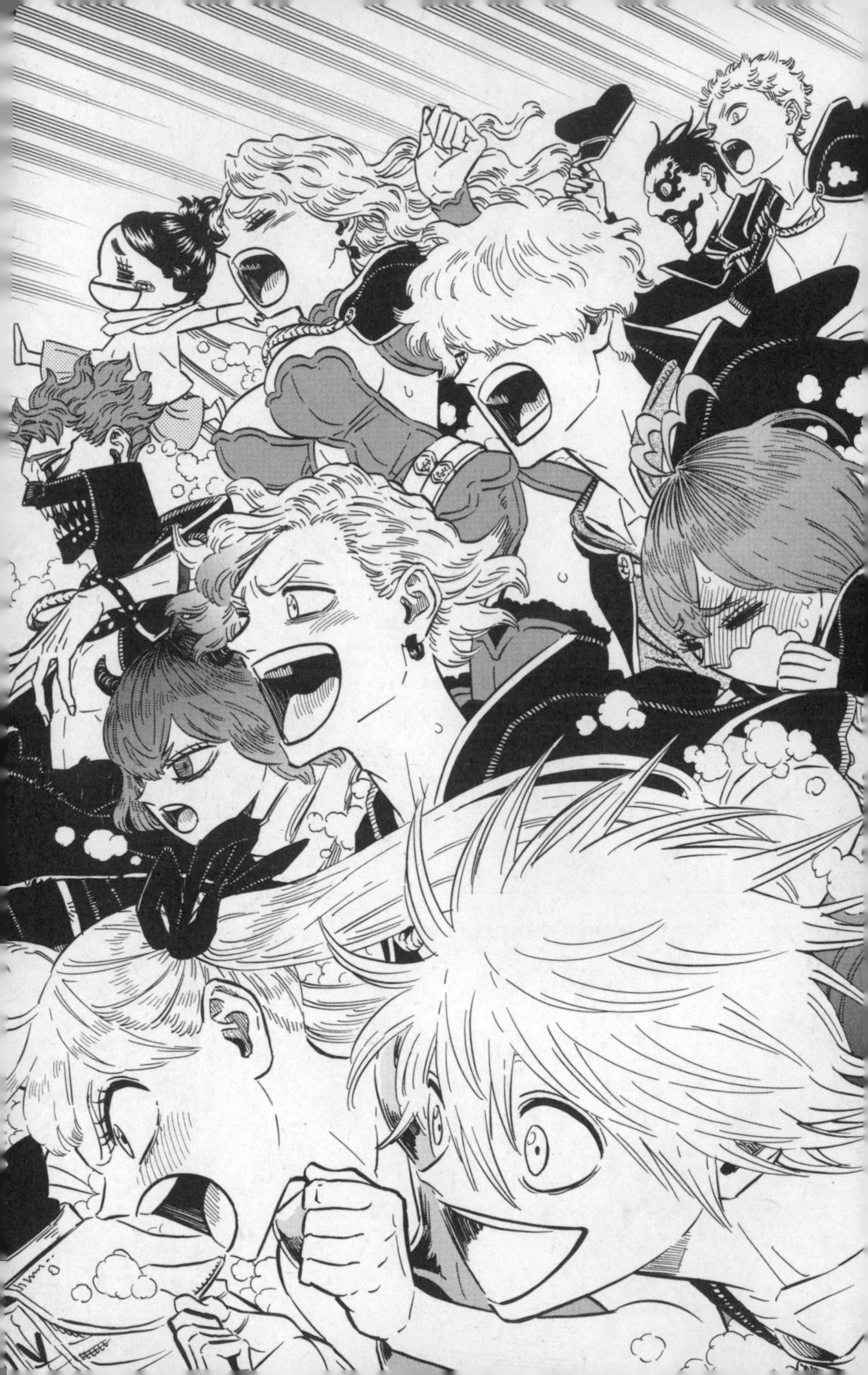

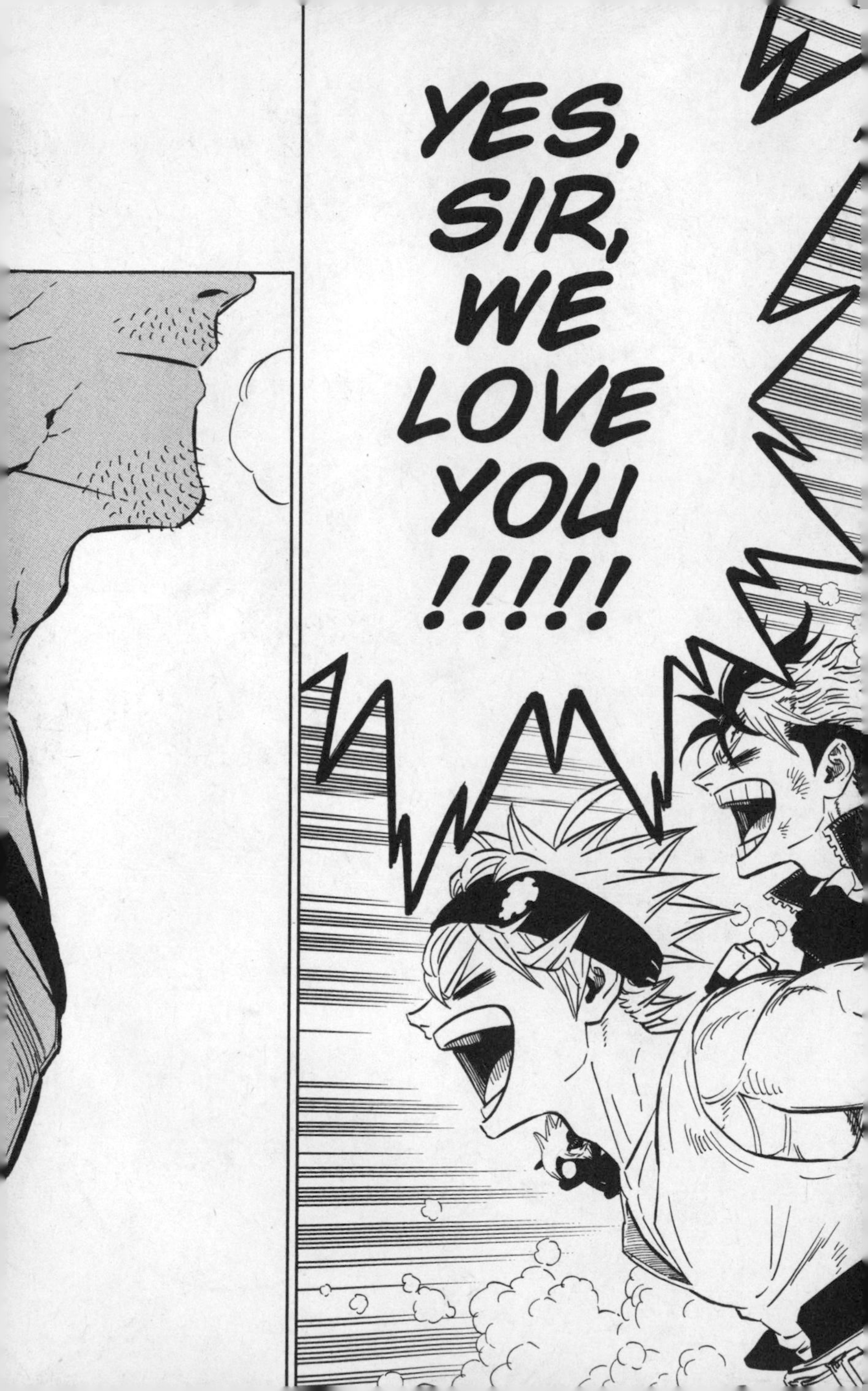
YES, SIR, WE LOVE YOU!!!!!

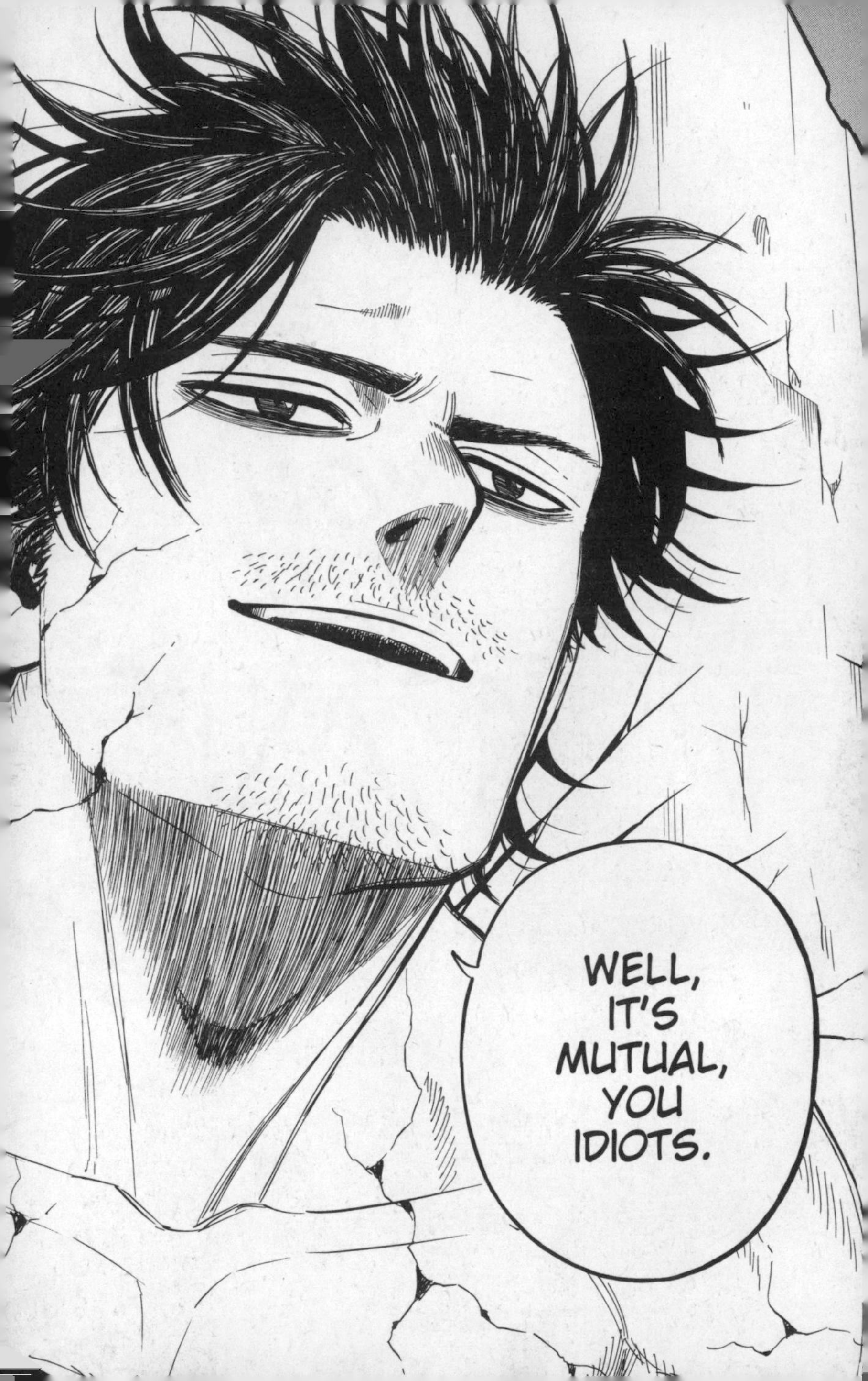
WELL, IT'S MUTUAL, YOU IDIOTS.

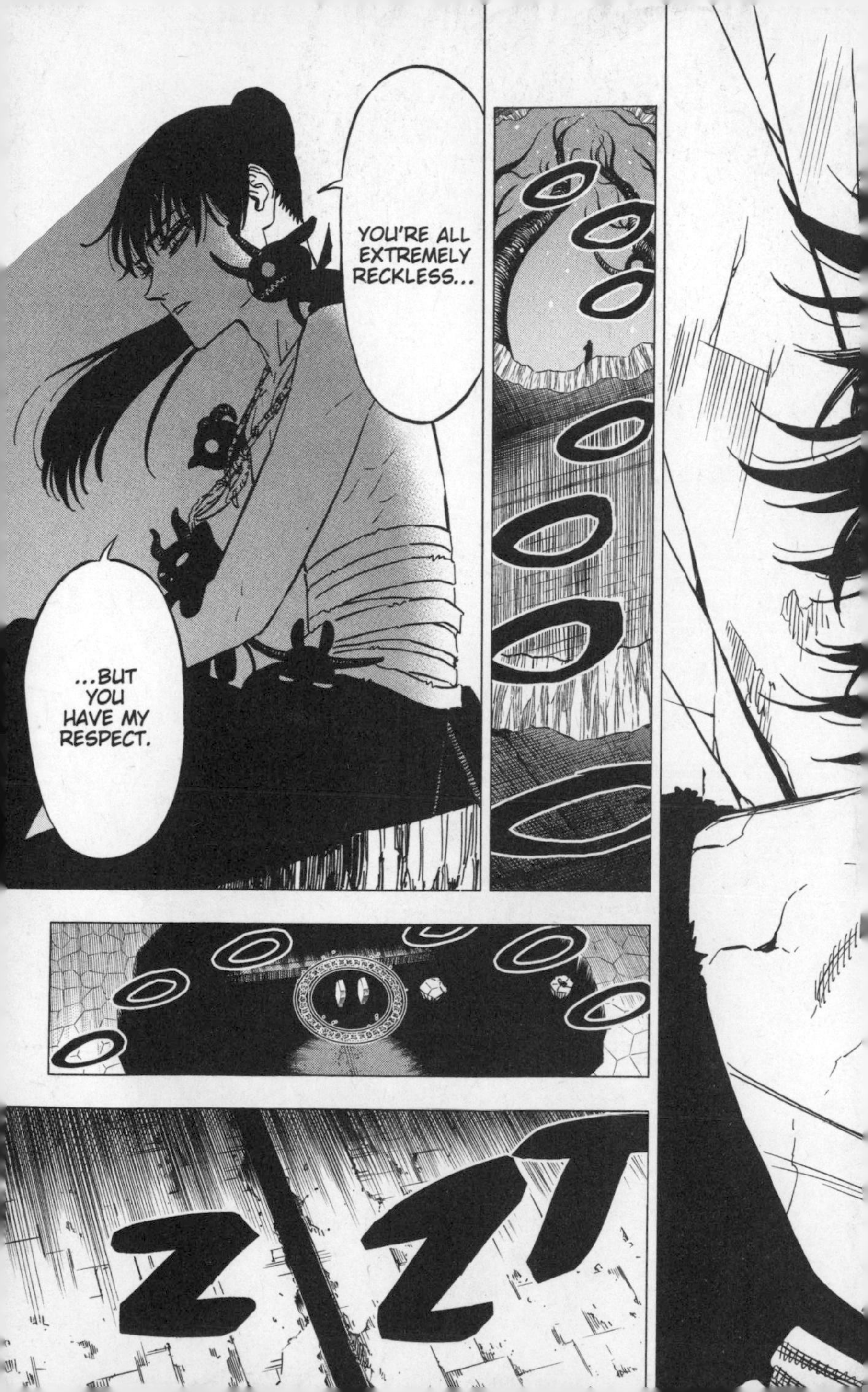
YOU'RE ALL EXTREMELY RECKLESS...
...BUT YOU HAVE MY RESPECT.

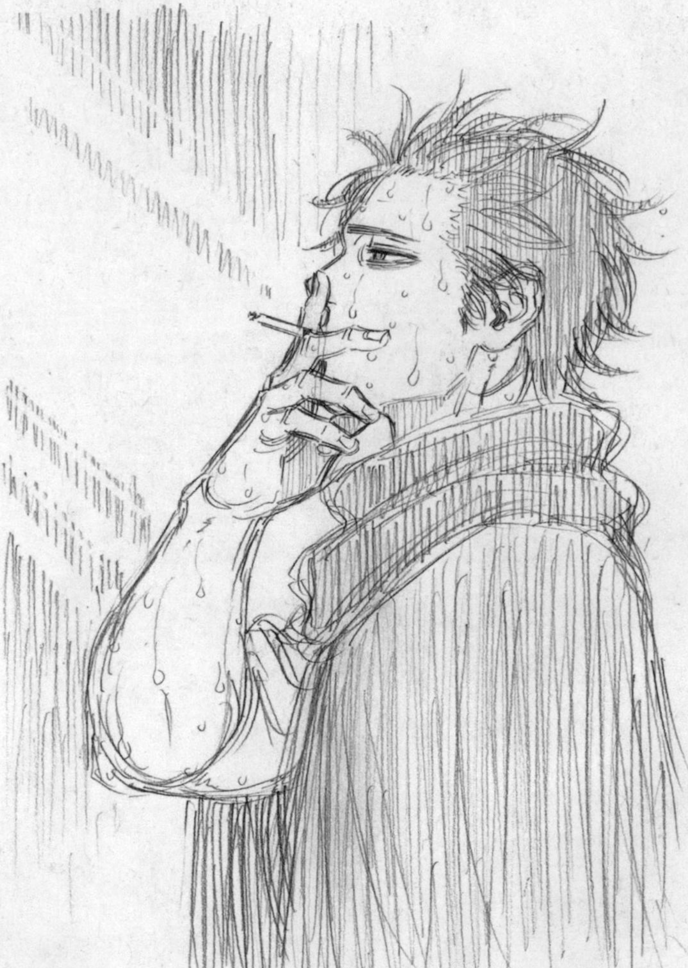

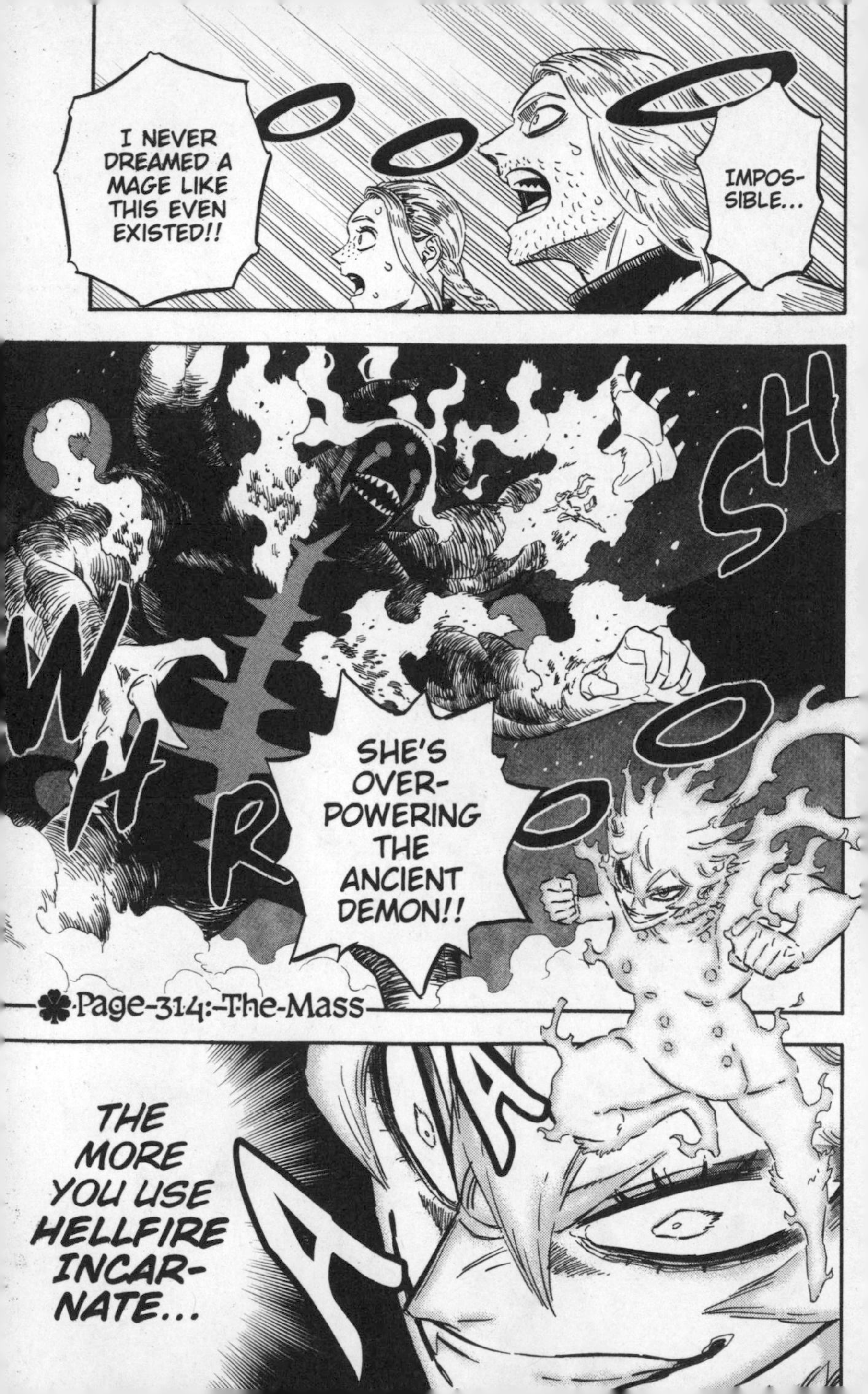
IMPOSSIBLE...
I NEVER DREAMED A MAGE LIKE THIS EVEN EXISTED!!
WHHROOOSH
SHE'S OVERPOWERING THE ANCIENT DEMON!!
Page 314: The Mass
THE MORE YOU USE HELLFIRE INCARNATE...

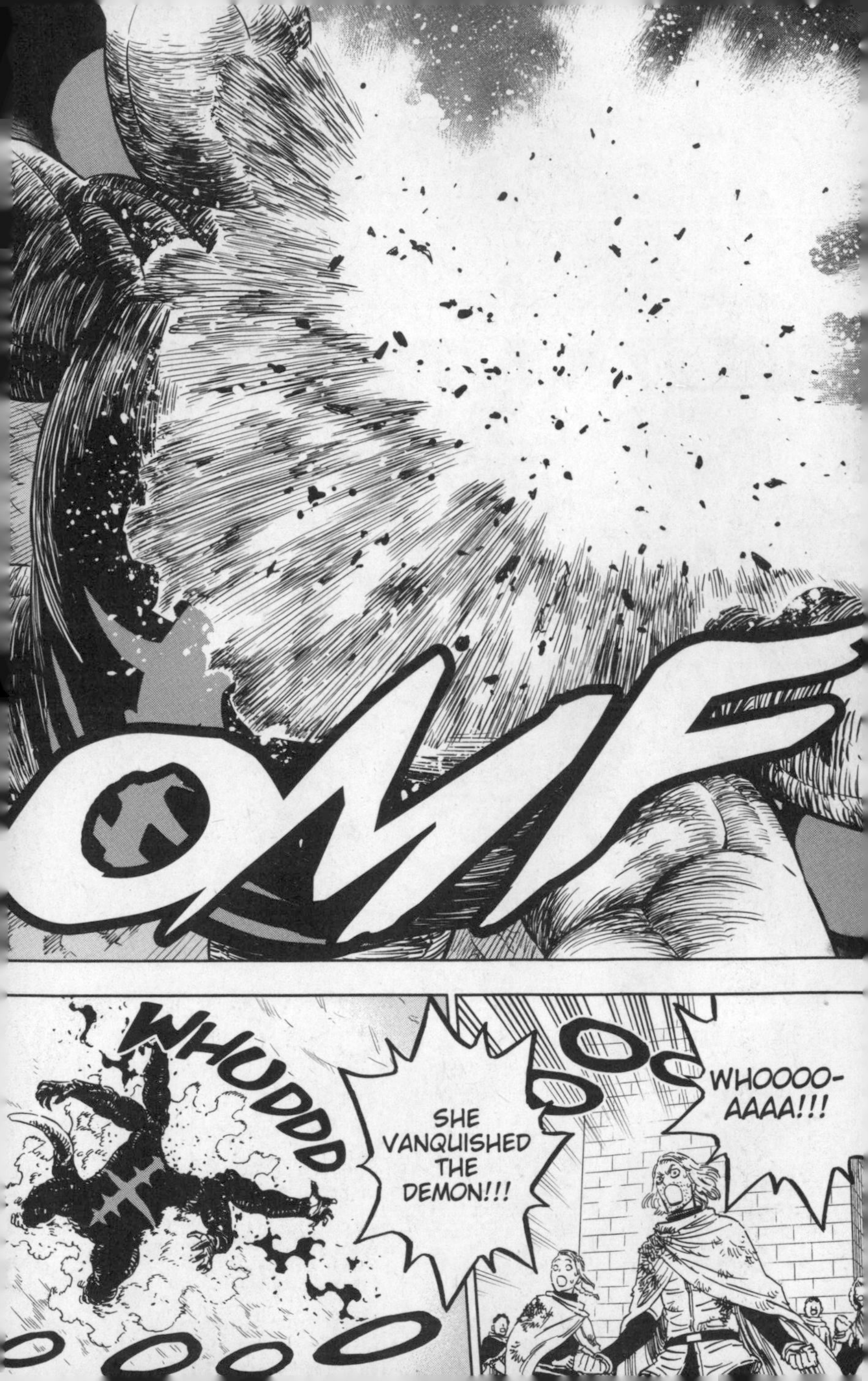
WHOOOO-
AAAA!!!
SHE VANQUISHED THE DEMON!!!
WHUDDD

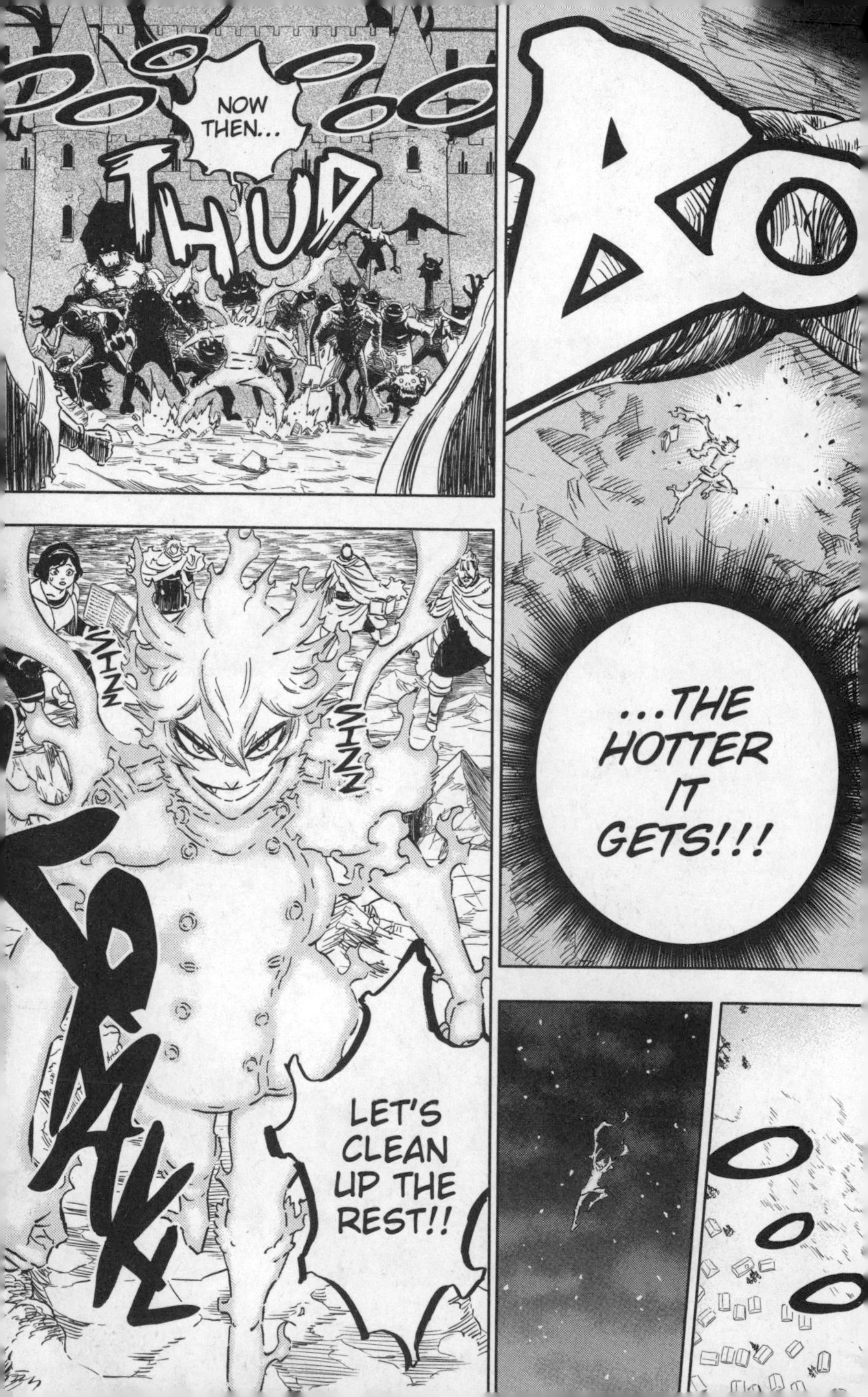
...THE HOTTER IT GETS!!!
NOW THEN...
THUD
SIZZ
SIZZ
LET'S CLEAN UP THE REST!!

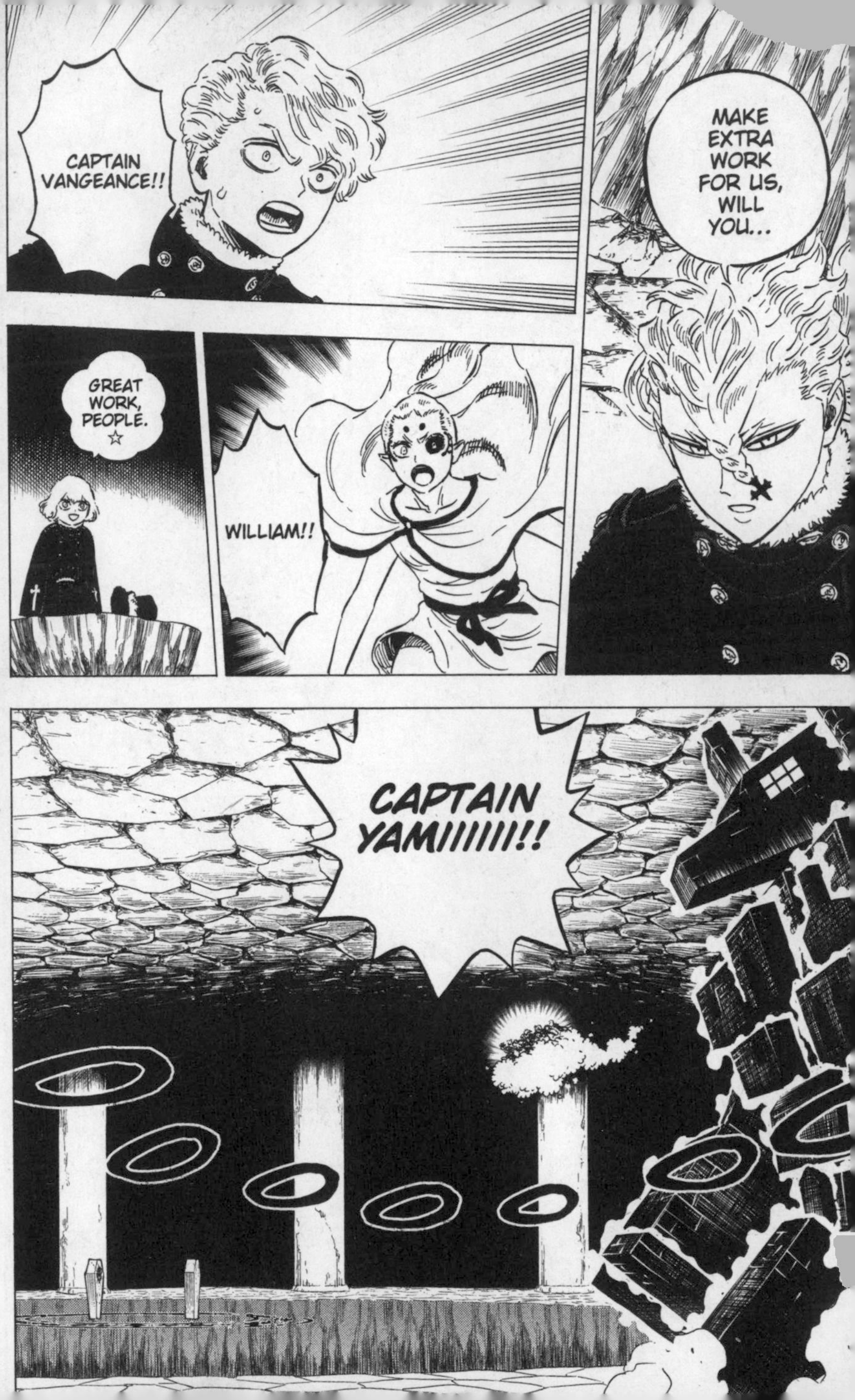
MAKE EXTRA WORK FOR US, WILL YOU...
CAPTAIN VANGEANCE!!
WILLIAM!!
GREAT WORK, PEOPLE. ☆
CAPTAIN YAMIIIIIII!!

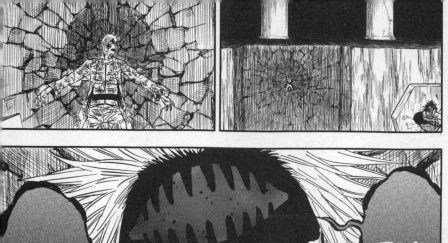

...human!!

Thank you for your service...

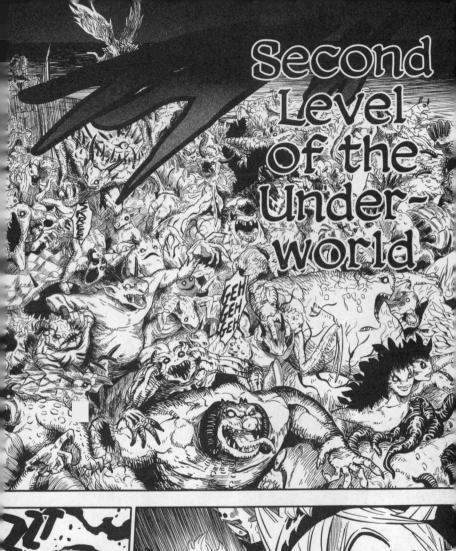

Second Level of the Underworld

The gates of the underworld are opening even faster...

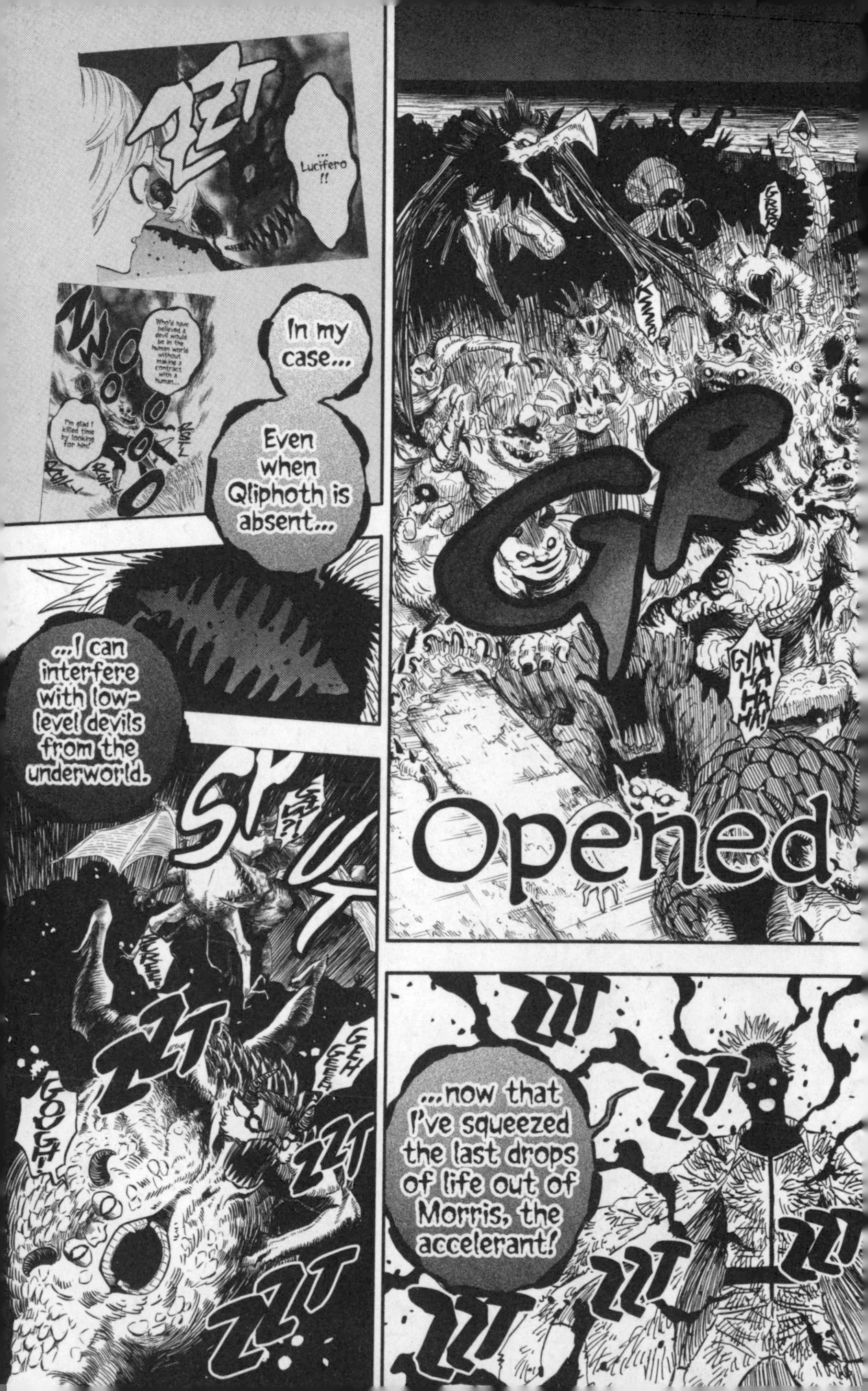
GRRR
KWAA
GYAH HA HA HA!
Opened
ZZZT
...Lucifero!!
Who'd have believed a devil would be in the human world without making a contract with a human...
I'm glad I killed time by looking for him!
WOOOOOO
In my case...
Even when Qliphoth is absent...
...I can interfere with low-level devils from the underworld.
...now that I've squeezed the last drops of life out of Morris, the accelerant!
ZZT
ZZT
ZZT
SPLUT
GAH?!
SKREE
GEH GEEH
GOUGH!
ZZT
ZZT

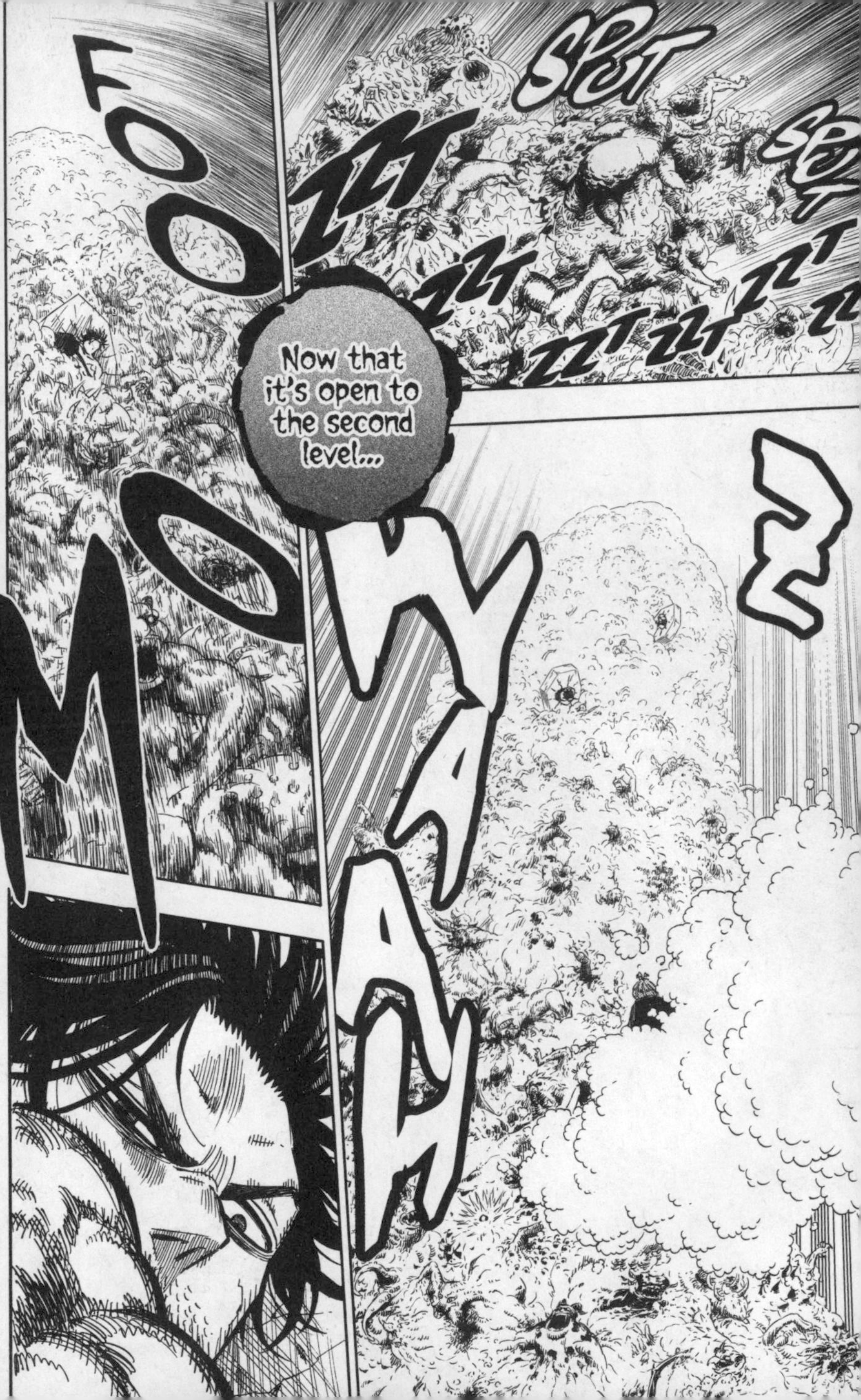
Now that it's open to the second level...

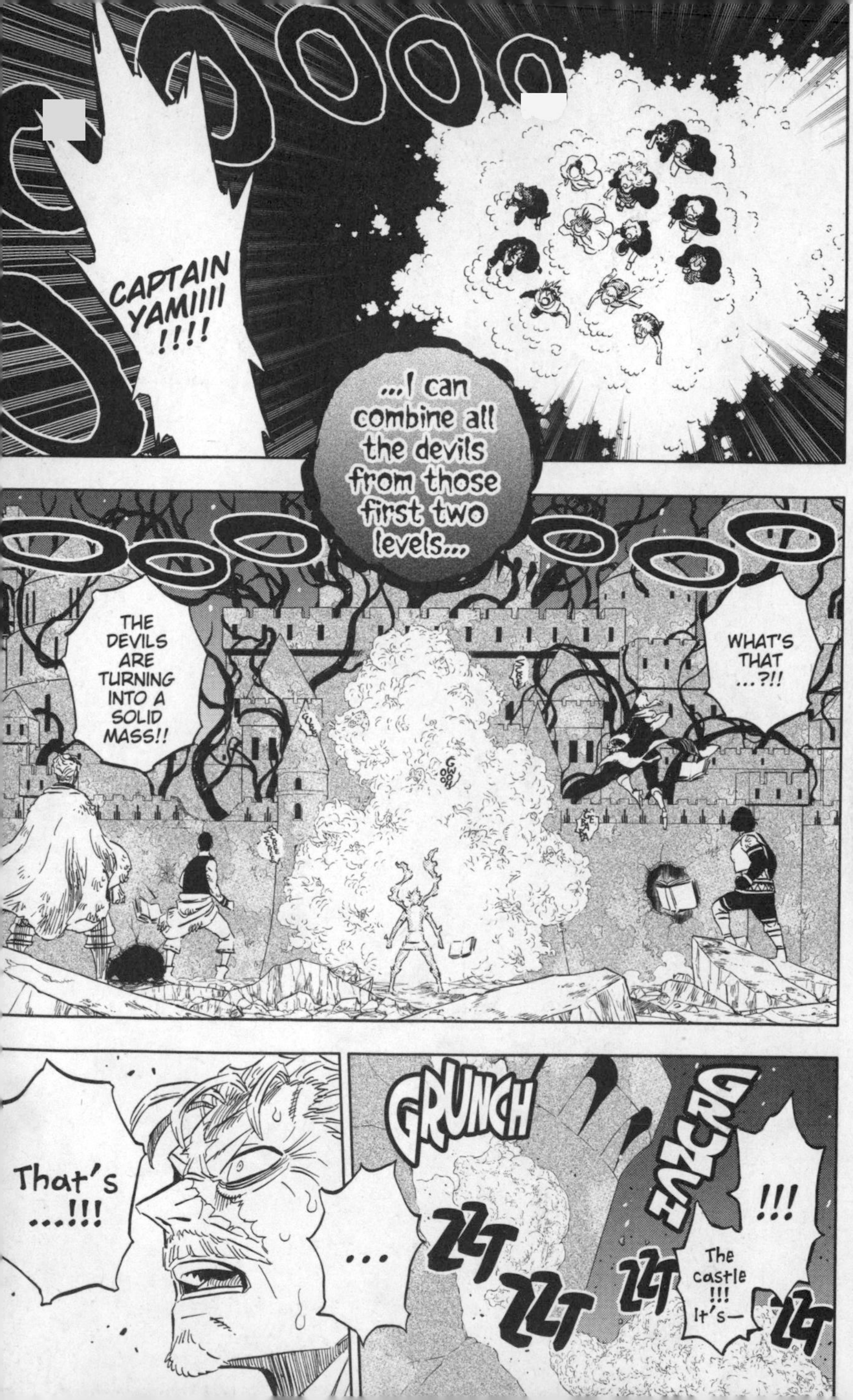
CAPTAIN YAMI!!!!! !!!!
...I can combine all the devils from those first two levels...
WHAT'S THAT ...?!!
THE DEVILS ARE TURNING INTO A SOLID MASS!!
GRUNCH
GRUNCH
!!!
The castle!!! It's—
ZZT
ZZT
ZZT
ZZT
...
That's ...!!!

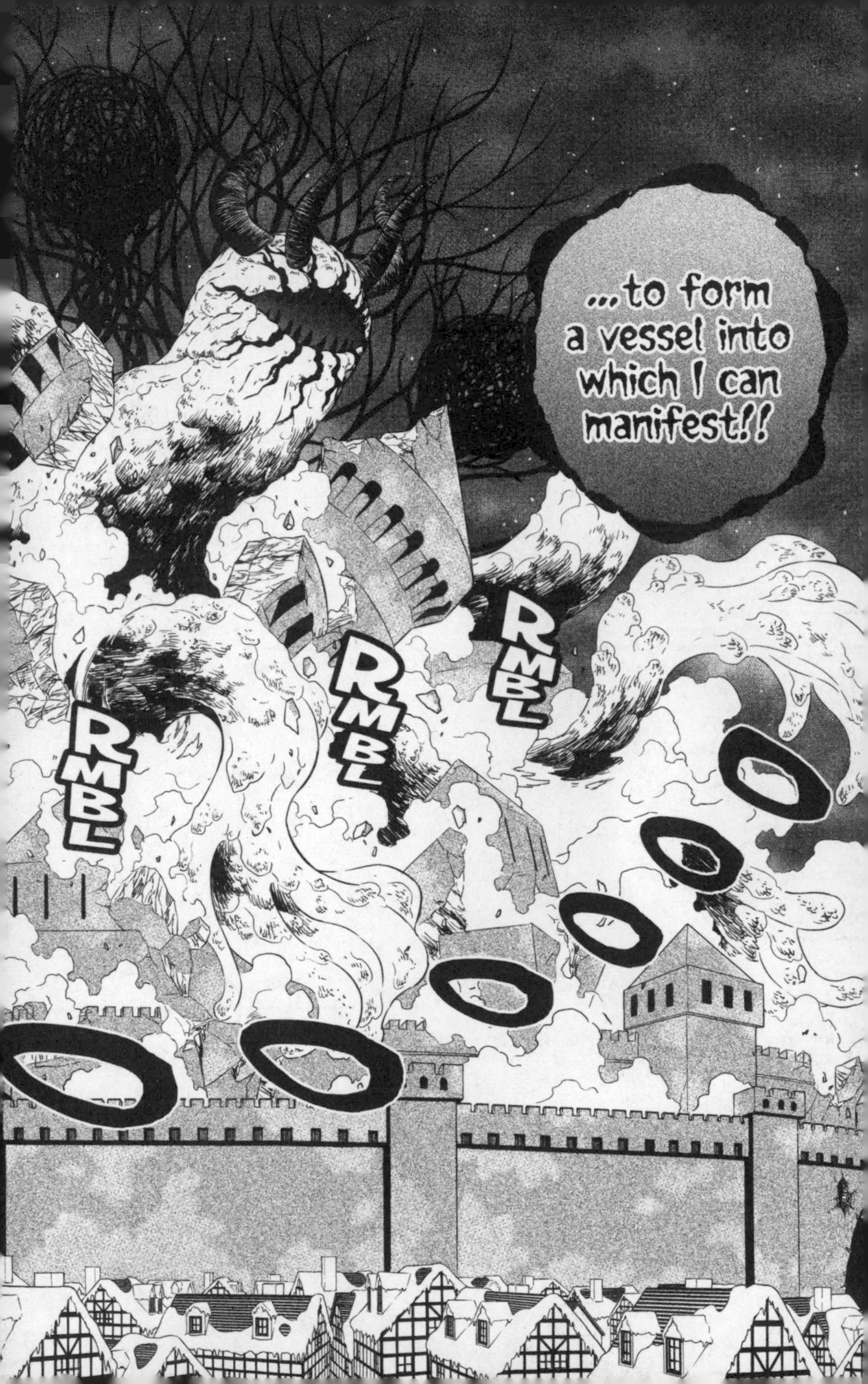
...to form a vessel into which I can manifest!!
RMBL
RMBL
RMBL
OOOOOOO

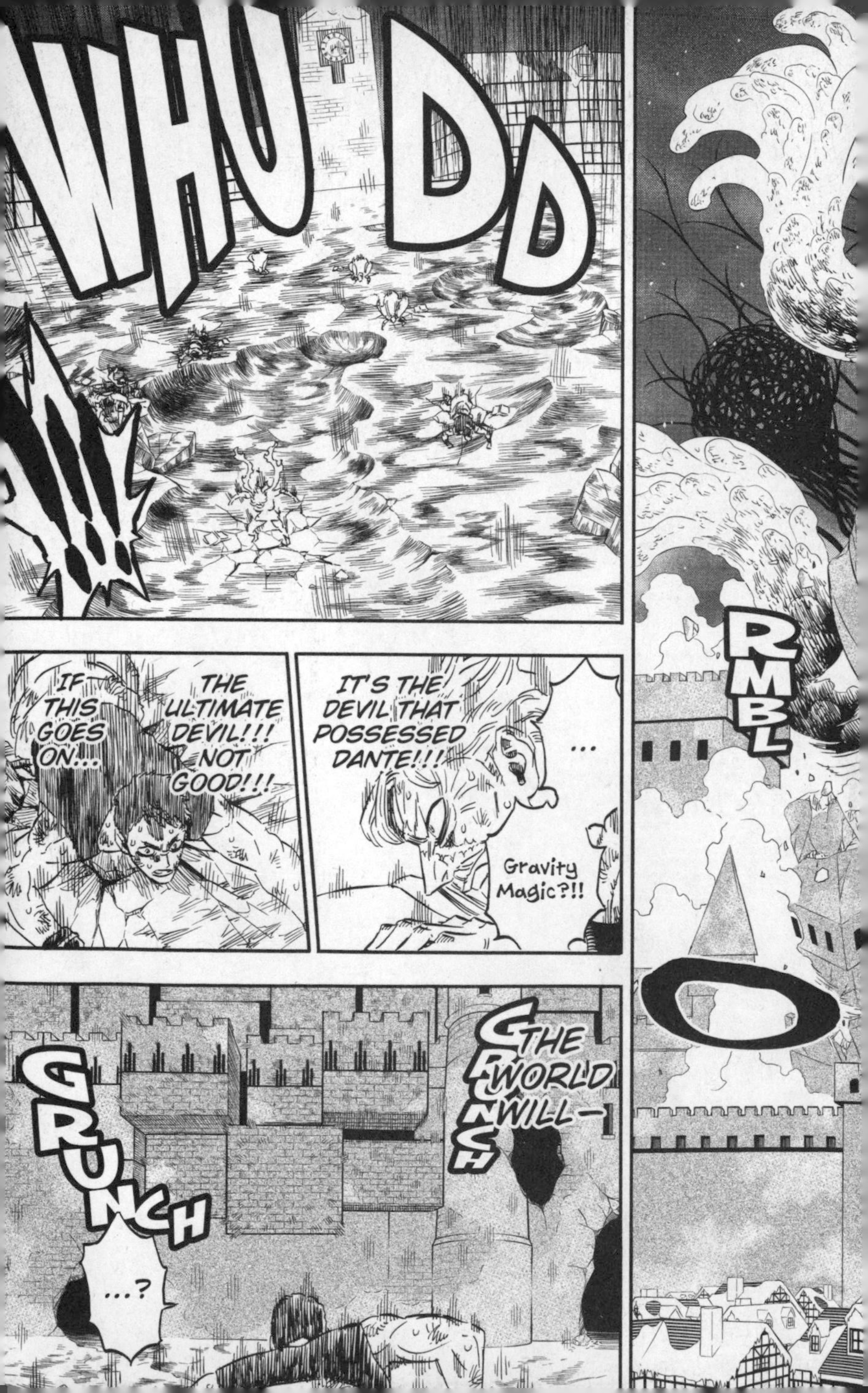
RMBL
WHUDD
IT'S THE DEVIL THAT POSSESSED DANTE!!!
...
Gravity Magic?!!
THE ULTIMATE DEVIL!!! NOT GOOD!!!
IF THIS GOES ON...
THE WORLD WILL—
CRUNCH
GRUNCH
...?

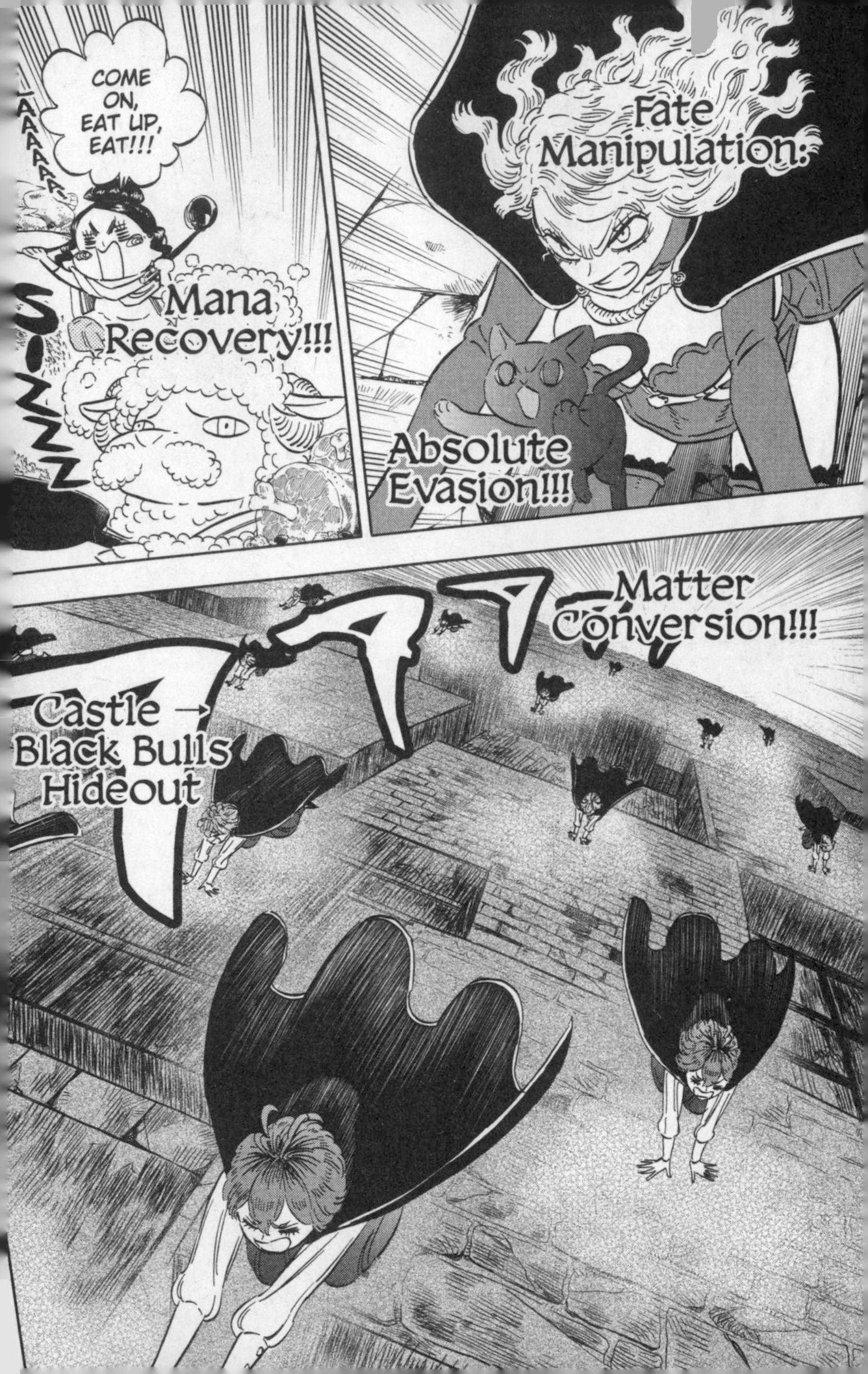
Fate Manipulation:
Absolute Evasion!!!
COME ON, EAT UP, EAT!!!
Mana Recovery!!!
SIZZZZ
—Matter Conversion!!!
Castle → Black Bulls Hideout

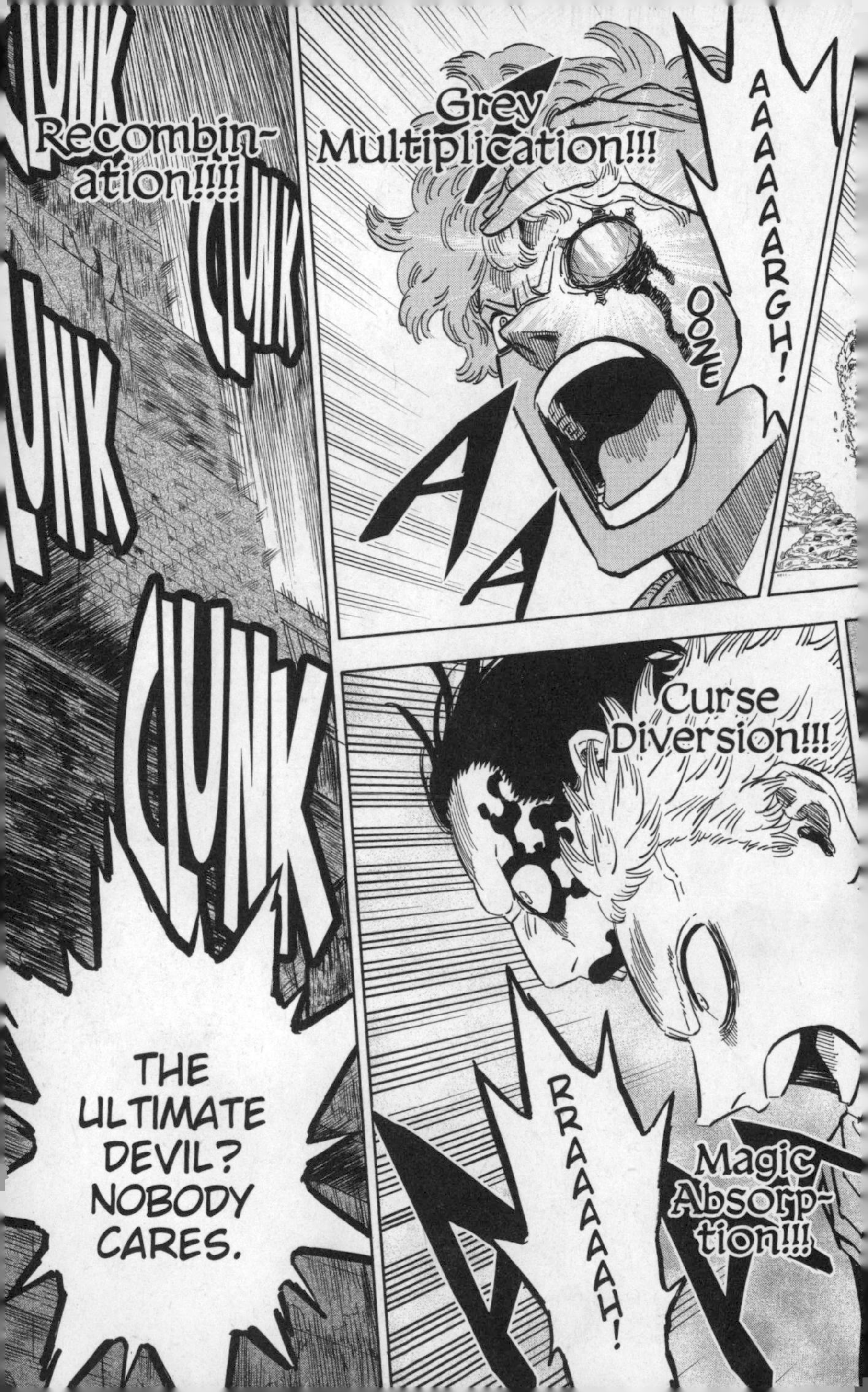
Grey Multiplication!!!
AAAAAARGH!
OOZE
AA
Curse Diversion!!!
RRAAAAAH!
Magic Absorption!!!
Recombination!!!!
CLUNK
CLUNK
THE ULTIMATE DEVIL? NOBODY CARES.

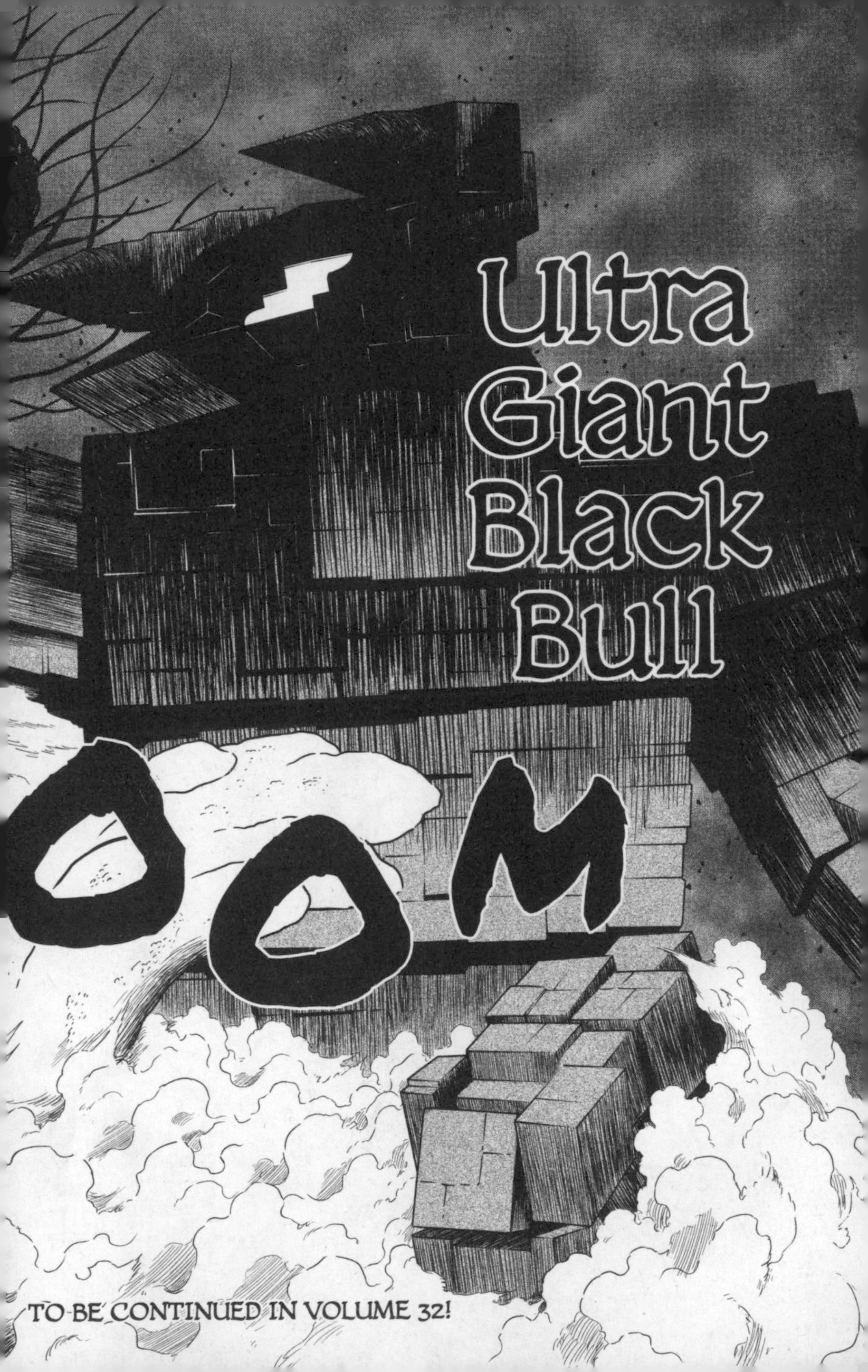
Ultra Giant Black Bull
DOOM
TO BE CONTINUED IN VOLUME 32!

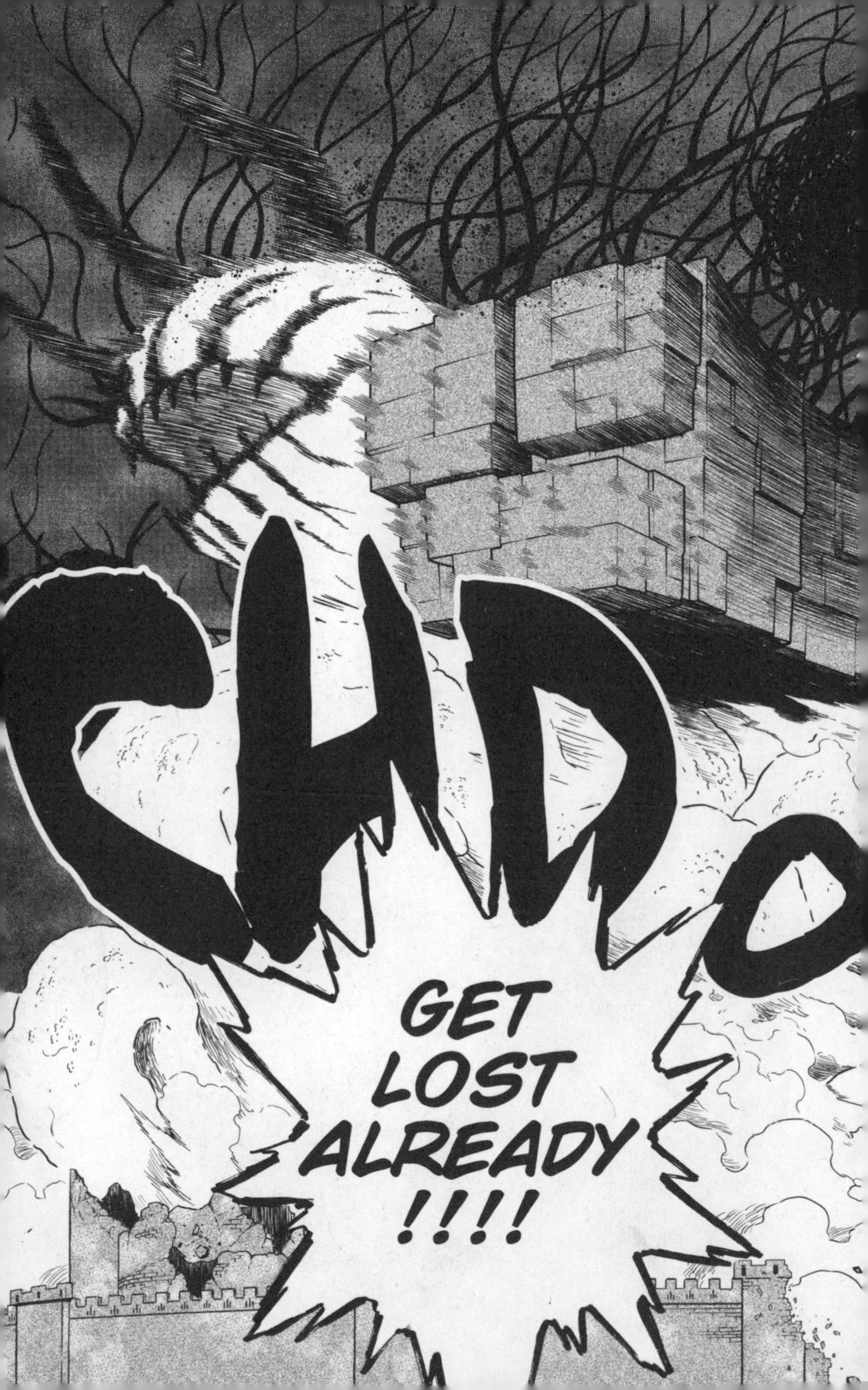
CHDO
GET LOST ALREADY!!!!

The Blank Page Brigade

This volume's topic: What surprised you recently?

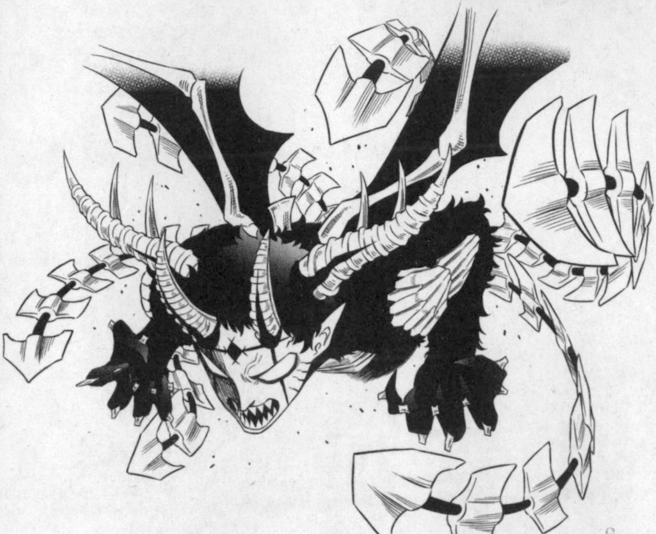

A color variant Pokémon turned up.

Tatsuya Hayashi

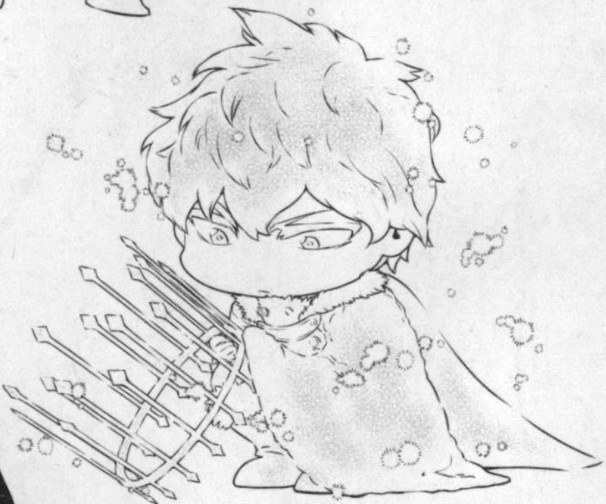

I got a phone call from my boss at my previous job.

Yū Ajina

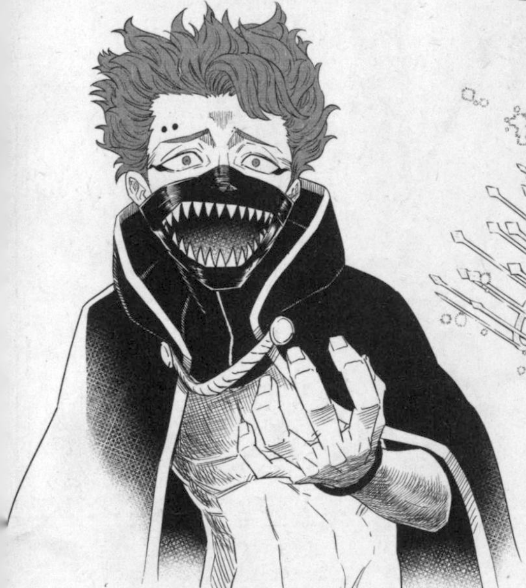

Sakai of Arco&Peace got married.

Shinobu Kasaya

I recently watched a movie called *The Castle of Cagliostro* for the first time, and it was so good it shocked me.

Seiya Miyamoto

FROM CHAPTER 314.

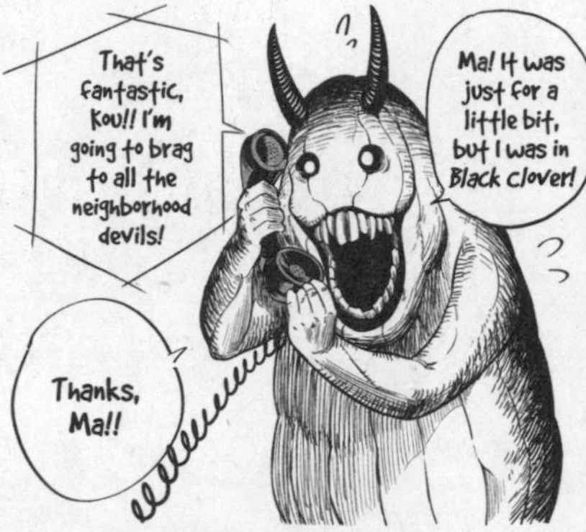
Ma! It was just for a little bit, but I was in Black Clover!
That's fantastic, Kou!! I'm going to brag to all the neighborhood devils!
Thanks, Ma!!

※ Try to find him in the chapter.

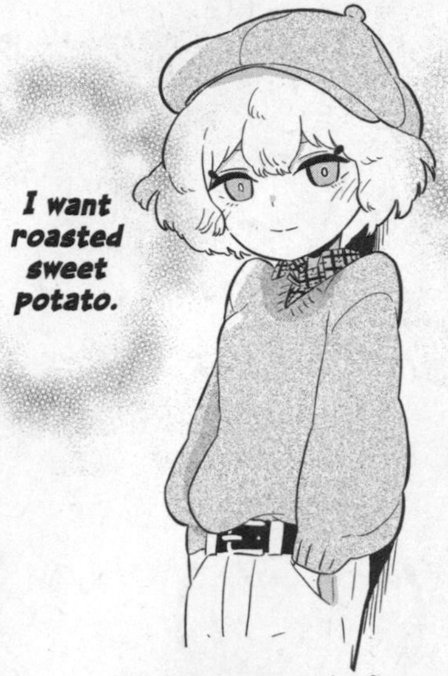
Roasted sweet potato.
I want roasted sweet potato.

The insane amount of time I lost watching short videos on YouTube.

Yōtarō Hayakawa

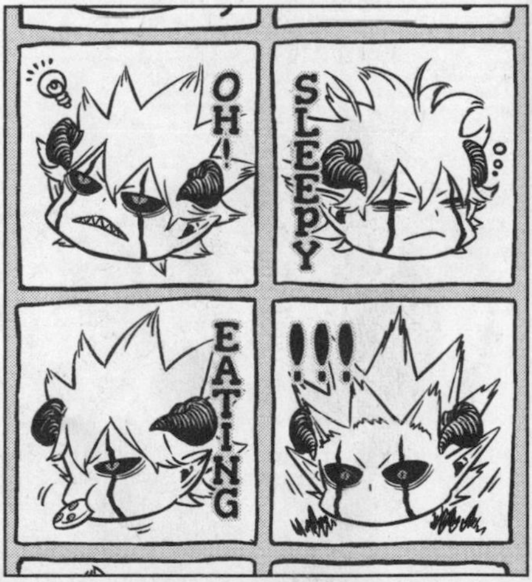
OH!
SLEEPY
...
!!!
EATING

My refrigerator started sounding like a construction site.

Yagasa

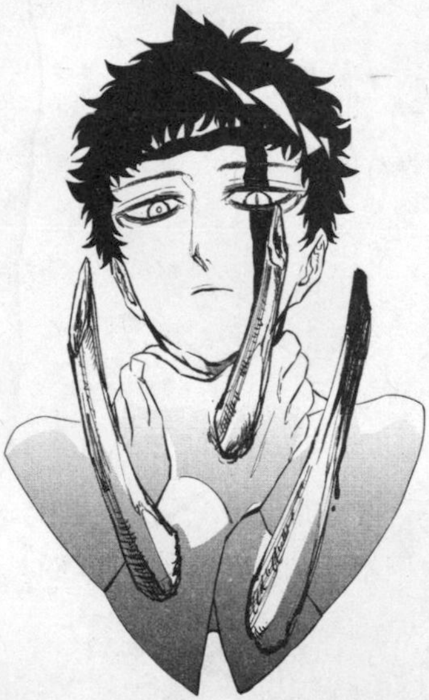

I learned that wombat poop is cube-shaped.

Sōta Hishikawa

The Blank Page Brigade

This volume's topic: What surprised you recently?

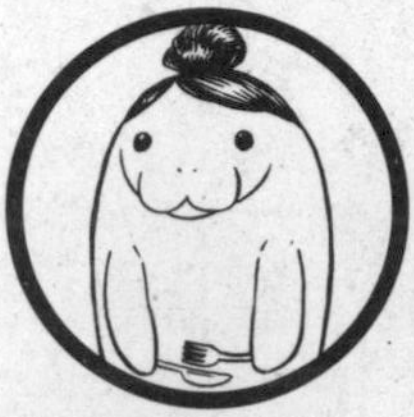

I thought I'd lost Amelie's walkies bag, looked all over the house for it, then realized it was hanging on my shoulder.

©

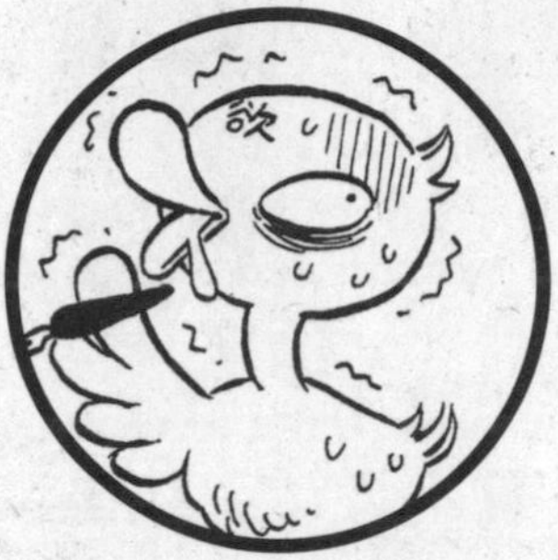
欲

When I was putting my daughter (age 2) into her PJs after her bath, and she whacked me upside the head with a wooden toy and made me literally bawl.

Captain Tabata

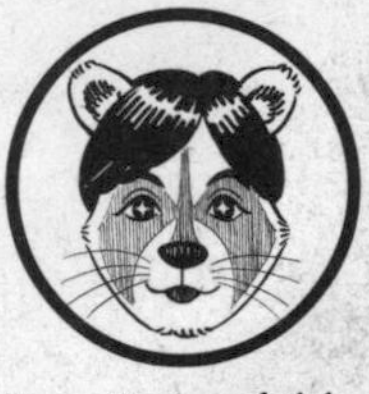

When the weight of Mr. K in the next seat over went from 120kg to 125 kg.

Media Supervisor Takahashi

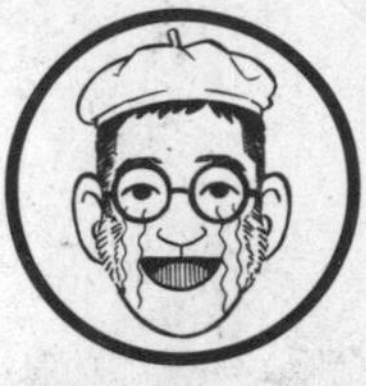

The extreme quality of the anime Hideaki Anno made in college.

Editor Fukuda

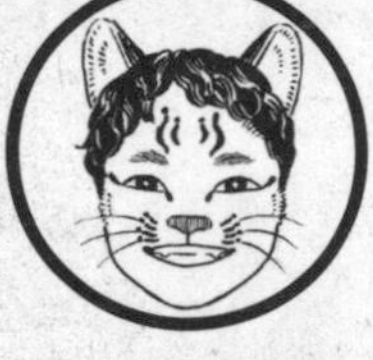

The hairiness of a convenience store clerk.

Comics Editor Chiba

AFTERWORD

✤

In my answer to the Blank Page Brigade topic,
I said I bawled, and I totally mean that. Me, a
grown man.

My daughter didn't mean any harm, of course.
She was just squealing and roughhousing, but I
cried for real. I was loud enough that my wife
jumped right out of the bath and ran to check
on us, and got weirded out.

I'd like to say I was exhausted from chasing
weekly deadlines and not in a great place mentally,
but I bawled quite a bit even before I had a series.

I love Tokyo now, but I was homesick for several
months after I moved here, and I cried in the
shower every night. We aren't talking a few silent
tears here—I sobbed.

Even after I met my wife, I'd cry every time I
messed up during something that mattered.

Don't give your wife trouble. Don't weird her out.

You've got a kid now, and you're still crying?
Knock it off already.

To any crybabies out there who are reading this,
don't worry.

I'm an adult, but I still cry all over the place!!!

And no matter how bad I ugly-cry, somebody
really tough watches over me and doesn't
abandon me!!! That is all!!!

Thank you, honey!!!

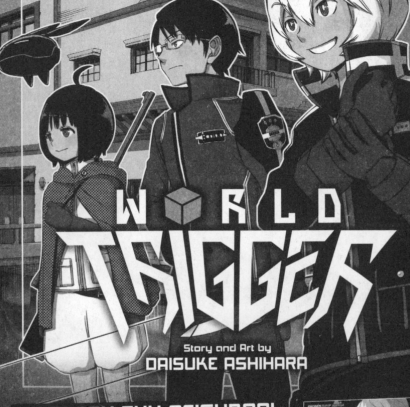

WORLD TRIGGER

Story and Art by
DAISUKE ASHIHARA

DESTROY THY NEIGHBOR!

A gate to another dimension has burst open, and invincible monsters called Neighbors invade Earth. Osamu Mikumo may not be the best among the elite warriors who co-opt other-dimensional technology to fight back, but along with his Neighbor friend Yuma, he'll do whatever it takes to defend life on Earth as we know it.

Story and Art by
KOYOHARU GOTOUGE

In Taisho-era Japan, kindhearted Tanjiro Kamado makes a living selling charcoal. But his peaceful life is shattered when a demon slaughters his entire family. His little sister Nezuko is the only survivor, but she has been transformed into a demon herself! Tanjiro sets out on a dangerous journey to find a way to return his sister to normal and destroy the demon who ruined his life.

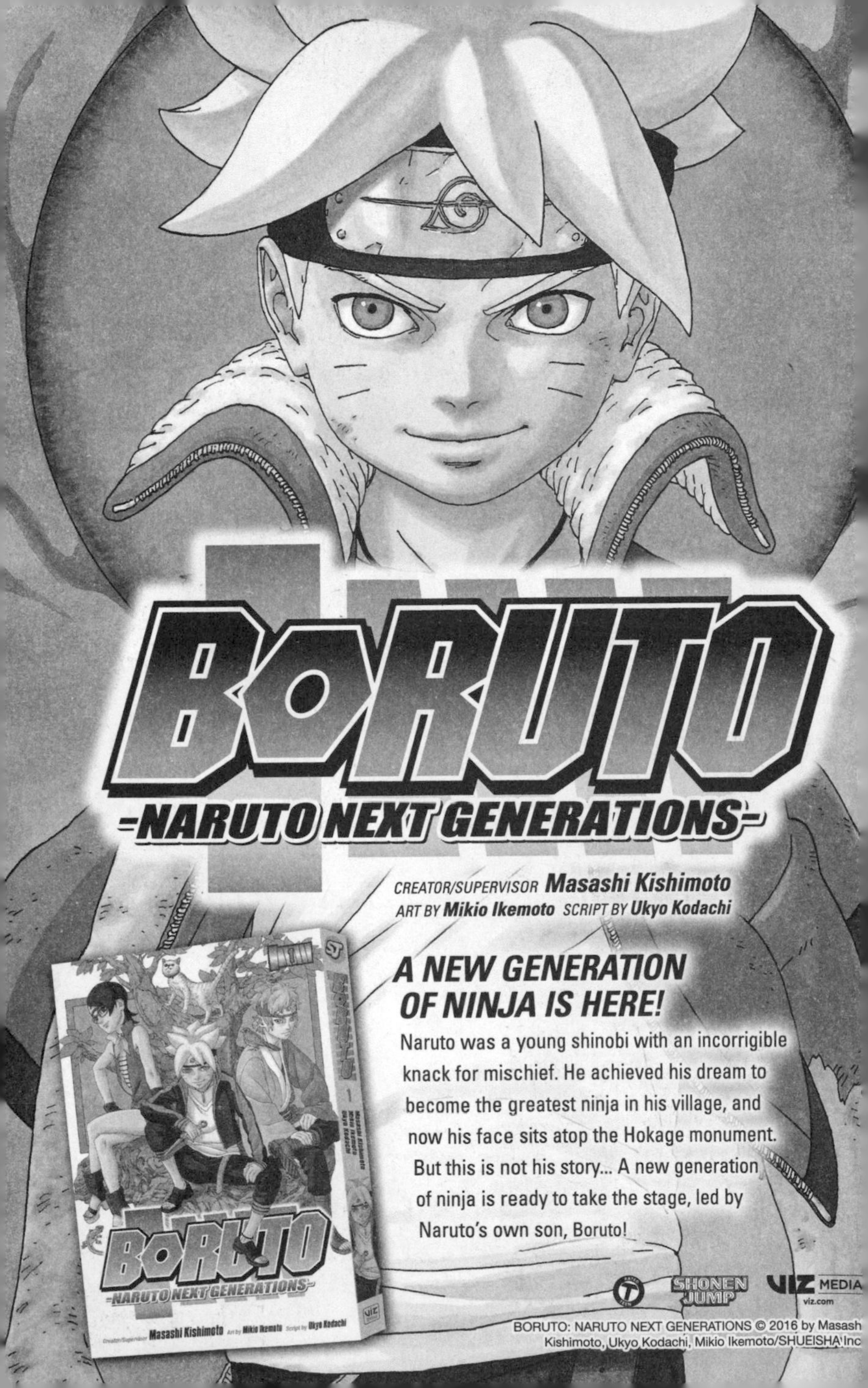
BORUTO
-NARUTO NEXT GENERATIONS-
CREATOR/SUPERVISOR Masashi Kishimoto
ART BY Mikio Ikemoto SCRIPT BY Ukyo Kodachi
A NEW GENERATION OF NINJA IS HERE!
Naruto was a young shinobi with an incorrigible knack for mischief. He achieved his dream to become the greatest ninja in his village, and now his face sits atop the Hokage monument. But this is not his story... A new generation of ninja is ready to take the stage, led by Naruto's own son, Boruto!
BORUTO
-NARUTO NEXT GENERATIONS-
SHONEN JUMP
VIZ MEDIA
viz.com
BORUTO: NARUTO NEXT GENERATIONS © 2016 by Masash Kishimoto, Ukyo Kodachi, Mikio Ikemoto/SHUEISHA Inc

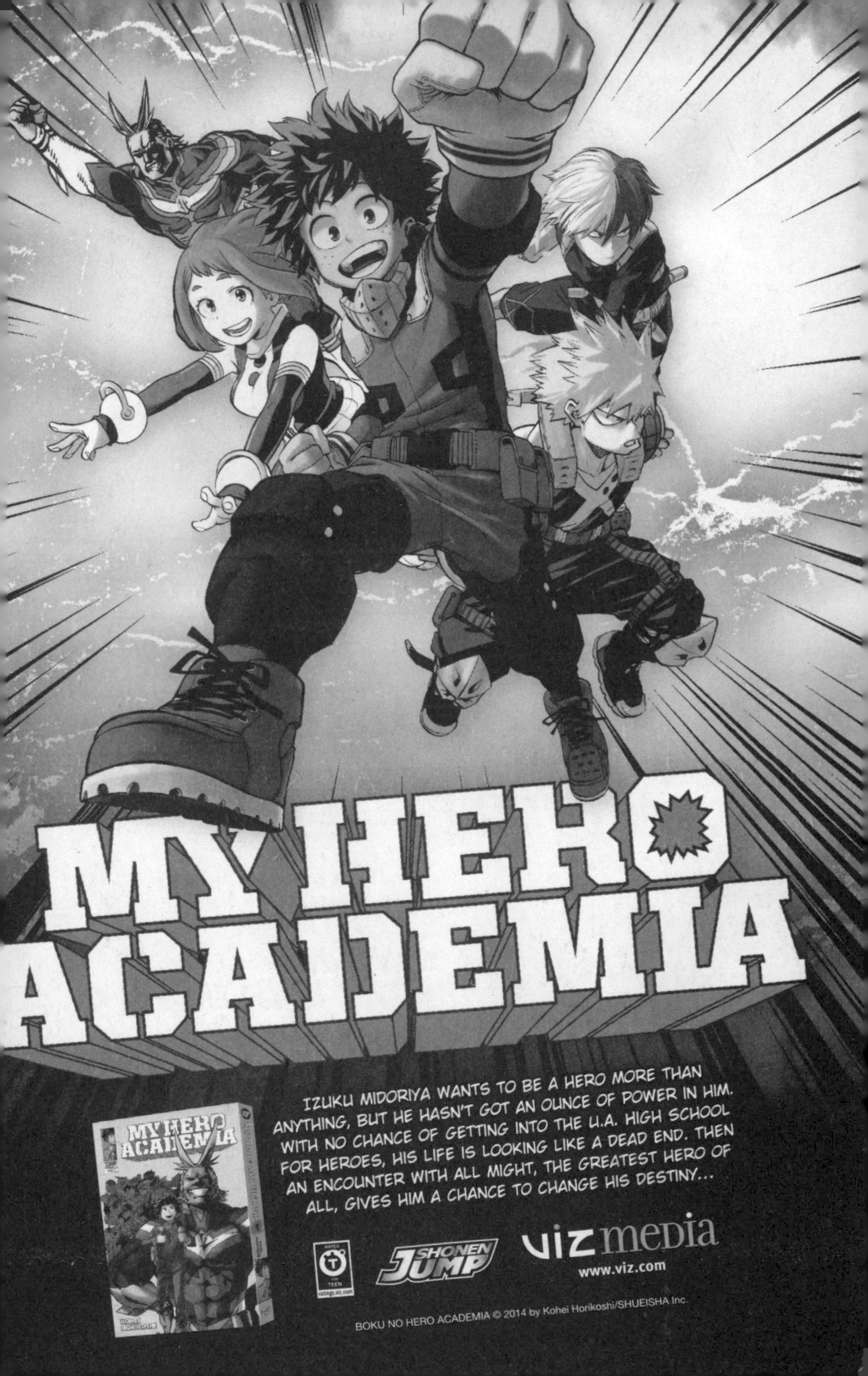
MY HERO ACADEMIA
IZUKU MIDORIYA WANTS TO BE A HERO MORE THAN ANYTHING, BUT HE HASN'T GOT AN OUNCE OF POWER IN HIM. WITH NO CHANCE OF GETTING INTO THE U.A. HIGH SCHOOL FOR HEROES, HIS LIFE IS LOOKING LIKE A DEAD END. THEN AN ENCOUNTER WITH ALL MIGHT, THE GREATEST HERO OF ALL, GIVES HIM A CHANCE TO CHANGE HIS DESTINY...
MY HERO ACADEMIA
RATED T FOR TEEN ratings.viz.com
SHONEN JUMP
viz media
www.viz.com
BOKU NO HERO ACADEMIA © 2014 by Kohei Horikoshi/SHUEISHA Inc.

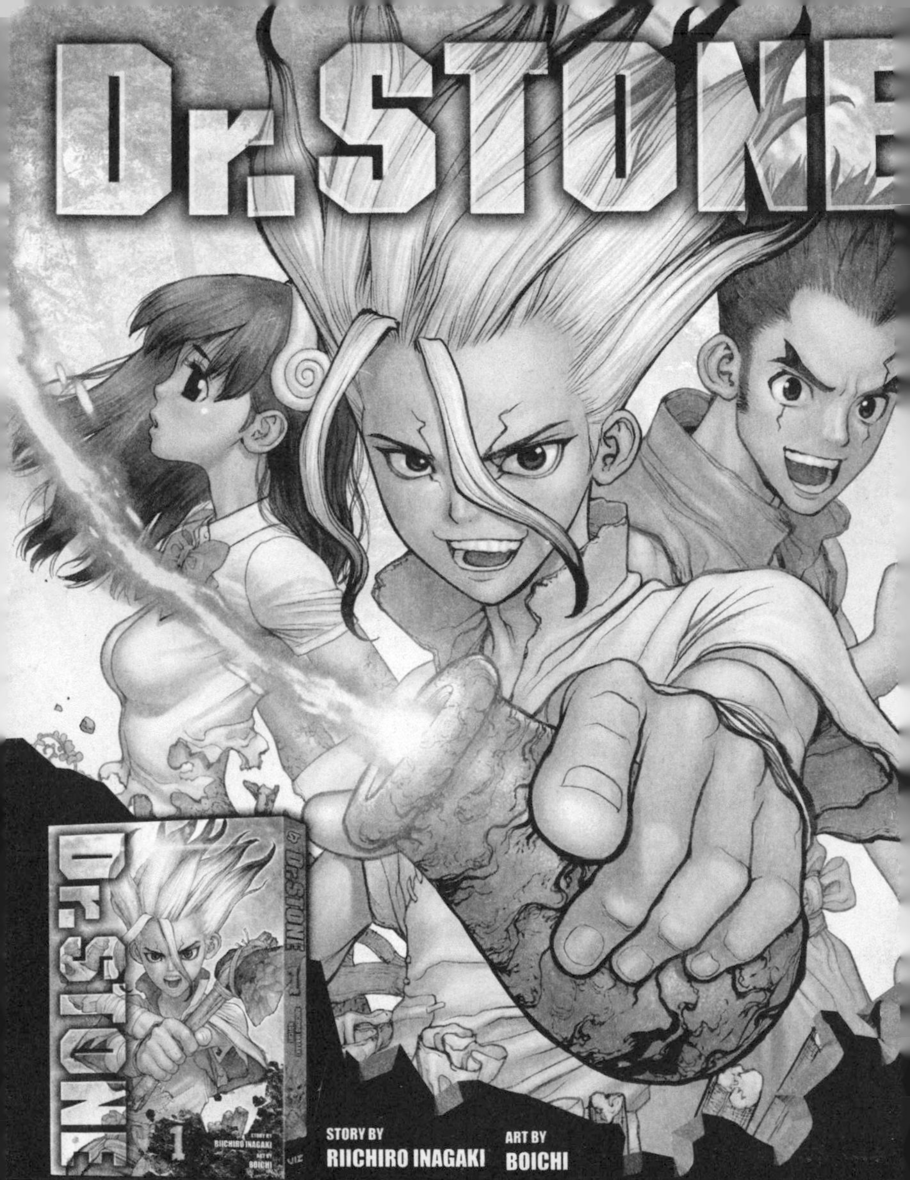

Dr. STONE

STORY BY
RIICHIRO INAGAKI

ART BY
BOICHI

One fateful day, all of humanity turned to stone. Many millenn
later, Taiju frees himself from petrification and finds himse
surrounded by statues. The situation looks grim—until he run
into his science-loving friend Senku! Together they plan to resta
civilization with the power of science!

Stop

YOU'RE READING
THE WRONG WAY!

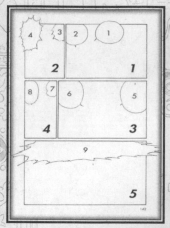

BLACK CLOVER

reads from right to left, starting
in the upper-right corner. Japanese
is read from right to left, meaning
that action, sound effects, and
word-balloon order are completely
reversed from English order.